Manual of Financial Reporting
and Accounting

Manual of Financial Reporting and Accounting

P J Stilling FCA, ACMA, MIMC
Partner in Charge of National Accounting
and Auditing, Touche Ross & Co

J B Stevenson CA
Partner in Charge of Audit Research,
Touche Ross & Co

A W Guida CPA
Senior Manager Audit Research,
Touche Ross & Co

LONDON
Butterworths
1985

England Butterworth & Co (Publishers) Ltd, 88 Kingsway, LONDON WC2B 6AB

Australia Butterworths Pty Ltd, SYDNEY, MELBOURNE, BRISBANE, ADELAIDE, PERTH, CANBERRA and HOBART

Canada Butterworth & Co (Canada) Ltd, TORONTO and VANCOUVER

New Zealand Butterworths of New Zealand Ltd, WELLINGTON and AUCKLAND

Singapore Butterworth & Co (Asia) Pte Ltd, SINGAPORE

South Africa Butterworth Publishers (Pty) Ltd, DURBAN and PRETORIA

USA Butterworth Legal Publishers, ST PAUL, Minnesota, SEATTLE, Washington, BOSTON, Massachusetts, AUSTIN, Texas and D & S Publishers, CLEARWATER, Florida

ISBN 0 406 50050 9

Printed in Great Britain by
Thomson Litho Ltd, East Kilbride, Scotland

PREFACE

It is now more than three years since our Reporting and Accounting Manual was first published by Butterworths. Its success has encouraged us to prepare for publication the revised edition necessitated by the outdating of the references to statute caused by the coming into force of the Companies Act 1985.

The changes made in this edition are more far-reaching than merely to change the references to statute. We have taken the opportunity to re-arrange the structure of the material and we hope our readers will find this an improvement. We have also tried to reflect other significant developments during the intervening period.

Important new Statements of Standard Accounting Practice have been issued, including those relating to Foreign Currency Translation and Leasing which have been accorded chapters of their own. By contrast, the withdrawal of the mandatory status of SSAP 16 on Accounting for Changing Prices has led us to diminish somewhat the previous coverage of this subject.

In 1982 there was no practical experience of the application of the accounting provisions of the Companies Act 1981. In our new edition we have modified our initial interpretations of the statute in some areas in the light of practices which have now achieved general acceptance.

We would like to thank the Consultative Committee of Accountancy Bodies for permission to reproduce material from the Statements of Standard Accounting Practice and the Auditing Standards and Guidelines, and from Counsel's opinion on 'true and fair' obtained from Leonard Hoffman and Mary Arden in September 1981, and the Council of The Stock Exchange for permission to reproduce material from 'Admission of Securities to Listing' and the USM General Undertaking.

August 1985 Touche Ross & Co.

REPORTING AND ACCOUNTING MANUAL

TABLE OF CONTENTS

10. STATEMENT OF SOURCE AND APPLICATION OF FUNDS

11. OTHER DISCLOSURE REQUIREMENTS

12. GROUP ACCOUNTS

13. ACCOUNTING FOR FOREIGN CURRENCY TRANSACTIONS

19. AUDITORS' AND ACCOUNTANTS' REPORTS Page

APPENDICES

1 INTRODUCTION

1.010 PURPOSE OF MANUAL

The purpose of this manual is to suggest best practice and acceptable alternatives as to:

(i) the form and content of financial statements;

(ii) the accounting policies and disclosures adopted for the presentation of financial information; and

(iii) the form and content of auditors' and accountants' reports.

1.020 NEW LEGISLATION

The Companies Act 1985 (the Act) consolidates the greater part of the Companies Acts 1948, 1967, 1976, 1980 and 1981. The Act, which comes into force on 1 July 1985, makes no substantive changes in company law as contained in the preceding Companies Acts. The legislation relating to the preparation, form and content, audit and publication of company and group accounts is contained in Part VII and Schedules 4 to 10 of the Act.

1.030 SOURCES AND STATUS

The sources and status of accounting principles and disclosures required of U.K. companies may be described under two headings (a) mandatory and (b) advisory.

1.031 MANDATORY

(i) Legal requirements are those contained in the Act or, for concerns which are not incorporated under the Companies Acts, any rules laid down by other regulatory Acts or bodies. EEC directives are only mandatory when enacted into legislation by Parliament. Other EEC directives are to be regarded as advisory.

(ii) The Stock Exchange requirements are those contained in the 'Admission of Securities to Listing' (Yellow Book) and in 'The Stock Exchange Unlisted Securities Market' (Green Book). These requirements relate respectively to listed companies and to companies whose shares are dealt in on the Unlisted Securities Market (USM). References in this manual to 'Stock Exchange companies' include those companies listed on The Stock Exchange and those whose shares are dealt in on the USM.

(iii) The U.K. Accountancy Bodies issue Statements of Standard Accounting Practice (SSAPs). These standards apply to all financial statements which are intended to give a true and fair view of financial position and profit or loss.

1.032 ADVISORY

(i) The ASC issues Statements of Recommended Practice (SORPs) which give guidance on current best practice on topics which are not of major or fundamental importance.

(ii) The Institute of Chartered Accountants in England and Wales and other accountancy bodies have issued accounting recommendations to their members. Although these recommendations are not mandatory, they are, nevertheless, strongly persuasive.

(iii) To test the climate of informed opinion the Accounting Standards Committee circulates an Exposure Draft in advance of the issue of the final SSAP or SORP. Although substantial alterations may be made in the light of comments received, these Exposure Drafts are a useful indicator of the eventual requirements. The ASC also issues Statements of Intent prior to the issuance of SSAPs and SORPs which give the likely direction to be taken by the ASC on a particular practice.

(iv) Pronouncements of professional bodies in other countries and international advisory committees (e.g. APBs of the American Institute of Certified Public Accountants, SFASs, studies issued by the Accountants International Study Group and exposure drafts issued by the International Accounting Standards Committee).

1.040 CONTENTS OF THIS EDITION

This edition of the manual includes the reporting and accounting requirements contained in:

(i) the Companies Act 1985;

(ii) relevant statutory instruments issued up to 1 July 1985;

(iii) Statements of Standard Accounting Practice numbers 1–23;

(iv) Auditing Standards and Guidelines issued up to 1 July 1985;

(v) Stock Exchange requirements as set out in 'Admission of Securities to Listing' (November 1984 edition) and in 'The Stock Exchange Unlisted Securities Market'.

1.041 SPECIALISED INDUSTRY PRACTICE

Special category companies (i.e. banks, insurance and shipping companies) may prepare their accounts in accordance with special rules which are contained in Part VII Chapter II, of the Act. This manual does not deal with these specialised rules nor with specialised accounting practices followed by various industries.

1.050 REFERENCES AND ABBREVIATIONS USED

Unless otherwise stated all references to statute in this manual are to the Companies Act 1985, e.g.:

s 227(2) – Section 227 subsection (2) of the Act

Sch 4: 58(3) – Schedule 4 to the Act paragraph 58 sub-paragraph (3)

A glossary of abbreviations used in the text of this manual is contained in Appendix 1.

1.060 DISCLOSURE CHECKLIST

A checklist of disclosures which are required by the Act, SSAPs and The Stock Exchange to be included in the directors' report and financial statements is included in Appendix 2. The checklist indicates the authority for each requirement. Where this authority is the Companies Act 1985, the corresponding reference in earlier legislation is also indicated.

2 GENERAL REQUIREMENTS AS TO FINANCIAL STATEMENTS

2.010 FINANCIAL STATEMENTS REQUIRED

The directors of every U.K. company registered under the Companies Acts (including an unlimited company) are required by s 241 to lay before the company in general meeting financial statements in respect of each accounting reference period and these financial statements must include a balance sheet, profit and loss account and additional information to be provided by way of notes. (See Chapter 17 for further requirements to produce and file financial statements and Chapter 12 for requirements in respect of consolidated financial statements.) These statements must comply with the requirements of the Act as to their form and content.

In addition to these statutory requirements, the financial statements should contain other financial information (i.e. a statement of source and application of funds and current cost accounts) and additional disclosures as required by SSAPs and by The Stock Exchange (if the company is a Stock Exchange company).

In certain cases, small and medium-sized companies may opt to prepare condensed versions of their financial statements solely for the purpose of filing with the Registrar of Companies. These 'modified' accounts are discussed in Section 17.020.

2.011 DEFINITIONS OF 'FINANCIAL STATEMENTS' AND 'ACCOUNTS'

The term 'financial statements' has been adopted by the ASC and defined as 'balance sheets, profit and loss accounts, statements of source and application of funds, notes and other statements which collectively are intended to give a true and fair view of financial position and profit or loss'.

The term 'accounts' has not been formally defined in the past but is usually taken to refer to the formal accounting statements, i.e. balance sheets and profit and loss accounts (both group and company), and possibly statements of source and application of funds. The notes which amplify the accounts are not part of the accounts. This is the meaning assigned to the term in this manual. Thus it is correct to refer to 'notes to the accounts' but not to 'notes to the financial statements'. (It should be noted that the Act does introduce a definition of 'accounts' for certain purposes, but under this definition both the directors' report and the auditors' report are included as part of the 'accounts'. This definition seems calculated to confuse and has not been used in this manual.)

2.020 TRUE AND FAIR VIEW

Financial statements are required to give a true and fair view of the profit or loss for the financial year and the state of affairs at the end of it. This requirement over-rides all the accounting requirements of the Act and SSAPs.

The requirements of ss 228(4) and 230(4) specify that if the financial statements drawn up in compliance with the Act do not provide sufficient information to give a true and fair view, then the necessary additional information must be given.

In rare circumstances it is possible that strict compliance with one or more requirements of the Act, even when supplemented by additional information, would prevent the financial statements from showing a true and fair view. In these cases the directors must depart from the specific requirements but must also disclose in a note the particulars of the departure, the reasons for it and its effect. It is clear from the Department of Trade statement on the Argyll Foods case that departures from the statutory requirements will only be acceptable in rare circumstances. Although it is desirable for financial statements to reflect the substance rather than the form of transactions, the Department of Trade statement specifically states that 'any emphasis on substance over form must not be at the expense of compliance with the law'.

The ASC has obtained a written opinion from counsel on the meaning of 'true and fair' with particular reference to the role of accounting standards. The full text of this opinion is reproduced in Appendix 7.

2.030 FUNDAMENTAL ACCOUNTING PRINCIPLES

Sch 4: 9 to 15 prescribes the fundamental accounting principles that are to be applied in determining the amounts to be included in respect of all items shown in financial statements. These follow closely the 'fundamental accounting concepts' recognised by SSAP 2. A departure from these accounting principles is only permitted if there are special reasons for it, in which case the financial statements must include a note giving particulars of the departure, the reasons for it and its effect. The prescribed accounting principles are dealt with below.

2.031 GOING CONCERN

The enterprise must be presumed to be carrying on business as a going concern. This assumes that it will continue operations in the foreseeable future and that there will be no significant liquidation of assets due to a reduction in the scale of operations (see page 271).

2.032 CONSISTENCY

Accounting policies must be applied consistently from one financial year to the next. The concept of consistency referred to in SSAP 2 is that there is consistency of accounting treatment of like items within each accounting period and from one period to the next (see Section 12.071 which deals with uniformity of accounting policies within a group of companies).

The only 'special reason' which would justify a departure from the principle of consistency of accounting policies is that indicated in SSAP 6, namely that the new policy is preferable to the one it replaces because it will give a fairer presentation of the results and of the financial position of the business. Normally this will arise from new legislation or the publication of a new SSAP or SORP.

Changes in accounting policies are sometimes confused with changes in estimates which arise from new information or developments. A change in accounting policy results from a choice between two or more accounting bases and not from the occurrence of transactions or events that are clearly different in substance from those previously occurring or which in the past were insignificant in their impact on the financial statements.

Where a corresponding amount in the financial statements is not comparable, Sch 4: 4(2) and 58(2) require that amount to be adjusted and the particulars of the adjustment and the reasons for it to be disclosed. This requirement appears to be similar to that contained in SSAP 6. As SSAP 6 makes clear, adjustment is only required in respect of (i) changes in accounting policies and (ii) correction of fundamental errors. Corresponding amounts should not be adjusted for changes in circumstances or estimates, which should normally be dealt with through the current year's profit and loss account.

2.033 PRUDENCE

The amount of any item must be determined on a prudent basis, specifically:

(i) only profits realised at the balance sheet date may be included in the profit and loss account; and

(ii) all liabilities and losses which have arisen or are liable to arise in respect of any period prior to the balance sheet date must be taken into account (including all those which become apparent before the balance sheet is signed on behalf of the directors).

Realised profits are defined as those which fall to be treated as realised in accordance with generally accepted accounting principles at the time when the accounts are prepared. [Sch 4: 91] The subject of realised profits is discussed in detail in Section 18.040(c).

The Act gives no indication of how one determines what principles are 'generally accepted' but the point was considered by the Court of Appeal in the case of Associated Portland Cement Manufacturers Ltd v Price Commission [1975 ICR 27]. The court concluded that generally accepted accounting principles are those principles which are generally regarded as permissible or legitimate by the accountancy profession irrespective of the degree of use.

All liabilities and losses which have arisen or are likely to arise in respect of the current or previous financial years must be taken into account (including those which subsequently become apparent up to the date on which the balance sheet is signed on behalf of the directors).

2.034 ACCRUALS

Income and charges relating to the financial year must be taken into account without regard to the date of receipt or payment. For this purpose the accruals concept in SSAP 2 is more explicit, i.e. the recognition of revenue and costs as they are earned or incurred not as money is received or paid. Revenue and profits dealt with in the profit and loss account are 'matched' by including in the same period the costs incurred in earning them.

Not infrequently there is a conflict between the prudence concept on the one hand and the accruals concept on the other. This conflict is not recognised in Sch 4, but is in SSAP 2 which indicates that where the accruals concept is inconsistent with the prudence concept, it is prudence which prevails.

2.035 SEPARATE DETERMINATION OF ITEMS

In determining the aggregate amount of any item, the amount of each individual asset or liability that falls to be taken into account shall be determined separately. Thus a 'portfolio' approach to the determination of asset values (e.g. those which are valued at the lower of cost and net realisable value, or at cost less permanent diminution in value) is not compatible with this principle.

2.040 GENERAL RULES AS TO FORM AND CONTENT OF FINANCIAL STATEMENTS

With the exception of special category companies (see Section 1.041), statutory financial statements are required to comply with the following general requirements as to their form and content.

A company is required to follow one of the two formats for the balance sheet and four formats for the profit and loss account prescribed in Sch 4. The formats chosen cannot be changed unless in the opinion of the directors there are special reasons for a change. A note to the accounts will then be required, giving particulars of the change of format and explaining the reasons therefor.

The Sch 4 formats are reproduced in Appendix 5 of this manual. Balance sheet Format 1 and profit and loss account Formats 1 and 2 follow the vertical arrangement of items which is customarily followed in the U.K. The alternative formats place the same items in a double-sided, or horizontal, arrangement. The double-sided formats, particularly the double-sided profit and loss account, are usually unsatisfactory as they tend to confuse rather than clarify (e.g. it is usually impossible to extend important sub-totals).

The general rules with respect to the form and content of a company's statutory financial statements, as contained in Sch 4 are as follows:

(i) Corresponding amounts for the preceding year must be shown. This applies to information stated in the notes to the accounts with the exception of the details of movements on fixed assets, reserves and provisions required by Sch 4: 42 and 46, proportion of share capital of subsidiaries or certain other companies, etc. required by Sch 5: 1, 7, 8 and 9, and particulars of certain loans etc. to directors as required by Sch 6.

(ii) Items listed in the formats (except those designated by Arabic numbers) must be shown in the financial statements and in the order and under the headings and sub-headings given in the format adopted (the letters and numbers are for identification purposes only and need not be shown in the statements). The precise headings and sub-headings specified in the formats must be used.

(iii) Items designated in the formats by Arabic numbers shall be adapted in terms of arrangement and headings where the special nature of the company's business requires. They may be combined if an amount is immaterial or the combination facilitates the assessment of the company's state of affairs or profit or loss, but in the latter case the items so combined must be disclosed in a note to the accounts.

(iv) If no amount falls to be shown under a heading for both the current and the preceding financial year, the heading may be omitted.

(v) Any amount which in the context of any provision of Sch 4 is not material may be disregarded.

Whether an amount is or is not material should be judged by reference to the needs of the users of the financial statements and in cases of doubt it should be treated as material. What must be decided is whether the item or matter is of significance to the user of the financial statements in relation to the specific provision of Sch 4 under consideration. No arbitrary percentage yardstick can be applied in judging whether an amount or other disclosure is not material. Qualitative factors must also be considered. In this respect disclosure of an item, such as auditors' remuneration, cannot be considered immaterial regardless of its size in relation to other costs shown in the profit and loss account.

(vi) Any item may be shown in greater detail than required by the format adopted, in which case a sub-total should be shown.

(vii) The financial statements may include an item not otherwise covered by the items listed in the format adopted (e.g. 'minority interests'), but preliminary expenses, expenses of and commissions on issue of shares or debentures, and cost of research cannot be shown as assets in the balance sheet.

(viii) Offsets of assets against liabilities or of income against expenditure are not allowed.

This requirement is interpreted as prohibiting the offset of any material amounts which fall into one of the items in the formats against another item. For example, amounts owed to a customer (credit balance) should not be offset within debtors against amounts owed by other customers. Similarly, a bank overdraft owing to one bank cannot be offset by cash held at another bank but it will be appropriate to offset overdrafts against bank balances held with the same bank where a legal right of offset exists.

(ix) Any information required by Sch 4 which is not shown on the face of the accounts must be given by way of note.

2.050 REPORTING CURRENCY

While it is customary for a U.K. company to produce its statutory financial statements in pounds sterling, there are no restrictions in U.K. company law which would prevent a company from using a foreign currency for this purpose (e.g. the currency in which most of its transactions are carried out). Where the reporting currency is changed to another currency, the new currency amounts for the current and preceding financial years should be determined using the temporal method of translation (see page 192). This method is preferred as it achieves the same currency balances as would have been obtained had the company accounted in the new currency from its inception.

The reporting currency, if it is other than sterling, should be disclosed in a prominent manner on every page in which financial figures are shown.

2.060 DATE OF APPROVAL OF FINANCIAL STATEMENTS

SSAP 17 requires the date on which the financial statements are approved by the board of directors (or the corresponding officers of an organisation which does not have directors) to be disclosed in the financial statements. This date is defined as the date when the board formally approves a set of documents as the financial statements (these need not be the final printed or typewriten documents to be submitted to members but they should be complete in all material respects). This date is important in establishing the date to which the directors are responsible for disclosing material post balance sheet events (see Section 11.070).

It is recommended that this date be shown either on the face of the balance sheet above the signature of the directors or as the first item in the notes to the accounts. Any other position within the financial statements will be acceptable but the date should not be disclosed in the directors' report. An example of appropriate wording would be:

EXAMPLE

Approved by the Board of Directors on 13 July 1985.

2.070 SIGNING OF BALANCE SHEET

Every balance sheet of a company must be signed on behalf of the board by two directors, or if there is only one director, by that director. [s 238] Some companies take the view that there is no requirement for the directors to sign the consolidated balance sheet. It is recommended that both the parent company and consolidated balance sheets are signed by the directors in accordance with current practice.

Financial statements of unincorporated concerns prepared with or without audit, should be approved by the client before the audit report is signed. The respective responsibilities of the client and the auditor should be clearly explained to the client at that time and he should be asked to sign a declaration on the face of the balance sheet. Normally this declaration would be simply 'I approve these financial statements' or 'approved'. There may be circumstances where a fuller declaration, such as 'I approve these financial statements and confirm that I have made available all relevant records and information for their preparation', would be appropriate.

In the case of partnerships, the declaration should be signed either by all partners or by the partner(s) duly authorised to sign on behalf of all the partners.

3 MODEL REPORT AND FINANCIAL STATEMENTS

3.010 INTRODUCTION TO MODEL

Section 3.030 illustrates the report and financial statements of a hypothetical listed company, Tramp Holdings p.l.c., which owns a group of manufacturing companies, showing a style and layout commonly adopted in the UK. *The purpose is to illustrate style and layout only.* A single model cannot of course illustrate all disclosure requirements. A comprehensive check list of disclosures can be found in Appendix 2.

The requirements of Sch 4 now impose a considerable degree of rigidity on the format and headings. However, advantage should be taken of such flexibility as is allowed by the Act to achieve the presentation which will be most useful to the reader. In any event the requirement to show a true and fair view may in rare cases require departure from the standard formats.

The financial statements are of course the responsibility of the directors and the auditor expresses his opinion on them. Although the auditor may participate in the accountancy work and draft the financial statements it is his client who ultimately decides the accounting policies to be adopted and the client may have preferences as to the format to be adopted or the extent to which disclosure may be made in the notes rather than on the face of the accounts. The auditor must respect his client's wishes in these respects provided he is satisfied that all legal requirements have been complied with and particularly that the financial statements show a true and fair view. If he is not so satisfied, he will issue a qualified report.

The 'Tramp Holdings p.l.c.' model report and financial statements are representative of the information contained in the published financial statements of a listed company. The arrangement of information as shown in the contents page (see page 14) follows an order which is commonly adopted, but it is, of course, open to the company to amend the package by, for example:

(i) excluding any of the optional sections, i.e. contents, directors' listing, chairman's statement, salient features and financial calendar, and ten year statistical record;

(ii) changing the order of the financial statements and auditors' report;

(iii) presenting the consolidated and parent company balance sheets on one page.

3.020 SOME CONSIDERATIONS OF STYLE AND PRESENTATION

3.021 LANGUAGE

Simple and concise language should be used which will be understandable by all readers of the financial statements.

3.022 USE OF CAPITAL LETTERS

The indiscriminate use of capital letters prevents attention being focused on significant words and should be avoided.

3.023 PERIOD COVERED BY FINANCIAL STATEMENTS

Each balance sheet forming part of the accounts should disclose prominently the date at which it is prepared. The directors' report, the remaining statements forming the accounts, and the first page of the notes to the accounts should disclose prominently the precise period covered. In all statements, the amounts for the current period and the preceding one should be identified at the top of each column. Where both the current and preceding accounting periods are of twelve months, the year in which the period ends is sufficient identification.

EXAMPLE

TRAMP HOLDINGS p.l.c.
BALANCE SHEET – 31 December 1984

	1984 *£'000*	*1983* *£'000*
Fixed assets	*720*	*695*

It is important that, in any set of financial statements in which the length of period covered by the current and comparative figures is different, a precise description of the period should be shown over the appropriate columns. This is necessary in order to alert the reader that the comparative figures are not comparable without taking into account the time differences.

EXAMPLE

TRAMP HOLDINGS p.l.c.
PROFIT AND LOSS ACCOUNT
Year ended 31 December 1984

	1984 *£'000*	*Six months ended 31 December 1983* *£'000*
Turnover	*36,615*	*14,998*

The use of the term 'period ended (date)' without further amplification is uninformative and should not be used. Examples of good description include:

Period from 15 November 1983 to 30 September 1984

15 November 1983 (date of incorporation) to 31 March 1985

Thirteen months ended 31 December 1984

53 weeks ended 2 January 1985

3.024 NOTES TO THE ACCOUNTS

Accounts on their own rarely provide all the financial information required to show a true and fair view. The Act specifies certain information to be shown either in the balance sheet and profit and loss account or in the notes to the accounts, and further requires that any additional information which is necessary to a true and fair view must be provided. Thus the notes form an integral part of the financial statements.

The Act does not dictate the manner or arrangement in which the notes are to be shown. The preparer of accounts should adopt a presentation which will provide the reader with an orderly arrangement of information which can be easily referenced to the relevant items in the accounts. The following approach is recommended:

(i) Notes should not be split between those relating to the profit and loss account and those relating to the balance sheet.

(ii) Notes relating to specific account balances should be shown in the order in which they appear in the accounts.

(iii) Notes should be numbered and cross-referenced to the relevant item(s) in the accounts.

(iv) Each note should be given a heading which identifies the subject matter of the disclosure.

(v) Notes should be placed after the accounts. The practice of placing the notes after the profit and loss account and balance sheet but before the statement of source and application of funds should be discouraged.

3.025 CROSS REFERENCE BETWEEN NOTES

Difficulties of understanding are caused by the relegation of supporting detail of one balance sheet or profit and loss account item to more than one note. This should be avoided as far as possible but where necessary the relevant notes should be cross-referenced.

3.026 ROUNDING AND REDUCING FIGURES

There are two main reasons why it is sensible to round and reduce figures:

- if they are stated to the last pound an illusory degree of accuracy is suggested.
- there is difficulty in understanding very large numbers.

It is therefore suggested that in place of detail such as:

	£
Raw materials and consumables	*1,851,784*
Work in progress	*7,933,241*
Finished goods and goods for resale	*5,839,473*
	15,624,498

the presentation should be:

	£'000
Raw materials and consumables	*1,852*
Work in progress	*7,933*
Finished goods and goods for resale	*5,839*
	15,624

3.027 USE OF BRACKETS

Opinions differ as to when figures should be bracketed and no set rules can be said to apply to all circumstances. In order to obtain some consistency, the following guidelines are suggested.

Where brackets are required to make mathematical sense out of a listing of numbers, the items which are mathematically opposite in direction to the nature of items in the list should be bracketed. For example, in a listing of expenses, a rebate credit or bad debt recovery should be bracketed.

No brackets are usually necessary when two items are subtotalled and their descriptions clearly indicate the mathematical direction of the amounts.

EXAMPLE

	1984	*1983*
	£'000	*£'000*
Profit on ordinary activities before taxation	*173*	*123*
Tax on profit on ordinary activities	*89*	*55*
Profit on ordinary activities after taxation	*84*	*68*

EXAMPLE

Contract work in progress	*1,283*	*937*
Less payments on account	*400*	*674*
	883	*263*

Where comparative figures are positive in one year and negative the next year, both the description of the appropriate item and amount should be bracketed.

EXAMPLE

	1984	*1983*
	£'000	*£'000*
(Loss)/profit on ordinary activities before taxation	*(84)*	*123*
Taxation (credit)/charge on (loss)/profit on ordinary activities	*(45)*	*155*
Loss on ordinary activities after taxation	*(39)*	*(32)*

Generally adverse balances in the balance sheet and profit and loss account should be bracketed: e.g. loss on ordinary activities before taxation, loss on ordinary activities after taxation, net current liabilities, debit balance on profit and loss account.

3.030 MODEL REPORT AND FINANCIAL STATEMENTS

Cover page

TRAMP HOLDINGS p.l.c.

REPORT AND FINANCIAL STATEMENTS

31 December 1984

Verry & Fire, Thrift House, Cheapside, London, EC2V 5TH

TRAMP HOLDINGS p.l.c.

REPORT AND FINANCIAL STATEMENTS 1984

CONTENTS

* Not produced for the purposes of this manual.

1.

TRAMP HOLDINGS p.l.c.

NOTICE OF MEETING

Notice is hereby given that the Annual General Meeting of Tramp Holdings p.l.c. will be held at The Connaught Rooms, Great Queen Street, London, W.C.2 on Thursday, 25 July 1985 at 12.00 noon for the following purposes:

1. To receive and adopt the financial statements for the year ended 31 December 1984, together with the reports of the directors and auditors thereon.

2. To declare a final ordinary dividend.

3. To elect directors.

4. To re-appoint the auditors and to fix their remuneration.

5. To transact any other ordinary business of the company.

By Order of the Board

A. VAGRANT

1 July 1985

Secretary

Notes:

1. A member entitled to attend and vote at this meeting is entitled to appoint a proxy or proxies to attend and vote instead of him. A proxy need not be a member of the company. Proxy forms must be lodged with the registrars not later than 48 hours before the time fixed for the meeting.

2. Copies of all directors' service contracts are available for inspection during business hours at the company's registered office, Thrift House, Cheapside, London EC2V 5TH and on the day of the Annual General Meeting at The Connaught Rooms, Great Queen Street, London, W.C.2 from 11.45 a.m. until the conclusion of that meeting.

(N.B. The Secretary may wish to include in the notice of meeting the wording of the actual resolutions to be placed before the members. The wording in 1 to 5 above represents the minimum requirement in respect of ordinary business.)

TRAMP HOLDINGS p.l.c.

OFFICERS AND PROFESSIONAL ADVISERS

Directors	J. Tramp (Chairman) M. Driver (Managing Director) A. Vagrant, F.C.A. J. Docker F. Sharp
Secretary	A. Vagrant, F.C.A.
Registered Office	Thrift House, Cheapside, London, EC2V 5TH
Auditors	Verry & Fire, Chartered Accountants
Bankers	Universal Bank Limited
Solicitors	Busola Peabody & Co.
Registrars	B & D Registrars Limited, 3 London Wall, London, EC2M 5PH

3.

TRAMP HOLDINGS p.l.c.

SALIENT FEATURES AND FINANCIAL CALENDAR

Year ended 31 December 1984

	1984 £'000	1983 £'000
TURNOVER	43,180	39,200
	======	======
PROFIT/(LOSS) AFTER TAXATION		
Before extraordinary items		
Historical cost	1,080	880
Current cost	(89)	90
After extraordinary items		
Historical cost	1,450	880
Current cost	120	90
	======	======
EARNINGS/(LOSS) PER ORDINARY SHARE		
Before extraordinary items		
Historical cost	13.5p	11.0p
Current cost	(1.1)p	1.1p
	======	======
DIVIDENDS PER ORDINARY SHARE	4p	3p
	======	======

RESULTS

First half year	:	Announced mid-September
Results for the year	:	Announced mid-June
Report and financial statements	:	Circulated early July

DIVIDENDS

Ordinary dividends		
Interim	:	Declared mid-October Paid early December
Final	:	Proposed mid-June Paid early August

TRAMP HOLDINGS p. l.c.

DIRECTORS' REPORT

The directors present their annual report and the audited financial statements for the year ended 31 December 1984.

1. ACTIVITIES

Tramp Holdings p.l.c. is the holding company of a group of companies engaged in the manufacture of accessories for the motor trade and artificial jewellery.

2. REVIEW OF DEVELOPMENTS

Group results

Despite difficult trading conditions in the motor industry throughout 1984, the directors are pleased to be able to report pre-tax profits up at £2.1m compared with £1.7m for the preceding year, an increase of 22%. Turnover increased by 10% to £43.2m and can be attributed to the exceptionally buoyant demand for our products in North America.

A geographical analysis of profits from ordinary activities before taxation is given below:

	1984		1983	
	£'000	%	£'000	%
United Kingdom	1,080	44	1,218	59
Other European countries	365	15	492	24
North America	1,005	41	340	17
	2,450	100	2,050	100

The group was able to sell land which was surplus to requirements, giving rise to an extraordinary profit after tax of £420,000. After losses arising from the closure of our metal trim division, extraordinary items added £370,000 to reserves.

Motor Products Division

This division is a major producer of accessories for the motor trade in the UK and in the US, with manufacturing plants in both countries producing a wide range of products for the car industry.

The sales volume and profits of the division showed considerable growth in North America, but this was offset by the decline in markets in the UK, reflecting the influence of price increases and loss in share of the car market to foreign competitors. Total sales of the division remained at the same level as last year, however, profits declined by 8%.

TRAMP HOLDINGS p.l.c.

DIRECTORS' REPORT
(continued)

2. REVIEW OF DEVELOPMENTS (continued)

Your directors plan extensive capital investments of £3m over the next three years to modernise and automate our UK plants. In order to concentrate resources on the more profitable plastics products, a decision was made to close production and marketing of our metal based product line. We are pleased that most employees who were affected by the closure were able to accept new jobs at our other plants.

Jewellery Division

The jewellery division manufactures low-priced jewellery which is sold to leading department stores and jewellery chains in the UK and the rest of Western Europe.

Sales and profits of this division exceeded all expectations, sales increasing by 27% to £19m and profits by 53% to £1.5m. We attribute this success to our line of teenage "stick-on" and "stick-through" trinkets introduced at the end of 1983 and the full benefits are now reflected in the 1984 results.

Acquisition

Shareholders approved the acquisition of all the issued share capital of C.P. Plastics Limited on 30 June 1984 for £2,000,000 cash. This subsidiary manufactures plastic trim for the motor trade and extends the range of products of the Motor Division. Its contribution to turnover and earnings is disclosed in note 2 to the accounts.

Unfortunately this company did not meet the level of profits forecast in the circular to shareholders, achieving a pre-tax profit of £215,000 compared to a forecast pre-tax profit of £330,000. The reduction in profitability was due primarily to the sharp downturn in the automotive market which could not have been anticipated at the time of the takeover.

Financial position

Shareholders' equity increased by £1.0m to £11.2m by profits retained in the year of £1.1m, by revaluation of properties of £0.5m, and after writing off goodwill of £0.6m. With working capital at £7.9m and cash balances in excess of bank overdrafts, the directors believe the group is soundly based to take advantage of opportunities for additional growth through further acquisition of companies.

TRAMP HOLDINGS p.l.c.

DIRECTORS' REPORT
(continued)

3. DIVIDENDS AND TRANSFERS TO RESERVES

The final dividend recommended by the directors is 2.5p per ordinary share, which together with the interim dividend paid of 1.5p per ordinary share, gives a total dividend for the year of 4.0p compared to 3.0p last year. After dividends, retained profits of £1.1m have been transferred to reserves.

4. RESEARCH AND DEVELOPMENT

Your group of companies continues an active programme of research and development, the costs of which in the year amounted to £722,000 (1983 - £605,000). We believe that our new line of shock-resistant bumpers introduced in 1984 will prove to be one of the main sources of turnover for the Motor Division in 1985. Our increased order book, which is due mainly to this product, should be reflected in next year's results.

We attribute much of the success of our Jewellery Division to the constant review and updating of our product lines to capitalise on the rapid changes in fashions.

5. IMPORTANT EVENT OCCURRING AFTER THE END OF YEAR

A fire destroyed production facilities in Meriden after the end of the year. The financial implications of this loss are disclosed in note 28 to the accounts.

6. FUTURE PROSPECTS

Your directors are optimistic about the long term prospects for continued growth. The destruction of production facilities mentioned in the preceding paragraph and in note 28 to the accounts will significantly affect the completion of orders for bumpers in the first half of 1984. The replacement of these facilities in the third quarter should result in the resumption of sales with no permanent loss of business anticipated.

7. FIXED ASSETS

A revaluation of freehold and long leasehold properties was undertaken this year by Messrs. K.T. and Co., chartered surveyors, resulting in a surplus of £500,000 over the previous valuation undertaken in 1981 and this surplus has been brought into the financial statements.

TRAMP HOLDINGS p.l.c.

DIRECTORS' REPORT
(continued)

7. FIXED ASSETS (continued)

The group spent £250,000 during the year on equipment for the Motor Division. Surplus land at Nottingham was disposed of and the Board took the opportunity of acquiring for £700,000 the site adjacent to the head office which will give room for expansion in the future.

8. DIRECTORS

The present membership of the Board is set out on page 2. All directors served throughout the year with the exception of Mr. A. Vagrant who was appointed a director on 30 June 1984. Mr. Vagrant retires and offers himself for re-election. His service contract with the company expires on 30 June 1986.

In accordance with the company's Articles of Association, Mr. J. Tramp retires by rotation and, being eligible, offers himself for re-election. He has no service contract with the company.

The directors' interests, as defined by the Companies Act, in the shares of the company at 1 January 1984 (or date of appointment) and 31 December 1984 were as follows:

	£1 ordinary shares			
	Beneficial		Non-beneficial	
	1.1.84 or date of appointment	31.12.84	1.1.84 or date of appointment	31.12.84
J. Tramp	1,000,000	1,000,000	-	-
F. Sharp	150,000	150,000	20,000	20,000
J. Docker	-	-	-	-
M. Driver	-	-	-	-
A. Vagrant	-	-	-	-

There has been no change in directors' holdings between the year end and 3 June 1985.

The directors had no interest in the 9% unsecured loan stock 1994/99 or the 12% debenture loan 1984/86.

(Note: Particulars of directors' holdings of shares and debentures may be disclosed in the notes to the accounts.)

9. SUBSTANTIAL INTERESTS

The Board is not aware of any person, other than a director, who is interested in 5 per cent. or more of the issued share capital of the company.

TRAMP HOLDINGS p.l.c.

DIRECTORS' REPORT
(continued)

10. DONATIONS

During the year the group made the following donations:

Political purposes	
Conservative Party	£1,000
Charitable purposes	£3,500

11. EMPLOYEE INVOLVEMENT

Quarterly meetings are held with employee representatives to discuss sales, financial position and prospects. Opportunity is given at these meetings for senior executives to be questioned about matters which concern the employees.

A monthly magazine is distributed to all employees which includes articles on the group's performance and plans.

12. EMPLOYMENT OF DISABLED PERSONS

The company and its subsidiaries have continued the policy regarding the employment of disabled persons. Full and fair consideration is given to applications for employment made by disabled persons having regard to their particular aptitudes and abilities. During the year, 350 disabled persons were employed compared to 312 in the preceding year. Appropriate training is arranged for disabled persons, including retraining for alternative work of employees who become disabled, to promote their career development within the organisation.

13. CLOSE COMPANY STATUS

So far as the directors are aware, the company is not a close company for taxation purposes.

14. AUDITORS

A resolution to re-appoint Verry & Fire as auditors will be proposed at the forthcoming Annual General Meeting.

By order of the Board

A. VAGRANT

1 July 1985

Secretary

AUDITORS' REPORT TO THE MEMBERS

of

TRAMP HOLDINGS p.l.c.

We have audited the financial statements on pages 10 to 33 in accordance with approved Auditing Standards.

In our opinion the financial statements on pages 10 to 28 give, under the historical cost convention as described in note 1(a), a true and fair view of the state of affairs of the company and the group at 31 December 1984 and of the profit and source and application of funds of the group for the year then ended and comply with the Companies Act 1985.

In our opinion the abridged supplementary current cost statements on pages 29 to 33 have been properly prepared, in accordance with the policies and methods described in notes 1 and 2, to give the information required by Statement of Standard Accounting Practice No. 16.

Verry & Fine

1 July 1985

Chartered Accountants
Thrift House
Cheapside
London
EC2V 5TH

10.

TRAMP HOLDINGS p.l.c.

CONSOLIDATED PROFIT AND LOSS ACCOUNT

Year ended 31 December 1984

	Note	1984 £'000	1983 £'000
Turnover	3	43,180	39,200
Cost of sales		35,080	32,120
Gross profit		8,100	7,080
Distribution costs		2,650	2,320
Administrative expenses		3,690	3,180
Other operating income		(350)	(260)
		5,990	5,240
Operating profit		2,110	1,840
Income from shares in associated companies		200	120
Income from other fixed asset investments		10	30
Other interest receivable and similar income	5	70	70
Interest payable and similar charges	6	(310)	(360)
Profit on ordinary activities before taxation	3, 7	2,080	1,700
Tax on profit on ordinary activities	8	980	800
Profit on ordinary activities after taxation		1,100	900
Minority interests		20	20
Profit on ordinary activities attributable to the members of Tramp Holdings p.l.c.		1,080	880
Extraordinary items	9	370	-
Profit for the financial year	10	1,450	880
Dividends paid and proposed	11	(320)	(240)
Profit retained, transferred to reserves		1,130	640
Earnings per ordinary share	12		
Before extraordinary items		13.5p	11.0p
After extraordinary items		18.1p	11.0p

TRAMP HOLDINGS p.l.c.

STATEMENTS OF MOVEMENTS ON RESERVES

Year ended 31 December 1984

	Share premium account £'000	Revaluation reserve £'000	Foreign exchange translation £'000	Profit and loss account £'000
THE GROUP				
Balance at 1 January 1984	978	468	260	1,272
Profit retained for the year	-	-	-	1,130
Surplus on revaluation of land and buildings	-	500	-	-
Write off of goodwill	-	-	-	(660)
Foreign exchange translation differences	-	-	30	-
Transfer of amount equivalent to additional depreciation on revalued assets	-	(8)	-	8
Scrip issue	(800)	-	-	-
Options exercised	2	-	-	-
Balance at 31 December 1984	180	960	290	1,750
THE COMPANY				
Balance at 1 January 1984	978	468		732
Profit retained for the year	-	-		150
Surplus on revaluation of land and buildings	-	500		-
Transfer of amount equivalent to additional depreciation on revalued assets	-	(8)		8
Scrip issue	(800)	-		-
Options exercised	2	-		-
Balance at 31 December 1984	180	960		890

TRAMP HOLDINGS p.l.c.

CONSOLIDATED BALANCE SHEET 31 December 1984

	Note	1984		1983	
		£'000	£'000	£'000	£'000
FIXED ASSETS					
Intangible assets	13	150		200	
Tangible assets	14	6,230		5,500	
Investments	15	250		150	
			6,630		5,850
CURRENT ASSETS					
Stocks	16	6,000		5,200	
Debtors	17	6,140		5,750	
Investments	18	500		500	
Cash at bank and in hand		1,500		1,988	
		14,140		13,438	
CREDITORS: AMOUNTS FALLING DUE WITHIN ONE YEAR					
Debenture loans	21	400		400	
Bank loans and overdrafts	21	1,060		2,000	
Obligations under finance leases and hire purchase contracts	21	230		180	
Trade creditors		3,295		2,090	
Other creditors including taxation and social security	19	900		780	
Proposed dividend	11	200		160	
Accruals and deferred income		415		370	
		6,500		5,980	
NET CURRENT ASSETS			7,640		7,458
TOTAL ASSETS LESS CURRENT LIABILITIES			14,270		13,308
CREDITORS: AMOUNTS FALLING DUE AFTER MORE THAN ONE YEAR	20, 21	1,970		2,420	
PROVISIONS FOR LIABILITIES AND CHARGES	22	900		520	
MINORITY INTERESTS		220		200	
			3,090		3,140
			11,180		10,168
CAPITAL AND RESERVES					
Called up share capital	23		8,000		7,190
Share premium account			180		978
Revaluation reserve			960		468
Other reserves			290		260
Profit and loss account			1,750		1,272
			11,180		10,168

These financial statements were approved by the Board of Directors on 1 July 1985.

J. TRAMP)
) Directors
M. DRIVER)

TRAMP HOLDINGS p.l.c.

BALANCE SHEET 31 December 1984

	Note	1984 £'000	1984 £'000	1983 £'000	1983 £'000
FIXED ASSETS					
Tangible assets	14	3,790		3,680	
Investments	15	5,060		3,060	
			8,850		6,740
CURRENT ASSETS					
Stocks	16	200		100	
Debtors	17	1,780		2,530	
Investments	18	200		200	
Cash at bank and in hand		450		1,148	
		2,630		3,978	
CREDITORS: AMOUNTS FALLING DUE WITHIN ONE YEAR					
Bank loans and overdrafts	21	300		490	
Trade creditors		400		200	
Amounts owed to group companies - subsidiaries		100		50	
Other creditors including taxation and social security	19	50		50	
Proposed dividend	11	200		160	
		1,050		950	
NET CURRENT ASSETS			1,580		3,028
TOTAL ASSETS LESS CURRENT LIABILITIES			10,430		9,768
CREDITORS: AMOUNTS FALLING DUE AFTER MORE THAN ONE YEAR	20, 21		400		400
			10,030		9,368
CAPITAL AND RESERVES					
Called up share capital	23		8,000		7,190
Share premium account			180		978
Revaluation reserve			960		468
Profit and loss account			890		732
			10,030		9,368

J. TRAMP)
) Directors
M. DRIVER)

TRAMP HOLDINGS p.l.c.

CONSOLIDATED STATEMENT OF SOURCE AND APPLICATION OF FUNDS

Year ended 31 December 1984

	1984 £'000	1983 £'000
SOURCE OF FUNDS		
Profit on ordinary activities before taxation	2,080	1,700
Adjustments for items not involving the movement of funds:		
Depreciation	850	630
Profit retained in associated companies	(200)	(80)
Total generated from operations	2,730	2,250
Increase in creditors	290	500
Borrowings under lease obligations and hire purchase contracts	250	160
Decrease in stocks	-	450
Proceeds of share option scheme	12	-
Proceeds of sale of land and other extraordinary item	1,500	-
	4,782	3,360
APPLICATION OF FUNDS		
Purchases of tangible fixed assets	1,000	800
Purchase of C.P. Plastics Limited *	1,600	-
Tax paid	580	460
Dividends paid	280	220
Increase in stocks	100	-
Increase in debtors	190	850
Repayment of loans, lease obligations, and hire purchase contracts	580	1,400
	4,330	3,730
INCREASE/(DECREASE) IN NET LIQUID FUNDS	452	(370)
	=====	=====

(Net liquid funds comprise bank balances less bank loans and overdrafts)

* ANALYSIS OF PURCHASE OF C.P. PLASTICS LIMITED:

	£'000		£'000
Net assets acquired		Discharged by	
Tangible fixed assets	1,000	Cash paid	2,000
Goodwill	660	Less cash included in assets acquired	(400)
Stocks	700		
Debtors	200		
Creditors	(960)		
	1,600		1,600
	=====		=====

TRAMP HOLDINGS p.l.c.

NOTES TO THE ACCOUNTS

Year ended 31 December 1984

1. ACCOUNTING POLICIES

(a) Accounting convention

The financial statements are prepared under the historical cost convention as modified by the revaluation of freehold and long leasehold properties.

(b) Basis of consolidation

The group financial statements consolidate the financial statements of the company and all subsidiaries for all financial periods ended 31 December 1984.

(c) Intangible fixed assets

Patents and trademarks are depreciated over a period of five years. Goodwill arising on consolidation is written off direct to reserves in the year in which it arises.

(d) Tangible fixed assets

Depreciation is not provided on freehold land. On other assets it is provided on cost or revalued amounts in equal annual instalments over the estimated lives of the assets. The rates of depreciation are as follows:

Freehold buildings	2% per annum
Leased assets	Over the term of lease
Plant	15% per annum
Motor vehicles	25% per annum
Equipment, fixtures and tools	10% - 33 1/3% per annum

(e) Investments

(i) In the accounts of Tramp Holdings p.l.c. investments held as fixed assets are stated at cost. Those held as current assets are stated at the lower of cost and net realisable value.

(ii) In the consolidated accounts, shares in associated companies are accounted for using the equity method of accounting. The consolidated profit and loss account includes the group's share of the before-tax profits and attributable taxation of the related companies based on audited financial statements for the year ended 31 October 1984. In the consolidated balance sheet, the shares in associated companies are shown at the group's share of the net assets, excluding goodwill, of the associated companies.

(iii) Other investments held as fixed assets are stated at cost. Investments held as current assets are stated at the lower of cost and net realisable value.

TRAMP HOLDINGS p.l.c.

NOTES TO THE ACCOUNTS

Year ended 31 December 1984

1. ACCOUNTING POLICIES, continued

(f) Stocks

Stocks are stated at the lower of cost and net realisable value. Cost represents materials, direct labour and appropriate production overheads.

(g) Deferred taxation

Deferred taxation is provided at the anticipated tax rates on differences arising from the inclusion of items of income and expenditure in taxation computations in periods different from those in which they are included in the financial statements to the extent that it is probable that a liability or asset will crystallise in the future.

(h) Foreign exchange

The financial statements of the foreign subsidiary are translated into sterling at the closing rate of exchange and the difference arising from the translation of the opening net investment in the subsidiary at the closing rate is taken direct to reserves. Other translation differences are dealt with in the profit and loss account.

(i) Pension costs

Retirement benefits to employees of most companies in the group are provided by defined benefit schemes which are funded by contributions from the group companies and employees. Payments are made either to pension trusts which are financially separate from the group or to insurance companies. These payments, which are made in accordance with periodic calculations by professionally qualified actuaries are charged against the profits of the year in which they become payable.

(j) Leases

Assets held under finance leases and the related lease obligations are recorded in the balance sheet at the fair value of the leased assets at the inception of the leases. The excess of the lease payments over the recorded lease obligations are treated as finance charges which are amortised over each lease term to give a constant rate of charge on the remaining balance of the obligation.

Rental costs under operating leases are charged to profit and loss account in equal annual amounts over the periods of the leases.

TRAMP HOLDINGS p.l.c.

NOTES TO THE ACCOUNTS

Year ended 31 December 1984

2. ACQUISITION

On 30 June 1984 the whole of the issued share capital of C.P. Plastics Limited was acquired for £2,000,000. The turnover and profit before taxation of this company for the six months ended 31 December 1984, amounting to £6,230,000 and £215,000 respectively, are included in the consolidated profit and loss account.

3. TURNOVER AND PROFITS

Analyses by class of business of turnover and historical cost profit before taxation are stated below:

	Turnover		Profit before taxation	
	1984	1983	1984	1983
	£'000	£'000	£'000	£'000
Class of business				
Jewellery	19,000	15,000	1,470	960
Motor products	24,180	24,200	1,100	1,200
	43,180	39,200	2,570	2,160
Less interest and other central costs			490	460
			2,080	1,700

Geographical analysis of turnover	1984	1983
	£'000	£'000
United Kingdom	31,300	29,650
Other European countries	5,200	5,110
North America	6,680	4,440
	43,180	39,200

TRAMP HOLDINGS p.l.c.

NOTES TO THE ACCOUNTS

Year ended 31 December 1984

4. INFORMATION REGARDING DIRECTORS AND EMPLOYEES

	1984 £'000	1983 £'000
Directors' emoluments:		
Fees	5	5
Other emoluments	73	64
Ex-gratia payments to former director	-	2
	78	71
Remuneration of the chairman	29	26
Remuneration of the highest paid director	35	33

Scale of directors' remuneration:	1984 No.	1983 No.
£ 0 - £ 5,000	3	3
£25,001 - £30,000	1	1
£30,001 - £35,000	1	1

	1984 £'000	1983 £'000
Employee costs during the year:		
Wages and salaries	22,910	18,840
Social security costs	2,210	1,840
Other pension costs	1,400	1,250
	26,520	21,930

Remuneration of senior employees which fall within the following range:	1984 No.	1983 No.
£30,001 - £35,000	2	1

	1984	1983
Average number of persons employed:		
Production	2,481	2,473
Sales and distribution	362	305
Administration	987	941
	3,830	3,719

5. OTHER INTEREST RECEIVABLE AND SIMILAR INCOME

	1984 £'000	1983 £'000
This heading includes:		
Income from listed investments	65	60

TRAMP HOLDINGS p.l.c.

NOTES TO THE ACCOUNTS

Year ended 31 December 1984

	1984 £'000	1983 £'000
6. INTEREST PAYABLE AND SIMILAR CHARGES		
Bank loans, overdrafts and other loans repayable within five years	150	210
Other loans	40	40
Finance charges - finance leases and hire purchase obligations	120	110
	310	360
	===	===
7. PROFIT ON ORDINARY ACTIVITIES BEFORE TAXATION		
Profit on ordinary activities before taxation is after charging:		
Rentals under operating leases		
Hire of plant and machinery	450	430
Other operating leases	220	200
	670	630
	===	===
Depreciation and other amounts written off tangible and intangible fixed assets:		
Own assets	783	572
Assets held under finance leases and hire purchase contracts	67	58
Auditors' remuneration	33	27
Exceptional charges and (credits):		
Redundancy costs	-	240
Employment grants	(30)	(170)
Exchange loss on conversion of dollar loan	-	65
8. TAX ON PROFIT ON ORDINARY ACTIVITIES		
United Kingdom corporation tax at 46.25% (1983 - 50.5%) based on the profit for the year	220	560
Less relief for overseas taxation	70	40
	150	520
Deferred taxation	400	80
Overseas taxation	370	140
Associated companies	100	60
	1,020	800
Adjustment to prior years' tax provisions	(40)	-
	980	800
	=====	=====

The taxation charge for the year has been reduced by £90,000 (1983 - £20,000) by capital allowances in excess of depreciation for which no deferred tax has been provided and by £34,000 (1983 - £180,000) in respect of stock relief.

TRAMP HOLDINGS p.l.c.

NOTES TO THE ACCOUNTS

Year ended 31 December 1984

9. EXTRAORDINARY ITEMS	1984 £'000	1983 £'000
Extraordinary income:		
Capital profit realised on sale of land	580	-
Extraordinary charges:		
Costs of closure of metal trim division	(80)	-
Extraordinary profit	500	-
Tax on extraordinary profit - corporation tax	130	-
	370	-

10. PROFIT OF PARENT COMPANY

As permitted by Section 228(7) of the Companies Act 1985, the profit and loss account of the parent company is not presented as part of these accounts. The consolidated profit for the financial year includes £470,000 (1983 - £290,000) which is dealt with in the accounts of the parent company.

11. DIVIDENDS	1984		1983	
	Per share	£'000	Per share	£'000
Interim	1.5p	120	1.0p	80
Proposed final	2.5p	200	2.0p	160
	4.0p	320	3.0p	240

12. EARNINGS PER ORDINARY SHARE

The calculation of earnings per ordinary share before extraordinary items is based on profits of £1,080,000 (1983 - £880,000) and on the average 7,995,000 (1983 - 7,990,000) ordinary shares in issue during the year, as adjusted for the scrip issue. No material dilution of earnings per share would arise if all outstanding share options were exercised.

13. INTANGIBLE FIXED ASSETS	Patents, trademarks £'000
Cost	
At 1 January 1984 and 31 December 1984	250
Accumulated depreciation	
At 1 January 1984	50
Provision	50
At 31 December 1984	100
Net book value	
At 31 December 1984	150
At 31 December 1983	200

TRAMP HOLDINGS p.l.c.

NOTES TO THE ACCOUNTS

Year ended 31 December 1984

14. TANGIBLE FIXED ASSETS

THE GROUP	Total £'000	Land and buildings: Freehold £'000	Land and buildings: Long leases £'000	Land and buildings: Short leases £'000	Plant and machinery £'000	Fixtures, fittings, tools & equipment £'000
Cost or Valuation						
At 1 January 1984	7,550	3,000	1,000	300	2,250	1,000
Foreign exchange translation differences	40	-	-	-	30	10
Additions						
Subsidiary acquired	1,000	-	-	-	500	500
Capital expenditure	1,000	700	-	-	200	100
Disposals	(1,050)	(1,000)	-	-	(50)	-
Adjustment arising on revaluation	30	180	(150)	-	-	-
At 31 December 1984	8,570	2,880	850	300	2,930	1,610
At valuation	3,100	2,250	850	-	-	-
At cost	5,470	630	-	300	2,930	1,610
	8,570	2,880	850	300	2,930	1,610
Accumulated depreciation						
At 1 January 1984	2,050	160	250	210	1,030	400
Foreign exchange translation differences	10	-	-	-	7	3
Provisions	800	40	20	30	510	200
Disposals	(50)	-	-	-	(50)	-
Adjustment arising on revaluation	(470)	(200)	(270)	-	-	-
At 31 December 1984	2,340	-	-	240	1,497	603
Net book value						
At 31 December 1984	6,230	2,880	850	60	1,433	1,007
At 31 December 1983	5,500	2,840	750	90	1,220	600
Comparable amounts determined according to the historical cost convention:						
Cost	8,140	2,300	1,000	300	2,930	1,610
Accumulated depreciation	2,870	260	270	240	1,497	603
Net book value						
At 31 December 1984	5,270	2,040	730	60	1,433	1,007
At 31 December 1983	5,032	2,372	750	90	1,220	600

TRAMP HOLDINGS p.l.c.
NOTES TO THE ACCOUNTS
Year ended 31 December 1984

14. TANGIBLE FIXED ASSETS, continued

THE COMPANY	Total £'000	Land and buildings Freehold £'000	Land and buildings Long leases £'000	Land and buildings Short leases £'000	Plant and machinery £'000
Cost or valuation					
At 1 January 1984	4,350	3,000	1,000	300	50
Additions	700	700	-	-	-
Disposals	(1,000)	(1,000)	-	-	-
Adjustment arising on revaluation	30	180	(150)	-	-
At 31 December 1984	4,080	2,880	850	300	50
At valuation	3,100	2,250	850	-	-
At cost	980	630	-	300	50
	4,080	2,880	850	300	50
Accumulated depreciation					
At 1 January 1984	670	160	250	210	50
Provisions	90	40	20	30	-
Adjustment arising on revaluation	(470)	(200)	(270)	-	-
At 31 December 1984	290	-	-	240	50
Net book value					
At 31 December 1984	3,790	2,880	850	60	-
At 31 December 1983	3,680	2,840	750	90	-
Comparable amounts determined according to the historical cost convention:					
Cost	3,650	2,300	1,000	300	50
Accumulated depreciation	820	260	270	240	50
Net book value					
At 31 December 1984	2,830	2,040	730	60	-
At 31 December 1983	3,212	2,372	750	90	-

Included in freehold land and buildings are property in course of construction amounting to £630,000 and land valued at £300,000 which are not depreciated.

Freehold and long leasehold land and buildings, excluding those under construction, were valued on 31 December, 1984 at open market value on the basis of existing use at £2,250,000 and £850,000 respectively by Messrs. K. T. and Co., Chartered Surveyors. The surplus over net book value of £500,000 has been transferred to Revaluation Reserve.

The net book value of the group's fixed assets includes £668,000 in respect of assets held under finance leases and hire purchase contracts.

TRAMP HOLDINGS p.l.c. 23.

NOTES TO THE ACCOUNTS

Year ended 31 December 1984

15. INVESTMENTS HELD AS FIXED ASSETS

	The Group		The Company	
	1984	1983	1984	1983
	£'000	£'000	£'000	£'000
Shares in group companies - subsidiaries	-	-	4,010	2,010
Loans to group companies - subsidiaries	-	-	1,035	1,035
Shares in associated companies	235	135	-	-
Other investments other than loans	15	15	15	15
	250	150	5,060	3,060
	===	===	=====	=====

All of the above investments are unlisted.

Additional information in respect of investments for which there have been movements during the year:

	£'000	£'000
Shares in group companies:		
Balance at 1 January 1984		2,010
Acquisition of subsidiary		2,000
Balance at 31 December 1984		4,010
		=====
Shares in associated companies:		
Cost		85
Group's share of undistributed post acquisition profits:		
Balance at 1 January 1984	50	
Profits retained for the year	100	
		150
Balance at 31 December 1984		235
		=====

16. STOCKS

	The Group		The Company	
	1984	1983	1984	1983
	£'000	£'000	£'000	£'000
Raw materials and consumables	1,120	1,850	200	100
Work in progress	1,630	1,950	-	-
Finished goods and goods for resale	3,870	2,500		
Less payments on account	(620)	(1,100)	-	-
	6,000	5,200	200	100
	=====	=====	=====	=====

The replacement cost of raw materials and consumables held by the group at 31 December 1984 was £830,000 greater (1983 - £730,000 greater) than the amount at which they are stated in the financial statements; there were no significant differences between the replacement cost and the values shown for other stock categories.

TRAMP HOLDINGS p.l.c. 24.

NOTES TO THE ACCOUNTS

Year ended 31 December 1984

17. DEBTORS

	The Group 1984 £'000	The Group 1983 £'000	The Company 1984 £'000	The Company 1983 £'000
Trade debtors				
Due within one year	5,150	5,100	1,230	2,270
Due after more than one year	300	110	300	110
Amounts owed by group companies - subsidiaries	-	-	100	50
Amount owed by associated company	60	60	-	-
Other debtors	250	190	150	100
Prepayments and accrued income	380	290	-	-
	6,140	5,750	1,780	2,530

18. INVESTMENTS HELD AS CURRENT ASSETS

	The Group 1984 £'000	The Group 1983 £'000	The Company 1984 £'000	The Company 1983 £'000
Other investments:				
Shares in listed companies				
In U.K.	200	100	200	100
Overseas	300	400	-	100
	500	500	200	200

The market value of listed investments held by the group was £750,000 (1983 - £680,000) and by the company was £250,000 (1983 - £220,000). A taxation liability of £75,000 for the group and £10,000 for the company would arise if these investments were sold at the stated market values.

19. OTHER CREDITORS INCLUDING TAXATION AND SOCIAL SECURITY

	The Group 1984 £'000	The Group 1983 £'000	The Company 1984 £'000	The Company 1983 £'000
This heading includes:				
Taxation and social security	683	614	15	13

20. CREDITORS: AMOUNTS FALLING DUE AFTER MORE THAN ONE YEAR

	The Group 1984 £'000	The Group 1983 £'000	The Company 1984 £'000	The Company 1983 £'000
Debenture loans	600	1,000	400	400
Bank loans	200	200	-	-
Obligations under finance leases and hire purchase contracts	590	570	-	-
Corporation tax due 1 January 1986	580	650	-	-
	1,970	2,420	400	400

TRAMP HOLDINGS p.l.c.
NOTES TO THE ACCOUNTS
Year ended 31 December 1984

25.

21. BORROWINGS

	The Group		The Company	
	1984	1983	1984	1983
	£'000	£'000	£'000	£'000
Debenture loans				
Secured loan - 12% 1984/86	600	1,000	-	-
Unsecured loan stock - 9% 1994/99	400	400	400	400
Bank loans and overdrafts				
Secured	1,260	1,550	300	490
Unsecured	-	650	-	-
Obligations under finance leases and hire purchase contracts	820	750	-	-
	3,080	4,350	700	890
Less amounts falling due within one year	1,690	2,580	300	490
Amounts falling due after more than one year	1,390	1,770	400	400
Analysis of loan repayments:				
Bank loans and overdrafts				
Within one year or on demand	1,060	2,000	300	490
Between two and five years	150	100	-	-
After five years	50	100	-	-
Other loans:				
Within one year or on demand	630	580	-	-
Between one and two years	350	542	-	-
Between two and five years	260	460	-	-
After five years	580	568	400	400
	3,080	4,350	700	890
Amounts wholly repayable after five years:				
Debenture loans	400	400	400	400
Amounts repayable by instalments some of which fall due after five years:				
Bank loan				
Total amount	200	200	-	-
Instalments due after five years	50	100	-	-
Finance leases and hire purchase contracts				
Total amount	502	495	-	-
Instalments due after five years	180	168	-	-

The debenture loan 1984/86 is secured by a first mortgage on the freehold factory premises held by the company. The long term bank loan bears interest at 2% above the bank's base rate. The bank loans and overdrafts are secured by fixed and floating charges on the assets of U.K. companies. Obligations under finance leases and hire purchase contracts are secured by related leased assets and bear finance charges at rates ranging from 15% to 25% per annum.

NOTES TO THE ACCOUNTS

Year ended 31 December 1984

22. PROVISIONS FOR LIABILITIES AND CHARGES

	Balance at 1 January 1984 £'000	Charged to to profit and loss account £'000	Applied £'000	Balance at 31 December 1984 £'000
THE GROUP				
Deferred taxation (a)	470	400	20	850
Unfunded pensions (b)	40	-	10	30
Product guarantees	10	20	10	20
Total provisions for liabilities and charges	520	420	40	900

(a) The amounts of deferred taxation provided and unprovided in the accounts are:

	Provided 1984 £'000	Provided 1983 £'000	Unprovided 1984 £'000	Unprovided 1983 £'000
THE GROUP				
Capital allowances in excess of depreciation	820	440	160	70
Surplus on revaluation	-	-	190	100
Other timing differences	130	110	50	90
	950	550	400	260
Less unrelieved Advance Corporation Tax	100	80		
	850	470		
THE COMPANY				
Surplus on revaluation	-	-	190	100

No provision has been made for taxation that would arise in the event of the overseas subsidiary distributing the balance of its reserves.

(b) The provision for unfunded pensions represents the balance of unpaid instalments recommended by the pension scheme actuaries to fund increases in benefits to existing pensioners to compensate for inflation in recent years.

TRAMP HOLDINGS p.l.c. 27.

NOTES TO THE ACCOUNTS

Year ended 31 December 1984

23. CALLED UP SHARE CAPITAL

	£'000
Authorised 10,000,000 ordinary shares of £1	10,000
Allotted and fully paid	
Balance at 1 January 1984	7,190
Options exercised	10
Scrip issue	800
Balance at 31 December 1984	8,000

During the year a scrip issue of 800,000 fully paid ordinary shares of £1 each was made at par value (£800,000) to shareholders out of share premium account on the basis of one new share for each nine shares held. The issue was made for the purpose of improving the marketability of the company's shares. Also 10,000 ordinary shares of £1 each (£10,000 par value) were issued for £12,000 under the share option scheme.

Under the Company's employee share option scheme, employees held options at 31 December 1984 for 306,525 ordinary shares as follows:

Number of shares	Option price per share	Option period ending
100,525	£1.20	31 December 1986
66,000	1.40	1 October 1987
140,000	1.45	30 September 1989

24. CAPITAL COMMITMENTS

	The Group		The Company	
	1984	1983	1984	1983
	£'000	£'000	£'000	£'000
Contracted for but not provided in the financial statements	250	750	50	50
Authorised but not yet contracted for	1,200	600	800	100

25. CONTINGENT LIABILITIES

Discounted bills of exchange	2,000	1,800	1,250	1,250

NOTES TO THE ACCOUNTS

Year ended 31 December 1984

26. OPERATING LEASE COMMITMENTS

At 31 December 1984 the group was committed to making the following payments during the next year in respect of operating leases:

	Land and buildings £'000	Other £'000
Leases which expire:		
Within one year	-	160
Within 2 to 5 years	-	350
After 5 years	220	-
	220	510

27. DIRECTOR'S CONTRACT

Mr. J. Tramp is the lessor in a contract expiring in 1991 whereby factory premises have been leased to the company at an annual rental of £220,000.

28. EVENT OCCURRING AFTER THE END OF YEAR

On 2 February 1985, facilities for the production of motor products at Meriden were destroyed by fire. While insurance coverage carried by the group exceeds the net book value of the assets destroyed, the replacement cost of new facilities is expected to require a large additional investment which cannot be quantified at this time. Reconstruction of these facilities should be completed by September 1985.

29. ADDITIONAL INFORMATION ON SUBSIDIARIES AND ASSOCIATED COMPANIES

SUBSIDIARIES

Jewellery
- Tramp (Diamonds) Limited
- Tramp Fashions Limited

Motor Trade
- Plastics Inc.
- Metals Limited
- C.P. Plastics Limited

All subsidiaries are incorporated in Great Britain and are wholly owned with the exception of Metals Limited, in which 75 per cent of the ordinary shares are owned, and Plastics Inc., which is incorporated in the United States of America. All companies operate principally in the country of incorporation.

ASSOCIATED COMPANIES

Motor Trade
- Tramp & Co. Limited
- Tramp Limited

Both companies are incorporated and operate in Great Britain and the group holds 40 per cent of the ordinary share capital of both companies. These companies have no other classes of share or loan capital outstanding.

TRAMP HOLDINGS p.l.c.

CONSOLIDATED CURRENT COST PROFIT AND LOSS ACCOUNT

Year ended 31 December 1984

	Note	1984 £'000	1983 £'000
Turnover		43,180	39,200
Profit before interest and taxation, as in the historical cost accounts		2,190	1,940
Current cost operating adjustments			
Cost of sales adjustment		590	450
Monetary working capital adjustment		360	290
Additional depreciation		470	340
		(1,420)	(1,080)
Share of current cost profits less losses of associated companies (after interest and gearing adjustment)		160	90
Current cost operating profit		930	950
Gearing adjustment		281	310
Interest		(310)	(360)
Current cost profit on ordinary activities before taxation		901	900
Taxation		(980)	(800)
Current cost (loss)/profit on ordinary activities after taxation		(79)	100
Minority interests		(10)	(10)
Extraordinary items	3	209	-
Current cost profit attributable to the members of Tramp Holdings p.l.c.		120	90
Dividends		320	240
Deficit transferred to reserves		(200)	(150)
Current cost (loss)/earnings per share		(1.1)p	1.1p

30.

TRAMP HOLDINGS p.l.c.

SUMMARISED CONSOLIDATED CURRENT COST BALANCE SHEET

31 December 1984

	Note	1984 £'000	1983 £'000
ASSETS EMPLOYED			
Fixed assets			
Intangible assets		150	200
Tangible assets	4	7,560	7,120
Investments		520	400
		8,230	7,720
Net current assets			
Stocks		6,900	6,000
Monetary working capital		1,980	3,200
		8,880	9,200
Other current liabilities, net		(140)	(782)
Proposed dividends		(200)	(160)
		8,540	8,258
		16,770	15,978
FINANCED BY			
Called up share capital		8,000	7,190
Reserves	5	5,700	5,658
		13,700	12,848
Minority interests		200	190
Creditors: amounts falling due after more than one year		1,970	2,420
Provision for liabilities and charges		900	520
		16,770	15,978

TRAMP HOLDINGS p.l.c.

NOTES TO THE CURRENT COST ACCOUNTS

Year ended 31 December 1984

1. DESCRIPTION OF THE CURRENT COST ACCOUNTS

The current cost accounts on pages 29 and 30 have been prepared in compliance with SSAP 16. The current cost system, whilst not a system of accounting for general inflation, allows for changes in cost prices specific to the business when reporting both assets employed and the profits earned by those assets.

The current cost operating profit is the surplus (before interest and taxation) arising from the ordinary activities of the business in the period. It takes account of the effect of price changes on the cost of replacing those productive assets which have been used up during the period. This is achieved by three adjustments to historical cost trading profit - a depreciation adjustment, a cost of sales adjustment relating to stock and a monetary working capital adjustment.

The current cost profit attributable to shareholders is the surplus (after interest and taxation) after allowing for the impact of price changes on only that proportion of the productive assets which shareholders have financed. The ratio of net borrowings to net operating assets is determined and applied to the total of the current cost operating adjustments to determine the gearing adjustment which is credited to profit. This gearing adjustment is regarded as attributable to shareholders because it represents that part of the operating adjustments which, on the evidence of the proportion of borrowed funds over the year, could be financed by borrowing.

2. ACCOUNTING POLICIES

(a) Plant and machinery situated in the U.K. have been valued at net current replacement cost, using appropriate external price indices.

(b) Land and buildings are included in the current cost balance sheet at professional valuation as at 31 December 1984.

(c) Depreciation has been based on the revalued amounts, using the same asset lives as in the historical cost accounts.

(d) Stocks have been valued using external price indices for raw materials, modified by internally-produced indices of direct labour costs and production overheads for work in progress and finished goods. The cost of sales adjustment has been calculated using the averaging method.

(e) Monetary working capital consists of trade debtors less trade creditors, and the monetary working capital adjustment has been calculated using the averaging method.

TRAMP HOLDINGS p.l.c. 32.

NOTES TO THE CURRENT COST ACCOUNTS

Year ended 31 December 1984

2. ACCOUNTING POLICIES (continued)

(f) The gearing adjustment has been calculated using a gearing ratio based on the average of opening and closing figures for net borrowings and net operating assets.

(g) The group's share of the associated companies' profits has been included after adjusting their profits to a current cost basis and after charging interest and gearing adjustment.

(h) The corresponding amounts are those which appeared in the current cost accounts for the preceding year, without adjustment.

(i) Other accounting policies are the same as those in the historical cost accounts.

3. EXTRAORDINARY ITEMS	1984 £'000
Gain on sale of land, as in the historical cost accounts	580
Less current cost adjustment based on existing use value at disposal, less gearing adjustment (£39,000)	(161)
	419
Cost of closure of Metal Trim Division	(80)
	339
Tax on extraordinary items	130
Extraordinary net gain	209

4. TANGIBLE ASSETS	31 December 1984			1983
	Gross £'000	Accumulated depreciation £'000	Net £'000	Net £'000
Land and buildings	3,880	-	3,880	3,740
Plant and equipment	9,090	5,410	3,680	3,380
	12,970	5,410	7,560	7,120

TRAMP HOLDINGS p.l.c. 33.

NOTES TO THE CURRENT COST ACCOUNTS

Year ended 31 December 1984

5. RESERVES

	1984 £'000	1983 £'000
Balance, 1 January	5,658	4,348
Current cost reserve movements:		
Surpluses on revaluation	1,000	1,040
Adjustments to historical cost profit	670	460
	1,670	1,500
Current cost deficit for year	(200)	(150)
Scrip issue	(800)	-
Write off of goodwill	(660)	-
Other movements	32	(40)
Balance, 31 December	5,700	5,658

6. FINANCING OF NET OPERATING ASSETS

The value to the business of the net operating assets and the manner in which they were financed are set out below:

	1984 £'000	1983 £'000
Fixed and intangible assets and investments	8,230	7,720
Working capital	8,880	9,200
NET OPERATING ASSETS	17,110	16,920
SHARE CAPITAL, RESERVES AND PROPOSED DIVIDENDS	13,900	13,008
MINORITY INTERESTS	200	190
NET BORROWING	3,010	3,722
	17,110	16,920

4 DIRECTORS' REPORT

4.010 INTRODUCTION

The information which is to be given in the directors' report is contained in s 235 and Sch 7. Comparative figures are not required but it is recommended that comparative information be given in the 'review of developments' section of the report. The matters required to be disclosed by Stock Exchange companies, which are also dealt with, are usually included in the directors' report but The Stock Exchange does not insist on this.

It is customary for the Secretary of the company to sign the directors' report 'by order of the board of directors' although the chairman or any other director authorised by the board may do so.

Difficulties of interpretation and application of the provisions of the Act arise particularly where disclosure is required only if an item is 'material' 'significant' or 'substantial' as no definition of these terms is given. It should be emphasised that except where the Act gives such an exemption the information should be given even if it is considered unimportant or immaterial by the directors.

4.020 ACTIVITIES AND RESULTS

4.021 ACTIVITIES

The report must state the principal activities of the company and its subsidiaries during the financial year and details of any significant change in these activities during the year. [s 235(2)] A definition of 'principal activities' or 'significant change' is not given in the Act but the following guidelines are suggested.

Principal activities disclosed are usually taken to mean categories of important horizontal diversification representing distinct classes of industry and commerce (e.g. textiles, oil, publishing, electrical equipment). Vertical analysis (e.g. wholesale; retail; manufacturing; factored; domestic; export) may be made for internal management and other reporting purposes but is usually not meaningful for the reader of the financial statements.

It is not always an easy matter to decide whether differing types of business are sufficiently significant to require separate disclosure. Although no precise rule can be laid down it is suggested that those activities which constitute less than 10% of the total of turnover or profits before taxation should be ignored.

EXAMPLE

The company and its subsidiaries are principally engaged in the manufacture, distribution and sale of food products, in hotel and catering operations, and in property development.

A change in activities which is disclosed usually involves the commencement or cessation of a complete activity rather than a change in degree of activity. Frequently a change in activities involves the acquisition or disposal of a subsidiary company. It is not sufficient to disclose details of such acquisitions or disposals without also disclosing any resultant change in the group's activities. Unless informed otherwise the reader will assume that the acquisition or disposal does not involve any such change.

EXAMPLE

The main activities of the group continue to be consumer electronics, music, films, video, software and leisure, and domestic appliances. During the year the group withdrew from the medical electronics business and from their hotel and restaurant activities.

Where no change in activities has taken place during the year, it is recommended that this fact be disclosed.

EXAMPLES

There has been no change in these activities during the year.

or

The principal activities of the company continue to be those of a holding company with subsidiaries engaged in....

4.022 ***REVIEW OF DEVELOPMENTS***

The report must contain a fair review of the developments of the business of the company and its subsidiaries during the financial year and of their position at the end of it. [s 235(1)]

(a) Review of developments during the year

What constitutes 'a fair review' for this purpose is a matter to be determined by the directors. Current reporting practices by public companies indicate a wide variation in the extent of disclosure, ranging from brief generalised statements to comprehensive reviews covering separately each major activity. There appears to be no uniformity as to where the review is shown in the report. Many companies include their reviews in the chairman's statement or in a review report separate from the directors' report. Most of these reviews are referred to in the directors' report and this seems necessary to comply with the requirements of the Act.

Thus no clear guidelines as to the form and content of the review of developments have emerged. It is suggested that it is good practice to deal with the matters which are discussed below.

(i) The review should highlight the significant measures of performance (i.e., turnover, profits from ordinary activities, exceptional and extraordinary items), indicating comparisons with the preceding year and, where relevant, with other prior years. The directors' report on the model financial statements of Tramp Holdings illustrates the use of percentage changes to emphasise the extent of growth in activities and performance.

(ii) The main factors which have contributed to any significant change in results should be disclosed. This can best be done by discussing the results and developments by significantly different activities. This should contribute to a better understanding of the financial breakdowns of turnover and profits which are required by the Act to be given in the notes to the accounts.

(iii) The review should include a discussion of any significant acquisitions and disposals of businesses and fixed assets, and exceptional trading conditions. Separate headings could be given to any of these topics.

(iv) The review might also comment on the results shown by any supplementary current cost accounts.

(b) Review of position at the end of year

To deal adequately with the position of the company and its subsidiaries at the end of the year the following matters should be considered:

(i) changes in and adequacy of working capital, levels of stocks, debtors, creditors and borrowings as compared with the preceding year.

(ii) proposals for financing any major commitments.

(iii) ratios such as gearing, current assets: current liabilities and net assets per share.

4.023 FUTURE DEVELOPMENTS

The report must contain an indication of the likely future developments in the business of the company and its subsidiaries [Sch 7: 6(b)] and this seems to require:

(i) a statement in general terms of the expectation of the directors regarding the trend of earnings in the forthcoming year.

(ii) details of decisions made which will have a significant impact on earnings or on the course of the business (e.g. new products, plans for expansion/rationalisation, proposed disposals/acquisitions).

(iii) the effect of significant events beyond the control of the company (e.g. restrictive legislation, technological changes, loss of markets or shortage of supplies, political or economic disturbances in the company's markets, interest rate changes).

4.024 RESEARCH AND DEVELOPMENT

The report must contain an indication of the activities (if any) of the company and its subsidiaries in the field of research and development. [Sch 7: 6(c)] This appears to require a description of the progress of projects which are expected to result in new or improved products, services, or production techniques. In addition, disclosure of the costs incurred in research and development in the current and preceding year will give the reader an indication of the level of activities in this field.

4.025 DIVIDENDS AND TRANSFER TO RESERVES

The report must state the amount, if any, recommended to be paid as dividend and the amount to be transferred to reserves. [s 235(1)] Where the directors do not propose a dividend, it is customary to state this.

4.026 POST BALANCE SHEET EVENTS

The report must contain particulars of any important events affecting the company or any of its subsidiaries which have occurred since the end of the financial year. [Sch 7: 6(a)] There is a similar requirement in SSAP 17 for disclosure in the notes to the accounts of 'non-adjusting post balance sheet events' which are of such materiality that their non-disclosure would affect the ability of users of financial statements to reach a proper understanding of the financial position. While an event might be thought sufficiently important to require disclosure in the directors' report, it may not be necessary for a proper understanding of the financial position and therefore would not need to be disclosed under

SSAP 17. But clearly any event which needs to be disclosed in the notes to the accounts under SSAP 17 is also an important event to be disclosed in the directors' report to comply with the Act. It is suggested that in these circumstances it is appropriate to make only a brief mention of the matter in the directors' report with a reference to the relevant note in the financial statements. This is exemplified in the directors' report on Tramp Holdings plc (see item 5 on page 20).

4.027 GEOGRAPHICAL ANALYSIS OF TURNOVER AND RESULTS

Stock Exchange companies are required to include in their report and accounts an analysis of net turnover and contribution to trading results of trading operations carried on outside the UK and the Republic of Ireland. Since the analysis of turnover may often be conveniently combined with the analysis by geographical markets and included in a note to the profit and loss account, it is dealt with in Section 5.022. However the information required by The Stock Exchange may equally well be included in the directors' report.

Any information required concerning contributions to trading results should normally be included in the directors' report rather than in the financial statements. The analysis of contributions to trading results by area is only required if the contribution to profit or loss from a specific area is abnormal in the sense that it is substantially out of line with the group's normal ratio of profit to turnover.

Although there is no requirement to do so, it is good practice to give in addition a geographical analysis of net assets, particularly if there are substantial assets in areas of abnormal political or economic risk.

4.028 PUBLISHED FORECASTS

Stock Exchange companies must give an explanation of any material difference between the trading results shown in the accounts and those given in any published forecast made by the company.

This latter requirement could refer not only to the obvious example of a forecast given in an offer or rebuttal document, but also any precise forecast given in an earlier chairman's statement or directors' report.

It is understood that a difference is usually regarded as material if it exceeds 10% of the forecast trading result although it is recognised that there may be circumstances (e.g. break-even situations) where this or a greater percentage will not be considered material. Where there is doubt the company should consult The Stock Exchange. The phrase 'trading results' is understood to mean profit before taxation, but clearly it is important when making the comparison with the forecast, to compare like with like.

4.030 FIXED ASSETS

The report is to contain particulars of:

(i) any significant changes in the fixed assets of the company or its subsidiaries during the year. [Sch 7: 1(1)]

Since the financial statements include the totals of acquisitions and disposals of fixed assets, this requirement is normally interpreted as relating to individual fixed assets, or groups of fixed assets, e.g. if connected with one particular activity. The information given should include an indication both of the nature of the assets and the cost of acquisition or proceeds of disposal. Examples of significant fixed assets might include major subsidiary companies, factories or other major productive units, (whether or not any change in activity was involved).

The practice, which is sometimes adopted, of meeting this requirement by referring to the note to the accounts about fixed assets seems inappropriate and should be discouraged. If acquisitions and additions of fixed assets are at a reasonably normal level, then no reference is necessary; if significant changes in fixed assets have taken place then a reference to the aggregate monetary amounts involved alone is not an adequate response to the requirement.

(ii) any substantial difference between the market value and balance sheet value of interests in land if the directors decide that this is significant to shareholders or debenture holders. [Sch 7: 1(2)] 'Land' is usually taken to include buildings and other capitalised building improvements such as car parks, drainage, etc.

No guidance is provided by the Act as to what is 'significant' and as to the circumstances in which the information should be regarded as significant. A substantial difference between book and market value is usually significant to shareholders or debenture holders where land and buildings are suitable for alternative uses or redevelopment so that their current value greatly exceeds book value.

Since such a difference is only significant on the basis that the company might sell the property in question, a fair presentation would also disclose any tax liabilities which would arise as a result of such a sale.

4.040 ACQUISITION OF OWN SHARES

Where a company purchases its own shares during the year, the following information must be given in the directors' report [s 235(4) and Sch 7: Part II]:

(i) the number and nominal value of shares purchased and the percentage of the called up share capital which those shares represent,

(ii) the consideration paid, and

(iii) the reasons for the purchases.

Other dealings in own shares, which must also be disclosed under Sch 7: 7, include own shares which:

(i) are acquired by the company through forfeiture or gift; or

(ii) are acquired by the company's nominee or by others with company financial assistance, where the company has a beneficial interest; or

(iii) are made subject to a lien or charge by the company.

The disclosures required in these circumstances, which are expected to be rare, are contained in Sch 7: 8.

The Stock Exchange requires listed companies to give the following additional information regarding arrangements for the acquisition of its own shares:

(i) any authority given by the shareholders for the company to purchase its own shares which exists at the end of the year (i.e. authority which has not yet been exercised and has not expired);

(ii) where acquisitions have been made (or are proposed) other than by a tender or partial offer to all shareholders, or by purchases through the market, the names of the sellers of the shares being purchased; and

(iii) the same particulars as are required in respect of purchases during the year (see above) of purchases, or options or contracts for purchase entered into since the end of the financial year covered by the report.

The circumstances under which a company may legally purchase or redeem its own shares and the requirements to ensure capital maintenance are discussed in Section 18.020.

4.050 DIRECTORS

4.051 DIRECTORS' NAMES

Disclosure is required of the names of the persons who were directors of the company at any time during the financial year. [s 235(2)] This can be achieved either by listing the names of the directors or referring the reader to the page where this information may be found. In practice, the dates of appointment or retirements during the period are also given. It is suggested that any changes after the year end should also be disclosed.

The following information, which is not required by the Act, or any regulation, is also often given:

(i) the dates of appointments or resignations occurring during the period;

(ii) changes in the directors since the end of the financial year;

(iii) the directors who retire at the annual general meeting and whether they offer themselves for re-election; and

(iv) the citizenship of non-UK directors.

4.052 DIRECTORS' INTERESTS IN SHARES OR DEBENTURES

The interests in shares or debentures of the company and other group companies of each person who was a director at the end of the financial year must be stated in the directors' report, or alternatively in the notes to the accounts. [Sch 7: 2]

Both the interests at the beginning of the year (or at the date of appointment) and the interests at the end of the year must be disclosed. If a director has no interest, this must be stated. The details to be disclosed are the interests of the directors as recorded in the register of directors' interests. Particulars of any duplication in holdings (i.e. joint holdings) should be given as interests of each of the holders.

Stock Exchange companies must also disclose any changes in these interests which have occurred between the end of the financial year and a date not more than one month prior to the date of the notice of the meeting. If there has been no change, this fact must be disclosed.

The interests of a director's spouse and infant children (other than any who are also directors of the company) are to be treated as interests of the director. [s 328] Part 1 of Sch 13 contains rules for interpretation of the requirement. It states that:

(i) an interest in shares or debentures includes any interest of any kind whatsoever;

(ii) any restraints or restrictions on the exercise of any rights attached to the interest is disregarded; and

(iii) it is immaterial that the shares or debentures in which a person has an interest are unidentifiable.

The following table summarises the specific rules for determining the interests which are included in and excluded from the disclosure requirements.

Included	***Excluded***
(i) An interest as a beneficiary under a trust. [Sch 13: 2]	(i) A person holding as a bare trustee or custodian trustee. (See definition below). [Sch 13: 10]
(ii) Joint interests (each notifiable). [Sch 13: 7]	(ii) Interests arising as a trustee or personal representative where the Public Trustee is also a trustee or personal representative. [SI 1985-802]
(iii) An interest arising from a contract for the purchase of shares or debentures. [Sch 13: 3]	(iii) A remainder interest in trust property, so long as the life interest subsists. [Sch 13: 9]
(iv) An entitlement to exercise any right conferred by the holding of shares or debentures (except as holder of a proxy for a specified meeting). [Sch 13: 3]	(iv) Interests of a director of a reporting company, which is a wholly owned subsidiary, and the director is also the director of the parent company which will report the interest. [SI 1985-802]
(v) A right to call for delivery of shares or debentures, a right to acquire an interest and an obligation to take an interest in shares or debentures (but excluding a right to subscribe for shares or debentures). [Sch 13: 6]	(v) Where a company is a wholly owned subsidiary of a company incorporated outside Great Britain, interests in any group companies incorporated outside Great Britain. [SI 1985-802]
(vi) An interest acquired through another company, if *that* company is interested and (a) that company or its directors are accustomed to act in accordance with the instructions of the notifying director; or (b) notifying director controls one third of the voting power in that company. [Sch 13: 4]	(vi) Interests in shares arising solely on account of a limitation in the memorandum or articles on a person's rights of disposal of shares. [SI 1985-802]
	(vii) Interests in shares or debentures of a society registered under the Industrial and Provident Societies Act 1965. [SI 1985-802]
	(viii) Interests as a trustee or beneficiary of an approved superannuation fund or retirement benefit scheme. [SI 1985-802]

The definitions of trustees for purpose of exclusion (i) above are:

Bare trustee – A trustee with no duties except to convey the assets to or by the direction of the beneficiaries. He should have no beneficial interest in the context of these rules (e.g. a nominee).

Custodian trustee – A trustee in whose name assets have been vested but who has no powers of administration. He is bound to act in accordance with the directions of the managing trustees as long as there is no breach of trust (e.g. a bank which holds the assets of a unit trust).

Each director is obliged, within 5 days of his appointment, to notify the company in writing of his interests in shares or debentures of the company and group companies. Any subsequent change in the interests must be notified to the company within 5 days of the 'event' which causes the change. An event is normally a sale, purchase or inheritance. Part III of Sch 13 covers most circumstances which constitute an event and specifies the information to be included in the notice.

A director for this purpose includes a shadow director (i.e. any person in accordance with whose directions or instructions the directors are accustomed to act unless they do so on advice given by this person in a professional capacity). It also includes an alternate director from the moment he is appointed to the time he is relieved of his post and not just when he is performing the duties of a director.

Stock Exchange companies are in addition required to distinguish between beneficial and non-beneficial interests. An interest should be shown as non-beneficial only if neither the director nor his spouse or infant children has any beneficial interest. Particulars should be given of the extent of any duplication which occurs.

4.053 DIRECTORS' SERVICE CONTRACTS

Listed companies are required by The Stock Exchange to state in the directors' report the unexpired period of any service contract of any director proposed for re-election at the annual general meeting. Where any such director does not have a service contract of more than one year's duration, a negative statement is required.

4.060 SUBSTANTIAL HOLDINGS

Stock Exchange companies are required to include in their annual report and accounts a statement of the substantial interests of any persons other than directors in the share capital of the company. The statement must be made of the position at a date not more than one month prior to the date of the notice calling the annual meeting and should state both the names of the persons interested and the amount of their interests. If no such substantial interests have been notified to the company, this should be stated. It is customary to give this information in the directors' report.

The interests which are to be stated are those which are recorded in the register which public companies are required to keep under s 211, i.e. substantial interests and changes in interests in the company's shares which are notified to it.

The rules for notification of substantial interests are complex and are contained in ss 198 to 210. Notification is required as soon as a person has an interest in 5% or more of the voting shares of a public company, and changes must be notified when they result in the interest to be reported changing by 1% or more. The term 'interest' is very widely construed; a person's interest is not restricted to a beneficial interest and it includes the interests of his close family and of bodies corporate which are accustomed to act on his instructions or of which he controls one-third of the voting power. In addition ss 204 to 206 catch the situation where two or more people agree together to acquire voting shares in a 'target company'.

4.070 EMPLOYEES

4.071 HEALTH AND SAFETY AT WORK

Sch 7: 10 requires the report to state, in the case of companies of such classes as may be prescribed in regulations made by the Secretary of State, such information as may be so prescribed about the arrangements in force in the financial year for securing the health, safety and welfare at work of employees of the company and its subsidiaries and for protecting other persons against risks to health or safety arising out of or in connection with the activities at work of those employees.

No regulations have yet been prescribed by the Secretary of State and therefore no information need be given although many companies are including some information in the directors' report.

4.072 DISABLED PERSONS

Sch 7: 9 requires the report to contain a statement describing the company's policy in respect of employment of disabled persons as it has been applied during the financial year:

(i) for giving full and fair consideration to applications for employment by the company made by disabled persons, having regard to their particular aptitudes and abilities;

(ii) for continuing the employment of, and for arranging appropriate training for employees of the company who have become disabled persons during the period when they were employed by the company, and

(iii) otherwise for the training, career development and promotion of disabled persons employed by the company.

This requirement only applies where the average number of persons employed during the financial year exceeds 250. The number of employees for this purpose is determined by dividing the sum of the number of employees employed under contracts of service in each week (whether throughout the week or not but excluding those persons who worked wholly or mainly outside the U.K.) by the number of weeks in the financial year. The Department of Trade has said that the disclosure is intended to refer to individual companies where such information would be relevant and not to groups of companies. Thus a holding company which employed less than 251 people need not make the above disclosure in the group directors' report even though the total of group employees exceeded 250.

An example of appropriate wording is contained in the financial statements of Tramp Holdings p.l.c. on page 22.

4.073 EMPLOYEE INVOLVEMENT IN AFFAIRS, POLICY AND PERFORMANCE

Sch 7: 11 requires the report to contain a statement describing the action that has been taken during the financial year to introduce, maintain or develop arrangements aimed at:

(i) providing employees systematically with information on matters of concern to them as employees;

(ii) consulting employees or their representatives on a regular basis so that the views of employees can be taken into account in making decisions which are likely to affect their interests;

(iii) encouraging the involvement of employees in the company's performance through an employees' Share Scheme or by some other means;

(iv) achieving a common awareness on the part of all employees of the financial and economic factors affecting the performance of the company.

This requirement applies to a company which employs more than 250 persons for each week of the financial year. The calculation of the number of employees for this purpose is the same as for the disclosures applicable to disabled persons (see Section 4.072 above).

As with the requirement to report the policy regarding disabled persons, this requirement applies only to individual companies which employ more than 250 people and not to groups (see Section 4.072 above).

4.080 POLITICAL AND CHARITABLE GIFTS

If a company and its subsidiaries have given money for political or charitable purposes, or both, which aggregate more than £200 in the financial year, then these must be disclosed in the report [Sch 7: 3]:

(i) the amount given for charitable purposes;

(ii) the amount given for political purposes;

(iii) the name of each person or political party to which an amount in excess of £200 was given for political purposes and the amount given.

Money given for charitable purposes to persons not ordinarily resident in the U.K. are left out of account for the purposes of this requirement.

Wholly owned subsidiaries of companies incorporated in Great Britain are exempt from this requirement.

4.090 INTERESTS IN CONTRACTS

The Stock Exchange requires listed companies to disclose any contracts of significance:

(i) where a director of the company is materially interested in such a contract (if there are no such contracts, this fact must be stated); and

(ii) between any group company and a corporate substantial shareholder, including a contract for the provision of services to a group company by a corporate substantial shareholder.

These requirements are discussed in detail in Section 11.083.

4.100 STANDARD ACCOUNTING PRACTICE

Stock Exchange companies are required to include a statement as to the reasons for any significant departures from standard accounting practices.

The Stock Exchange expects the accounts of listed companies incorporated within the U.K. and the Republic of Ireland to comply with accounting standards approved by the principal accounting bodies of the U.K. and Ireland. It also expects the accounts of companies incorporated outside the U.K. and the Republic of Ireland but listed in the U.K. to be drawn up in conformity with International Accounting Standards, with the exception of IAS 14 on segmental analysis. Any significant departure from or non-compliance with the applicable standards must be disclosed and explained.

4.110 CLOSE COMPANY STATUS

Stock Exchange companies must include a statement as to whether or not, so far as the directors are aware, the company is a close company for taxation purposes and whether there has been any change in that respect since the year end. Where there is doubt as to the company's status the statement should indicate the existence of the doubt and the basis on which taxation provisions have been made.

EXAMPLE

So far as the directors are aware, the company is not a close company for taxation purposes.

4.120 RE-APPOINTMENT OF AUDITORS

Although there is no statutory requirement for the directors' report to refer to the re-appointment of the auditor it is normal for it to do this.

EXAMPLE

A resolution to re-appoint Verry & Fire as auditors will be proposed at the forthcoming Annual General Meeting.

5 PROFIT AND LOSS ACCOUNT

5.010 GENERAL REQUIREMENTS

The Act provides that every profit and loss account shall give a true and fair view of the profit or loss for the financial year and shall comply with Sch 4 as to its form and content. [s 228]

Guidance is given in this chapter on the accounting treatment and disclosures required in respect of the items to be shown on the face of the profit and loss account or in the notes to the accounts.

5.011 FORMATS

Sch 4 permits four alternative formats. These formats are reproduced in Appendix 5. Format 1 classifies operating expenses by function in a vertical arrangement and relegates details of certain expenditure to the notes. Format 2, also vertical in arrangement, summarises expenditure by type rather than by function. The headings for operating expenditure used under the different formats are as follows:

Format 1	*Format 2*
Cost of sales	Changes in stocks of finished goods and work in progress
Distribution costs	Own work capitalised
Administrative expenses	Raw materials and consumables
	Other external charges
	Staff costs
	Depreciation and other amounts written off tangible and intangible fixed assets
	Exceptional amounts written off current assets
	Other operating charges

Formats 3 and 4 are two-sided arrangements of the items in Formats 1 and 2 respectively. Format 1 may be more suitable for a manufacturing company since Format 2 does not permit the calculation of cost of sales and gross profit which is a significant measure of performance for such a company. It is also suggested that vertical formats give a more logical presentation than two-sided formats in most cases. However companies are free to select whichever format is most suitable to them, but the selected format may not be changed in subsequent years unless there are special reasons (see Section 2.040 above).

The items discussed below are dealt with in the order of items shown in Format 1 which is reproduced below. The additional items required under Formats 2 and 4 are discussed in Section 5.230.

Format 1

1. Turnover
2. Cost of sales
3. Gross profit or loss
4. Distribution costs
5. Administrative expenses
6. Other operating income
7. Income from shares in group companies
8. Income from shares in related companies
9. Income from other fixed asset investments
10. Other interest receivable and similar income
11. Amounts written off investments
12. Interest payable and similar charges
13. Tax on profit or loss on ordinary activities
14. Profit or loss on ordinary activities after taxation
15. Extraordinary income
16. Extraordinary charges
17. Extraordinary profit or loss
18. Tax on extraordinary profit or loss
19. Other taxes not shown under the above items
20. Profit or loss for the financial year

5.012 HEADINGS

All the headings in the profit and loss account formats have Arabic numerals and accordingly they may be combined on the face of the profit and loss account, with the sub-divisions shown in the notes if this combination facilitates the assessment of the profit or loss of the company. Further the directors are required to adapt the arrangement and headings required 'in any case where the special nature of the company's business requires such adaptation'. In practice full advantage has been taken of this flexibility and there is little uniformity of presentation, but the most common combinations of items under Format 1 seem to be:

4, 5 & 6	– distribution costs, administrative expenses, and other operating income
7, 8, 9 & 10	– investment income
15, 16, 17 & 18	– extraordinary items

It is an almost universal practice to strike a sub-total entitled 'Operating profit' or 'Trading profit' which is not required by the format. It is the profit after all operating costs and income but before investment income and interest.

There are three headings not included in the formats which Sch 4: 3(6)(7) states must be shown separately in each profit and loss account, namely:

(i) profit or loss on ordinary activities before taxation;

(ii) the aggregate amount of dividends paid and proposed; and

(iii) any amount set aside to or withdrawn from reserves.

5.020 TURNOVER

All formats given in Sch 4 require the disclosure of turnover and this item is almost invariably shown on the face of the profit and loss account.

Turnover is defined in Sch 4: 95 as the amounts derived from the provision of goods and services falling within the company's ordinary activities after deduction of trade discounts, VAT and any other taxes based on amounts so derived.

Under this definition the turnover of agents, such as insurance brokers, stockbrokers, and estate agents, consists of gross commissions receivable and not the total amounts billed to customers; the turnover of a stockjobber on the other hand consists of sales of investments; the turnover of a construction company would exclude the value of work done on speculative developments not sold at the year-end. It is important that the turnover reported in the profit and loss account should be measured in such a way that there is a proper matching between sales, costs and the related profit. For example, a construction company which recognises the attributable profit in long term contract work in progress should measure its turnover in long term contracts by reference to the work done during the year rather than by reference to contracts completed. On the other hand a company engaged in shorter term contracts which recognises profit only on completion should measure its turnover by reference to the value of contracts completed during the year.

Where turnover with group companies (including associated companies and companies under common control or ownership) constitutes a significant proportion of total turnover, it is good practice to disclose this fact in the notes, preferably by stating the amount of intercompany turnover included in the total turnover.

In consolidated financial statements, turnover will exclude intra-group transactions.

5.021 TURNOVER AND PROFITS BY CLASS OF BUSINESS

The notes to the accounts must disclose the amount of turnover and profit or loss before taxation attributable to each class of business that, in the opinion of the directors, differs substantially from any other class of business carried on by the company or group. [Sch 4: 55].

The Act does not define what is meant by 'class of business'. It is suggested that this term might reasonably be regarded as equivalent to the 'principal activities' of the company which must be disclosed in the directors' report (see Section 4.021). Thus it should be interpreted as meaning important horizontal diversification representing distinct classes of industry and commerce (e.g. textiles, oil, publishing, electrical equipment).

Only those classes which contribute materially to turnover and profits need be disclosed and a useful guide is to consider as material a class of business with turnover or profits comprising 10% or more of the total. The amounts which are not material may be included in amounts stated in respect of another class.

Where, in the opinion of the directors, disclosure of this information would be seriously prejudicial to the interests of the company it need not be given but the fact that the information has not been disclosed must be stated.

An area which in practice causes concern and difficulty is the fair allocation of head office expenses, such as interest and general administration costs and miscellaneous income. Many companies overcome this problem by showing gross earnings from each activity and then deducting any unallocated expenses in total.

EXAMPLE

	Turnover				Profits			
	1984		*1983*		*1984*		*1983*	
	£'000	*%*	*£'000*	*%*	*£'000*	*%*	*£'000*	*%*
Agricultural services	*10,550*	*(50)*	*9,750*	*(70)*	*1,200*	*(39)*	*1,350*	*(77)*
Building materials	*2,000*	*(9)*	*1,860*	*(13)*	*475*	*(15)*	*360*	*(21)*
Property development	*8,770*	*(41)*	*2,400*	*(17)*	*1,800*	*(58)*	*488*	*(28)*
	21,320	*(100)*	*14,010*	*(100)*	*3,475*	*(112)*	*2,198*	*(126)*
Interest and parent company expenses less other income					*(390)*	*(12)*	*(456)*	*(26)*
					3,085	*(100)*	*1,742*	*(100)*

5.022 GEOGRAPHICAL ANALYSIS OF TURNOVER

If the company supplies geographical markets which in the opinion of the directors differ substantially from each other, then the amount of turnover, if material, attributable to each such market must be stated in the notes to the accounts. [Sch 4: 55] The criteria for determining whether markets differ substantially from each other are not specified but it is thought that they are related to the market and other conditions under which a company does business in each area rather than to mere geographical disparity. Thus in appropriate circumstances it appears to be open to the directors to determine that no part of its worldwide market is substantially different from any other and therefore to make no disclosure under this heading.

However, there is an additional requirement imposed on Stock Exchange companies to give a geographical analysis of net turnover of trading operations carried on outside the U.K. and the Republic of Ireland. Direct exports from the U.K. and the Republic of Ireland are treated as trading operations carried on overseas. The Stock Exchange requirements suggest that the analysis should be by continent unless more than 50% of total overseas operations is in one continent in which case there should be a further analysis by country.

Clearly it will often be possible and convenient to meet both the requirements of the Act and The Stock Exchange in a single note to the accounts. However, The Stock Exchange does not specify where the information it requires is to be given, and if the turnover information is not presented in a way which also meets the requirements of the Act, it is preferable that it is included in the directors' report. If the information is not included in the financial statements then a broad geographical analysis by percentages instead of figures is sufficient.

Stock Exchange companies are also required to give an analysis of the contribution to trading results of those operations carried on outside the U.K. and the Republic of Ireland. Since this information is generally given in the directors' report rather than in the financial statements, it is discussed in Section 4.027.

5.030 COST OF SALES

The cost of sales will normally include the following elements of cost of ordinary activities:

Opening stocks and work in progress

Direct materials and other external charges

Direct labour

Fixed and variable production overheads, including depreciation or diminution in value of productive assets

Research and development costs

Variances from standard where a standard costing system is in use

Less: Own work capitalised

Less: Closing stocks and work in progress

The practice of excluding production overheads from cost of sales is not permitted by the Act.

The elements of cost of sales identified above are appropriate for companies which manufacture or purchase for re-sale tangible products. It is also appropriate for companies which provide a service to include under this head the costs of providing that service; the costs should normally be identified as those which are carried forward in work in progress if the related service has not been completed. Where costs cannot be identified reasonably easily with units of service provided, it may well be that Format 2 is more appropriate to the needs of the company.

5.040 GROSS PROFIT OR LOSS

Under Format 1, the gross profit or loss, being the difference between turnover and the cost of sales, must be shown as a separate item. The gross profit or loss can also be determined from Format 3 but it need not be shown in the profit and loss account.

The manner in which expenditure is analysed in Formats 2 and 4 generally prevents the determination of gross profit or loss unless additional information beyond that required by the Act is given.

5.050 DISTRIBUTION COSTS

Distribution costs should include all expenses related to the holding of goods for sale, selling costs and the transfer of goods to the customer, such as:

Sales salaries and commissions and related N.I. and pension costs

Advertising, trade shows

Warehousing costs of finished products

Travelling and entertainment

Outward transportation costs including depreciation of vehicles

Rent, rates, insurance, utilities, depreciation and maintenance of sales outlets

Cash discounts on sales

5.060 ADMINISTRATIVE EXPENSES

This category includes all other operating costs except those associated with the production and distribution of products and services and interest costs which are shown under separate headings. The following expenditure is normally included in administrative expenses:

Salary costs of administrative personnel (such as accounting department, directors' salaries attributable to the general management of the company) and related N.I. and pension costs

Rent, rates, insurance, utilities, depreciation and maintenance of administration buildings

Professional fees

Bad debts

5.070 OTHER OPERATING INCOME

'Other operating income' includes all other income derived from sources associated with the ordinary activities of the business with the exception of income from investments and other interest receivable which must be shown under separate headings unless they are immaterial. Examples of other operating income include:

Canteen sales

Rental income from surplus facilities

For many companies the amount of other operating income will not be material and will be included as part of turnover.

5.080 INCOME FROM SHARES IN GROUP COMPANIES

'Income from shares in group companies' should include dividends received and receivable (i) from subsidiaries where the holding company is required to prepare its own profit and loss account (e.g. where group accounts need not be prepared) and (ii) from fellow subsidiaries where a company holds shares in a group company. In a consolidated profit and loss account the heading should include the group's share of earnings of unconsolidated subsidiaries which are accounted for on the equity method and dividends received and receivable in respect of other unconsolidated subsidiaries.

5.090 INCOME FROM SHARES IN RELATED COMPANIES

Related companies are defined in Section 6.044. It will usually be the case that related companies are associated companies as defined by SSAP 1 and it is common to find the heading 'Income from shares in associated companies' instead of 'Income from shares in related companies'.

If a company prepares its own profit and loss account, the amount to be shown under this heading is the amount of dividends received and receivable from associated companies. In any consolidated profit and loss account, the associated companies would be accounted for by the equity method (see Section 12.083) and this heading would include the group's share of the pre-tax profit or loss of those companies.

5.100 OTHER INVESTMENT INCOME

The headings under which other investment income must be shown are:

(i) Income from other fixed asset investments;

(ii) Other interest receivable and similar income.

Any amounts of income and interest from group companies included under either heading must be shown separately.

In addition the amount of income from listed investments must be disclosed.

5.110 AMOUNTS WRITTEN OFF INVESTMENTS

The amount to be included under this heading should be that portion of the amount written off which reduces the carrying value of an investment below its cost; any write off of amounts previously credited to the revaluation reserve in respect of the same investment should be deducted from that reserve. Where a provision to write down an investment below cost is subsequently written back, the relevant credit should be shown under this heading and separately identified.

5.120 INTEREST PAYABLE AND SIMILAR CHARGES

'Interest payable and similar charges' should include:

Interest charged on borrowings

Amortisation of discount or premium on bills, debentures, etc.

Imputed interest element of finance leases and similar obligations

Commitment fees in connection with obtaining loans and unused credit facilities

Less: interest capitalised

The amounts payable to group companies must be shown separately and other amounts analysed between interest and similar charges:

(i) on bank loans and overdrafts and loans wholly repayable within 5 years whether by instalments or not, and

(ii) on any other loans. [Sch 4: 53(2)]

EXAMPLE

Interest payable and similar charges are in respect of:

	1984 *£'000*	*1983* *£'000*
Group company loans	*390*	*125*
Bank loans and overdrafts and other loans repayable within 5 years	*1,445*	*974*
Other loans	*202*	*200*
	2,037	*1,299*

Under certain circumstances interest on borrowings to finance the production of an asset may be added to the cost of production rather than be written off as an expense and this subject is discussed in detail on page 95. Stock Exchange companies are required to disclose the amount of interest capitalised during the year and the treatment of any related tax relief, and although there is no legal requirement to do so, it is recommended that entities not subject to The Stock Exchange requirement should provide similar information. One convenient method of meeting the requirement is to include it in the note regarding interest payable, as in the following example:

EXAMPLE

	1984	*1983*
	£'000	*£'000*
Interest payable and similar charges:		
Interest on bank loans and overdrafts and other loans repayable within 5 years	*7,200*	*6,400*
Other interest	*2,500*	*2,200*
	9,700	*8,600*
Deduct amount of interest added to cost of investment properties under development	*1,430*	*544*
	8,270	*8,056*

The tax relief obtained in the year in respect of interest costs capitalised has reduced the tax charge by £744,000 (1983 – £283,000). No provision has been made for the potential tax liability which might arise in respect of the capitalised interest element of investment properties if these properties are sold (see note 15).

5.130 PROFIT OR LOSS ON ORDINARY ACTIVITIES BEFORE TAXATION

Sch 4: 3(6) requires the profit and loss account to show the company's profit or loss on ordinary activities before taxation. Unlike the items listed in the profit and loss account formats, this figure may not be relegated to the notes. It will represent the balance of all items mentioned in the previous sections which relate to the ordinary activities of the company, including exceptional items, but excluding taxation and extraordinary items.

5.140 EXCEPTIONAL ITEMS

The effect must be stated of any transactions that are exceptional by virtue of size or incidence though they fall within the ordinary activities of the company. [Sch 4: 57(3)]

ED 36, which is a proposed replacement for SSAP 6, also contains a requirement for the disclosure of exceptional items which are defined as 'those items which, whilst deriving from events or transactions that fall within the ordinary activities of the company need to be disclosed separately by virtue of their size or incidence if the financial statements are to give a true and fair view'. Since exceptional items fall within the ordinary activities of the company, it follows that they must be charged or credited in arriving at the 'profit or loss on ordinary activities'. The provisions of ED 36 concerning the manner of disclosure of exceptional items are not clear and it is to be hoped that this will be rectified in any amendment to SSAP 6 that is adopted.

In the meantime, it is suggested that it will normally be sufficient to disclose exceptional items in the notes to the accounts which supplement the profit and loss account; however they should be clearly identified as exceptional items and not merely included in a list of statutory disclosures. There may be rare circumstances where exceptional items are so large in relation to the profit of the year that they should be disclosed as separate items on the face of the profit and loss account to avoid the possibility of a reader being misled as a result of his failing to read the notes to the accounts with sufficient care.

Practical problems sometimes arise in distinguishing between exceptional items and extraordinary items and this matter is discussed in Section 5.190 below.

5.150 OTHER SUPPLEMENTARY PROFIT AND LOSS INFORMATION

5.151 EMPLOYEE INFORMATION

(a) Number of employees

Sch 4: 56(1) requires disclosure of the total average number of employees in the financial year and a division of this total by categories determined by the directors having regard to the manner in which the company's activities are organised.

The average number of employees is derived by dividing the sum of the number of employees employed under contracts of service in each week by the number of weeks in the financial year.

The term 'under contracts of service' is not defined but presumably is not restricted to those employees who have a written service contract. It is thought that all employees, other than occasional casual workers, must be regarded as being employed under contracts of service. However, a director who acts purely in a non-executive capacity is probably not employed under a contract of service for this purpose. It should be noted that employees to be included are not restricted to those who are employed in the U.K.

The directors have considerable flexibility as to how they divide employees into categories, e.g. by function (production, selling and distribution, administration), by activity (drilling and exploration, chemicals, textiles), by job description (managers and supervisors, factory workers, clerical staff, salesmen, researchers).

(b) Staff costs

Sch 4: 56(4) requires disclosure of the following costs in respect of all employees who are taken into account in determining the number of employees in (a) above:

(i) wages and salaries paid and payable;

(ii) social security costs incurred by the company;

(iii) other pension costs.

Under Formats 2 and 4, this information is to be shown separately in the profit and loss account. Wages and salaries should include bonuses and other incentive payments whether payable under contract or not and the emoluments of directors (other than non-executive directors). Redundancy payments should be excluded as they do not constitute wages or salaries but, they should be disclosed as an exceptional or extraordinary item, as appropriate, if the amount is material.

(c) Remuneration of higher paid employees

The number of employees who worked wholly or mainly in the United Kingdom and whose emoluments exceeded £30,000 must be disclosed. The number is to be subdivided in bands of emoluments of £5,000 over £30,000, i.e. £30,000–£35,000, £35,001–£40,000, etc. [Sch 5: 35]

'Emoluments' are defined as any amount paid to or receivable by the employee from the company, the company's subsidiaries and any other person, in respect of his services as a person in the employment of the company or a subsidiary thereof (except sums to be accounted for to the company or any of its subsidiaries) and includes fees and percentages, and any sums paid by way of an expense allowance in so far as those sums are charged to U.K. income tax and the estimated money value of any other benefits received by him otherwise than in cash.

The emoluments to be taken into account are the amounts paid to or receivable by the employee during the financial year. Thus where the accounts cover a financial year which is shorter or longer than twelve months, the emoluments will not be those of a twelve month period. To avoid misinterpretation of comparative information, the periods covered by the information should be clearly described. The emoluments should not be annualised.

It must be emphasised that, in the consolidated financial statements of a group of companies, the requirement is for disclosure only of remuneration of employees of the holding company who exceed the above limit. However, it is quite common for groups to deal with group employees and to include in this category directors of subsidiaries who are not directors of the parent. There is no objection to this providing it is made clear that it is group information that is given and information about the parent company alone is given as well.

5.152 DIRECTORS' EMOLUMENTS

The Act requires disclosure in the notes to the accounts of the aggregate amounts of each of the following:

(i) directors' emoluments, distinguishing between emoluments in respect of services as director (whether of the company or its subsidiaries) and other emoluments [Sch 5: 22];

(ii) directors' and past directors' pensions, distinguishing between pensions in respect of services as a director and other pensions [Sch 5: 28]; and

(iii) compensation to directors or past directors in respect of loss of office, distinguishing between compensation in respect of the office of director and other offices. [Sch 5: 29]

The amounts to be disclosed under each head must include all relevant sums paid by or receivable from:

(i) the company,

(ii) the company's subsidiaries, and

(iii) any other person. [Sch 5: 30(3)]

It should be noted that the information to be given concerns directors of the reporting company. Thus in the notes to the accounts of a group it is only payments to the directors of the parent company that should be included. Payments made to a person who is a director of a subsidiary company, but not of the parent, should be excluded even if he receives some or all of his remuneration from the parent company.

Further details of the requirements are given below.

(a) Emoluments

Emoluments are to include any amounts paid to or receivable by any person in respect of his services as director of the company or in respect of his services, while director of the company, as director of a subsidiary or otherwise in connection with the management of the affairs of the company or any subsidiary. [Sch 5: 22(2)]

Emoluments are to include fees and percentages, any sum paid by way of expense allowance which has been charged to U.K. income tax, any contribution paid in respect of the director under any pension scheme, and the estimated money value of any other benefits received by him otherwise than in cash. [Sch 5: 22(3)]

The following points should be noted:

(i) Total emoluments are to be divided between emoluments as directors (whether of the company or its subsidiaries) and other emoluments. [Sch 5: 22(b)] This is often interpreted as requiring distinction between directors' fees on the one hand and salaries and other payments on the other. However, this is not the only possible interpretation and Sch 5: 32 provides that directors may apportion any payments between the matters in respect of which they have been paid in such manner as they think appropriate.

(ii) The amounts to be shown include amounts receivable by a director in respect of the year, even if not actually paid during it. [Sch 5: 31(1)] For example if a director is entitled to receive a share of the profits which cannot be ascertained until after the end of the year, the amount should be included as emoluments for the year. Similarly directors' fees paid in respect of the financial year should be included at their proposed amount even if they do not become due until approved by the shareholders in general meeting.

(iii) All emoluments payable in respect of a director's services must be included even if they are paid to a third party, e.g. a service company set up to receive the emoluments, or a firm or company of which the director is a partner or employee.

(iv) Whether the director is receiving emoluments for services as a director of a company or otherwise in connection with the management of its affairs is a question of fact. The presumption must be that any payments he receives from the company (which are not re-imbursements of expenses) must come within this category unless it can be clearly demonstrated that they do not. One exception could be payments made to a director in a professional capacity (e.g. as a solicitor) as payment for professional services performed for the company. Here it is usually a question of degree. For example, if a solicitor is a director and occasionally performs (or his firm performs) intermittent conveyancing work for which the normal scale fees are paid, it could be accepted that these payments were not caught by Sch 5: 22, particularly if the director was non-executive. However, if his main work for the company was conveyancing (e.g. as director of a property company), it would be difficult to accept this view.

The position is less obvious if a non-executive director is a management consultant. It can be argued that intermittent advice given by the director to the chief executive for which the director's firm charges professional fees on its normal basis does not involve services in connection with the management of the company and therefore such fees should not be included as directors' emoluments. Obviously the facts must be considered closely.

Sometimes the details of a service agreement between the company and the director confirm that certain payments are part of his emoluments and the minutes also may give confirmation. Absence of such confirmation is of course not conclusive nor would a negative agreement (e.g. confirming that the payments made to a director were not in respect of his services as a director) provide irrefutable evidence.

(v) Emoluments include any sum paid by way of expenses allowance which has been charged to U.K. income tax. This might arise if a director was granted a round sum allowance for expenses which he could not justify to the Inland Revenue. A more common example is the reimbursement of travelling expenses incurred in attending meetings by a non-executive director, which are normally treated as remuneration for tax purposes. If any payments of this nature are not disclosed in the appropriate year (on the grounds that they are not expected to be charged to tax) but they are charged to tax subsequently then they must be shown separately in the first accounts in which it is practicable to do so.

(vi) Contributions paid in respect of directors under any pension scheme must be included. This is generally interpreted as also requiring the inclusion of the employers' National Insurance contributions in respect of every director.

(vii) Emoluments include the estimated value of any other benefits received otherwise than in cash. A common example is the private use by a director of a company car. Because benefits in kind enjoyed by a director are assessable to income tax, this requirement is often interpreted as requiring disclosure of any of those amounts which are assessed to income tax. While in most cases the amount will be the same it is emphasised that the disclosure requirement is not directly related to assessment to income tax and that the estimated value of all benefits in kind, even if they are not so assessed, must be included.

(viii) Where a company is a member of a group other than the parent, care is necessary to identify the amounts to be disclosed as directors' emoluments. The following should be noted:

- only emoluments of directors of the company should be included:
- the amounts should be restricted to emoluments in respect of services to the company and its subsidiaries (if any); emoluments in respect of services to the parent company or any fellow subsidiaries must be excluded, whether or not the director concerned is also a director of these companies.

EXAMPLES:

Mr X is a director of ABC Ltd and receives remuneration of £8,000 in respect of his services to ABC Ltd plus £10,000 in respect of his services to its subsidiary company A Ltd. The emoluments to be included in the financial statements of ABC Ltd are £18,000. The emoluments to be included in the financial statements of A Ltd are £10,000 if Mr X is a director of A Ltd and nil if he is not.

Mr Y is employed as a manager of ABC Ltd at a salary of £9,000 per year. He also acts as a director of its subsidiary B Ltd at a fee of £5,000. No disclosure is required in the financial statements of ABC Ltd since Mr Y is not a director of that company. The emoluments to be disclosed in the financial statements of B Ltd are £5,000.

A situation which sometimes arises and which can cause difficulty is where directors of subsidiary companies are paid a single salary in respect of their services to the whole group and no allocation is made between the separate companies.

EXAMPLE:

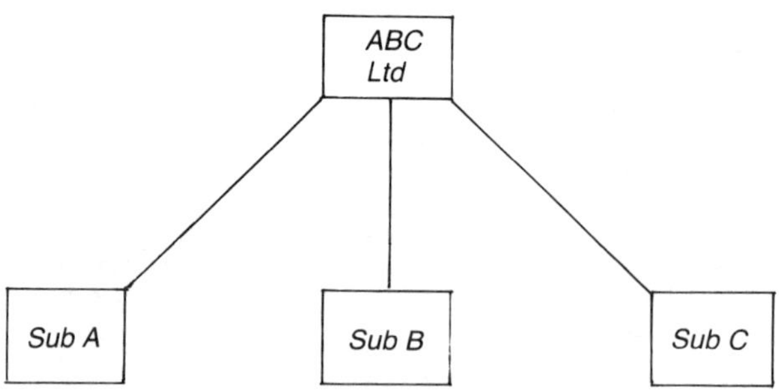

X, Y and Z are directors of each of the subsidiaries and executives of ABC Ltd, the holding company. ABC Ltd pays X, Y and Z £20,000 per annum each, but no allocation between their services, as executives of ABC Ltd and directors of each of the subsidiaries, is made nor is ABC Ltd prepared to attempt such allocation.

The best disclosure in the financial statements of each of the subsidiaries would be a recital of the facts:

EXAMPLE

The directors are executives of the holding company, ABC Ltd, and are also directors of A Ltd, B Ltd and C Ltd. The directors received total remuneration of £60,000 from ABC Ltd during the year but it is not practicable to allocate this between their services as executives of ABC Ltd and their services as directors of A Ltd, B Ltd and C Ltd.

(b) Directors' or past directors' pensions

The amount disclosed in respect of directors' or past directors' pensions should not include any pension paid or receivable under a funded pension scheme contributions to which are required to be included in 'emoluments', but must include any other pensions paid or receivable by the former director himself, his nominee or dependant, or any other person. [Sch 5: 28(2)] 'Pension' includes any superannuation allowance, superannuation gratuity or similar payment.

Total pensions are to be divided between pensions in respect of services as directors (whether of the company or its subsidiaries) and pensions in respect of other services. [Sch 5: 28(3)]

(c) Compensation to directors or past directors in respect of loss of office

The amount disclosed must include any sums paid to or receivable by a director or past director by way of compensation for the loss of office as director of the company or for the loss, while director of the company or in connection with his ceasing to be a director of the company, of any other office in connection with the management of the company's affairs or of any office as director or otherwise in connection with the management of the affairs of any subsidiary. [Sch 5: 29(2)]

Total compensation disclosed must be divided between compensation in respect of the office of director (whether of the company or any subsidiary) and compensation in respect of other offices.

The total compensation must also be divided between sums paid by:

(i) the company,

(ii) the company's subsidiaries, and

(iii) any other person.

Compensation for which the director concerned is liable to account to the company or its subsidiaries under ss 314 and 315 is to be excluded (i.e. compensation paid to a director for loss of office in connection with an offer for the company's shares unless it is disclosed to and approved by the shareholders before the transfer of the shares). However, if the director's liability is subsequently released or is not enforced within two years, then the amount involved must be disclosed separately in the first accounts in which it is practicable to disclose it. [Sch 5: 31(2)]

(d) Remuneration of individual directors

The following additional information regarding directors' emoluments must be disclosed in the notes to the accounts [Sch 5: 24 to 26]:

(i) remuneration of the chairman;
(ii) remuneration of the highest paid director; and
(iii) number of directors receiving remuneration in each band of £5,000 (starting from £0–£5,000 and upward).

This additional information is not required if the company is not a member of a group and the total of directors' emoluments disclosed under the Act does not exceed £60,000. [Sch 5: 23]

The following points should be noted:

(i) Remuneration includes all the items included as emoluments for the purpose of Sch 5: 22 (see (a) above) with the exception of contributions paid in respect of directors under any pension scheme.

(ii) Any directors who performed their duties wholly or mainly outside the United Kingdom are ignored for the purpose of this requirement.

(iii) The emoluments to be disclosed are the amounts paid to or receivable by the director during the financial year. Thus, where the accounts cover a financial year which is shorter or longer than twelve months the emoluments will not be those of a twelve month period. To avoid misinterpretation of comparative information, the periods covered by the information should be clearly described. The amounts should not be annualised.

(iv) The Act [Sch 5: 25] seems to require that all directors including the chairman and the highest paid director (other than any who performed their duties wholly or mainly outside the U.K.) should be included in the numbers shown in the various bands of remuneration. Some companies disclose the numbers in the different bands excluding the chairman and the highest paid director. It is important therefore that the note should make clear which approach is being adopted.

(v) Directors who have not received any remuneration should be included in the £0–5,000 band.

(vi) If there has been a change in chairman during the year the emoluments of each chairman for the period in which he acted in that capacity should be shown.

(vii) It is only necessary to disclose the emoluments of the highest paid director separately if he was not also the chairman. Where there has been a change of chairman during the year, disclosure is only necessary if there is a director whose emoluments exceeded the aggregate emoluments of the different chairmen during their respective periods of office.

(e) Waiver of emoluments

The Act requires disclosure of the number of directors who have waived any emoluments which would have had to be included in total emoluments if they had not been waived together with the aggregate amount waived. [Sch 5: 27] This requirement does not apply if the company is not a member of a group and the aggregate directors' emoluments disclosed do not exceed £60,000. [Sch 5: 23]

Stock Exchange companies are required to disclose 'particulars of any arrangement under which a director has waived or agreed to waive any emoluments'. This requirement extends to particulars of any agreement to waive future emoluments as well as waivers of emoluments in respect of the financial year.

5.153 DEPRECIATION

Under Formats 1 and 3, depreciation does not appear as a separate item in the profit and loss account, but the amount of any provisions for depreciation and diminution in value of tangible and intangible fixed assets must be disclosed in a note to the accounts. Under Formats 2 and 4 this amount is shown as a separate item on the face of the profit and loss account.

If an asset has been revalued in the balance sheet, then depreciation must be calculated by reference to the revalued amount but the total depreciation in respect of the revalued asset may be included in the profit and loss account in two parts, that based on historical cost and that based on the revaluation surplus. [Sch 4: 32(3)] Depreciation on historical cost must be included under the appropriate heads in the profit and loss account Formats, i.e. under cost of sales, distribution costs and administrative expenses in Formats 1 and 3, or under depreciation in Formats 2 and 4. No indication is given as to where depreciation on revaluation surplus is to be included but it is suggested that it should either (i) be included under the same headings as depreciation on historical cost and separated in the notes to the accounts or (ii) be shown as a separate heading in the profit and loss account, charged before arriving at profit on ordinary activities before taxation.

Some prominent companies and their auditors have interpreted Sch 4: 32(3) as permitting the depreciation on the revaluation surplus to be charged direct to reserves and not set against annual profits at all. Although the relevant paragraph is far from clear the authors believe that this interpretation is wrong: certainly it is contrary to the requirements of the Fourth Directive which the statute purports to enact. It also seems to be contrary to the intention of SSAPs 6 and 12 although the matter is not referred to specifically in either statement. However the ASC has now issued ED 37 which is a proposed replacement of SSAP 12. ED 37 makes clear that the depreciation charge in the profit and loss account should be based on the carrying amount of the asset in the balance sheet, whether that be the historical cost or revalued amount, and that no part of the depreciation charge should be set directly against reserves. Accordingly it is strongly recommended that the practice of charging depreciation on a revaluation surplus direct to reserve should not be followed.

5.154 AUDITORS' REMUNERATION

The amount required to be disclosed in the notes is the sum of the audit fee and the related expenses charged in the profit and loss account. [Sch 4: 53(7)] This amount will be after adding or deducting, respectively, any under or over provisions for the previous accounting period. Fees and expenses for special services, such as accountancy, taxation and other matters, should not be included.

5.155 HIRE OF PLANT AND MACHINERY

It is a requirement of Sch 4: 53(6) that the amount charged to revenue for the hire of plant and machinery should be disclosed in the notes to the accounts. It is believed that this requirement is intended to disclose a charge comparable to that of depreciation where fixed assets are owned, and accordingly the term 'plant and machinery' should be interpreted broadly to include such items as motor vehicles.

5.156 RENTS FROM LAND

If a substantial part of the company's revenue comprises rents from land, the amount of rents receivable, less ground rents, rates and other outgoings must be disclosed in the notes. [Sch 4: 53(5)] Most rental agreements do not distinguish between rents from land and from buildings and therefore most companies include rents from buildings and improvements to land in this disclosure.

5.157 PROVISIONS FOR DIMINUTION IN VALUE OF FIXED ASSETS

The following must be disclosed separately in the profit and loss account or in the notes to the accounts [Sch 4: 19]:

(i) any provision made for diminution in value of a fixed asset investment;

(ii) any provision made for the permanent diminution in value of any other fixed asset (separate from and in addition to the systematic provision for depreciation); and

(iii) any such provisions previously made which are written back on the grounds that they are no longer required.

5.160 TAX ON PROFIT OR LOSS

The presentation and disclosure of taxation in the profit and loss account are discussed in Chapter 14 (see specifically Section 14.022).

5.170 PROFIT OR LOSS ON ORDINARY ACTIVITIES AFTER TAXATION PROFIT OR LOSS FOR THE FINANCIAL YEAR

All the formats require separate disclosure of 'Profit or loss on ordinary activities after taxation' and 'Profit or loss for the financial year'. If there are no extraordinary items or minority interests in both the current and preceding financial years, then these amounts will be the same and it is suggested that it is unnecessary to show both headings. The amount might be disclosed as 'Profit or loss for the financial year'.

5.180 MINORITY INTERESTS

Since the formats were designed to deal with companies (but not groups), they make no provision for 'minority interests'. The minority's share of profits from ordinary activities after taxation should in accordance with SSAP 14 be shown as a 'one line' item immediately after 'Profit or loss on ordinary activities after taxation'.

5.190 EXTRAORDINARY ITEMS

All the formats require separate disclosure on the face of the profit and loss account or in the notes to the accounts of:

Extraordinary income

Extraordinary charges

Tax on extraordinary profit or loss

Formats 1 and 2 require a further subtotal for 'Extraordinary profit or loss'. The combining of the above items under one heading of 'Extraordinary items', with details of each item and the total of taxation on extraordinary items given in the notes, is often preferable on the grounds that it facilitates the assessment of results, particularly if minority interests or associated companies are involved.

In a group profit and loss account, any minority interests in extraordinary items should be deducted from the related items [SSAP 14] and the group's share of any extraordinary items of associated companies should be disclosed separately from other extraordinary items where that share is material in the context of the group's results [SSAP 1].

Extraordinary items are not defined in the Act, but are defined in the Fourth Directive as 'income and charges that arise otherwise than in the course of the company's ordinary activities'. The definition contained in SSAP 6 is 'items which derive from events or transactions outside the ordinary activities of the business and which are both material and expected not to recur frequently or regularly'. The definition in SSAP 6 is thus apparently more restrictive than that in the directive since it introduces the additional test concerning the expectation as to the frequency and regularity of recurrence. It is a pity that ED 36 repeats the definition in SSAP 6 and that the opportunity to adopt a definition which coincides with that adopted by the E.E.C. has not been taken. However 'frequently' and 'regularly' are both subjective terms and no guidance is given as to how they should be interpreted, so it is unlikely that the difference between the two definitions will give rise to practical difficulties.

The critical distinction between an extraordinary item and one that is exceptional (see Section 5.140 above) is whether it derives from events or transactions that fall outside the ordinary activities of the company or from events or transactions that fall within those activities. This is often a difficult judgement to make and different views are sometimes possible. Further, it is recognised that what is extraordinary in one company will not necessarily be extraordinary in another. For example the disposal of surplus land might be regarded as being outside the ordinary activities of a manufacturing company but within those of a property development company. However in order to minimise the incidence of different treatments of similar items, the ASC proposes in ED 36 to clarify the requirements to be met before an item is treated as extraordinary. This is done primarily by including more comprehensive lists of items which may be exceptional and of those which would be extraordinary. The examples listed are set out below:

Exceptional Items

- Redundancy and reorganisation costs unrelated to the discontinuance of a business segment
- Development expenditure written off (other than routine charges for amortisation)
- Profits appropriated to employee share schemes
- Profits or losses on disposal of fixed assets
- Abnormal charges for bad debts, stock obsolescence or losses on long-term contracts
- Surpluses arising on settlement of insurance claims
- Amounts received in respect of insurance claims for consequential loss of profits

Extraordinary Items

- The discontinuance of a significant business segment
- The sale of an investment not acquired for resale (e.g. in a subsidiary or associated company)
- Provision for permanent diminution in value of a fixed asset because of unusual events during the period
- The expropriation of assets

The most difficult distinction to draw is between redundancy and reorganisation costs on the one hand, and costs associated with the discontinuance of a 'significant business segment' on the other. A business segment is defined as a separately identifiable component of a company whose activities, assets and results can be clearly distinguished from those of the company as a whole. It may be in the form of a subsidiary or associated company, a joint venture, a division, a plant, or a department. In marginal cases there will clearly be room for difference of opinion as to whether a particular event constitutes a reorganisation or the closure of a department which can be treated as a significant business segment.

It remains to be seen how effective any revised standard based on ED 36 will be in achieving greater consistency in the recognition of items as exceptional or extraordinary, but in view of the judgemental nature of the decision it seems unlikely that inconsistencies can be eliminated entirely. It is suggested therefore that it is particularly important that the notes to the accounts should include descriptions of all exceptional and extraordinary items which are unambiguous and which make clear the precise nature of each item. The informed reader of the financial statements should be in a position to make his own evaluation of how each item should be treated and to make any necessary adjustment to earnings per share for his own purposes if the treatment of any item is different from the one which he prefers.

5.191 TERMINATED ACTIVITIES

It is proposed in ED 36 to define more clearly how to determine the amount of the extraordinary item to be recognised in respect of the discontinuance of a significant business segment, with a view to achieving greater consistency in approach. The proposal is that, where a decision has been made to discontinue a business segment, provision should be made for the consequences of all decisions taken up to the balance sheet date. The following are listed as items that should normally be included:

- provision for redundancy payments
- retention payments to key personnel during the run-down period
- profits or provisions for losses arising from the disposals of assets, including anticipated ongoing costs prior to disposal (e.g. rent, rates and security)
- pension costs
- bad debts arising from the decision to close
- results of any trading after commencement of implementation of the decision to discontinue
- losses due to penalty clauses in contracts

It is specifically proposed that such items may be treated as extraordinary even if they are recognised over a number of accounting periods. This implies that, if provisions which are created for the costs of discontinuance at one date subsequently prove to be inaccurate or incomplete, any necessary material adjustment in a subsequent period should also be treated as extraordinary. It also appears to recognise that separate decisions may be taken to close different business segments over a period and that these decisions would each result in the recognition of extraordinary items.

5.200 PRIOR YEAR ITEMS

Sch 4: 57(1) requires that where any amount relating to any preceding financial year is included in the profit and loss account, the effect shall be stated.

The majority of prior year items arise mainly from the corrections and adjustments which are the natural result of estimates inherent in the accounting process and particularly in the periodic preparation of financial statements. Such items should be dealt with in the profit and loss account of the year in which they are recognised and shown separately if material. It is specifically stated in SSAP 6 that prior year items are not extraordinary merely because they relate to a prior year.

Prior year adjustments, which are not reflected in the profits of the current year, are required and permitted by SSAP 6 only in two rare sets of circumstances:

(i) where there has been a change in accounting policy; and

(ii) where it is discovered that the prior year's accounts have included a fundamental error.

As is indicated in Section 2.032 above, accounting policies must be applied consistently from one financial year to the next and policies should be changed only when this can be justified on the grounds of better financial reporting.

A fundamental error is defined as one which is of such significance as to destroy the true and fair view and hence the validity of the accounts, and which would have led to their withdrawal had the errors been recognised at the time. It is suggested therefore that a fundamental error should be recognised only in the very rare circumstances when it is acknowledged that the accounts should not have been issued in the form in which they were. An error in an accounting estimate, however large, which is apparent with the benefit of hindsight is not a fundamental error if the estimate was reasonably made on the basis of the information available at the time.

Such changes in accounting policy or correction of fundamental errors are adjusted for by restating prior years with the result that the opening balance of retained profits is adjusted accordingly. The effect of the change should if practicable be disclosed by showing separately in the restatement of the previous year the amount involved. An example of the accounting presentation and disclosure of a prior year adjustment arising from a change in accounting policy is given below.

EXAMPLE

STATEMENT OF MOVEMENTS ON RESERVES

Year ended 31st December 1984

	Note	*Revaluation Reserve £'000*	*Profit and loss account £'000*
Balance at 1 January 1984			
As previously reported		*500*	*12,674*
Prior year adjustment	*21*	—	*(698)*
As restated		*500*	*11,976*
Profit retained for the year		—	*2,005*
Balance at 31 December 1984		*500*	*13,981*

NOTE 21 – PRIOR YEAR ADJUSTMENT

The policy for accounting for goodwill has been changed during the year and the asset is now amortised in equal amounts over five years commencing in the year of acquisition, whereas the previous policy was for goodwill to be carried forward indefinitely unless a permanent diminution in value was recognised. It is considered that the new policy will give a fairer presentation of the results and financial position of the group. Amounts for prior years have been adjusted in accordance with the new policy, resulting in a reduction in the balance of retained profits at 1 January 1984 of £698,000, and of the profit for 1983 of £386,000.

5.210 DIVIDENDS

The aggregate amount of dividends paid and proposed must be shown separately in the profit and loss account. [Sch 4: 3(7)(b)] Dividends should be deducted from 'Profit or loss for the financial year'.

Dividends should be expressed in the profit and loss account at the actual cash amount paid (or proposed to be paid) to the shareholders. The rate of dividend as well as the amount should be shown.

Stock Exchange companies are required to disclose particulars of any arrangement under which a shareholder has waived or agreed to waive any dividends. This requirement applies to waivers of future dividends as well as to waivers of dividends payable during the past financial year. Waivers of minor amount may be disregarded provided some payment has been made on each share during the year.

5.220 RETAINED PROFIT

It is widespread practice to conclude the profit and loss account with a figure derived by deducting the amount of dividends paid and proposed from the profit or loss for the financial year. This figure is commonly described by a title such as 'Retained profit/deficit' or 'Transferred to/from reserves'. Other transfers, such as transfers from revaluation reserve to distributable profits are not disclosed on the face of the profit and loss account but are dealt with in the statement of movements on reserves. This treatment may not comply with a strict interpretation of the requirement in Sch 4: 3(7)(a) that every profit and loss account must show separately as an additional item any amount set aside to, or withdrawn from, reserves. However, it seems unobjectionable and perhaps to be preferred, particularly if, as is recommended in Section 9.021, a statement of movements on reserves appears on the face of, or immediately follows, the profit and loss account.

5.221 OTHER ADJUSTMENTS TO RESERVES

Only in exceptional circumstances should items be charged or credited direct to reserves without being included in the profit and loss account. These cases are discussed under reserves in Section 9.022.

SSAP 6 deals with the problem of special instances where items of a revenue or expense nature are permitted or required either by law or by a company's constitution to be taken to reserves. For example the Act permits certain items to be written off against share premium account rather than against profits and the articles of property or investment holding companies frequently require that profits on sale of properties or investments should be taken to capital reserve. SSAP 6 suggests that such items should be dealt with by recognising them in the profit and loss account and transferring an equivalent amount between the profit for the year and the appropriate reserve. The requirement proposed in ED 36 is for this approach to be applied only to items where the special treatment is permitted or allowed by the company's constitution, not where it is permitted or allowed by law. There seems to be little merit in this requirement, particularly since investment trusts are specifically excluded from it, and it is to be hoped that this aspect of ED 36 will be removed before it is converted into a SSAP. Fortunately the circumstances envisaged will occur only rarely.

5.222 REDEMPTION OF SHARE CAPITAL AND LOANS

Sch 4: 53(3) requires disclosure in the notes of amounts set aside out of profit and loss account for redemption of share capital and loans. A company may be required by law or by agreement, or may decide for reasons of prudence, to set aside funds for purposes of redemption of shares or loans, but this action merely restricts the amount of distributable reserves available for other purposes and does not affect the reported profit or loss for the period.

5.230 ADDITIONAL DISCLOSURES UNDER FORMATS 2 AND 4

Formats 2 and 4 require more detailed disclosure of certain profit and loss items. The headings required under these formats which have not been dealt with in the preceding sections are:

Changes in stocks of finished goods and work in progress

Own work capitalised

Raw materials and consumables

Other external charges

Staff costs

Depreciation and other amounts written off tangible and intangible fixed assets

Exceptional amounts written off current assets

Other operating charges

5.231 CHANGES IN STOCKS OF FINISHED GOODS AND WORK IN PROGRESS

The difference between opening and closing stocks of finished goods and work in progress is to be shown under this heading. Finished goods would include factored stock as well as items manufactured by the company. Progress payments, which would be deducted from the valuation of stocks for balance sheet purposes, are not to be taken into account but profits earned and included in the valuation of long term contract work in progress should be included. Since this heading requires a clear distinction between stocks of finished goods and work in progress on the one hand and stocks of purchased items (such as raw materials and consumables) on the other, it seems that it will only be used by manufacturing companies.

5.232 OWN WORK CAPITALISED

This caption will include the value of direct materials and labour and appropriate interest and other overhead costs capitalised in connection with the company's own construction of tangible fixed assets. The cost elements shown under the other profit and loss headings will be shown at their gross amount.

5.233 RAW MATERIALS AND CONSUMABLES

The difference between the opening and closing stocks of raw materials and consumables will be deducted from or added to the total cost of purchases of these items in arriving at the amount to be shown under this heading. Purchases of components should be included as forming part of raw materials. Companies in the retail trade which adopt this format should use more appropriate wording for this heading, e.g. 'Goods for resale'.

5.234 OTHER EXTERNAL CHARGES AND OTHER OPERATING CHARGES

No guidance is provided as to what items should be included in 'Other external charges' as opposed to 'Other operating charges'. Since it is linked in the formats with raw materials and consumables, it is suggested that as a minimum 'Other external charges' must include those production costs from external sources which are not included as raw materials and consumables, e.g. purchased cost of factored goods, sub-contractors' costs, equipment rentals and appropriate production overheads. 'Other operating charges' would then include selling and administrative costs which were not shown under the other headings. But it is impossible to refute the argument that any charge which is neither a staff cost nor depreciation must be an external charge; on this basis everything that was not specifically included elsewhere would be included in 'Other external charges' and 'Other operating charges' would become redundant.

It is unlikely that any authoritative interpretation of the division between these two headings will ever be attempted and companies should adopt whatever reasonable division is most convenient to them. The important point is that whatever division is adopted must be adhered to consistently from year to year.

5.235 STAFF COSTS

The information required to be shown under this heading is explained in Section 5.151. The formats indicate that staff costs be divided between (i) wages and salaries paid or payable (ii) social security costs and (iii) other pension costs. It is probably clearer to show staff costs as one amount in the profit and loss account and the required details in the notes.

5.236 DEPRECIATION AND OTHER AMOUNTS WRITTEN OFF FIXED ASSETS

The information required to be shown under this heading is explained in Section 5.153.

5.237 EXCEPTIONAL AMOUNTS WRITTEN OFF CURRENT ASSETS

This heading seems to be intended to record necessary reductions from the cost of current assets to arrive at net realisable value, for example amounts written off debtors. However it seems equally possible to deal with these items in some other way: amounts written off debtors could be included in 'Other operating charges' and reductions in net realisable value of stocks under either 'Changes in stocks of finished goods and work in progress' or 'Raw materials and consumables' as appropriate. It is only necessary to deal with exceptional amounts under this heading.

5.240 EARNINGS PER SHARE

SSAP 3 requires companies listed on a recognised stock exchange for any class of equity capital (except banking, shipping and insurance companies claiming exemption from disclosure requirements) to disclose earnings (loss) per share on the face of the profit and loss account together with comparative figures for the previous year.

Both 'basic' earnings per share and 'fully diluted' earnings per share (i.e. after taking account of conversion of convertible loan stock, exercising of options, etc.) should be shown. Comparative fully diluted earnings per share should not be shown unless the assumptions on which it was based are still applicable. It is not necessary to show fully diluted earnings per share if the dilution is less than 5% of the basic earnings per share.

The basis of calculation of both basic and fully diluted earnings per share should be shown and the amount of the earnings and the number of equity shares used in the calculation should be disclosed.

The calculation of basic earnings per share is: profit/(loss) on ordinary activities after tax, minority interests and preference dividends divided by the weighted average number of equity shares in issue and ranking for dividend.

The appendix to SSAP 3 includes an example of the method of calculating earnings per share and also deals with the treatment of changes in equity share capital such as rights issues. The appendix to the original standard contains a number of other examples of earnings per share calculations.

Where extraordinary items are material, disclosure of earnings per share after taxation and extraordinary items, together with the comparative figures should be encouraged. The proposed revision of SSAP 6 (ED 36) supports this view, although this will not be a requirement of the proposed standard.

5.250 PROFITS AND LOSSES ON REALISATION OF FIXED ASSETS

There may occasionally be circumstances in which the sale of a fixed asset should be classified as an extraordinary item (see Section 5.190) but generally profits and losses arising on the realisation of fixed assets should be dealt with as part of the profit or loss on ordinary activities.

Some authorities consider that the profit or loss arising on the disposal of depreciable assets which are replaced in the normal course of business reflects the over- or under-estimate of depreciation and accordingly should be treated in the profit and loss account as an adjustment of depreciation. This treatment is clearly appropriate for the normal minor adjustments that arise as a matter of routine, although the alternative treatment of including such profits under 'other operating income' and losses under an appropriate expense classification is equally acceptable. But if the adjustments which arise are large, it is probable that they are caused by circumstances other than the lack of precision in depreciation estimates, and treating them as adjustments to depreciation will distort the annual charge for depreciation and is not appropriate. In such circumstances the amounts should be included under 'Other operating income' or a suitable expense heading, and if they are sufficiently significant the amounts should be disclosed separately as exceptional items.

Where a fixed asset that has been revalued is subsequently realised, there have been differing views as to whether the gain or loss to be recognised in the profit and loss account should be measured by reference to the depreciated original cost of the asset or to its revalued amount. ED 36, the exposure draft of a proposed revision to SSAP 6, takes the position that the gain or loss should be determined by reference to depreciated original cost. This seems the most logical approach and it is suggested that it should be followed.

Accounting for revaluation of assets is dealt with in Section 9.025.

6 BALANCE SHEET: GENERAL AND FIXED ASSETS

6.010 GENERAL REQUIREMENTS

The Act provides that every balance sheet shall give a true and fair view of the state of the company's affairs at the end of its financial year and shall comply with Sch 4 as to its form and content. [s 228]

Guidance is given in this and other chapters of the accounting treatment and disclosures required in respect of items to be included under each balance sheet heading.

6.011 FORMATS

Two alternative formats are permitted and these are reproduced in Appendix 5. Format 1 arranges the balance sheet headings vertically, which is the practice customarily followed in the U.K. and is the preferred arrangement. Format 2 presents a two-sided arrangement, with assets on one side and liabilities, capital and reserves on the other.

In practice most companies which have adopted Format 1 strike a total for total assets less liabilities, balanced by a total for capital and reserves, and this treatment is considered best practice. However, some companies rule off at the heading 'Total assets less current liabilities' and combine long-term creditors and provisions with capital and reserves to give a total which is sometimes described as 'capital employed'. As the format does not include a heading equivalent to 'Total assets less total liabilities', this presentation cannot be said to be contrary to law but it is not recommended.

6.012 HEADINGS

Balance sheet headings which have been assigned letters or Roman numerals must be shown in the order and under the headings and sub-headings given in the format adopted. No flexibility is permitted in the description of the headings or in their position in the balance sheet, except that the headings for 'Prepayments and accrued income' and 'Accruals and deferred income' may be shown either as main headings or as sub-headings of debtors and creditors, respectively.

Sub-headings preceded by Arabic numerals are permitted greater flexibility. The arrangement and description of these items shall be adapted to meet the special nature of the company's business. In addition, they may be combined as one amount where such combination facilitates the assessment of the state of affairs provided that the details of each item so combined are shown by way of note to the accounts; items which are not material for such assessment may be combined with other items without disclosure.

6.013 CLASSIFICATION OF ASSETS AND LIABILITIES

(a) Current assets and fixed assets

The balance sheet formats require classification of all assets under the heading of 'Current assets' or 'Fixed assets'. Two exceptions to this requirement are: 'Prepayments and accrued income' and 'Called up share capital not paid'. Amounts included in each of these items may be shown as separate main headings or as sub-headings under 'Debtors'. It is unlikely that such amounts will be material enough to justify being shown as separate main headings.

The definition of fixed and current assets given in Sch 4 is based on the intended use of the asset in the business. A fixed asset is one which is intended for use on a continuing basis in the company's activities and a current asset is one which is not intended for such use.

(b) Current liabilities

The classification of liabilities in the balance sheet formats is made by reference to whether the liability falls due within one year or after more than one year. An exception to this rule is that 'Accruals and deferred income' may be shown separately as a main heading or as a sub-heading under the two 'Creditors' headings.

(c) Net current assets (liabilities)

The balance sheet Format 1 requires a sub-total for current assets less current liabilities, designated 'Net current assets (liabilities)'. This sub-total must include 'Prepayments and accrued income' even when this item is shown under a heading separate from that of current assets.

Since the sub-heading 'Net current assets (liabilities)' may include certain assets not realisable within one year while it will recognise only those liabilities which are payable within one year, it may well not give a meaningful indication of liquidity.

6.014 ASSET VALUATION RULES

Sch 4 lays down rules for the valuation of balance sheet items. These, for the most part, are consistent with the valuation bases required by SSAPs. The rules distinguish between the historical cost convention and alternative conventions. The alternative rules permit companies to adopt the current cost accounting valuations stated in SSAP 16 in the preparation of their statutory financial statements or to adopt a mixture of historical and alternative valuations.

The general valuation rules are stated below. The rules applicable to specific assets are given in the sections of the manual dealing with those assets.

(i) Gross value of assets

Under the historical cost accounting rules, the gross value of assets shall be their purchase price or production cost.

The alternative accounting rules permit assets to be valued on the following bases:

Tangible fixed assets	– at market value determined as at their last valuation date or at current cost.
Intangible fixed assets, excluding goodwill	– at current cost.
Investments included in fixed assets	– at market value determined as at their last valuation date or at a value determined on any basis considered by the directors to be appropriate in the circumstances.
Investments included in current assets	– at current cost.
Stocks	– at current cost.

(ii) Depreciation

The cost or alternative valuation of all fixed assets with limited useful lives shall be reduced by a provision for depreciation to write off the difference between cost or alternative valuation and residual amount systematically over the asset's useful economic life.

(iii) Provision for reduction in value

All fixed assets	– a provision for diminution in value must be made where the reduction is expected to be permanent.
Fixed asset investments	– a provision for diminution in value may be made (even if not expected to be permanent).
Current assets	– a write down to net realisable value shall be made if lower than cost or alternative valuation.

Where the reasons for making any of these provisions no longer apply to any extent, the provisions shall be written back to the extent that they are no longer necessary.

(iv) Price or cost unknown

Where the purchase price or production cost of an asset cannot be determined from the records without unreasonable expense or delay, the value ascribed to it in the earliest available record of its value made on or after its acquisition or production shall be used in place of the purchase price or production cost. (The Act repeats the Companies Act 1981 requirement that particulars shall be given of any case where the purchase price or production cost of an asset is for the first time determined in this way. [Sch 4: 51(1)] This requirement is unlikely to have any practical significance other than on the first accounts prepared in accordance with the Companies Act 1981.)

6.020 INTANGIBLE FIXED ASSETS

6.021 DISCLOSURE REQUIREMENTS

(a) Statutory headings

'Intangible assets' is a main heading which must appear on the face of the balance sheet. The following sub-headings are required but may be shown either on the face of the balance sheet or in the notes.

Development costs

Concessions, patents, licences, trademarks, and similar rights and assets

Goodwill

Payments on account

(b) Movements

For each sub-heading there must be shown [Sch 4: 42]:

in respect of the gross amount:

- the balances at the beginning and end of the year;
- acquisitions and disposals during the year;
- transfers of assets to and from that item during the year.

in respect of provisions for depreciation or diminution in value:

- the balances at the beginning and end of the year;
- provision made during the year;
- adjustments of provisions arising from disposals;
- any other adjustments made.

Comparative figures for the preceding year are not required.

(c) Accounting policies

Sch 4: 36 requires disclosure of the accounting policies with respect to the depreciation and diminution in value of assets, including intangibles. Generally this will include disclosure of the method of depreciation and period of write off.

(d) Other disclosures

Disclosures applicable to specific intangible fixed assets are given in the sections below.

6.022 BASIS OF VALUATION

Sch 4 requires the valuation of intangible fixed assets at purchase price or production cost and, except in the case of goodwill, allows the alternative of the current cost basis. However, it seems inappropriate to use the current cost basis except in current cost accounts.

All intangible assets, with the exception of goodwill on consolidation, must be depreciated over their useful economic life. [Sch 4: 18, 66] Purchased goodwill may be written off over a shorter period (see Section 6.024 below).

Although it is not provided for in the Act, it is considered good practice in respect of any intangible fixed asset which has been fully written down to remove both the cost and the corresponding depreciation from the aggregate amounts disclosed.

6.023 DEVELOPMENT COSTS AND EXPENDITURE ON RESEARCH

(a) Disclosure

If any amount is included under 'Development costs' there must be stated in a note to the accounts [Sch 4: 20]:

(i) the period over which costs originally capitalised are being or are to be written off; and

(ii) the reasons for capitalising the development costs.

A development expenditure note which meets these requirements would be:

EXAMPLE

Development costs on product X which came into production in 1983 are being amortised in equal amounts over the three years 1983–1985 since most of the benefit of the development is expected to fall in these years.

Development costs on product Y are capitalised and carried forward since product Y is not yet in commercial production. The costs will be amortised over two years commencing with commercial production which is expected to be in 1986.

SSAP 13 requires that the accounting policy followed in relation to expenditure on research and development should be clearly explained.

(b) Accounting methods

The Act provides that the costs of research may not be treated as assets in any company's balance sheet [Sch 4: 3(2)] and that an amount may only be included in a balance sheet in respect of development costs in special circumstances. [Sch 4: 20(1)] It thus gives statutory authority to the principles of SSAP 13.

SSAP 13 subdivides research and development expenditure under three headings:

(i) Pure (or basic) research: original investigation undertaken in order to gain new scientific or technical knowledge and not primarily directed towards any specific practical aim or application.

(ii) Applied research: original investigation undertaken to gain new scientific or technical knowledge and directed towards a specific practical aim or objective.

(iii) Development: the use of scientific or technical knowledge to produce new or substantially improved materials, devices, products, processes, systems or services prior to the commencement of commercial production. Specifically excluded from this definition is expenditure incurred in locating and exploiting mineral deposits in the extractive industry; however, it would seem reasonable that development or improvement of processes and techniques in this industry including those employed in drilling and extraction should be included in this definition.

Expenditure which is reimbursable by third parties either directly or under a firm contract should be treated in the same way as stocks and work in progress.

Expenditure on pure and applied research should be written off as incurred except that the cost of tangible fixed assets acquired in order to provide facilities for research and development should be treated in the same way as other tangible fixed assets. Development expenditure should also be written off as incurred except where all the following circumstances apply:

(i) there is a clearly defined project, and

(ii) the related expenditure is separately identifiable, and

(iii) the outcome of the project has been assessed with reasonable certainty as to its technical feasibility and its ultimate commercial viability considered in the light of factors such as likely market conditions (including competing products), public opinion, consumer and environmental legislation, and

(iv) if further development costs are to be incurred on the same project the aggregate of such costs together with related production, selling and administration costs are reasonably expected to be more than covered by related future revenues, and

(v) adequate resources exist, or are reasonably expected to be available, to enable the project to be completed and to provide any consequential increases in working capital.

Where these circumstances apply, development expenditure may be deferred to the extent that its recovery can reasonably be regarded as assured.

If development costs are deferred to future periods, their depreciation should commence with the commercial production of the product or process and should be allocated on a systematic basis to each accounting period, by reference to either the sale or use of the product or process, or to the time period over which the product or process is expected to be sold or used.

It is recommended that the period of depreciation should be short so that there may be a reasonable certainty of recovery. At the end of each year the balance of deferred development expenditure should be reviewed in the light of latest available information (e.g. actual sales compared with estimates) and where recovery is considered doubtful, the undepreciated balance in respect of doubtful projects should be written off immediately.

Development expenditure written off in previous periods should not be reinstated even though the uncertainties which had led to its being written off no longer apply.

6.024 GOODWILL

(a) Introduction

Goodwill is defined as the difference between the value of a business as a whole and the aggregate of the fair value of its separable net assets. It usually arises where the profits earned by the business represent more than a fair return on the value of its net assets other than goodwill. Many businesses generate their own goodwill through commercial connections, regular customers, good reputation, efficient management, etc., but such goodwill does not appear in the financial statements. The Act provides that goodwill may only be included in a balance sheet to the extent that it was acquired for valuable consideration. [Sch 4: Note 3 to balance sheet formats]

Goodwill may arise as a result of the purchase of a business or undertaking either directly or through the purchase of shares in a company.

It is necessary at the outset to distinguish between transactions for the purchase of a business, in which goodwill may or may not arise, and the purchase of specific assets. It is considered that the appropriate criteria of the purchase of a business are whether customers' accounts are assigned and employees agree to contracts of service with the acquiring company. In other words, the business carries on substantially as before under the responsibility of the new owners.

Where specific assets are purchased, the total consideration represents the cost of those assets to the purchaser irrespective of the values attributed to them in the books of the vendor and therefore no goodwill arises. Where there is more than one asset or group of assets being acquired, it will be necessary to allocate the purchase price to the respective assets on the basis of fair values. Where there is a vending agreement, this may give some guidance, but the values attributed therein to the various assets should always be carefully considered in the light of all the circumstances to ensure that they represent fair and arms length prices.

Where a business is purchased, the consideration will reflect not only the net assets being acquired but also goodwill that the purchaser recognises in the corpus of the business. It will therefore be necessary to determine the fair value to the purchaser of the net assets acquired before the amount of goodwill can be identified. Provision should be made for all liabilities expected to arise as a result of the acquisition (e.g. plant closure and other reorganisation costs). These fair values, not the historical book values of the vendor as shown in the financial statements of the acquired business, should be reflected in the balance sheet. Any excess of the purchase consideration over the fair value of the net assets acquired represents purchased goodwill. Where the purchase consideration represents the cost of investment in a subsidiary or related company, the goodwill element arises in the consolidation process and is commonly referred to as 'goodwill on consolidation'.

It sometimes happens that the aggregate of the fair values of the net assets acquired, (after making provision for all costs which were taken into account in determining the purchase price, such as anticipated future losses or costs of reorganisation) exceeds the consideration paid. This excess when it arises is referred to as 'negative goodwill'.

Although the Act contains a requirement to amortise any goodwill treated as an asset over a period which does not exceed its useful economic life, this requirement does not apply to goodwill arising on consolidation. In practice therefore a variety of methods for accounting for goodwill has continued to be seen. Some reduction in this variety should however result from the publication of SSAP 22 'Accounting for goodwill', which is effective in respect of financial statements relating to accounting periods beginning on or after 1 January 1985.

SSAP 22 provides for two alternative standard practices to be followed in relation to purchased goodwill arising after the introduction of the statement and a wider range of choices for dealing with goodwill existing in accounts at the date of its introduction.

(b) Accounting for purchased goodwill

(i) Immediate elimination

The normal method of accounting for purchased goodwill recommended in SSAP 22 is to eliminate it from the accounts on acquisition directly against reserves, and not as a charge in the profit and loss account.

The statement does not specify which reserves should be used for the elimination of goodwill and some disparity of practice seems likely. Clearly goodwill may not be set against a share premium account and it is thought that it should not be set against a revaluation reserve except to the extent that the revaluation reserve represents realised profit (i.e. to the extent that the revaluation reserve exceeds the unamortised surpluses on revaluation of assets still held by the company). It is suggested that the set off should normally be against reserves which represent retained profits of the company or group.

(ii) Amortisation

The alternative method of accounting for purchased goodwill is to amortise it on a systematic basis over its useful economic life. If this method is adopted the charges for amortisation must be recognised in arriving at the profit or loss on ordinary activities before tax. It is specifically stated that purchased goodwill may not be revalued except that any permanent diminution in value below its net book amount should be recognised by an immediate charge to profit and loss account. The useful economic life must be estimated at the time of acquisition, and this estimate may subsequently be revised downwards but not upwards.

No restriction is imposed on what may be regarded as the economic life of purchased goodwill and only vague general guidance is provided on the factors to be considered in making the assessment. It is suggested that the life of purchased goodwill is short and that the amortisation period should normally be not more than five years. However, there is an alternative view (which SSAP 22 rejects) that goodwill once created continues indefinitely provided it is maintained and therefore that a very long life may be recognised: this view received significant support from ASC's earlier discussion paper which canvassed a maximum period of 40 or 50 years, and it is also supported by the general practice in the U.S.

(iii) The choice of method

It is suggested that goodwill is an asset like any other fixed asset which is purchased for the purpose of earning profits and which does in fact contribute to profitability provided no more than a fair price has been paid. Accordingly the cost of goodwill should be accounted for by charges against profits over the period expected to benefit from it, which as indicated above is relatively short. The alternative policy permitted by the standard of amortisation of goodwill through the profit and loss account over its (short) useful economic life is therefore preferred.

However it must be recognised that in practice the overwhelming majority of companies will opt for the approach of immediate elimination against reserves, since under this approach they are not required to charge against future profits all the payments made to obtain these profits. The reported profits (which are generally regarded as much more significant than the net asset position) will therefore be much better than they would be if goodwill were amortised.

SSAP 22 recognises that the alternative treatments of immediate elimination and amortisation are based on different ways of looking at goodwill, yet it permits both treatments to be used in the same financial statements for different acquisitions. How such an approach is reconciled with the fundamental accounting concept of consistency as described in SSAP 2 is not explained. The acknowledged purpose is to enable a company to depart from a policy of immediate elimination in the case of a large payment for goodwill where the resultant effect on reserves would be unacceptable. Such a mixture of accounting policies is clearly very undesirable and it is to be hoped will occur only rarely but, in view of the terms of SSAP 22, must be regarded as acceptable. It should be borne in mind that the reserves disclosed in a consolidated balance sheet have no relevance to the determination of the distributable profits of the holding company; there is no reason therefore why a consistent policy of immediate elimination should not be followed in consolidated accounts, even if this results in an adverse balance on reserves. It is only in the accounts of an individual company that the problem of adequate distributable profits may arise.

(c) The treatment of negative goodwill

Negative goodwill arising on an acquisition should be credited direct to reserves. Appendix 2 to SSAP 22 suggests that where negative goodwill arises in the accounts of an individual company (not a group) the credit should be to an unrealised reserve, from which it may be transferred in line with the depreciation or realisation of the tangible assets acquired as part of the acquisition of the business.

(d) Treatment of existing goodwill

When a company has goodwill in its balance sheet at the date when SSAP 22 first applies there is a choice of methods available for eliminating it:

(i) Where the general policy of immediate elimination is adopted:

- The preferred approach is immediate elimination against reserves of all pre-existing goodwill.

- Acceptable alternatives are:

  prospective amortisation of the balance over its remaining useful economic life, or

  partial immediate elimination and partial amortisation.

(ii) Where the general policy of amortisation is adopted:

- The preferred approach is to restate the existing goodwill at the amount at which it would have appeared in the balance sheet if the new policy had always been in force. The normal approach of making a prior year adjustment in respect of a change in accounting policy would apply.

- Acceptable alternatives are:

  prospective amortisation of the balance over its remaining useful economic life (without any restatement), or

  partial restatement in line with the new policy and partial amortisation commencing at the date of the accounts.

It is considered that the preferred approaches indicated above are so overwhelmingly preferable that they should always be adopted except in very rare circumstances. The alternatives which allow different items of goodwill brought forward to be treated in different ways are contrary to the consistency principle and should be avoided.

A particular problem that may arise is that of a group which has carried goodwill on acquisition as a permanent item and a very large balance of goodwill has been created as a result of acquisitions which would have been accounted for as mergers had they taken place after the coming into force of the Companies Act 1981. It is suggested that the best approach to this problem is immediate write off against reserves in the group accounts even if this results in a substantial adverse balance on a reserve account. The total reserves will normally remain in credit since there will usually be a large share premium account, and in any case distributable reserves are not affected. There is no reason why the effect of the write off of goodwill should not be disclosed in a note to the accounts if this is thought desirable for an understanding of the group reserve position. This approach seems preferable to the alternative of amortisation against group profits even on the basis of a relatively long useful economic life.

(e) Disclosure requirements

In addition to the general requirements to disclose movements both in gross amounts and depreciation of intangibles, the following information should be given:

(i) the accounting policy followed in respect of goodwill, and of any pre-existing goodwill if this is different.

(ii) the amount where material of goodwill arising as a result of each separate acquisition which took place during the year.

(iii) the period chosen by the directors over which purchased goodwill is to be written off (i.e. the estimated useful economic life) and 'the reasons for choosing that period'. A statement that the period chosen represents the estimated useful economic life seems to satisfy the second requirement.

(f) Fair value of net assets

Where goodwill is eliminated immediately against reserves, the determination of the fair values (other assets and liabilities assumes particular importance since the value ascribed to the net assets other than goodwill must be charged against earnings either immediately or by amortisation over a period. Any inappropriate valuation can therefore have a significant effect on reported earnings. The appropriate approach to the determination of fair value is discussed in Section 12.092.

6.025 CONCESSIONS, PATENTS, LICENCES, TRADEMARKS AND SIMILAR RIGHTS

The items included under this heading represent rights granted under a contract with a third party or by legal registration. They generally permit a company to manufacture or sell a product or service or to enjoy the exclusive use of an invention or name. Most rights expire after a specified period of time but there may be a renewal option.

Note 2 to the balance sheet formats states that the amounts may only be included in a balance sheet under this item if either (i) the assets were acquired for valuable consideration and are not required to be shown under goodwill or (ii) the assets were created by the company itself.

The economic useful life over which these intangibles are to be depreciated should be the shorter of the anticipated period of profitable exploitation and the period to the expiry of the right. Renewal periods should only be included if the holder has the option to renew which he is likely to exercise and any additional costs are small in relation to costs carried forward.

6.030 TANGIBLE FIXED ASSETS

6.031 DISCLOSURE REQUIREMENTS

(a) Statutory headings

'Tangible assets' is a main heading which must appear on the face of the balance sheet. The following sub-headings are required but may be shown either on the face of the balance sheet or in the notes:

Land and buildings

Plant and machinery

Fixtures, fittings, tools and equipment

Payments on account and assets in course of construction

(b) Movements

For each sub-heading there must be shown [Sch 4: 42]:

in respect of the gross amounts (i.e. cost or other valuation basis):

- the balances at the beginning and end of the year;
- any revision of the amount made during the year arising from a revaluation;
- acquisitions and disposals during the year;
- transfers of assets to or from that asset category during the year.

in respect of provisions for depreciation or diminution in value:

- the balances at the beginning and end of the year;
- provisions made during the year;
- adjustments of provisions arising from disposals;
- any other adjustment made in respect of such provisions during the year.

Comparative figures for the preceding year are not required.

(c) Information on valuation bases

Where tangible fixed assets are valued in accordance with the alternative valuation rules permitted in Sch 4 (i.e., market value or current cost) (see Section 6.033), the following information is to be given:

(i) the assets affected and the basis of valuation [Sch 4: 33(2)];

(ii) the year of revaluation and the values; also in the year of valuation, the name of the valuers (or particulars of their qualifications) and basis of valuation [Sch 4 :43];

(iii) the comparable historical cost amounts, or the difference between these amounts and the valuation, including the comparable amount or difference in the cumulative provision for depreciation. [Sch 4: 33(3)] If the historical cost of any asset is not readily ascertainable, then as indicated on page 84 the value ascribed to it in the earliest available record of its value may be used instead.

SSAP 19 further requires that if the valuer of investment properties is an employee of the company or group, this fact should be disclosed.

An example of good disclosure in respect of property revaluation is as follows:

EXAMPLE

The company's freehold property was valued by Messrs. King & Co., Chartered Surveyors on 31st July, 1984. In their opinion the market value for existing use at that time was £750,000 as compared with the net book amount of £218,000. A potential tax liability of £105,000 will become due if the property is sold at the above value. The valuation has been incorporated in the balance sheet and the surplus over net book amount of £532,000 has been added to the revaluation reserve. Depreciation for the year has been based on the amount of the valuation, resulting in an increased depreciation charge of £5,100.

(d) Analysis of land and buildings

The item of 'Land and buildings' must be analysed between freeholds, long leaseholds (not less than 50 years unexpired) and short leaseholds. [Sch 4: 44, 83]

(e) Interest capitalised

Where interest has been included in the cost of an asset (see Section 6.032(h)), the amount of interest so included must be disclosed in a note to the accounts. [Sch 4: 26(3)] The effect of this requirement appears to be that the amount of interest included in the cost of any fixed asset must continue to be disclosed as long as that asset is held by the company.

Stock Exchange companies are required to state the amount of interest capitalised during the year, together with the amount and treatment of any related tax relief.

(f) Depreciation

The accounting policies with respect to the depreciation and diminution in value of assets must be disclosed. [Sch 4: 36] SSAP 12 also requires that there should be disclosed for each major class of depreciable asset, the depreciation methods used, the useful economic lives or the depreciation rates used, and the total depreciation charged for the period. Where a number of different lives or rates are used in one major class of assets, it is customary to indicate the extent of the range, e.g. 'rates of between 10% and 25%' or 'estimated useful lives of between 4 and 10 years'.

If a change is made from one method of depreciation to another, SSAP 12 requires disclosure of the effect, if material, in the year of change. The statement also requires disclosure of the effect, if material, on the provision for depreciation of revaluations made in the year.

(g) Provision for diminution in value

Any provisions for diminution in value of fixed assets which are required in addition to normal charges for depreciation (see Section 6.035) must be disclosed separately either in the profit and loss account or in a note to the accounts. [Sch 4: 19(2)]

(h) Gross amount of depreciable assets

SSAP 12 requires disclosure for each major class of depreciable asset of the gross amount and the related accumulated depreciation. The principal fixed asset which is not usually depreciated is land and this asset is often combined in the item of 'Land and buildings'. The amount of depreciable assets therefore cannot be derived from the customary tabulation of fixed asset information unless the land element not subject to depreciation is separately disclosed. The other significant asset categories which are not depreciated are investment properties and assets in course of construction, and if these are shown separately the disclosure in the accounting policies that these assets are not depreciated is adequate to comply with SSAP 12.

6.032 DETERMINATION OF COST

(a) General

As indicated above, under the historical cost accounting rules the amount to be included in any fixed asset is its purchase price or production cost. [Sch 4: 17]

Purchase price is the actual price paid plus any expenses incidental to the acquisition.

Production cost consists of the purchase price of the raw materials and consumables used plus the amount of the costs incurred which are directly attributable to the production of the asset. In addition production cost may include (i) a reasonable proportion of indirect costs of the production of the asset, but only to the extent that they relate to the period of production and (ii) interest on capital borrowed to finance the production of the asset to the extent that it accrues in respect of the period of production. [Sch 4: 26]

The application of the rules to specific fixed assets is discussed below.

(b) Land

Cost of land includes the purchase price, estate agents' commission, legal fees, surveying, draining, clearing and landscaping, and demolition costs of buildings not intended for use at time of purchase. Any development land tax (which is discussed more fully in Section 14.100) should be added to the cost of land.

(c) Buildings

If a building is purchased, cost is the purchase price (excluding the cost of the land) plus all repair charges incurred in making good dilapidations which occurred before the building was purchased, as well as all costs of alterations and improvements.

If a building is constructed instead of being purchased, the capitalised amount should include the cost of work sub-contracted, the cost of materials, labour, supervision and other direct production overheads, and other incidental costs, such as:

costs of excavation.

costs of building permits and licences.

cost of temporary buildings used for construction offices. The cost of temporary buildings used for operations during the construction of the permanent buildings should be absorbed in operations.

professional fees.

Overheads which are indirectly attributable to the production of the building may be included to the extent they relate to the period of production.

(d) Plant and machinery

The cost of plant and machinery includes the purchase price, freight, duty and installation costs. If machinery has to be operated for a time for the purpose of running it in and testing it, the costs of such work may be capitalised. In-built plant and machinery will include labour, materials and appropriate production overheads.

The costs of relocating machinery within a factory or to another location should not be capitalised.

(e) Tools

Tools may be divided into two classes: machine tools and hand tools. Machine tools are a part of the machine and should be capitalised. However, because they usually wear out much more rapidly than the machine and have to be replaced, they should be recorded separately from the machine. Hand tools, because of their short life, are similarly recorded in a separate tool account or written off in the year of purchase.

Two bases of accounting for tools which are frequently used are (i) to make periodic counts and value them at cost less depreciation and (ii) to value them at a fixed amount (see Section 6.033(f)).

(f) Furniture and fixtures and equipment

This group of assets should include the cost of relatively permanent property, such as show-cases and counters, shelving, display fixtures, safes, office equipment and furniture.

The cost of computer equipment may include software costs. Because of the likelihood of rapid operating and technological changes, these costs are often expensed as incurred or, if capitalised, are written off over a short period of time.

(g) Payments on account and assets in course of construction

This heading should include deposits against delivery of fixed assets and payments made to contractors for work completed to date.

Although all formats include a separate heading of 'Payments on account and assets in course of construction', in many cases the amounts involved are insufficiently material to justify separate disclosure and are included in the heading appropriate to the asset being acquired. Where the amounts are material they should be disclosed in a separate column in the fixed asset tabulation in the notes to the accounts.

(h) Capitalisation of interest

As indicated above there may be included in the production cost of an asset interest on capital borrowed to finance the production of that asset, to the extent that it accrues in respect of the period of production. [Sch 4: 26(3)]

In general it is not possible to identify that part of a company's borrowing facilities which has been used to finance the production of a specific asset and the normal practice is to write off all interest charges to the profit and loss account in the year in which they are incurred. However, circumstances in which capitalisation may be appropriate are discussed below.

(i) Where a business undertakes a major capital project and incurs heavy interest costs while the asset under construction is making no contribution to income, the immediate write off of these interest costs may cause reported profits to be distorted. In such circumstances interest should be included in the cost of the fixed asset provided that the capital borrowed to finance the production can be identified with sufficient precision to enable the corresponding interest charge to be determined accurately. This normally requires the arrangement of a line of credit specifically to cover the expenditure on the project. Alternative approaches, such as charging 'notional' interest on the capital expenditure incurred or making an allocation from the company's general interest charge, are unlikely to provide a measure of the interest incurred on capital borrowed to finance the project that is sufficiently accurate to be acceptable. Interest may only be added in respect of the period of production of the asset; no interest should be added after physical completion even if the asset is not brought into use immediately.

(ii) The company's business may consist wholly or substantially of major projects in which there is a long period during which expenditure is incurred before any amount is received as income; a particular example is a property developer which typically will incur expenditure over a long period before there is an asset available either for sale or to provide rental income. In these circumstances it is unreasonable to suggest that separate borrowing arrangements should be made for each separate project, and it is likely that all, or substantially all, of the company's borrowing is for the purpose of financing projects. Therefore an allocation of the company's general interest charge which is related to the capital invested in the project may well provide an acceptable measure of the interest on capital borrowed to finance the project.

However the application of 'notional' interest which has not actually been incurred is not acceptable. This point must be noted particularly in group accounts. Some groups have centralised banking arrangements whereby the 'banking' company charges or credits interest to the group companies on the basis of its balances with these companies. Interest charged by one group company to another cannot be capitalised except to the extent that it represents interest actually borne by the group on capital borrowed to finance the production of the relevant asset.

Interest can only be capitalised to the extent that it accrues during the period of production. In the case of a property company it can be argued that the asset which is being produced is not merely a property but a tenanted rent-earning property and that the period of production does not end with the completion of construction but extends for a reasonable period thereafter until suitable tenants are obtained. This approach is acceptable provided that a reasonable policy is consistently followed; such a policy would require interest to cease being accrued as soon as a substantial proportion of the property is let or after the expiry of a specified period from completion of construction. Each case must be considered separately but it is suggested that the substantial proportion of the property let should normally not be more than 75% and the specified period from completion of construction should normally not be more than one year.

6.033 ALTERNATIVE BASES OF VALUATION

(a) General

As an alternative to historical cost, tangible fixed assets may be included at market value determined at the date of their last valuation. Thus the valuation need not be a current valuation. However ED 37 indicates in the draft explanatory note that where a policy of revaluing assets is adopted, the valuations should be kept up-to-date.

A further permitted alternative is valuation at current cost but this basis is not normally appropriate in the context of historical cost accounts and should only be used in the context of current cost accounts which are discussed in Chapter 16.

When a company becomes a subsidiary company of another unless merger accounting is used, the group accounts must reflect the fair values of the net assets to the acquiring company at the date of acquisition (see Section 12.092). In these circumstances it is a common practice to revalue the fixed assets in the books of the subsidiary at these fair values in order to simplify the preparation of consolidated accounts. When this is done any revaluation surpluses must be dealt with through the revaluation reserve as discussed in Section 9.025.

(b) Revaluation of properties

It is customary to revalue properties in a historical cost balance sheet on the basis of a valuation provided by a qualified valuer, but before a valuation is used for this purpose it is essential to consider the basis of valuation adopted to ensure that it is suitable. This problem has been greatly eased as a result of the issue and revision from time to time by the RICS of guidance notes on the valuation of assets.

The only basis of valuation which clearly provides an acceptable measure of market value for inclusion in a company's accounts is market value for existing use. This is an estimate of market value which takes account, amongst other things, of evidence of open market transactions in similar property and which is based on the assumption of the use of the property for the same or similar purposes as hitherto.

Another basis is market value for alternative use. This is an estimate of market value which also takes account of evidence of open market transactions in similar property but which reflects its prospective use for other purposes. Such valuations have no relevance to financial statements based on the going concern assumption and therefore are unsuitable for inclusion in such statements. Where there is a major difference between the book amount and the market value assuming alternative use, it might be appropriate to disclose this in the directors' report (see Section 4.030).

It is possible that the valuation may refer simply to 'open market value' without the qualifying words 'for existing use' or 'for alternative use'. The guidance notes of the RICS indicate that such a valuation will have regard to both existing and alternative uses to the extent to which these are reflected in the price obtainable on the open market. It seems that such a valuation should not be used unless sufficient additional information to confirm its suitability can be obtained from the valuer.

A further basis which is recognised by the RICS for use under the historical cost convention is depreciated replacement cost. This requires an estimate of the open market value of the land for its existing use and an estimate of the new replacement cost of the building from which deductions are made to allow for age, condition and functional obsolescence. A valuation made on this basis will include a statement that in the judgment of the valuer an open market value for existing use cannot be applied to the particular asset. The value will also be expressed as 'subject to adequate profitability'. On a strict interpretation of the Act a valuation on this basis seems to be unacceptable for inclusion in financial statements since it is clearly not a market value. On this interpretation revaluation of highly specialised buildings for which there is no market value would be prohibited: it seems likely that companies who have in the past used depreciated replacement cost as a basis for revaluation of properties will continue to do so, and unlikely that the practice will be challenged.

(c) Valuation of investment properties

Investment properties, as defined below, are required by SSAP 19 to be included in the balance sheet at their open market value (to be determined annually) and, except for leased property having an unexpired term of 20 years or less, are not subject to depreciation. The failure to depreciate investment properties is a departure from the requirement of Sch 4: 18 to depreciate fixed assets having limited useful economic lives. Disclosure of such departure and its effect is required by the Act to be given in the notes. An example of disclosure in these circumstances is given in Section 11.012. Wording similar to that contained in the example has been suggested by the APC and reviewed by the Department of Trade as meeting the requirements of the Act. It will not be necessary to show the effects of depreciation, even on an arbitrary basis.

An investment property is defined by SSAP 19 as an interest in land and/or buildings:

(i) in respect of which construction work and development have been completed, and

(ii) which is held for its investment potential, any rental income being negotiated at arm's length.

Property owned and occupied by a company for its own use and property let to and occupied by group companies are specifically excluded from this definition.

While the standard does not require the valuer of investment properties to hold professional qualifications or to be independent, the explanatory notes to SSAP 19 suggest that where investment properties represent a substantial proportion of the total assets of a major enterprise (e.g. a listed company) their valuation would normally be carried out annually by persons who do hold a recognised professional qualification with experience in the location and category of the properties concerned and at least every five years by an external valuer.

(d) Revaluation of other tangible fixed assets

Although the practice of including tangible fixed assets other than properties in the balance sheet at market value is comparatively rare, it is clearly permitted by the Act. There are significant practical problems; in particular it is only very rarely that it is practicable to establish a meaningful market value of partly used plant and machinery, fixtures, fittings, tools and equipment. It is often not practicable to purchase the items required by the business in a partly used state at all. Further, the value at which they can be sold may well be less than their net book amount, but this is not usually of any significance in the context of a going concern. In the rare cases where other tangible fixed assets have been revalued, the basis of valuation used has probably been depreciated replacement cost. On a strict interpretation of the Act, it seems that, since depreciated replacement cost is not normally equivalent to market value, valuation on this basis is not acceptable unless it is carried out annually, in which case it represents a valuation at current cost. However, it seems likely that revaluation on the basis of depreciated replacement cost will continue to take place when a company becomes a subsidiary of another as discussed in (a) above. The practice is unlikely to be challenged.

(e) Fixed assets surplus to requirements

Fixed assets are defined as those which are intended for use on a continuing basis in the company's activities. [Sch 4: 77] Thus when a particular asset is no longer intended for use on a continuing basis, it ceases to be a fixed asset and must be reclassified as current.

The definition is open to various interpretations. It is suggested that an item which has been defined as a fixed asset should normally continue to be so defined as long as it in fact continues to be used, even if there is an intention to dispose of it on suitable terms. Thus it is not uncommon for a company to conclude that it would like to sell a particular piece of plant, but to continue to use it perhaps not constantly and at less than full capacity in the meantime: such an item should continue to be classified as a fixed asset. Only if the piece of plant is actually taken out of use should it be reclassified as a current asset. Similarly an investment property should be treated as a fixed asset until negotiations for its sale are sufficiently far advanced for the sale to be reasonably assured. It is a feature of investment properties that they are always available for sale at the right price, but until a sale takes place, they are held for the purposes of the company's business – to obtain rental income and capital appreciation.

When it is necessary to reclassify a fixed asset as current, it must be revalued at the lower of cost and net realisable value. [Sch 4: 23(1)] If the asset is an item of plant which has been carried at historical cost less depreciation, it seems appropriate to treat the net book amount as equivalent to cost for this purpose: it represents the balance of cost which has not yet been charged against profits. In any case it is unlikely that this amount will be significantly less than net realisable value. If net realisable value is lower than the net book amount, the difference must be charged in the profit and loss account as a provision for diminution in value. However where as a result of a revaluation, the asset (normally a property) is included in the balance sheet at an amount which is greater than original cost, it is necessary to reduce it to cost by a transfer from revaluation reserve.

(f) Assets included at a fixed amount

A further alternative basis of valuation is permitted for tangible fixed assets provided that they:

(i) are not material to assessing the company's state of affairs,

(ii) are constantly being replaced, and

(iii) are not subject to material variation as to quantity, value or composition.

Fixed assets which meet the above conditions may be stated at a fixed quantity and value. [Sch 4: 25] It is likely that this method of valuation will only apply to low value, short-life assets, such as tools and moulds.

6.034 DEPRECIATION OF TANGIBLE FIXED ASSETS

(a) General

If a tangible fixed asset has a limited useful economic life, then its cost or market value, if appropriate, must be reduced to estimated residual value by systematic provisions for depreciation over the asset's useful economic life. [Sch 4: 18, 32]

Where a tangible fixed asset has diminished in value below its net book value, and that reduction in value is expected to be permanent, then additional provision for that diminution in value must be made. If any such provision for diminution in value has been made, but is no longer fully required, then it must be written back to the extent that it is not required. [Sch 4: 19]

These legal requirements give statutory support to SSAP 12 which requires that provision for depreciation of fixed assets having a finite useful life should be made by allocating the cost (or revalued amount) less estimated residual value as fairly as possible to the periods expected to benefit from their use. An exception is made in the case of investment properties (see Section 6.033(c)).

In order to comply with SSAP 12, it is necessary to identify:

(i) the cost or valuation of each asset,

(ii) the estimated residual value,

(iii) the length of time during which the asset will be commercially useful to the undertaking.

The definition of residual value proposed in ED 37 is the realisable value of the asset at the end of its useful economic life based on prices prevailing at the date of acquisition or revaluation.

It is also necessary to select the method of applying depreciation which results in the cost being allocated as fairly as possible to the periods expected to benefit from the use of the asset.

(b) Methods of depreciation

There are various methods of apportioning depreciation over the anticipated useful life of the asset. Those most commonly employed are the straight-line method and the reducing balance method. The straight-line method is favoured as most suitable for general application. To provide depreciation on the reducing balance method, the percentage applied needs to be approximately twice that applied under the straight-line method.

Another acceptable basis is the production method which apportions the cost of the fixed asset over its productive life measured in terms of the units produced or machine hours utilised in relation to the total of such units or hours estimated to comprise the productive life of the asset. Although this method is theoretically superior to the straight-line or reducing balance methods in that it more accurately matches costs with revenue, it is not often used because of the additional record keeping involved.

Some considerations regarding the methods of depreciation are discussed below:

(i) Freehold land

Freehold land does not have a limited useful life and therefore should not be depreciated. In consequence it is necessary where freehold property is purchased to allocate the purchase consideration between the value of the land and that of the buildings. Similarly any revaluations of freehold property should distinguish between land and buildings.

(ii) Freehold buildings

Normally buildings have limited useful economic lives and they are generally depreciated on the straight-line basis. However, in ED 37, the ASC proposes to recognise the rare instances where an asset is maintained to such a standard that (a) the estimated residual value is equal to or greater than its net book amount, or (b) its estimated useful economic life is infinite or such that any depreciation charge would be insignificant. In such circumstances no depreciation should be charged. In making this assessment it will be necessary to consider not only the physical condition of the asset but also the risk of obsolescence. Maintenance must be undertaken on a regular basis and the cost charged to the profit and loss account.

(iii) Leasehold properties (including improvements)

Provision for amortisation should be made on the straight-line basis over the unexpired period of the lease, or useful life of the asset, if shorter. Allowance should be made for the estimated cost of making good any dilapidations.

Where there are rent reviews any premium paid should be amortised over the period to the next review date.

(iv) Plant and machinery, tools and equipment, ships, vehicles, etc.

Provision for depreciation should, in general, be computed on the straight-line method. The declining balance and production methods are also suitable in appropriate circumstances. Assets of very short effective lives, such as loose tools, jigs and patterns, may however be dealt with more satisfactorily by other methods such as revaluation or valuation at a fixed amount.

(v) Mines, oil wells, quarries and similar assets of a wasting character

Provision for depreciation and depletion should be made according to the estimated exhaustion of the asset concerned (i.e. units extracted compared with estimated total units to be extracted) and should include provision for estimated cost of environmental reinstatement where appropriate.

(c) Change in depreciation method

A change from one method of providing depreciation to another is permissible only on the grounds that the new method will give a fairer presentation of the results and of the financial position. When the method is changed, the unamortised amount at the date of change is to be written off by the new method over the remaining useful life commencing with the period in which the change takes place. (In this respect SSAP 12 seems to be inconsistent with SSAP 6 since the latter statement requires that on the adoption of a change in accounting policy, prior years should be restated.)

(d) Changed estimates of useful lives

A requirement of SSAP 12 is that the estimate of useful lives should be reviewed annually by management but in ED 37 the requirement is that they should be reviewed regularly and at least every five years. Estimates of useful lives require adjustment from time to time in the light of changes in experience and knowledge. These changes may reflect extension of estimated useful lives due to exceptional maintenance expenditure, curtailment due to excessive use, or obsolescence not allowed for in the original estimates of the commercially useful lives of the assets. When the original estimate of useful life is revised, the unamortised cost (or valuation) should be charged to revenue over the revised remaining useful life.

(e) Fully depreciated assets

If the estimates of useful life of assets are made realistically and kept under annual review as required by SSAP 12, the problem of fully depreciated fixed assets (i.e. fixed assets which are still in use but have already been written down to nil or residual value) should not arise, or at least should not be material. If fully depreciated fixed assets are no longer in use the cost and related depreciation should be written out of the books.

On rare occasions it may happen that the amount of fully depreciated fixed assets still in use is such that the financial statements are seriously distorted. ED 37 indicates that the assets should be reinstated but does not explain how this should be done. It is suggested that in these circumstances the appropriate course is to recognise that there has been a fundamental error in earlier years in the form of the failure to comply properly with SSAP 12 and to reinstate a proportion of the cost by a prior year adjustment (see Section 5.200). This is best done by making a revised estimate of the total useful life and allocating cost less residual value over that period.

(f) Depreciation of revalued assets

Where fixed assets are revalued, the charge for depreciation thereafter should be based on the revalued amount and current estimate of remaining useful life. The treatment of depreciation on the revaluation surplus in the profit and loss account is discussed in Section 5.153.

6.035 PROVISION FOR PERMANENT DIMINUTION IN VALUE

If at any time the net book amount of a fixed asset is seen to be irrecoverable, a provision for permanent diminution in value should be made immediately to write the asset down to its estimated recoverable amount, which should then be depreciated over the remaining useful life (see Section 6:014(iii)).

In addition to reviewing asset lives (see (d) above), management will need to consider whether the depreciation charges over the remaining useful life of an asset will be recovered from revenues generated from the asset's future use; if they cannot be recovered, a provision is necessary. Such a review is essential when, as a result of rapid technological changes or change in economic environment, a decision is made to use an asset over a much shorter period than originally considered as the asset's normal economic life.

6.036 LEASED ASSETS

There are special rules for accounting for leases which define the circumstances under which leased assets should be treated as fixed assets in the accounts. The appropriate treatment is determined by the nature of the lease rather than by the nature of the asset. The subject is dealt with in detail in Chapter 15.

6.040 INVESTMENTS

6.041 DISCLOSURE REQUIREMENTS

(a) Statutory headings

'Investments' is a main heading which must appear on the face of the balance sheet. It appears twice, both under fixed assets and current assets. The following sub-headings are required but may be shown either on the face of the balance sheet or in the notes.

Fixed assets	***Current assets***
Shares in group companies	Shares in group companies
Loans to group companies	Own shares
Shares in related companies	Other investments
Loans to related companies	
Other investments other than loans	
Other loans	
Own shares	

Shares in group companies are normally fixed assets of the company and would only appear as current assets in the exceptional circumstance where a decision had been made to dispose of all or part of a holding in a group. In normal circumstances the only investments to be classified as current assets will be 'other investments' consisting of the investment of a company's surplus funds on a relatively short-term basis.

This section deals with investments classified as fixed assets, though the disclosures listed in (d)–(h) below are also required in respect of investments treated as current assets.

(b) Movements

For each sub-heading there must be shown [Sch 4: 42]:

in respect of the gross valuation (i.e. cost or other valuation basis):

- the balances at the beginning and end of the year;
- any revision arising from a revaluation made during the year;
- acquisitions and disposals during the year;
- transfers of assets to or from fixed asset investments.

in respect of provisions made for diminution in value:

- the balances at the beginning and end of the year;
- provisions made during the year;
- adjustments of provisions arising from disposals;
- any other adjustment made in respect of such provisions during the year.

Comparative figures for the preceding year are not required.

(c) Information on valuation bases

Where fixed asset investments are valued in accordance with the alternative valuation rules of Sch 4 (i.e., market value, or any basis considered appropriate by the directors), the following information is to be given in the notes to the accounts:

(i) the investments affected and the basis of valuation [Sch 4: 33(2)],

(ii) in respect of investments other than listed investments, the year of valuation and the values; also in the year of valuation, the name of the valuers (or particulars of their qualifications) and basis of valuation [Sch 4: 43]; where any basis other than market value is used, the reasons for adopting the alternative basis is to be disclosed [Sch 4: 31(3)];

(iii) the comparable historical cost amount for both cost and provision for diminution in value, or the difference between these amounts and the alternative valuation. [Sch 4: 33(3)]

(d) Listed investments

The following additional information about listed investments must be given [Sch 4: 45]:

(i) the amounts of listed investments included in each sub-heading, divided between those listed on a recognised stock exchange and those otherwise listed;

(ii) for each sub-heading, the aggregate market value of listed investments, where this differs from the amount at which it is stated in the financial statements;

(iii) where the market value of any listed investments is used for purposes of the financial statements and this value is higher than the stock exchange value, both the market value and stock exchange value must be stated.

A 'recognised stock exchange' as defined by the Act is one which is so recognised for the purposes of the Prevention of Fraud (Investments) Act 1958. At present only The Stock Exchange is so recognised.

Companies dealt with on the USM are not listed companies.

(e) Group investments

The sub-headings 'Shares in group companies' and 'Loans to group companies' must be further sub-divided between:

(i) interests in a holding or fellow subsidiary company, and

(ii) interests in subsidiaries. [Sch 4: 59]

(f) Holdings which exceed 10%

In respect of investments in shares where (i) the nominal value of the holding in a company exceeds 10% of the allotted share capital (ii) the nominal value of the holding of any class of equity share capital of a company exceeds 10% of the nominal value of that class, or (iii) the value of the holding as shown in the investing company's accounts exceeds 10% of the assets of the investing company, the following information is to be given in the notes to the accounts [Sch 5: 1, 7 to 9]:

(i) the name of each company;

(ii) the country of incorporation if other than Great Britain; if incorporated in Great Britain, the country of registration (i.e. England or Scotland) is to be given unless this is the same as that of the investing company;

(iii) the identity and proportion of the nominal value of each class of shares held.

In addition SSAP 14 and SSAP 1 require in respect of each principal subsidiary and associated company an indication of the nature of its business.

Corresponding information for the preceding year need not be given.

In addition to the above, holdings in subsidiaries must be distinguished between direct holdings of the investing company and those of its subsidiaries.

Companies incorporated abroad or carrying on business abroad may be excluded if, in the opinion of the directors, disclosure would be harmful and the Secretary of State agrees to the exclusion.

If the companies referred to above are too numerous, the directors need only give the information for companies which principally affect the group's profit or loss or the amount of its assets. They must then include a statement to this effect and give the balance of the information in the next annual return.

Stock Exchange companies are required to disclose the following additional information in respect of each company not being a subsidiary in which holdings of equity capital amount to 20% or more:

(i) the principal country of operation;

(ii) particulars of and the percentage of each class of debt security directly or indirectly held by the company. For this purpose, debt security includes debenture or loan stock, debentures bonds and notes, whether secured or unsecured.

If the number of companies is large, particulars with regard to those of less importance may be omitted, i.e. information may be given for companies which principally affect the group's profit or loss or the amount of its assets.

(g) Investment in shares not accounted for by the equity method

The following additional information must be stated about each unconsolidated subsidiary and about each other investment in which the shares held represent more than 20% of the allotted share capital [Sch 5: 15 to 17]:

(i) the total of its share capital and reserves as at the end of its financial year ending with or last before the financial year of the company; and

(ii) its profit or loss for that financial year.

This information need not be given if the investment in the subsidiary or other company is included in the accounts or the notes by the equity method of valuation, or:

(i) it is not material; or

(ii) the holding relates to subsidiary companies and the holding company is exempt from preparing group accounts by virtue of its being a wholly owned subsidiary of a company incorporated in Great Britain; or

(iii) the holding is in respect of any body corporate which is exempted by the Act from the requirement to deliver a copy of its balance sheet to the Registrar of Companies and does not otherwise publish that balance sheet in Great Britain or elsewhere; or

(iv) in respect of minor companies where the company has taken advantage of the concession given in the Act and has limited the disclosure of particulars required by (f) above to principal investments. The information about such minor companies must be annexed to the next annual return.

(h) Subsidiaries not dealt with in group accounts

Where a holding company does not prepare group financial statements or excludes a subsidiary from the group financial statements, additional disclosures are required by Sch 4: 69 which are dealt with in Section 12.031. The principal requirement of this section is the disclosure in the notes of the total value, determined by the equity method, of the investment in those subsidiaries which have not been dealt with in the group financial statements.

A company which is a wholly owned subsidiary of a company incorporated in Great Britain does not have to give this information if the notes include a statement that in the opinion of the directors the aggregate value of the shares and amounts owing from the company's unconsolidated subsidiaries is not less than the total amount at which they are stated in the balance sheet.

6.042 BASIS OF VALUATION

(a) Historical cost convention

Under the historical cost accounting rules investments classified as fixed assets are valued at cost, but:

(i) provision must be made for any diminution in value which is expected to be permanent, and

(ii) provision may be made for a diminution in value even if it is not expected to be permanent.

Where the reasons for making any such provisions no longer apply to any extent, they must be written back to the extent that they are no longer necessary.

(b) Alternative valuation bases

Under the alternative valuation rules investments classified as fixed assets may be valued either:

(i) at market value as at the date of their last valuation, or

(ii) at a value determined on any basis which the directors consider appropriate in the circumstances.

6.043 SHARES IN GROUP COMPANIES

Shares in group companies held as fixed assets are usually included in an investing company's balance sheet at cost less provision for any permanent diminution in value. The problem of determining the 'cost' of shares acquired by share exchange is discussed in Section 12.092.

The alternative valuation bases are rarely used and are generally not appropriate. One practice which is sometimes seen is for the carrying value of investments in subsidiaries in the books of the holding company to be adjusted to the amounts of the net assets shown in the historical cost balance sheets of the individual subsidiaries. The effect of this is to make the total reserves shown in the holding company's own balance sheet identical to those shown in the group balance sheet. This practice is clearly contrary to the intentions of SSAP 22 (see paragraph 18 of the explanatory notes) and should now be discouraged.

6.044 SHARES IN RELATED/ASSOCIATED COMPANIES

Sch 4: 92 defines a related company as any corporate body (other than a group company) in which an investing company holds on a long-term basis a sufficient interest in the equity share capital carrying full voting rights to secure 'a contribution to that company's own activities by the exercise of any control or influence arising from that interest'. It further provides that a holding of 20% or more shall be presumed to provide such an interest unless the contrary can be shown.

This definition is very similar to the definition of an associated company in SSAP 1 (see Section 12.083). The major difference is that the definition in SSAP 1 is extended to include a non-corporate joint venture or consortium if the appropriate conditions apply.

Normally related companies and associated companies are identical and it is a common practice to refer only to 'associated companies' (as is done in the model financial statements of Tramp Holdings p.l.c.).

Shares in associated companies should normally be valued in the investing company's own balance sheet at cost less provision for any permanent diminution in value.

The treatment of investments in associated companies in group accounts and the application of the equity method of accounting are dealt with in Section 12.080.

6.045 OTHER INVESTMENTS

This category will comprise all investments, other than group and related companies, and will include:

listed and unlisted securities

partnerships and joint ventures

building society deposits

time deposits with banks

life insurance policies

Other investments must be classified under either fixed or current assets according to the definition contained in Sch 4: 77 (see Section 6.013(a)). In practice investments which are not intended for use on a continuing basis in the company's activities are likely to be restricted to those representing the investment of surplus funds on a relatively short term basis. Thus of the above items, interests in partnerships and joint ventures and life insurance policies are normally fixed assets, while building society deposits and time deposits with banks are normally current assets. Listed securities and unlisted securities in which there was a ready market could be either depending on the nature and purpose of the investment.

6.046 LOANS

Loans to third parties should only be treated as fixed assets where they are made for a significant period, normally exceeding twelve months, and for a purpose clearly connected with the company's activities, such as to establish a trading link with an important customer or supplier. Normally the loan would be the object of a formal agreement as to repayment arrangements and interest would be payable. Short term advances and any which are unconnected with the company's activities should be included under 'Debtors' (with any amount falling due after more than one year being separately disclosed).

The classification of loans to group and associated companies must be determined by reference to the facts in each case. Loans which are in the nature of current accounts and loans that are made on the clear understanding that they will be repaid within a relatively short period should be treated as current assets and shown as amounts due by group or associated companies. However many loans between companies in a group are made on an informal basis with no agreed repayment terms but in practice are used to meet the capital requirements of the borrower, and there is no realistic expectation of early repayment. Such loans are in effect investments intended for use on a continuing basis in the lender company's activities and should be classified as fixed assets.

6.047 OWN SHARES

U.K. legislation permitting the purchase or redemption of own shares also requires such shares to be cancelled. It is therefore difficult to see under what circumstances an investment would be included under the heading of 'Own shares'. The rules regarding the purchase or redemption by a company of its own shares are discussed in Section 18.020.

7 BALANCE SHEET: CURRENT ASSETS

7.010 STOCKS

7.011 DISCLOSURE REQUIREMENTS

(a) Statutory headings

Stocks is a main heading which must appear on the face of the balance sheet. The sub-headings required, which may be shown either on the face of the balance sheet or in the notes to the accounts, are:

Raw materials and consumables

Work in progress

Finished goods and goods for resale

Payments on account

These legal requirements are more specific than the corresponding disclosure requirement in SSAP 9 that stocks and work in progress should be sub-classified in a manner which is appropriate to the business and so as to indicate the amounts held in each main category. However there is an over-riding requirement [Sch 4: 3(3)] that the directors must adapt the arrangement and headings in any case where the special nature of the company's business requires such adaptation. An example of an adaptation that might be appropriate for a contracting and property development company is as follows:

EXAMPLE	*£'000*	*£'000*
Raw materials and consumables		*597*
Land held for development		*2,724*
Work in progress		
Contracting, less progress claims of £3,200,000	*4,700*	
Commercial developments	*1,400*	
Housing	*928*	
		7,028
Completed developments and houses for sale		*3,500*
		13,849

(b) Accounting policies

There is a statutory requirement [Sch 4: 36] for the disclosure of accounting policies adopted in determining the amounts to be included in respect of the items shown in the balance sheet. The requirements of SSAP 9 in regards to stocks are that the accounting policies that have been used in calculating cost, net realisable value, attributable profit and foreseeable losses (as appropriate) should be stated.

The description of the accounting policies should be as brief as possible whilst making clear to the reader which of the different policies permissible under the Act have been adopted. An example of a form of disclosure which would be acceptable in a simple situation is:

EXAMPLE

Stocks and work in progress are stated at the lower of cost and net realisable value. Cost represents direct materials and labour and production overheads.

Strict adherence to SSAP 9 appears to require that the method of determining net realisable value should also be stated, but this should only be necessary if the amount included at net realisable value is significant, or if an unusual method of calculating net realisable value has been adopted.

(c) Disclosure of replacement cost or most recent cost

Where stocks are determined by one of the acceptable methods other than the ascertainment of actual cost (see Section 7.014 below), the difference between the amount determined by that method and the 'relative alternative amount' must be disclosed in a note to the accounts if the difference is material. [Sch 4: 27]

The 'relative alternative amount' is the replacement cost of the stock at the balance sheet date or the amount determined by reference to the most recent actual purchase price or production cost before the balance sheet date if this appears to the directors to constitute a more appropriate standard of comparison in the circumstances.

Only the difference between the carrying value and the 'relative alternative amount' of those stock items valued at FIFO, LIFO, weighted average, or any other similar method need be disclosed. There is no requirement to disclose the amount of stock actually carried on any particular basis. An appropriate wording for the disclosure in such a situation would be:

EXAMPLE

Included in the amount shown above for stocks of raw materials and consumables are items valued at cost calculated on a first in first out basis. The replacement cost of these items at 31 December 1984 was £X greater (1983 – £Y greater) than the amount at which they are included in the accounts.

Although determination of the value of stock on the basis of actual cost is rare, there are very few examples in practice of published financial statements including this disclosure. Presumably it has been omitted on the grounds that it is not material. It is difficult to determine what is material in this context since it is difficult to identify the possible usefulness of the information to readers of financial statements. It is suggested that in most circumstances a difference which is less than 10% of the total amount of stocks can reasonably be regarded as not material.

(d) Interest capitalised

The amount of interest capitalised in the cost of stocks is required by Sch 4: 26(3) to be disclosed in a note to the accounts.

(e) Long-term contract work in progress

The special disclosure requirements applicable to long-term contracts are discussed in Section 7.016.

7.012 BASIS OF VALUATION

(a) Historical cost rules

Stocks must be valued at their purchase price or production cost unless their net realisable value is lower, in which case the latter basis must be used. [Sch 4: 22, 23] The comparison of net realisable value with cost should in principle be carried out on an item by item basis but, if this is impracticable, groups of similar items may be considered together. It is unacceptable to compare the total net realisable value of all stocks with their total purchase price or production cost. Where the reasons for making a provision in a previous year to write down stocks to net realisable value have ceased to apply to any extent, the Act requires that provision to be written back to the extent that it is no longer necessary. [Sch 4: 23(2)]

Net realisable value represents the actual or estimated selling price net of trade discounts and after deduction of all further costs to completion and of marketing, selling and distribution.

The purchase price of stocks is to be determined by adding to the actual price paid any expenses incidental to their acquisition.

Production cost is to be determined by adding to the purchase price of raw materials and consumables used the amount of the costs incurred by the company which are directly attributable to the production of the stock. In addition there may be included (i) a reasonable proportion of the costs which are only indirectly attributable to the production of the stock, but only to the extent that they relate to the period of production and (ii) interest on capital borrowed to finance the production of stock.

SSAP 9 deals in more detail with the valuation of stocks and work in progress. With the exception of the question of the treatment of long term contract work in progress, which is discussed below, this statement is consistent with the statutory requirements and should be followed.

In SSAP 9 cost is defined as that expenditure which has been incurred in the normal course of business in bringing the product or service to its present location and condition. It includes both the cost of purchase (which includes import duties, transport and handling costs and any other indirectly attributable costs) and costs of conversion. Costs of conversion include direct costs, production overheads and other overheads 'attributable in the particular circumstances of the business to bringing the product or service to its present location and condition'.

(b) Alternative valuation rules

Sch 4 permits stocks to be valued at current cost, but this basis is normally only appropriate in the context of current cost accounts, which are discussed in Chapter 16.

7.013 ELEMENTS OF COST

The various elements of cost to be included in the value of stock are discussed under the headings below.

(a) Material costs

Normally these will consist of the actual invoice price of the material, together with the ancillary costs of purchase, such as import duties, transport and handling costs, etc. Trade discounts, rebates and subsidies should be deducted.

Where raw material is subject to wastage and spoilage during production, it may be convenient to include the cost of such normal scrapping and wastage as part of the material cost of the product. Alternatively the costs of material scrapped or wasted may be included in overheads.

(b) Direct labour costs

The cost of wages of employees directly engaged in production must be allocated to production on the basis of normal operating conditions. Labour costs which are the result of operating inefficiencies, such as abnormal idle capacity or abnormal rectification work, should not be included in the stock valuation. This will require the costs of these abnormal inefficiencies to be identified in the company's accounting records.

(c) Overhead costs

SSAP 9 requires that all production overheads should be included in stock valuations. The practice of omitting some or all overheads from valuation on the grounds of prudence is not acceptable. Equally the valuation of stocks on a 'marginal costing' basis, whereby only costs which vary directly with volume of output are included and costs which accrue on a time basis are excluded, is not acceptable. Overheads other than production overheads should only be included in stock valuation where this is justified by exceptional circumstances: those which are properly classified as selling or administrative overheads should not be included. An exception is made in circumstances where firm sales contracts have been entered into in advance of manufacture for the provision of goods or services to customer specification; in these circumstances overheads relating to design, and marketing and selling costs incurred before manufacture may be included.

The problem of determining the amount of overhead to be carried forward in stocks may be considered under two headings (i) identifying the overheads to be included and (ii) applying these overheads to production in a logical manner. It is necessary first to analyse overheads by function between production, marketing and distribution, and administration. There are practical problems in making this analysis. For example, management salaries may include an element of supervision of production as well as of administration, and pension costs are likely to cover employees in the production sphere as well as those in sales and general administration departments. Central services departments, such as accounts, may provide identifiable services for production. Costs should be allocated over the functions on a reasonable basis which should be consistently applied.

The method of applying overheads to production must be one that is appropriate to the nature of the product and the method of production. The most popular methods of applying overheads are:

(i) by way of a labour hour or machine hour rate,

(ii) in proportion to direct labour costs,

(iii) in proportion to material costs,

(iv) in proportion to prime cost,

(v) equally to each unit of production (this is only appropriate where a single product is being produced in a given cost centre).

Whichever method of applying overheads is adopted, the overheads must be applied on the basis of the company's normal level of activity. Overhead costs which are the result of operating inefficiencies, such as abnormal idle capacity or abnormal rectification work, should not be included in the stock valuation.

(d) Interest

Sch 4: 26(3) permits the inclusion in the valuation of stock of interest on capital borrowed to finance its production to the extent that the interest accrues in respect of the period of production (but if this is done the amount of interest included must be disclosed in a note to the accounts). Generally interest on capital should not be included in stock valuations since capital is borrowed to finance the activities of the business as a whole and not specifically to finance stocks during the period of production. Appendix 1 to SSAP 9 indicates that in ascertaining the cost of long term contract work in progress it is not normally appropriate to include interest payable on borrowed money, but that this may be acceptable in infrequent circumstances where sums borrowed can be identified as financing specific long term contracts. Generally speaking interest may only be included in the cost of long term contract work in progress under the same conditions as are appropriate for including interest in the cost of fixed assets (see page 95).

An exception to the general rule that interest should not be included in stock valuations arises when a company holds significant quantities of maturing stocks such as whisky. The maturing period is clearly part of the period of production and the addition of interest is therefore permissible under Sch 4. Similarly interest incurred is clearly attributable to bringing the product to its existing condition and should therefore be included under SSAP 9. Provided that it can be demonstrated that the whole, or at least a large proportion of the company's borrowings is invested in maturing stocks, it is appropriate to include the whole or an appropriate proportion of the company's interest charges in the value of such stocks. The interest included in stocks must be the appropriate proportion of the company's actual interest expense; a 'notional' charge for interest on capital should not be added.

It is sometimes difficult to determine when the 'period of production' ends, i.e. when stocks are being held for sale as opposed to being held for maturing. For example, stocks of whisky 'mature' after three years but go on improving with age for many more years. It is considered acceptable to continue adding interest to the value of maturing stocks for as long as it can be demonstrated that the particular stock item continues to increase in value solely on account of age rather than because of market fluctuations or inflation. This increase in value must be greater than the interest cost incurred to achieve it. If this cannot be demonstrated then the stocks should be regarded as held for sale and no further interest should be added.

(e) Transfer price

Where the manufacturing process involves the transfer of work from one department to another, the transfer may be made at a price different from the cost incurred by the transferring department, either for reasons of convenience in accounting or as part of the system of management control. Where this takes place it is necessary for the purpose of valuing closing stocks to adjust the valuations to actual cost by eliminating any profits or losses arising at the separate department levels.

7.014 METHODS OF DETERMINING COST

Stocks should be valued wherever possible by attributing costs directly to specific items. This requires the identification of each item in stock with a particular purchase invoice or specific costs of production. In the vast majority of cases such specific identification is not practicable and Sch 4 permits cost to be determined by any one of the following methods:

(i) first in, first out (FIFO);

(ii) last in, first out (LIFO);

(iii) weighted average price;

(iv) any other method similar to these.

Although the Act permits the LIFO basis of valuation, this is not permitted by SSAP 9.

The generally preferred methods are: (i) FIFO, which is based on the assumption that the earliest purchased stock is the first to be disposed of, and the stock on hand, therefore, represents the most recent purchase or production; or (ii) weighted average price which is determined by dividing the total cost of units by their number to arrive at a weighted average price. This average price may be arrived at by a continuous calculation, a periodic calculation, or a moving average.

Many companies use predetermined estimates of costs in advance of production based on expected levels of costs, efficiency and operational activity. These estimates, usually referred to as 'standard costs' are used for internal management accounting purposes and sometimes also as a basis for year end stock valuation. Standard costs can only be used for year end stock valuation purposes if they are adjusted to actual cost which usually involves taking account of the variances (differences between actual cost and standard arising from price, volume and other factors) which have arisen.

Other methods of valuation which are sometimes adopted include:

(i) *Latest invoice price*

Under this method the latest invoice price is applied to the total volume of stocks held. SSAP 9 states that this method is not acceptable in principle since the result does not normally represent cost; it may only be accepted where it can be demonstrated that price fluctuations during the stock holding period have been so insignificant that the result is a reasonable approximation of cost.

(ii) *Retail method*

This method is frequently adopted by retail establishments. The total stock on hand is valued at current selling price and then reduced to approximate cost by deducting the normal gross margin. The method results in a valuation of stocks that approximates to average price and is, therefore, acceptable subject to certain constraints.

Approximately the same profit margin should be derived from all lines held by the department or alternatively it should be demonstrable that the proportions of the different types of stock held do not vary significantly. For example, the stocks of a newsagent and confectioner normally include lines of widely differing profit margins and to arrive at an acceptable stock figure by the retail method, it is necessary to divide the stocks into categories according to the profit margin achieved. A further problem with the retail method arises if the selling price on slow moving items has been marked down. If the normal gross profit percentage is then deducted from such items this will result in their being valued below cost. It is therefore necessary to ensure that the volume of marked down items is insignificant or alternatively they must be segregated and valued separately.

(iii) *Selling price less profit margin*

This method is similar to the retail method and is sometimes applied in the absence of a satisfactory costing system. In a multi-product environment, it is unlikely to be acceptable since it will not normally be possible to demonstrate that the method gives a reasonable approximation of actual cost.

(iv) *Fixed amount*

Sch 4: 25 also permits certain items to be included in stocks of raw materials and consumables at a fixed quantity and value. This treatment is acceptable provided that:

(i) the items are of a kind which are constantly being replaced,

(ii) their overall value is not material to assessing the state of the company's affairs, and

(iii) their quantity, value and composition are not subject to material variation.

7.015 PAYMENTS ON ACCOUNT

One of the sub-headings of stocks is 'Payments on account'. Identical sub-headings are included under both tangible and intangible fixed assets, while the sub-heading 'Payments received on account' appears under creditors. It therefore appears that this sub-heading relates to payments made, not to payments received, and it would only be used in the rare circumstance where payments have been made in advance in respect of items ordered for stock but not yet delivered.

However the legislation [note 8 on the balance sheet formats] permits and SSAP 9 requires payments received on account to be shown as deductions from stocks.

7.016 LONG TERM CONTRACTS

SSAP 9 requires that long term contract work in progress should be stated in financial statements at 'cost, plus attributable profit ......'. This is in conflict with the Sch 4 requirement that stocks (which includes work in progress) should be included in the balance sheet at the lower of cost and net realisable value. However, although Sch 4 defines the method of valuation of work in progress in the balance sheet, it does not prohibit the recognition of profit on long term contract work in progress. Sch 4: 91 indicates that profits are to be regarded as realised on the basis of generally accepted accounting principles at the time the financial statements are prepared and the recognition of realised profit on uncompleted long term contracts is well established and generally accepted, as well as being required by SSAP 9.

SSAP 9 defines a long term contract as one in which the time taken 'is such that a substantial proportion of all such contract work will extend for a period exceeding one year'. Difficulties have been encountered in interpreting this definition. It is suggested that contracts of the same type should all be treated in the same way and that it is not correct to make an arbitrary distinction between a contract which takes slightly less than one year to complete and a similar contract which takes slightly more. Accordingly if a substantial proportion of all contract work of one type will extend for a period exceeding one year, then all work in progress of that type constitutes long term contract work in progress even if some individual contracts will be completed in less than twelve months.

Conversely, if a company's business consists predominantly of short term contracts, the fact that one or two extend for a period slightly exceeding twelve months would not justify segregating them and treating them as long term contracts. It sometimes happens, however, that a company normally engaged solely in short term contracts exceptionally becomes involved in one or more very large contracts which extend for more than twelve months and which account for a substantial proportion of the company's activity. Bearing in mind the objective of reflecting a fair view of the activity of the company during the year, it will often be appropriate to account for the large contracts as long term contracts while treating the remainder as short term.

Frequently companies are engaged in two or more clearly identifiable types of contracts, of which some types are clearly short-term in nature, whereas others qualify as long term contracts. In those circumstances each type of contract should be considered separately. For example companies in the construction industry are generally involved in long term contracts, but many of them also undertake small repair and jobbing contracts which are short-term in nature. The latter should not be treated as long term contracts since they are clearly different in type.

Work in progress that does not qualify as long term contract work in progress must be valued at the lower of cost and net realisable value, and only in rare circumstances will it be appropriate to include an element of profit. To justify such a departure from both the Companies Acts and SSAP 9 it would be necessary to show that the recognition of profit only on completion resulted in serious distortions of profits on a regular basis; this circumstance is only likely to arise in very small enterprises.

(a) Attributable profit

Attributable profit is that part of the total anticipated profit 'which fairly reflects the profit attributable to that part of the work performed at the accounting date'. There are two principal approaches to the determination of attributable profit:

(i) the total anticipated profit is spread over the contract in direct proportion to the work carried out: there are in turn various methods of measuring the work carried out, e.g. in terms of value, elapsed time, or labour cost or hours;

(ii) the actual profit on that portion of the work completed at the balance sheet date is determined and regarded as the attributable profit.

Both methods are used but the first is preferable provided the method of measuring the work carried out is appropriate. A problem with the second method, particularly in the construction and civil engineering industries, is that tenders are often 'front-end loaded', i.e. while the total price is competitive, items for completion early in the contract are priced more highly than those to be completed later on. This improves the cash flow from the contract, but if the tender prices are used to measure profit, the contract will appear to be very much more profitable in the early stages than it does on completion. Indeed, an apparent loss may be sustained on later work in some cases.

It is important that prudence should be exercised in estimating both the total anticipated profit on the contract and the proportion thereof attributable to the work completed during the period. For example, claims for additional work or losses caused by the customer should not be accrued unless they have been agreed or established and claims against the company by the customer for penalties, rectification work, etc. should be accrued where it is likely that such costs will be incurred. SSAP 9 emphasises that many businesses carry out contracts where the outcome cannot reasonably be assessed before conclusion of the contract and in such cases no profit should be taken up. There can be no attributable profit until the outcome of the contract can be assessed with reasonable certainty.

(b) Loss making contracts

All foreseeable losses on contracts entered into before the balance sheet date must be provided in full and this applies even if work has not commenced. Provision for a foreseeable loss should be deducted from the cost of the contract work in progress in the balance sheet, unless the amount of the loss exceeds the cost incurred to date on the contract less progress payments received, in which case the excess should be shown as a liability in the balance sheet.

(c) Presentation in the accounts

While the recognition of profit on long-term contract work in progress is permissible under Sch 4, it is nonetheless required that work in progress should be included in the balance sheet at the lower of cost and net realisable value. This requirement appears to be in direct conflict with SSAP 9 which states: 'The amount at which long-term contract work in progress is stated in periodic financial statements should be cost plus any attributable profit, less any foreseeable losses and progress payments received and receivable'.

Since the Companies Act 1981 was enacted, the apparent conflict between the legislation and the

SSAP has caused substantial controversy as to the correct treatment of long-term contract work in progress in financial statements. A variety of different approaches have been proposed and adopted. No authoritative pronouncements have yet been issued on the subject but it is understood that a review of SSAPs in the light of the Companies Act 1981 requirements and with particular reference to SSAP 9 is being undertaken by ASC. It is to be hoped that a statement will not be long delayed but in the meantime it seems that at least the approaches discussed below must be regarded as acceptable.

The first approach is to exclude from work in progress the cost of that part of the contract which has been billed to the customer and similarly to exclude the payments on account received. Any retentions on the amounts billed or any payments on account receivable but unpaid would then be included in debtors. In effect the amounts billed to the buyer are treated as sales rather than as payments on account of uncompleted contracts. If this method is adopted care must be taken to ensure that too much profit is not recognised in the early stages of the contract, particularly as a result of the front-end loading of tenders which is referred to above. Where this has occurred it may well be necessary to make a provision to defer some of the apparent profit to later in the contract. Provided this point is borne in mind this method is particularly suitable in those cases where ownership of the work passes to the buyer as it is carried out and he is billed at regular intervals for work completed. This is the position with most construction and civil engineering contracts. This method clearly complies with the law and does not conflict with SSAP 9 or any other accounting standard since none of them specifically address the issue of when a sale should be recognised. However it does not solve the problem of the position where it is desired to recognise profit on a long term contract in circumstances where the work done cannot be the subject of an interim billing or a request for a payment on account to the customer.

The approach which appears to have been adopted by most companies is to take the view that it is necessary to comply with SSAP 9 in order to show a true and fair view and that they are required by s 228(5) of the Act to depart from the detailed requirements of Sch 4. They have therefore continued to include long term contract work in progress in the balance sheet at 'cost plus any attributable profit less any foreseeable losses and progress payments received and receivable'. Since this involves a departure from the requirements of Sch 4, it is necessary to disclose particulars of the departure, the reasons for it, and its 'effect'. There are major differences of view as to what is the 'effect' of the departure and how it should be disclosed.

One way is to disclose the total amount of attributable profit included in work in progress as in the following example:

EXAMPLE: Stocks	*1984*	*1983*
	£'000	*£'000*
Raw materials and consumables	*704*	*599*
Work in progress		
At cost less provision for future losses	*2,424*	*2,238*
Attributable profit on long term contracts	*192*	*441*
	2,616	*2,679*
Payments on account	*(1,856)*	*(2,110)*
	1,464	*1,168*

As indicated in the accounting policies the attributable profit is included in long term contract work in progress in accordance with SSAP 9. This constitutes a departure from the valuation rules contained in Schedule 4 to the Companies Act 1985, which is necessary to enable the balance sheet to give a true and fair view of the state of the company's affairs and is therefore required by Section 228(5) of that Act. The amount of profit included in work in progress is disclosed above.

There is however a strong body of opinion that the total amount of attributable profit included in the gross value of work in progress is not an appropriate method of measuring the effect of the departure. The supporters of this view argue that payments are received on account of the value of work done at contract prices, not merely on account of costs incurred; in consequence much, probably most, of the attributable profit added to the gross value of work in progress has already been realised in the payments received on account. The only effect of the departure is the amount by which the net work in progress (after deducting payments received on account) exceeds the lower of cost and net realisable value; because payments on account are not directly related to cost and no meaningful allocation between cost and attributable profit is practicable, this amount is not measurable.

This approach is illustrated in the following example:

EXAMPLE: Stocks

	1984	*1983*
	£'000	*£'000*
Raw materials and consumables	*704*	*599*
Contract work in progress, after deducting payments received on account of £1,856,000 (1983 £2,110,000)	*760*	*569*
	1,464	*1,168*

As indicated in the accounting policies the attributable profit on long term contracts is included in work in progress in accordance with SSAP 9. This constitutes a departure from the valuation rules contained in Schedule 4 to the Companies Act 1985, which is necessary to enable the balance sheet to show a true and fair view of the state of the company's affairs and is therefore required by Section 228(5) of that Act. As it is not possible to allocate progress payments received on contracts meaningfully between costs and profit it is impracticable to quantify the effect of this departure on the amount attributable to contract work in progress in the balance sheet.

Another approach involves including work in progress at cost in 'Stocks' and the attributable profit element in 'Prepayments and accrued income'. Under this method the treatment of payments received on account is a problem. For the reasons discussed above it is not appropriate to deduct them in total from the cost of work in progress and it is probably not practicable to allocate them meaningfully between work in progress and prepayments and accrued income. A possible solution is to include them in creditors under the heading 'Payments received on account'.

This method is rarely used but it is appropriate in circumstances where it is desired to recognise profit on a long term contract but the work done cannot be treated as a sale because no interim billing or request for payment on account can be made under the contract. It is clearly not in accordance with SSAP 9 and therefore can only be adopted on the basis that the requirement to comply with the law constitutes a good reason for departing from a statement of standard accounting practice.

7.020 DEBTORS

7.021 DISCLOSURE REQUIREMENTS

(a) Statutory headings

'Debtors' is a main heading which must appear on the face of the balance sheet. The sub-headings required, which may be disclosed on the face of the balance sheet or in the notes, are:

Trade debtors
Amounts owed by group companies
Amounts owed by related companies
Other debtors
Called up share capital not paid
Prepayments and accrued income

(b) Amounts falling due after more than one year

Any amounts which fall due after more than one year must be shown separately for each sub-heading. [Note 5 of balance sheet formats]

(c) Other disclosures

Additional disclosure which is required of certain items included under various sub-headings is discussed below.

7.022 TRADE DEBTORS

This item generally includes amounts invoiced to customers, accrued sales for goods delivered but not billed, contract retentions, suppliers' debit balances, less provision for bad debts and credits for returns, allowances, cash discounts and rebates. Amounts owed by group and related companies should not be included in this category.

7.023 AMOUNTS OWED BY GROUP COMPANIES

This item includes all amounts owed by group companies (i.e. parent, subsidiary or fellow subsidiary companies) with the exception of loans which are recorded as fixed assets (see Section 6.046) e.g. loans, current accounts and dividends receivable.

The netting of intercompany balances due from one group company against intercompany balances due to another group company is not permitted.

This sub-heading must be further sub-divided between (i) amounts owed by holding and fellow subsidiary companies and (ii) amounts owed by subsidiary companies. [Sch 4: 59]

7.024 AMOUNTS OWED BY RELATED COMPANIES

As with group companies this item includes all amounts owed by related companies with the exception of loans which are recorded as fixed assets (see Section 6.046).

7.025 OTHER DEBTORS

This heading generally includes debtors resulting from non-trading activities, such as amounts due from the sale of fixed assets, loans not included under other headings, insurance claims, and refundable deposits. Advances or partial payments (not to be confused with deposits which are to be refunded) made towards the purchase or construction of fixed assets or stocks are more appropriately included under those captions.

Loans which include an interest element as part of the principal balance should be shown net of the related unearned interest. The treatment of debtors under lease or hire-purchase contracts is discussed in Section 15.042.

Where amounts are due by directors and officers of the company or its holding company or by other related parties, disclosure may be necessary to meet specific statutory requirements or the general requirement for the accounts to show a true and fair view. This subject is dealt with in Section 11.080 - disclosure of transactions with interested parties.

Loans to finance acquisition of own shares

Where a company has any loans outstanding at the balance sheet date arising from:

(i) the provision of money made in accordance with an employee's share scheme for the acquisition of fully paid shares; or

(ii) loans made to bona fide employees (not directors) to enable them to purchase shares in the company or its holding company to be held by them by way of beneficial ownership; or

(iii) loans made by a private company for the purpose of the acquisition of its shares or those of its holding company or for the purpose of reducing or discharging any liability incurred in the acquisition of such shares;

the aggregate amount of those loans must be disclosed in the notes to the accounts. [Sch 4: 51(2)]

The restrictions on the ability of a company to provide financial assistance for the purchase of its own shares are discussed in Section 18.030.

7.026 CALLED UP SHARE CAPITAL NOT PAID

The unpaid balance of a call must be shown separately either as a sub-heading under 'Debtors' (which will normally be the more appropriate) or as a main heading.

7.027 PREPAYMENTS AND ACCRUED INCOME

'Prepayments and accrued income' must be shown as a separate item either as a sub-heading under 'Debtors' or as a main heading. It is unlikely that the total of this item will be of sufficient size or importance to deserve the prominence which a main heading would give to it. Often the separate sub-heading is not used since the amount concerned is not material and it can be combined with another sub-heading, such as trade debtors or other debtors.

(a) Prepayments

In accordance with the fundamental accounting concept of matching revenue with the expenditure incurred to earn it, it is appropriate in certain circumstances and with certain safeguards for expenditure to be carried forward and charged in the profit and loss account in the period in which the related benefits are received.

The following principles should be considered:

(i) No expenditure should be carried forward unless it can be shown that:

(a) the expenditure does not relate to any revenue already brought into the profit and loss account but to revenue which it is anticipated will be earned in the future, and

(b) the expenditure will directly generate, in the future, profits which will amply cover the amortisation of the expenditure over the period during which benefits will be received. Alternatively, the expenditure carried forward has an intrinsic realisable value of its own which will at least equal the cost.

(ii) The period of amortisation should be short enough to allow a reasonable certainty of recovery of such costs.

(iii) The unamortised balance of expenditure must be kept under continuous review and written off immediately to the extent that its recoverability becomes open to doubt.

Two particular problem areas are:

Advertising costs

Advertising costs usually cannot be identified with specific revenue as required by (i)(a) above and these expenses should not normally be carried forward. An exception to this might be advertising expenditure directly related to the launching of a new product but there would need to be powerful evidence of future benefits and the period of write off should be short. The cost of brochures relating to next seasons goods or services can be carried forward. Catalogues and show cards might be considered on a stock basis providing the material is not out of date and quantities are not excessive in relation to expected consumption.

Contract cancellation costs

Expenditure incurred to cancel an onerous contract, even when apparently linked to the obtaining of another profitable contract should not be carried forward. The purpose of the expenditure is not directly related to the generation of future profits.

Prepayments will include amounts paid in advance of benefits to be received (e.g., unexpired portion of rents, insurance and interest, advertising costs paid in advance).

(b) Discount of loans

Sch 4: 24 provides that where the amount repayable on a debt is greater than the value of the consideration received the difference may be treated as an asset. The difference must be written off by annual instalments before the debt is repaid and the amount not yet written off at each balance sheet date must be disclosed. The Act does not specify the heading under which this 'asset' is to be shown, and it is suggested that 'Prepayment and accrued income' will normally be the most appropriate. Accounting for discount on loans is discussed in Section 8: 014(c).

(c) Accrued income

Accrued income includes amounts earned at the balance sheet date but which the company is not yet entitled to bill or receive (e.g., interest and rental income; it should normally exclude sales accruals for goods shipped but not invoiced, which should be shown as trade debtors, since these usually arise from delays in invoicing or premature closing of the sales journal; they do not represent amounts which the company is not entitled to bill to the customer.

7.030 INVESTMENTS

The classification of investments between fixed assets and current assets is discussed in Section 6.040 (specifically 6.041(a), 6.045 and 6.046). Investments classified as current assets will normally consist either of deposits or short term loans to institutions, such as building societies or banks, or of marketable shares or securities.

The amount of listed investments must be disclosed separately together with their market value at the balance sheet date. [Sch 4: 45] The precise requirements are detailed in Section 6.041(d).

Under the historical cost accounting rules each separate investment held must be valued at the lower of cost and net realisable value. Any provision for diminution in value must be charged to the profit and loss account.

A problem arises where the market value of listed investments which have a ready and active market is above cost at the balance sheet date. Clearly the excess of market value over cost is a realised profit in accordance with generally accepted accounting principles. It may therefore be recognised in the profit and loss account and best practice is to do this. However the historical cost accounting rules apparently prohibit adding the excess of market value over cost to the amount at which the investment is shown in the balance sheet. The obvious treatment is to include the excess over cost under the heading 'Prepayments and accrued income', but there is a serious danger of this treatment being misleading because of the separate requirement to disclose the market value of the investment. A reader of the financial statements might compare market value to cost without appreciating that the difference had already been recognised and therefore draw an incorrect conclusion.

A possible solution is to include the accrued income element under investments in the balance sheet. Strictly this is probably a breach of the required formats which include prepayments and accrued income either under debtors or as a separate main heading, but it is not likely to constitute a material breach and can certainly be justified as being in the interests of clarity and fair disclosure.

EXAMPLE

Investments	*£*
Listed investments at cost (market value £150,000)	*120,000*
Accrued income: excess of market value of listed investments over cost	*30,000*
	150,000

An alternative approach which is less clear but which cannot be criticised as being a breach of the Act is to include the investment at cost, and the excess of market value over cost as prepayments and accrued income under debtors, but to explain this treatment in the note disclosing market value.

EXAMPLE

The market value of the listed investments was £150,000 and the excess of this amount over cost of £30,000 is included in the balance sheet under 'prepayments and accrued interest'.

There are additional disclosure requirements in respect of substantial investments i.e. investments which represent more than 10% in nominal value of a company's allotted share capital or of any class of its equity capital or whose value in the investing company's accounts exceeds 10% of the investing company's assets. The detailed requirements in such circumstances are described in Section 6.041(f)-(h).

Shares in group companies will only appear under current assets in very exceptional circumstances (see Section 6.041(a)), but if they do then they must be sub-divided between shares in a holding or fellow subsidiary company, and shares in subsidiary companies.

7.040 CASH AT BANK AND IN HAND

In addition to legal tender and amounts due by banks, items such as cheques, postal orders and bank credit card vouchers held in the ordinary course of collection should be included under this heading.

Demand deposits and deposits on seven day call with banks should be included but similar sums placed with building societies and other deposit taking institutions should be included under current asset investments. The list of recognised banks in the U.K. published by the Bank of England can be used to determine whether any particular U.K. institution should be regarded as a bank for this purpose, but it is often more difficult to determine the status of foreign institutions. It is suggested that in order to be treated as a bank for this purpose a foreign institution should meet the tests laid down in U.D.T. v Kirkwood [1966], i.e. it must (i) take money on current account, (ii) pay cheques drawn on itself, and (iii) collect cheques for customers.

Advances to employees on account of expenditure should be included in 'Other debtors' and not cash.

Normally the amounts to be shown under this heading should be the amounts recorded in the company's accounting records, i.e. amounts should be treated as withdrawn from the bank when cheques are drawn rather than when they are presented.

Some companies show the amount in the bank statement at the year end as the balance sheet figure; cheques drawn and not presented are added back to creditors and unbanked receivables are included in debtors. One reason advanced for this treatment is that in the event of a liquidation, all movements on bank accounts would be frozen, but this seems inconsistent with the fundamental accounting principle that the company should be presumed to be carrying on the business as a going concern. Accordingly this treatment is not recommended.

However the practice is sometimes encountered whereby cheques are drawn in settlement of liabilities but these cheques are not released to the creditors until a later date. In such circumstances it may be necessary to reverse the entries recording payment in order that the financial statements should show a true and fair view.

If any funds are held in specially designated bank accounts which may only be used for certain restricted purposes, it is good practice to disclose these amounts separately from the unrestricted funds. Restrictions may be imposed by statute, by the rules of a professional body or trade association, by the articles or by an agreement, such as a loan agreement. Common examples are the client accounts of solicitors and the 'insurance broking' accounts of insurance brokers.

8. BALANCE SHEET: LIABILITIES

8.010 CREDITORS

8.011 GENERAL DISCLOSURE REQUIREMENTS

(a) Statutory headings

In Format 1 there are two separate main headings: 'Creditors: amounts falling due within one year' and 'Creditors: amounts falling due after more than one year'.

In Format 2 there is only one main heading 'Creditors', but the amounts falling due within one year and after one year must be shown separately for each sub-heading and in aggregate.

The sub-headings which may be shown separately on the face of the balance sheet (the presentation followed by most U.K. companies) or in the notes to the accounts are:

Debenture loans
Bank loans and overdrafts
Payments received on account
Trade creditors
Bills of exchange payable
Amounts owed to group companies
Amounts owed to related companies
Other creditors including taxation and social security
Accruals and deferred income

As an alternative 'Accruals and deferred income' may be shown as a separate main heading, rather than as a sub-heading of creditors, but this alternative is rarely followed.

(b) Other statutory requirements

For each item shown under creditors which is payable wholly or partly after 5 years from the balance sheet date, there must be stated [Sch 4: 48]:

(i) the aggregate amount payable otherwise than by instalments;

(ii) the aggregate amount payable by instalments, and the aggregate amount of instalments which fall due after 5 years; and

(iii) the terms of payment and rates of interest payable.

Where the number of debts is large, a general indication of the terms of payment and rates of interest payable is sufficient.

There must also be stated for each sub-heading of creditors the aggregate amount of debts for which any security has been given by the company and an indication of the nature of those securities. [Sch 4: 48(4)]

(c) Stock Exchange requirement

Stock Exchange companies are required in addition to include a statement showing the aggregate amounts repayable:

(i) in one year or less, or on demand;

(ii) between one and two years;

(iii) between two and five years; and

(iv) in five years or more.

The amounts are to be sub-divided between (a) bank loans and overdrafts and (b) other borrowings.

An example of an appropriate note to the accounts which meets these requirements as they affect creditors falling due after more than one year is given below.

EXAMPLE

CREDITORS: AMOUNTS FALLING DUE AFTER MORE THAN ONE YEAR	*1984 £millions*	*1983 £millions*
Debenture loans (secured)	*40.43*	*43.24*
Bank loans (secured)	*13.60*	*12.40*
Other creditors including taxation and social security:		
Lease obligations (secured)	*1.40*	*1.75*
Other loans	*3.52*	*3.04*
Corporation tax due 30 September 1986	*3.50*	*1.87*
	8.42	*6.66*
	62.45	*62.30*
Repayable wholly after five years		
Bank loans	*8.00*	*8.00*
Repayable by instalments, some of which fall due after five years:		
Debenture loans, instalments due		
between one and two years	*2.81*	*2.81*
between two and five years	*17.43*	*17.43*
after more than five years	*20.19*	*23.00*
Total amount	*40.43*	*43.24*
Bank loans, instalments due		
between one and two years	*.80*	*.80*
between two and five years	*2.40*	*2.40*
after more than five years	*.40*	*1.20*
Total amount	*3.60*	*4.40*
Loans wholly repayable within five years:		
Bank loans repayable between one and two years	*2.00*	*–*
Other loans repayable		
between one and two years	*.92*	*1.25*
between two and five years	*2.60*	*1.79*
Total amount	*3.52*	*3.04*

	1984 £millions	1983 £millions
Lease obligations		
Total amount payable under finance leases	*1.82*	*2.36*
Less future finance charges	*.42*	*.61*
	1.40	*1.75*
Amounts payable		
between one and two years	*.37*	*.55*
between two and five years	*1.03*	*1.20*
Details of loans not wholly repayable within five years		
4 1/2% debenture stock 1975/94 repayable by annual instalments of £1,450,000	*15.95*	*17.40*
5 1/2% debenture stock 1980/98 repayable by annual instalments of £1,360,000	*24.48*	*25.84*
Bank loan repayable 1990, interest at 1 1/2% above the bank's base lending rate	*8.00*	*8.00*
Bank loan repayable by half yearly instalments of £400,000 with interest at 1% above the bank's base lending rate	*3.60*	*4.40*

The debenture stocks are secured by a floating charge on all the assets of the group. Bank loans are secured by first mortgages on the group's freehold and leasehold properties in Crewe and by guarantees given by all companies in the group. Lease obligations are secured by retention of title to the relevant plant and machinery.

8.012 CLASSIFICATION OF LOANS

For the purpose of complying with the statutory disclosure requirements, loans are to be regarded as due for repayment on the earliest date on which the lender could require repayment if he exercised all options and rights available to him. [Sch 4: 85]

This point is particularly significant in relation to the following matters:

(i) *Bank loans*

It is not uncommon to find that, although arrangements are made for a bank loan to be repaid by a regular schedule of periodic repayments over a period of years, the agreement gives the bank the right to demand repayment at any time.

(ii) *Balances with group companies*

Frequently large balances are built up between one group company and another with no foreseeable likelihood of them being repaid; but unless there is a formal agreement between the two companies which restricts the creditor company's right to demand repayment the amount must be shown as due within one year in the balance sheet of the debtor company.

(iii) *Default*

Where a company has defaulted on the terms of a loan, the creditor is normally entitled to demand immediate repayment, and in these circumstances the whole of the outstanding loan must be classified as falling due within one year. It is thought that this is not necessary if before the directors approve the financial statements, the default has been cured and the creditor's rights arising from the default either have been waived or have lapsed.

8.013 DEBENTURES

A debenture is defined as including debenture stock, bonds and any other securities of a company, whether constituting a charge on the assets of the company or not. [s 744]

Where the company has the power to re-issue any redeemed debentures, the particulars must be disclosed in the notes to the accounts. [Sch 4: 41(2)]

Sch 4: 41(1) requires disclosure of the following particulars of debentures issued during the financial year in the notes to the accounts:

(i) the reason for making the issue;

(ii) the classes of debentures issued; and

(iii) the amount issued and the consideration received.

The amount of any convertible loans (which will almost invariably fall within the definition of debentures) must be shown separately. [Note 7 of balance sheet formats]

In addition the following details of the conversion rights must be stated [Sch 4: 40]:

(i) the number, description and amount of the shares in relation to which the right is exercisable;

(ii) the period during which the conversion rights may be exercised; and

(iii) the price to be paid for the shares allotted.

EXAMPLE

The convertible unsecured loan stock may be converted into fully paid ordinary shares of £1 each in any year up to 1988 at the rate of one ordinary share for every £2.50 of convertible stock. Full conversion of the outstanding rights will result in the issue of 5,250,000 ordinary shares.

8.014 OTHER ASPECTS OF LOAN AGREEMENTS

(a) Restrictive clauses

Although it is not customary for loans negotiated with U.K. financial institutions to include clauses which restrict the activities of the company, foreign loans sometimes contain such restrictions. In such cases, the notes to the accounts should disclose the significant restrictions, such as those which limit the payment of dividends or establish minimum working capital.

(b) Refinancing of long-term loans

Where a long-term loan is within twelve months of its maturity date, it must, according to the rules of Sch 4 be included as a creditor falling due within one year. Normally the company will make arrangements to re-finance this loan on a medium or long-term basis, or by the issue of equity. Since the reality of the position is that this finance has been provided on a long term basis throughout, this seems to be one of the rare situations where in the special circumstances of the company it is necessary to depart from the rules of Sch 4 in order to show a true and fair view.

Provided that by the date of approval of the financial statements the company has made binding arrangements to obtain a further long term loan or issue shares to re-finance this borrowing, it is suggested that it should preferably be included in creditors falling due after more than one year. If this approach is adopted, it is necessary to disclose in the notes particulars of the departure, the reasons for it and its effect.

It is thought that the circumstances where this approach is justified are restricted to those where a pre-existing long-term liability would otherwise be re-classified as current. It would not be justified where a company's bank borrowings and other current liabilities had built up to the point at which it is necessary to arrange longer term funding. In such a situation the borrowings should continue to be shown as current liabilities in the balance sheet. If funding arrangements have been made between the date of the balance sheet and the date of approval of the financial statements, this fact can be disclosed by a note.

(c) Amortisation of discount

As an issue of debentures at a discount will be made at a lower interest rate than would apply if the equivalent debentures were issued at par, the discount is in effect an additional cost of borrowing. The most appropriate accounting treatment is to amortise the discount by annual charges to profit and loss account over the period of the loan. It is normally acceptable to amortise the discount by equal annual charges over the period of the loan, but if the loan is repayable by instalments and the amounts involved are material it is preferable to compute the annual charge by an actuarial method so that the charge bears a constant relationship to the amount of the loan outstanding in each year. As indicated in Section 7.027(b) the unamortised amount will normally be included under 'Prepayments and accrued income' but must be separately disclosed.

Although annual amortisation of a discount is the most appropriate treatment in principle, the general practice is to write off any discount immediately either direct to share premium account, as permitted by s 130, or to profit and loss account.

In general any discount that has been allowed on the issue of debentures by companies has been small, but there is a growing practice of issuing 'zero coupon' or 'deep discount' debentures, i.e. debentures which carry a nil or very small rate of interest during their lives but where the lender's reward consists largely of a repayment at the end of the period very much higher than the amount advanced. In effect the company meets all or most of the cost of its borrowing when repayment is due. In these circumstances it seems that the immediate write off of the discount would result in the financial statements not showing a true and fair view, and that the annual amortisation approach must be adopted. Otherwise the cost of borrowing will not be reflected in the profit and loss accounts of the periods which benefit from the use of the borrowed funds.

8.015 BANK LOANS AND OVERDRAFTS

As noted above in Section 8.012 above, many bank loans give the bank an unconditional right to demand payment, in which case they must be classified as creditors falling due within one year.

If bank accounts with both debit and credit balances are maintained at the same bank and there is a right of set off, the net amount should be shown under current assets or liabilities as appropriate. Where the right of set off does not exist, the assets and liabilities should both be shown at their full amount in the balance sheet, regardless of whether the balances are with the same bank or different banks.

8.016 PAYMENTS RECEIVED ON ACCOUNT

Payments received on account of orders (e.g. progress payments on contracts) are usually first set off against any stocks relating to the same contracts. Any balance remaining should be shown under this heading. [Note 8 of balance sheet formats]

8.017 TRADE CREDITORS

Although bills of exchange payable and accruals are separate sub-headings their amounts are often insufficiently material to justify separate disclosure. When this arises, they are usually included with trade creditors. Debit balances on suppliers' accounts, if the aggregate amount is significant, should be included in debtors.

(a) Reservation of title clauses

Following the judgment in the 'Romalpa' case in 1976, suppliers of goods have increasingly sought to protect their position on the insolvency of a customer by inserting 'reservation of title' clauses into their terms of trade. These clauses take various forms but all have the objective of establishing that the goods remain the property of the seller until they are paid for. A number of cases have arisen subsequent to the Romalpa judgment, indicating that the legal effect of such clauses is not always clear. In any case they have no practical effect except in the event of the insolvency of the debtor.

Accordingly, goods purchased subject to a reservation of title clause, should be accounted for in precisely the same way as goods purchased without such a clause, i.e. the goods should be recorded as being the property of the company and the amount payable recorded as a trade creditor.

While the above treatment was recommended in a guidance statement issued by the accountancy bodies in 1976, the same statement also recommended:

(i) that where accounts are materially affected by adopting this accounting treatment, it should be disclosed, and

(ii) that the fact that liability to suppliers may be secured in this way should also be disclosed.

In spite of the use of these clauses being now widespread, disclosures of the type suggested in the guidance statement are almost never seen in published accounts. This is not surprising since the suggested disclosures are usually unnecessary and frequently impracticable. Financial statements prepared on a going concern basis are not required to disclose matters which are only relevant in the event of insolvency. It is common in routine commercial dealings for the precise contractual terms between the parties to be uncertain, since they only become significant in the event of a dispute or other difficulty; most managements of commercial entities neither know nor care whether the goods which they purchase are subject to valid reservation of title.

It is understood that the accountancy bodies are re-considering their guidance on this subject. In the meantime it is suggested that no reference to the existence of reservation of title clauses need be included in financial statements except in the rare circumstances where the directors are prepared to acknowledge that valid reservation of title arrangements exist with one or more major creditors and the continuation of the enterprise as a going concern is in doubt.

8.018 BILLS OF EXCHANGE

Bills of exchange are negotiable instruments usually entered into to obtain longer than normal credit terms, or to facilitate transactions with overseas suppliers. Such bills, if material, must be distinguished separately from other trade creditors in the balance sheet or in the notes.

8.019 AMOUNTS OWED TO GROUP COMPANIES

The aggregate amount owed to group companies must be subdivided in the balance sheet or in a note between amounts owed to (i) subsidiary companies and (ii) the holding company and fellow subsidiaries. [Sch 4: 59]

As indicated in Section 8.012 above, all amounts owed to group companies must be treated as due within one year unless there is a formal agreement which restricts the creditor company's right to demand repayment.

8.020 OTHER CREDITORS INCLUDING TAXATION AND SOCIAL SECURITY

'Other creditors including taxation and social security' is a 'catch-all' heading for all liabilities which do not come under any other sub-heading.

The amount included in respect of taxation and social security must be disclosed separately from the amount for other creditors. [Note 9 of balance sheet formats] This requirement is usually met by disclosing in the notes to the accounts one figure representing the total amount due to central governments by the company: thus it would include corporation tax, income tax, ACT, VAT, PAYE, and NI contributions and any similar liabilities to foreign governments. It is not necessary to subdivide these items in any way.

Loans, other than debenture loans and bank loans which must be included under separate sub-headings, may be included in other creditors. Details of loans from directors should be separately disclosed (see page 155).

8.021 ACCRUALS AND DEFERRED INCOME

Accruals and deferred income may be shown either under creditors or as a separate heading. Where the total of these items is not material, they may be included in another category of creditors, such as 'Trade creditors' or 'Other creditors including taxation and social security'.

(a) Accruals

An accrual, as distinguished from a liability shown under trade creditors, is an estimate of an actual liability which at the time the accounts are prepared is not supported by an invoice or other request for payment. Examples of accruals which might be included under this heading are: unpaid salaries, pension costs, vacation pay, rents and royalties, interest. Accruals relating to taxation liabilities should be included under the heading 'Other creditors including taxation and social security'.

(b) Deferred income

Income, such as rents and interest, may be received in advance of the period to which it relates. The portion of such income relating to periods after the balance sheet date should be deferred and included under this heading.

8.022 DIVIDENDS

The aggregate amount of dividends which are recommended to be distributed must be stated. [Sch 4: 51(3)] A proposed dividend is not strictly a liability in law until it has been declared and therefore it is not appropriate to include it under any of the items listed in the balance sheet formats. Instead it should be shown as an additional item under the heading 'Creditors: amounts falling due within one year' as permitted by Sch 4: 3(2). Dividends declared but unpaid at the balance sheet date should, however, be included under the item 'Other creditors including taxation and social security'.

8.030 PROVISIONS FOR LIABILITIES AND CHARGES

8.031 DISCLOSURE REQUIREMENTS

(a) Statutory headings

'Provisions for liabilities and charges' is a main heading which must appear on the face of the balance sheet. The following sub-headings are required but may be shown either on the face of the balance sheet or in a note to the accounts:

Pensions and similar obligations

Taxation, including deferred taxation

Other provisions

(b) Movements

Where a transfer has been made to any provision for liabilities and charges, or from such a provision for a purpose otherwise than that for which the provision was established, the following information is required by Sch 4: 46 to be given by way of note:

(i) opening and closing balances,

(ii) amounts transferred to or from the provisions during the year, and

(iii) the source and application, as appropriate, of the amounts so transferred.

Comparative amounts for the preceding year do not have to be shown.

(c) Provision for taxation

Sch 4: 47 requires disclosure in the the notes of the amount of any provision for taxation other than deferred taxation.

Taxation is dealt with in Chapter 14.

(d) Provision for pensions

Particulars of any pension commitments included under provisions, together with separate particulars of any such commitments relating to pensions payable to past directors of the company, must be given. [Sch 4: 50(4)] This matter is further discussed in Section 11.062.

(e) Particulars of 'Other provisions'

Particulars of any material provision included in 'Other provisions' are to be stated. [Sch 4: 46(3)]

8.032 DEFINITION OF PROVISIONS

Provision for liabilities and charges is defined by Sch 4: 88 as 'any amount retained as reasonably necessary for the purpose of providing for any liability or loss which is either likely to be incurred, or certain to be incurred but uncertain as to amount or as to the date on which it will arise'.

It is sometimes difficult to determine whether any particular item should be included under creditors or under provisions. It is suggested that if a liability is 'certain to be incurred', this normally implies that it has been incurred already and even if the amount is uncertain it should be included in creditors at the best estimate possible, probably under accruals. It is particularly important that an item which is payable within twelve months should not be treated as a provision on the grounds that the amount is uncertain; this would probably be misleading and if Format 1 was being used would result in net current assets being overstated.

8.033 LOSSES ON PURCHASE COMMITMENTS

Where a company has unfilled purchase commitments which are non-cancellable and not protected by hedging contracts, provision for losses in respect of such contracts should be made in the accounts. Losses, as measured by the excess of the contract price over replacement cost, should not be recognised where it can be demonstrated that future sales of the finished product containing the committed purchase will realise a profit.

9 BALANCE SHEET: SHARE CAPITAL AND RESERVES

9.010 CALLED UP SHARE CAPITAL

The amount of 'Called up share capital' must be shown on the face of the balance sheet under the heading 'Capital and reserves'.

9.011 DISCLOSURE REQUIREMENTS

The following must be stated in the notes to the accounts:

(i) The amount of the authorised share capital. [Sch 4: 38]

(ii) The amount of the allotted share capital and the amount of called up share capital which has been paid must be shown separately. [note 12 of balance sheet formats] Since partly paid shares are rare in the U.K., this provision has little significance and the requirement can normally be met by using the words 'allotted and fully paid' after the heading.

(iii) Where more than one class of shares has been allotted, the number and aggregate nominal value of shares of each class. [Sch 4: 38]

(iv) If the allotted capital includes redeemable shares:

- (a) the earliest and latest dates on which the company has power to redeem these shares;
- (b) whether those shares must be redeemed in any event or may be redeemed at the option of the company or of the shareholder; and
- (c) whether any (and if so, what) premium is payable on redemption. [Sch 4: 38]

(v) If any shares have been allotted during the year:

- (a) reasons for the allotment;
- (b) the classes of shares allotted; and
- (c) regarding each class of shares, the number allotted, their aggregate nominal value, and the consideration received. [Sch 4: 39]

(vi) If there are any options to subscribe for shares or any other rights to require the allotment of shares to any person (including conversion rights of other securities):

- (a) the number, description and amount of shares in relation to which the right is exercisable;
- (b) the period during which the right is exercisable; and
- (c) the price to be paid for the shares. [Sch 4: 40]

(vii) If fixed cumulative dividends are in arrears, the amount and period of arrears for each class of shares. [Sch 4: 49]

(viii) The number, description and amount of shares in and debentures of the company held by its subsidiaries or their nominees. [Sch 4: 60]

9.012 DIRECTORS' INTERESTS IN SHARES AND DEBENTURES

The particulars of directors' interests in shares and debentures may be given by way of note to the accounts instead of in the directors' report. [Sch 7: 2(3)] These particulars are discussed in Section 4.052.

9.020 RESERVES

Reserves represent the excess of assets over liabilities of a company after deducting its called up share capital. The following reserves must be shown on the face of the balance sheet:

Share premium account
Revaluation reserve (but a title other than this may be used)
Other reserves
Profit and loss account

The main heading 'Other reserves' has the following sub-headings which must be shown either on the face of the balance sheet or in a note to the accounts:

Capital redemption reserve
Reserve for own shares
Reserves provided for by the articles of association
Other reserves

9.021 DISCLOSURE REQUIREMENTS

Where any amount is transferred to or from any reserves, the following must be shown in respect of each reserve affected [Sch 4: 46]:

(i) opening and closing balances;

(ii) amounts transferred to or from reserve during the year; and

(iii) the source and application, respectively, of the amounts so transferred.

Comparative amounts for the preceding year do not have to be shown.

Because the information concerning movements on reserves is often significant to an understanding of an enterprise's results and state of affairs, it is recommended that it is given in a separate statement of movements on reserves which appear in a prominent position in the financial statements. In simple cases the statement might appear on the face of the profit and loss account itself; in group accounts where the reserve structure is complex, it may be preferable for it to appear on a separate page immediately following the profit and loss account. The inclusion of the information as one of the notes supporting the balance sheet is permissible but is not recommended. ED 36 proposes a requirement that the profit and loss account must indicate where the information is to be found if it does not immediately follow the profit and loss account. An example of an appropriate presentation in the financial statements of a group is shown in the model financial statements of Tramp Holdings p.l.c. in Chapter 3.

9.022 ITEMS CHARGED OR CREDITED DIRECT TO RESERVES

As indicated in Section 5.221 items should only be charged or credited to reserves without being included in the profit and loss account in exceptional circumstances. The following circumstances have been identified as justifying this treatment:

(i) items charged direct against share premium account, as permitted by law (Section 9.024);

(ii) valuation adjustments dealt with through the revaluation reserve (Section 9.025);

(iii) foreign currency translation differences where the financial statements of foreign enterprises are translated by the net investment method (Section 13.031);

(iv) the immediate elimination of purchased goodwill (Section 6.024(b));

(v) prior year adjustments arising from changes in accounting policy or correction of fundamental errors (Section 5.200);

(vi) investment gains and losses, realised and unrealised, of investment trust companies.

9.023 DISTRIBUTABLE RESERVES

SSAP 14 requires in relation to group accounts that if there are significant restrictions on the ability of the holding company to distribute the retained profits of the group (other than those shown as non-distributable) because of statutory, contractual or exchange control restrictions, the extent of the restrictions should be indicated. Clearly similar information should also be given if the retained profits of a single company are subject to such restrictions. This matter is discussed in detail in Section 12.075.

The Act imposes restrictions on the amounts which may legally be distributed by a company by way of dividend or otherwise; these restrictions are described in Section 18.040. There is no requirement to disclose the actual amount of a company's reserves which are legally available for distribution, and it is normally impracticable to do so in the case of a group. Except in the rare case where it is necessary to do so because the effect of the legal requirements is to impose severe restrictions on the company's ability to distribute its retained profits, the amount of reserves legally available for distribution should not be disclosed.

9.024 SHARE PREMIUM ACCOUNT

Where a company issues shares (whether for cash or otherwise) for a consideration in excess of their par value, the excess is to be placed in a share premium account. [s 130(1)]

Exceptions to this rule are discussed in Section 12.100 on merger accounting.

The share premium account can be used for the following purposes laid down in s 130(2):

(i) to issue fully paid bonus shares (scrip issue);

(ii) to write off the preliminary expenses of the company;

(iii) to write off the expenses, commission, or discount, on any issue of shares or debentures of the company;

(iv) to provide for any premium payable on the redemption of debentures of the company.

The share premium account may be used in the special circumstances described on page 247 to write off the excess of the 'permissible capital payment' over the nominal value of shares redeemed or purchased by a private limited company. [s 171(5)]

Where a company redeems or purchases its own shares which were issued at a premium, any premium payable on redemption or purchase may be paid out of the proceeds of a fresh issue of shares made for the purpose up to an amount equal to the lesser of the premium received by the company on the issue of the shares being redeemed or purchased and the current amount of the company's share premium account. [ss 160(2), 162] The practical effect of these sections is to permit the reduction of the share premium account under these circumstances.

9.025 REVALUATION RESERVE

This is the only balance sheet heading with a Roman numeral designation in the Sch 4 formats which may be given another name.

Sch 4: 34 requires the amount of the profit or loss arising from the valuation of any asset by any of the alternative methods prescribed by Sch 4 to be credited or debited to the revaluation reserve. This paragraph further provides that the directors shall reduce the revaluation reserve by any amounts that in their opinion are no longer necessary for the purposes of the accounting policies adopted, but an amount may only be transferred from this account to the profit and loss account if either (i) it represents a realised profit or (ii) it is in respect of an amount previously charged to the profit and loss account.

An exception is made in the case of an investment company; any profit or loss arising from a revaluation of an investment company need not be transferred to revaluation reserve. [Sch 4: 71(1)]

The appropriate treatment of the various items which may be dealt with in the revaluation reserve is discussed below.

(a) Surplus on revaluation

Any surplus arising from the use of the alternative methods of valuation must be credited to a separate revaluation reserve. [Sch 4: 34(1)] The surplus represents the excess of the revalued amount over the historical cost (or the previously revalued amount) less depreciation up to the latest valuation date. Where, for example, a fixed asset costing £100,000 and having accumulated depreciation based on cost of £20,000 is revalued at £110,000, the surplus of £30,000 (£110,000 – (£100,000 – £20,000)) is to be credited to the revaluation reserve.

The foregoing interpretation of the statutory requirements has not been accepted by all authorities, and it has been suggested that it is permissible to regard as a realised profit that proportion of the revaluation surplus which represents depreciation previously charged in the profit and loss account. Thus in the above example the transfer to revaluation reserve would be £10,000 only while the depreciation of £20,000 would be credited to profit and loss account. However ED 37 proposes that a revision of SSAP 12 should make clear that this approach should not be followed and that the difference between the net book amount and the revalued amount should be transferred to a revaluation reserve. The one exception to this is that if a provision for a diminution in value has been made (in addition to normal depreciation) and this provision has been shown by the revaluation to have been unnecessary, it should be credited to profit and loss account.

(b) Deficit on revaluation

Where an asset is revalued and the revalued amount is less than the corresponding book amount, then in order to account correctly for the difference between the two (the revaluation deficit) it is necessary to determine the amount at which the asset would have been included in the accounts under the historical cost accounting rules.

The first step is to establish the net book amount on the historical cost basis. If this amount is less than the revalued amount, then the whole of the revaluation deficit represents the reduction in a previous revaluation surplus and should be debited to the revaluation reserve. If the revalued amount is less than the historical cost net book amount, then it is necessary to consider whether in the light of the valuation any further provision is necessary for diminution in value. Any provision for diminution in value which is necessary under the historical cost accounting rules should be charged in the profit and loss account.

In the case of tangible and intangible fixed assets provision should only be made under the historical cost accounting rules for a diminution in value which is expected to be permanent; a valuation made at a particular time does not necessarily give rise to the expectation of a permanent fall in value. Provision for a fall in value of a fixed asset investment may be made under the historical cost accounting rules even if it is not expected to be permanent. It is suggested therefore that, if an investment is revalued at market value and the market value is below cost, then the difference between cost and market value should be charged in the profit and loss account as an amount written off investments (see Section 5.110). However if the reduction in market value below cost is not expected to be permanent, this treatment is optional. If an investment is revalued on some other basis which appears to the directors to be appropriate, it is unlikely that the resulting valuation will represent the value of the investment under the historical cost accounting rules, and accordingly no charge to profit and loss account will be appropriate.

Once the appropriate net book amount under the historical cost accounting rules has been established, any difference between that amount and the revalued amount should be transferred to the revaluation reserve. To the extent that the revalued amount is below the adjusted historical cost amount, the balance on the revaluation reserve in respect of that particular asset will be a debit.

The approach described above is different from that proposed in ED 36 which is that deficits on the revaluation of fixed assets should be debited to the profit and loss account for the year to the extent that they exceed any surplus held in reserves and identified as relating to previous revaluations of the same assets. This requirement seems to be contrary to the intentions of the Act which distinguishes between permanent diminution in value, which must be recognised in the profit and loss account, and value adjustments made under the alternative accounting rules, which should be dealt with through the revaluation reserve. Until this part of ED 36 is included in a current SSAP, it is suggested that the treatment described in this section should be followed.

In practice it is very unlikely that a revaluation would establish a reduction in value below the historical cost amount of a depreciable asset and there would be good reason for not regarding that diminution in value as permanent. The point is more significant in relation to assets with a ready market and a fluctuating market value which are held for investment rather than for use in a manufacturing or trading activity.

(c) Adjustment of depreciation

As indicated in Section 5.153 the depreciation to be charged in the profit and loss account in respect of an asset which has been revalued should be based on the revalued amount. However to the extent that depreciation on the revalued amount exceeds the corresponding depreciation based on historical cost, the excess represents a realised profit. [s 275(2)] Therefore an amount equal to the excess of the depreciation charged over the depreciation based on historical cost should be transferred annually from revaluation reserve to profit and loss account. This is best done as a movement in reserves as illustrated in the model financial statements of Tramp Holdings p.l.c. on page 25.

In the rare circumstance where a depreciable asset is revalued at an amount below its carrying amount under the historical cost accounting rules, the charge for depreciation based on the revalued amount would be insufficient to amortise the balance of the historical cost over its remaining useful life. In these circumstances a transfer should be made from profit and loss account to revaluation reserve of an amount equal to the difference between the depreciation charged and the depreciation based on historical cost.

(d) Sale of revalued assets

When a fixed asset which has been revalued is to be sold, its net book value must be adjusted to the net book value on the historical cost basis (i.e. to the depreciated cost which would have been shown if no revaluation had taken place) by a transfer from revaluation reserve. Provided that amounts in respect of excess depreciation have been transferred annually to profit and loss account as indicated in (c) above, the amount required to reduce the asset from its net revalued amount to its net historical cost amount will be equal to the balance included in the revaluation reserve in respect of that asset. If this is not the case (e.g. because the transfers in respect of annual depreciation have not been made) any further balance in the revaluation reserve in respect of that asset should be transferred to profit and loss account as a movement in reserves.

The gain or loss on realisation is the difference between the amount realised and the depreciated original cost of the asset and this should be included as part of the profit or loss for the year as indicated in Section 5.250.

If any provision has been made for deferred tax out of revaluation reserve in respect of the asset being sold, this provision should be reversed on sale (i.e. deferred tax should be debited and revaluation reserve credited with the amount involved). Deferred tax is discussed in Section 14.080.

EXAMPLE

A fixed asset is revalued at £10,000 on 31 December 1981 at which time its depreciated book amount is £6,000. At the date of revaluation it is estimated to have a further useful life of ten years and no residual value. In January 1985 the asset is sold for £6,500.

At 31 December 1981 the valuation surplus transferred to revaluation reserve is	*£* *4,000*
This is reduced by annual transfers to profit and loss account of £400, which in three years amount to	*1,200*
The revaluation reserve in respect of the asset at 31 December 1984 is	*2,800*
The book amount of the asset at 31 December 1984 is [£10,000 – (3 x £1,000)]	*7,000*
which is reduced by the transfer from revaluation reserve of	*2,800*
to its depreciated original cost of	*4,200*
[the depreciated original cost is the amount at 31 December 1981 £6,000 less three years' depreciation at £600]	
The asset was sold for	*6,500*
The gain on realisation credited to profit and loss account for the year is	*2,300*

It should be noted that if the gain or loss had been measured by reference to the revalued amount, the result would have been a loss of £500.

As indicated in Section 6.033(e) it sometimes happens that a fixed asset has to be reclassified as current because it is no longer intended for use on a continuing basis; in these circumstances its book amount must be adjusted by a transfer from revaluation reserve as if the asset were being sold at that date. This assures consistency in the measurement of profit or loss on the sale of assets and compliance with the requirement that current assets must not be valued above cost.

(e) Investment properties

SSAP 19 requires that investment properties should be included in balance sheets at their open market value (see Section 6.033(c)) and that changes in value should be dealt with in an 'investment revaluation reserve'. This heading should appear in the balance sheet if the only revalued assets are investment properties. However, if other assets have also been revalued in the financial statements so that the amount in the revaluation reserve does not relate solely to investment properties then it is preferable to show the revaluation reserve as one amount in the balance sheet and the sub-division between the investment revaluation reserve and the rest in a note to the accounts.

SSAP 19 also requires that all changes in value should be dealt with in the investment revaluation reserve unless the total of that reserve is insufficient to cover a deficit, in which case the balance of the deficit should be charged to profit and loss account. This treatment is clearly inconsistent with the approach proposed in ED 36 which is referred to above. At first sight it also appears to be contrary to the Act which requires that provision for permanent diminution in value are made in the profit and loss account and that the amount of each individual asset must be determined separately. However it is thought that, in general, compliance with this aspect of SSAP 19 does not involve a departure from the legal requirements since it is only permanent diminution in value that must be recognised in the profit and loss account and, as indicated above, a revaluation made at a particular time does not necessarily give rise to the expectation of a permanent fall in value. Given that investment properties are generally held at least as much for capital appreciation as for rental income, it is unlikely that an investment property would continue to be held if it was no longer expected to increase in value. Falls in value of investment properties can usually reasonably be regarded as temporary in nature due to fluctuations in the property market generally or in relation to the particular location and nature of the property concerned. In the rare circumstance where an investment property has fallen in value below cost and the reduction in value is expected to be permanent, there appears to be a direct conflict between the Act, which requires the diminution in value to be charged to the profit and loss account, and SSAP 19, which requires it to be charged to investment revaluation reserve. If this situation arises it is suggested that the treatment required by the Act should be followed since it is hard to argue that the departure required by SSAP 19 is necessary to a true and fair view.

SSAP 19 is silent as to how gains and losses arising from the realisation of investment properties should be accounted for. It is suggested therefore that the approach described in (d) above should be followed.

(f) Taxation

The treatment for taxation purposes of amounts credited or debited to the revaluation reserve must be disclosed in a note to the accounts. [Sch 4: 34(4)] The appropriate treatment is discussed in Section 14.087.

(g) Application of revaluation reserve

Since the balance on the revaluation reserve represents unrealised surpluses, it follows that it is not a distributable balance and its application is restricted. It is suggested that the only way in which the revaluation reserve should be applied, other than as indicated above, is in paying up new shares to be issued to the members as fully paid bonus shares. The view has been expressed that the elimination of goodwill against this reserve is also permitted. The fourth directive makes clear that the revaluation reserve may be reduced only by capitalization or in accordance with rules laid down by the Member States. The Act provides that the reserve is to be reduced to the extent that it is 'no longer necessary for the purpose of the accounting policies adopted by the company' [Sch 4: 34(3)] Although the point is not totally clear in the legislation, in view of the terms of the directive, the intention must have been that this is the only circumstance under which reduction in the revaluation reserve is permitted. If this view is correct, then the elimination of goodwill against the revaluation reserve seems contrary to law.

It is possible if the practices outlined above are followed for the revaluation reserve to become a debit balance, particularly if it has been used in whole or in part for the purpose of a scrip issue. There appears to be nothing to prohibit such a debit balance from appearing in the balance sheet. However a better presentation is not to have a heading for revaluation reserve in the balance sheet at all, but to set the revaluation debit against the balance on profit and loss account or another distributable reserve.

9.026 CAPITAL REDEMPTION RESERVE

The capital redemption reserve is a sub-heading under 'Other reserves' in the balance sheet formats and may be shown either on the face of the balance sheet or in the notes.

The provisions of s 170 require the amount by which the issued share capital of the company is diminished through the purchase or redemption of its own shares, otherwise than out of capital or out of the proceeds of a new issue made for that purpose, to be credited to the capital redemption reserve.

The Act does not allow this reserve to be used for any purpose other than to pay up fully paid bonus shares. [s 170(4)]

9.027 RESERVE FOR OWN SHARES

While it is expected that this heading will be rarely used, it might be required in respect of amounts set aside from distributable profits for the purpose of the future redemption of redeemable shares. The creation of such a reserve may be required by the terms of allotment of the redeemable shares.

9.028 RESERVES PROVIDED FOR BY THE ARTICLES OF ASSOCIATION

This reserve should be confined to amounts required specifically by the company's articles of association to be set aside. These will include, for example, the profits on sale of investments which are required by the articles of many investment trusts to be transferred to a non-distributable 'capital' reserve.

9.029 OTHER RESERVES

In normal circumstances the only item which might appear in other reserves would be translation differences arising on the consolidation of foreign subsidiaries which are dealt with in Chapter 13. The practice of creating other reserves out of distributable profits serves little useful purpose.

10 STATEMENT OF SOURCE AND APPLICATION OF FUNDS

10.010 GENERAL REQUIREMENTS

There is no statutory requirement for companies to produce a statement of source and application of funds (the 'funds statement'). However, SSAP 10 requires such a statement to be included in financial statements which are intended to give a true and fair view of financial position and profit or loss (small businesses with turnover of less than £25,000 are exempt from this requirement). Where a company has subsidiaries, the statement should deal with the source and application of funds of the group but not of the holding company alone. Corresponding amounts for the preceding period should be given.

The objective of the funds statement is to show the manner in which the operations of a company have been financed and in which its financial resources have been used.

SSAP 10 sets out certain sources and applications of funds which must be shown, if material, but does not prescribe any particular format for the statement or the terminology to be used. Considerable variations in the funds statement have therefore evolved in practice. This chapter gives guidance as to best practice in those areas where alternative methods are available.

10.020 FORMAT

By far the most popular form of funds statement is that which explains changes in net liquid funds. An example of this layout is shown in the model financial statements on page 28. An alternative form of statement which balances to a figure of increase/decrease in working capital is illustrated in the appendix to SSAP 10.

The definition of net liquid funds in SSAP 10 embraces not only cash at bank and in hand but also cash equivalents (e.g. investments held as current assets) less bank overdrafts and other borrowings repayable within one year of the accounting date. The exact items included should be identified in the statement of source and application of funds but in practice other than cash, only short term funds are usually included (e.g. money at 7 day call) and only short term borrowings such as bank overdrafts are deducted.

10.030 CONTENT

SSAP 10 requires the funds statement to show the profit or loss for the period together with adjustments for items not involving the use of funds (e.g. depreciation, deferred taxation). In addition the following other sources and applications of funds should, where material, be shown:

(i) dividends paid;

(ii) acquisitions and disposals of fixed and other non-current assets;

(iii) funds raised by increasing, or expended in repaying or redeeming, medium or long-term loans or the issued capital of the company;

(iv) increase or decrease in working capital sub-divided into its components, and movements in net liquid funds.

It is not appropriate to show losses as negative sources of funds unless there is a net source of funds after adjusting for depreciation and other items in the profit and loss account which do not involve the movement of funds. If the balance remains negative after adjusting for items not involving the movement of funds, it should be shown as an application of funds, not as a 'negative source'.

In general there should be no 'netting' of important items. For example purchases and disposals of fixed assets should be shown as two separate amounts, i.e. cost of acquisitions and proceeds from disposals. However, small unimportant items can be combined.

10.040 RESTRICTIVE DEFINITION OF FUNDS

Some compilers of the funds statement have interpreted 'funds' to be working capital, cash or its equivalent and have therefore excluded certain financing and investing activities which do not directly affect working capital or cash. Examples of these would be the issue of shares to acquire fixed assets or the conversion of convertible loan stock into ordinary shares.

Such activities represent both a financing and an investing transaction and details should appear in the statement. For example in the fixed asset acquisition referred to above, the acquisition would be shown as a use of funds and the issue of shares as a source of funds.

However, items such as transfers to and from reserves, valuation surpluses and scrip issues, which do not affect the financial resources of the company should not be reflected in the funds statement.

10.050 TAXATION

SSAP 10 does not lay down precise rules on the subject of taxation. Many companies follow the treatment of taxation shown in the example in the appendix to the standard. This deals with taxation on a paid basis and no regard is given to deferred taxation or to unpaid taxes. Thus the movements in working capital exclude taxation liabilities and the source of funds starts with the figure of profit on ordinary activities before taxation. This method, which is recommended, is simple and avoids some of the anomalies which arise in respect of ACT payments and the movements of taxation liabilities between current and long-term.

An alternative method (which is the generally accepted method in the U.S.) follows the strict accruals concept which takes into account movements of all taxation balances. Under this method the statement should start with profit from ordinary activities after taxation to which should be added the deferred taxation element which does not require the use of funds. The increase or decrease in corporation tax liabilities will be shown as a source or application of funds.

10.060 EXTRAORDINARY ITEMS

Although extraordinary items are not specifically dealt with in SSAP 10, they should be separately disclosed in the funds statement if they involve the movement of funds. Taxation applicable to extraordinary items should be dealt with on a basis consistent with the treatment of tax on trading profits (see Section 10.050 above).

10.070 MINORITY INTERESTS

Although SSAP 10 makes no specific recommendations on the treatment of minority interests, the appendix to the standard gives an example which starts with profit before tax and extraordinary items, less minority interests and then adds back the minority interests retained as an item not involving the movement of funds.

An alternative presentation is to start with profit and extraordinary items before minority interests (before or after taxation, depending upon the approach adopted in the treatment of taxation) and to make no further adjustment for minority interests except to the extent that dividends were paid to minority shareholders.

10.080 ASSOCIATED COMPANIES

There are two methods of treating the results of associated companies in the funds statement. The method illustrated in the appendix to SSAP 10 includes as a source of funds only those earnings of the associated company which are received or receivable. This is achieved by showing as an adjustment not involving the movement of funds the undistributed portion of associated company results (i.e. share of associated company profits less dividends received and receivable). The supporters of this treatment consider that profits of associated companies are not a source of funds until dividends are received.

The second method includes the full share of earnings of the associated companies as part of the funds provided by operations and the unremitted part of those earnings as an application of funds. Supporters of this method hold the view that the investing company, by virtue of its influence is in a position to determine the timing of the conversion of earnings into cash and the unremitted earnings are regarded as a reinvestment in the associated company.

SSAP 10 makes no specific recommendation but the first method appears to conform more closely to reality.

10.090 ACQUISITION AND DISPOSAL OF SUBSIDIARIES

SSAP 10 suggests two ways of disclosing the purchase or sale of subsidiaries in the funds statement and examples of both presentations are given in the appendix to the SSAP. Under one method, the purchase or sale consideration is shown as a separate item and the movements in group assets and liabilities exclude the assets and liabilities of the subsidiary at the date of acquisition or disposal. Under the other method, each of the individual assets and liabilities acquired or disposed of is included in the movements of group assets and liabilities in the normal way. Regardless of which method is used, the explanatory note recommends that in all cases the effects of the acquisition, and an analysis of the purchase price between the amount paid in cash and the amount satisfied by the issue of shares should be disclosed by way of note.

Where shares are issued to purchase a subsidiary, the value of the shares issued should be shown as a source of funds.

Arguments can be advanced in favour of each of the alternative methods of presentation. However the second method has disadvantages if only a majority of the shares in the subsidiary are acquired, since in these circumstances it will be necessary to show the minority interest in the new subsidiary as a source of funds; many readers are likely to find such an item hard to understand. This method also gives rise to difficulties if a company which has previously been accounted for as an associated company becomes a subsidiary. In these circumstances the carrying value of the associated company investment in the group accounts has to be shown as a source of funds. Such an item is also hard to understand in circumstances where the investment has not been realised but has been increased. In both these situations the first method seems clearly preferable since only the cost of the additional investment is entered in the funds statement and the analysis of the acquisition is disclosed as a note. This may be an argument in favour of adopting the first method for all acquisitions in the interest of consistency.

10.100 FOREIGN EXCHANGE DIFFERENCES

SSAP 10 gives no guidance on the treatment of foreign exchange differences in the funds statement. The following matters should be considered when foreign exchange differences are significant.

When the accounts of overseas subsidiaries are translated using the net investment method described in SSAP 20 (see Section 13.031), all translation differences are reflected in reserves. Since translation does not involve any movement of funds, no adjustment is required in the funds statement. However in order to identify the increases and decreases in the assets and liabilities of overseas subsidiaries during the year it is necessary to eliminate the effect of translation differences. This may be done either (i) by measuring the changes in the assets and liabilities of the overseas subsidiaries in their local currency and translating these changes at the closing exchange rate, or (ii) by re-translating the assets and liabilities of the overseas subsidiaries at the beginning of the year at the rate ruling at the end of the year before measuring the changes that have taken place.

It is good practice to indicate that this has been done since otherwise readers may be puzzled by the fact that amounts shown as increases or decreases in various balances are not the same as the difference between the amounts disclosed in the group balance sheet and the corresponding amount for the previous year.

> ***EXAMPLE***
>
> *The above statement excludes the effect of adjustments arising on the translation of the financial statements of overseas subsidiaries at different rates of exchange. In consequence the amounts shown as increases and decreases in assets and liabilities are not equal to the differences between the corresponding opening and closing balance sheet amounts.*

A commonly adopted alternative practice which is acceptable and easier to apply, although less theoretically correct, is to measure the movement in assets and liabilities by reference to the sterling amounts appearing in the group balance sheet and to bring in an exchange rate adjustment either as a source or an application of funds, as appropriate. The amount of the exchange rate adjustment will normally be equal to the movement on reserves in respect of the translation of the net investment at the beginning of the year at the closing rate, less the proportion of that adjustment which affects fixed assets and is usually separately identified and excluded from the funds statement.

A practice which is sometimes seen is to include the exchange rate adjustment in arriving at the amount of 'funds generated from operations'. This is incorrect since no funds are generated as a result of this adjustment; unless the amount is immaterial it is preferable that it should be included either as a source or an application of funds, or as a separate item.

10.110 OVERSEAS EARNINGS NOT REMITTABLE

Where material overseas earnings are derived from countries which restrict remittances to the U.K., the net monetary funds so blocked should be excluded from the calculation of movements in working capital or net liquid funds. To the extent that such earnings are included in profits, they should be shown in the funds statement as an adjustment to the funds generated from operations. To the extent that blocked funds increase as a result of additional investment in such currencies, they should be shown as an application of funds.

11 OTHER DISCLOSURE REQUIREMENTS

11.010 ACCOUNTING POLICIES

The Act prescribes certain fundamental accounting principles to be followed in the preparation of a company's accounts and these are discussed in Section 2.030. Within the framework of these fundamental principles, there is room for some measure of choice in regard to the specific accounting policies to be applied, though this choice is significantly reduced both by the statutory valuation rules and by statements of standard accounting practice. The effect of these rules and statements is discussed under the appropriate headings throughout this manual.

Accounting policies are the specific accounting bases selected and consistently followed by a business enterprise (not necessarily a company) for the purpose of financial statements, in particular (i) for determining the accounting periods in which revenue and costs should be recognised in the profit and loss account and (ii) for determining the amounts at which material items should be stated in the balance sheet.

SSAP 2 states that the accounting policies followed for dealing with items which are judged material or critical in determining profit or loss for the year and in stating financial position should be disclosed. This requirement is similar to the legal requirement in Sch 4: 36 to disclose accounting policies adopted by the company.

It is recommended that the accounting policies used should be identified in the first note to the accounts. An alternative presentation which is often found is to have a separate statement of accounting policies, possibly inserted before the accounts. A further approach is to state the policies applicable to individual items in the notes on each item along with other required information. If the latter approach is adopted, it is advisable to explain this in the first note.

EXAMPLE

The accounting policies adopted are disclosed in the appropriate notes below.

It must be borne in mind that a policy which is not significant in one company (or industry) may be highly significant in another company (or industry). For example, the method of accounting for investments will normally not be significant in a manufacturing company but would be significant in an investment company.

In a large group or complicated situation, the explanations of accounting policies may have to be greatly enlarged. However, SSAP 2 specifies that the explanations should be clear, fair and as brief as possible. Policy notes should deal solely with policy matters; they should not deal with information concerning the make-up of amounts dealt with in the financial statements.

Examples of policies which could have a material effect on reported results and financial position include the treatment of the following:

- consolidation principles
- income recognition
- associated companies
- * translation of foreign currencies
- * depreciation and diminution in value of assets
- stock and work in progress
- long term contracts
- valuation of investments
- deferred taxation
- hire purchase or instalment transactions
- property development transactions
- leasing and rental transactions
- warranties for products or services
- pension costs
- government grants

* These are specifically required to be disclosed by Sch 4.

Reference should be made to the policy note in the model financial statements of Tramp Holdings p.l.c. for examples of wording.

11.011 ACCOUNTING CONVENTION

The particular accounting convention used in preparing the financial statements should be disclosed in the accounting policy note.

EXAMPLE

The financial statements have been prepared under the historical cost convention as modified by the revaluation of land and buildings.

Companies who value the majority of their assets by reference to a convention other than historical cost will not normally deem it appropriate to refer to the historical cost convention. Investment trust companies which carry their investments at market value and property investment companies which carry properties at valuations are two examples. In such cases, the accounting policy note should describe the valuation bases used.

11.012 DEPARTURE FROM REQUIREMENTS OF THE ACT IN ORDER TO SHOW A TRUE AND FAIR VIEW

As discussed in Section 2.020, in rare circumstances it may be necessary to depart from the requirements of the Act in order for the financial statements to show a true and fair view. If such a departure is necessary, the Act requires that the particulars of the departure, the reasons for it and its effect are given in a note to the accounts. [S 228(6)] In practice it is often not practicable to disclose the effect in monetary terms as in the following example.

EXAMPLE: Accounting policy – investment properties

Investment properties are revalued annually and the aggregate surplus or deficit is transferred to revaluation reserve. No depreciation is provided in respect of investment properties; this constitutes a departure from the statutory rules requiring fixed assets to be depreciated over their economic useful lives and is necessary to enable the financial statements to give a true and fair view. Depreciation is only one of many factors reflected in the annual valuation and the amount which might otherwise have been shown cannot be separately identified or quantified.

11.013 CHANGE IN ACCOUNTING POLICY

In the year in which an accounting policy has been changed, the accounting policy note should disclose the nature of the change from the policy previously adopted and that the preceding year's figures have been restated in accordance with the new policy. The Act requires that the particulars of any departure from the principle of consistency, the reasons for it and the effect shall be given in a note to the accounts. Furthermore, SSAP 6 requires the effect of the change to be disclosed where practicable by showing separately in the restatement of the previous year the amount involved. An example of disclosure is given in Section 5.200.

11.020 GOVERNMENT GRANTS

SSAP 4 requires that government grants relating to fixed assets should be credited to revenue over the expected useful life of the asset. Two alternative presentations are permitted:

(i) to reduce the cost of the asset by the amount of the grant; or

(ii) to treat the grant as a deferred credit, a portion of which is transferred to revenue annually, based on the expected useful life of the asset.

Although the second method is probably theoretically superior, the first is most used in practice.

The SSAP indicates that the amount of any deferred credit should, if material, be shown separately in the balance sheet. In most circumstances, however, it seems that the most appropriate treatment would be to include the credit in 'Accruals and deferred income' and disclose the amount separately in a note.

No other formal guidance on accounting for government grants is provided, but clearly the principle that should be followed is that the accounting for any grant must reflect its purpose and nature. In some circumstances it may also be necessary to consider special conditions attached to the grant. The following treatment is recommended:

(i) Grants specifically given to assist with revenue expenditure should be matched as far as possible with the expenditure to which they relate. Normally this will result in the grants being credited in arriving at the profit or loss on ordinary activities, but this may not always be the case, e.g. grants towards development expenditure which is properly carried forward (see Section 6.023) would be deducted from the amount carried forward. Interest relief grants should be credited in the periods in which the interest relieved is suffered; if this is not readily identifiable because the amount recoverable is unconnected with any interest charges that the company has suffered, then careful consideration should be given to whether in the light of all the circumstances, it should really be treated as a revenue grant at all.

(ii) As indicated above, grants relating to fixed assets should be credited to revenue over the expected useful life of the asset. Although it is not specified in SSAP 4 it is thought that this requirement should only be applied to tangible fixed assets and not to fixed asset investments, which do not have an expected life.

(iii) Grants which do not relate either to revenue expenditure or to tangible fixed assets should normally be credited to profit and loss account as extraordinary items. Examples of such grants are grants towards working capital, grants to assist in the acquisition of an investment (usually a controlling investment) in a company, grants which are unrelated to any specific expenditure such as those directly related to the number of new jobs created.

(iv) There is a growing practice of grants given to assist in a project being made on condition that the grant or a proportion of it is capitalised and applied in increasing the issued and fully paid up share capital of the recipient company. Any amounts restricted in this way should be taken direct to a non-distributable reserve to be used in the agreed manner.

(v) Many grants are given on condition that the grants are repayable in whole or in part on certain events occurring within a specified period. These conditions must be considered and evaluated in the same way as other contingencies (see Section 11.050). Normally the contingency is likely to be so remote as not to require disclosure, but if an event which is largely outside the control of the company would cause repayment, the contingency should be disclosed in a note to the accounts. However, if the contingency is the company's ceasing to trade within a specified period, this need not be referred to since it is not relevant to financial statements prepared on a going concern basis.

Apart from regional development grants which clearly relate to fixed assets, most grants seem to be given under the schemes for national or regional selective assistance. The legislation gives the granting authority very wide discretion as to the nature of assistance that can be given and it is not always easy to place such a grant in one of the above categories. Each case must be considered on its merits in the light of a careful reading of the agreement. The stated purpose of such grants is often to assist in a 'project' which is defined in general terms. Regard must be had to the manner in which sums payable are to be determined, the timing of the payment, and the nature of the information to be submitted with grant applications. Often it will be necessary to divide one grant over two or more of the categories discussed above.

With the exception of regional development grants, which are tax-free, most grants are taxable in the hands of the recipient and this fact is sometimes advanced as a reason for treating them as income as received. It is suggested that the taxable status of a grant should not affect its accounting treatment except that care must be taken to ensure that any tax liabilities are properly provided.

11.030 ULTIMATE HOLDING COMPANY

Where a company is a subsidiary of another company, the notes to the accounts must disclose the name of the company's ultimate holding company and, if known to the directors, the country in which it is incorporated. The Secretary of State may give an exemption from this requirement where the company carries on business outside the United Kingdom and disclosure would be harmful to the business of the group. [Sch 5: 20, 21]

11.040 PARTICIPATION OF HOLDING COMPANY IN VENDOR PLACING

If a listed company is a subsidiary of another company, The Stock Exchange requires disclosure of particulars of the participation by the parent company in any vendor consideration placing made during the year. This situation arises where the company acquires assets in exchange for the issue of its own shares to vendors who, under a prior arrangement, then place the shares with selected investors (one of which is the parent company) for cash.

11.050 CONTINGENCIES

Accounting for contingencies is dealt with by SSAP 18. This statement defines a contingency as a condition which exists at the balance sheet date, where the outcome will be confirmed only on the occurrence or nonoccurence of one or more uncertain future events. Examples would include: recourse on bills discounted, guarantees to third parties, law suits, possible calls on partly paid shares. Contingencies do not include uncertainties connected with accounting estimates (e.g. lives of fixed assets, outcome of long-term contracts).

11.051 ACCOUNTING TREATMENT

It is necessary to estimate the outcome and financial effect of all significant contingencies existing at the balance sheet date and these estimates should be based on the consideration of all information available up to the date on which the financial statements are approved by the board of directors. The estimate of the outcome involves assessing the likelihood of a loss or gain arising from the contingency. The assessment determines the appropriate accounting treatment.

(a) Contingent losses

(i) Where it is probable that a future event will confirm a material contingent loss, the loss should be accrued in the financial statements. The amount accrued may take account of the probable outcome of related counter-claims against third parties. This is in accordance with the statutory requirement that all liabilities and losses which are likely to arise in respect of periods prior to the balance sheet date must be taken into account. [Sch 4: 12(b)]

(ii) Where a material contingent loss has not been accrued, it must be disclosed in the notes to the accounts, unless it is excluded on the grounds of remoteness (see (iii) below).

(iii) A contingency which is remote need not be disclosed, but the definition of remote for this purpose in SSAP 18 should be noted - 'the possibility of the ultimate outcome having a material effect on the financial statements is so remote that disclosure would be misleading'.

(b) Contingent gains

There is no requirement in the Act to disclose contingent gains. SSAP 18 requires that material contingent gains should be disclosed in the notes to the accounts only if it is probable that the gain will be realised. A gain should only be accrued in the financial statements if its realisation is reasonably certain (so that it is not a contingency) and it may properly be regarded as having been realised at the balance sheet date.

No disclosure should be made of other contingent gains where realisation cannot be assessed as probable.

11.052 DISCLOSURE REQUIREMENTS

The information to be disclosed about contingent liabilities and other contingencies which may result in losses is as follows:

(i) the nature of the contingency;

(ii) the uncertainties which are expected to affect the ultimate outcome (this will include separate disclosure of any counter-claims or related claims against third parties);

(iii) a prudent estimate of the financial effect, or statement that it is not practicable to make an estimate. Sch 4: 50(2) requires disclosure of the estimated amount of the liability and apparently does not contemplate the possibility that it may not be practicable to make such an estimate;

(iv) particulars of any valuable security provided by the company in connection with any contingent liability. [Sch 4: 50(2)] There is a further requirement for particulars to be given of any charge on the assets of the company to secure the liabilities of any other person including, when practicable, the amount secured. [Sch 4: 50(1)] This further requirement seems to be superfluous since the existence of the charge seems to create a contingency requiring disclosure in any event.

Contingencies which arise from undertakings entered into on behalf of or for the benefit of other group companies (e.g. guarantees or bills discounted) must be disclosed separately, sub-divided between those benefiting (a) the holding company and fellow subsidiaries and (b) subsidiary companies.

The financial effect in (iii) above should be reduced by amounts accrued and amounts considered remote, and it is this net amount before taking account of taxation which should be disclosed. The tax implications should be explained if considered necessary for a proper understanding of the financial position.

The financial effect and other disclosures relating to contingencies which are common to a large number of similar transactions may be based on the group of transactions.

11.060 FINANCIAL COMMITMENTS

Particulars of the following financial commitments must be disclosed in the notes. [Sch 4: 50] Any such commitments undertaken on behalf of or for the benefit of (a) any holding company and fellow subsidiary and (b) subsidiary companies must be disclosed separately under each of the appropriate headings.

11.061 CAPITAL COMMITMENTS

The disclosure requirements of Sch 4: 50(3) are:

(i) the aggregate amount of capital expenditure contracted for at the balance sheet date, to the extent that this amount has not been provided in the accounts (some companies accrue their capital commitments but this is not best practice);

(ii) the aggregate amount of capital expenditure which, although not the subject of a firm contract, has been authorised by the directors.

An example of appropriate disclosure is given in the model financial statements of Tramp Holdings p.l.c. on page 41.

SSAP 21 requires disclosure of any commitment existing at the balance sheet date in respect of finance leases which have been entered into but whose inception occurs after the balance sheet date.

11.062 PENSION COMMITMENTS

Particulars of any pension commitments which:

(i) are provided in the balance sheet, and

(ii) for which no provision has been made,

should be disclosed. [Sch 4: 50(4)]

Separate particulars must be given where any of these commitments relate to past directors of the company.

It is not clear precisely what is intended by this requirement but it seems that it does not require disclosure of pensions payable from a pension scheme which is funded outside the company or of annual contributions to such a scheme. Clearly any commitments covered by such a scheme are not provided in the balance sheet, nor are they commitments for which no provision has been made.

It seems that the legal requirement is probably restricted to disclosing particulars of pensions presently being paid to former employees and directors where these pensions have not been funded externally.

Although probably not required on a strict interpretation of the law it is suggested that the following additional information should be given under this head:

(i) particulars of any undertakings to pay pensions on retirement to existing employees, where such pensions have not been funded externally or provided in the balance sheet; such undertakings are unlikely to be legally binding and in any case do not constitute commitments since they are presumably contingent on the employees affected surviving and remaining in the company's employment to pension age; however such undertakings may in practice constitute a significant obligation of the company of which users of the financial statements should be aware;

(ii) undertakings to make special payments over and above the normal annual contributions in respect of current service to an external pension fund either to make good a funding deficiency or to provide enhanced benefit. Such payments will affect the company's cash flow over the period, and if the amounts have not already been provided, will also affect its reported profits; if the amounts involved will give rise to significant fluctuations in pension costs, the information is clearly significant to users of the financial statements.

The whole subject of accounting for pension costs is currently under study by ASC, and it is likely that the requirements for disclosure in this area will increase significantly in the future.

11.063 OTHER FINANCIAL COMMITMENTS

Particulars of other financial commitments which have not been provided for in the financial statements and are relevant to assessing the company's state of affairs are also to be disclosed. [Sch 4: 50(5)] These might include:

(i) purchase commitments in excess of normal requirements (especially speculative positions) to the extent not covered by hedging agreements.

(ii) exposed foreign currency positions.

(iii) commitments to lend money or to guarantee future loans to third parties by companies which do not customarily provide financial services.

(iv) commitments as lessee under leasing agreements (See Section 15.036(c)).

11.070 POST BALANCE SHEET EVENTS

11.071 DEFINITION

The Act requires that all liabilities and losses relating to a period prior to the balance sheet date must be taken into account, including those which only become apparent between the balance sheet date and the date on which it is signed on behalf of the board of directors. [Sch 4: 12] This requirement does no more than give statutory authority to part of the standard practice required under SSAP 17.

Post balance sheet events are defined by SSAP 17 as those which occur between the balance sheet date and the date on which the financial statements are approved by the board of directors. A distinction is made between two principal types of post balance sheet events: (i) adjusting events, being those which require adjustment of the financial statements and, (ii) non-adjusting events which may require disclosure but do not require adjustment to the financial statements. The statement also discusses the treatment of 'window dressing' transactions.

11.072 ADJUSTING EVENTS

Adjusting events are defined in SSAP 17 as post balance sheet events which provide additional evidence of conditions that existed at the balance sheet date. The financial statements must be changed to take account of the additional evidence provided by such events.

Examples of adjusting events are:

- the bankruptcy of a customer after the year-end, but not resulting from an adverse post balance sheet event affecting the customer.
- a fall in selling price of a product, causing the net realisable value of stocks to fall below cost.
- the settlement of litigation arising from events which took place prior to the year-end.
- changes in rates of taxation based on profits taken up in the financial statements.

Other examples of adjusting events are contained in the Appendix to SSAP 17.

Special consideration must be given to post balance sheet events such as a deterioration in operating results and in the financial position of the company which, although they do not provide direct evidence of conditions existing at the balance sheet date, may raise doubts as to whether the accounts can properly be prepared under the going concern concept. SSAP 17 requires that financial statements must be changed if post balance sheet events indicate that application of the going concern concept to the whole or a material part of the company is not appropriate.

11.073 NON-ADJUSTING EVENTS

Non-adjusting events are defined in SSAP 17 as post balance sheet events which concern conditions which did not exist at the balance sheet date. They do not create a need for changes in the financial statements but should be disclosed if they are so material that non-disclosure would affect the ability of users of the financial statements to reach a proper understanding of the financial position.

Examples of non-adjusting events are:

- a change in exchange rates.
- a fall in value of property or investments which has occurred after the year end.
- the acquisition or disposal of a business.
- the issue of shares or loan capital.

Other examples are contained in the Appendix to SSAP 17.

It should be borne in mind that circumstances surrounding some of the events listed as non-adjusting may alter their classification and require adjustment of the financial statements. For example, the sale of an investment after the year end is normally a non-adjusting event. However, if no information as to the market value (or other basis of valuation) at the balance sheet date was available, the sale price might provide valid evidence of the net realisable value of the investment at the year end. It might be appropriate to adjust the carrying value of the investment to net realisable value, if lower than its book value, in such circumstances.

11.074 DISCLOSURE

SSAP 17 requires disclosure by way of note of the nature of a non-adjusting event and an estimate of the financial effect before taxation or a statement that it is not practicable to make such an estimate. The tax implications should be explained if necessary for a proper understanding of the financial statements.

The Act also requires disclosure in the directors' report of particulars of important events affecting the company and its subsidiaries which have occurred after the end of the year. [Sch 7: 6(a)]

11.075 WINDOW DRESSING

Window dressing is the term used to describe transactions whose primary purpose is to alter the appearance of the balance sheet. These include legitimate transactions entered into before the year-end which are reversed after the year-end. For example, a loan to a related party may be paid back a few days prior to the year-end but re-lent back to the same party in the first days of the new financial year, the result being to hide the existence of the loan and to increase cash at bank.

The 'window dressing' transaction is the one entered into before the balance sheet date, while the post balance sheet transaction reverses it. SSAP 17 includes in the definition of non-adjusting events a material post balance sheet event which is the reversal or maturity after the year end of a transaction entered into before the year end whose substance was primarily to alter the appearance of the balance sheet. In consequence, the nature of such a transaction and its financial effect must be disclosed in the notes.

It is important to distinguish between a window dressing transaction which only affects the balance sheet, and a transaction which also affects the profit and loss account. The latter will almost certainly be an adjusting event. For example, the reversal in the post balance sheet period of significant sales recorded prior to the balance sheet date should be treated as an adjusting event, the sales and debtors at the balance sheet date should be reduced and stocks increased appropriately.

11.080 DISCLOSURE OF TRANSACTIONS WITH INTERESTED PARTIES

Disclosure of transactions with interested parties is required:

(i) by the general requirement that financial statements must show a true and fair view;

(ii) by statute; and

(iii) by The Stock Exchange.

Material transactions entered into with interested parties are clearly of significance to readers of financial statements and should therefore be disclosed in order for the accounts to show a true and fair view. The decision on what must be disclosed is a difficult one on which precise rules cannot be laid down. It is suggested that cases of doubt should be resolved in favour of disclosure.

Interested parties include directors, officers, substantial shareholders and persons, companies or other bodies, such as trusts or partnerships connected with any of these. There may also be circumstances in which some person or body which does not fall within that definition should be regarded as an interested party.

Transactions which should be disclosed should include all material transactions even if they arise in the ordinary course of business, such as lease agreements, purchase and sales of fixed assets, loans or guarantees made, loans or financial support received. They should also include routine purchases and sales of goods or services, if these are significant to the company's business or carried out at other than normal terms.

The disclosure should be sufficient to enable the reader to understand the nature of the relationship between the parties, the nature of the transaction and its significance to the company. It is not normally necessary to name any of the parties involved.

In addition to the overall requirement that financial statements must show a true and fair view, the Act contains specific requirements for disclosure of transactions with directors and officers. [Sch 6] These requirements are summarised below but the legislation is complex and in cases of doubt reference should be made to the Act itself. It may also be necessary to obtain legal advice as to its interpretation. The requirements specified do not apply to recognised banks for which there are special rules. The required disclosures must be included as part of the financial statements, normally in the notes to the accounts. Corresponding amounts for the previous financial year are not required.

The Stock Exchange imposes certain requirements in regard to disclosure of 'contracts of significance'. These requirements, which to some extent overlap those imposed by statute are discussed in Section 11.083.

11.081 DISCLOSURE OF TRANSACTIONS WITH DIRECTORS

(a) Persons affected

Disclosure is required of relevant transactions with:

- persons who were directors, including 'shadow directors', of the company or its holding company, at any time during the financial year, and

- persons connected with them.

A shadow director is a person in accordance with whose directions or instructions other directors are accustomed to act.

Persons connected with a director include [s 346]:

(i) his spouse;

(ii) his child under the age of 18 (including a step-child or illegitimate child);

(iii) a body corporate with which he is associated, i.e. he and other persons connected with him are interested in 20% or more of the company's equity share capital, or are entitled to exercise 20% or more of the votes at a general meeting: a director is treated as being entitled to exercise votes if they may be exercised by a company under his control (i.e. a company in which he or a person connected with him is entitled to exercise some of the voting power and he, persons connected with him and the other directors of the company together can exercise more than half the voting power);

(iv) a person acting in his capacity as trustee of a trust whose beneficiaries include the director or anyone falling within (i) - (iii) above (including a trustee of a discretionary trust which includes the persons as potential beneficiaries but excluding a trustee under an employees' share scheme or a pension scheme);

(v) a person acting in his capacity as partner of the director or anyone falling within (i)–(iii) above;

(vi) a Scottish firm in which the director or anyone falling within (i)–(iv) above is a partner.

A person is not treated as being 'connected with a director' if that person is himself a director of the company.

(b) Transactions which require disclosure

The following transactions must be disclosed [Sch 6: 1,2] if they were made for any person affected (as described above) by the company or any of its subsidiaries:

(i) loans;

(ii) quasi-loans (i.e. arrangements whereby the company pays or agrees to pay sums on behalf of the person affected to be reimbursed at a later date; e.g. credit card transactions);

(iii) credit transactions (i.e. leasing transactions, hire purchase transactions, conditional sales and other sales on deferred payment terms);

(iv) guarantees or provisions of security for any loans, quasi-loans or credit transactions made by a third party;

(v) any agreement to enter into any of the transactions listed in (i)–(iv) above; and

(vi) any other transaction or arrangement in which the person affected had directly or indirectly a material interest (see below).

It is specifically enacted that disclosure is required even if:

- the transaction or arrangement is prohibited under the Act (the prohibitions with regard to loans, etc. in favour of directors and connected persons are discussed in Section 18.050);
- the person for whom it was made was not a director or connected person at the time it was made; or
- the company making the transaction is a subsidiary company which was not a subsidiary at the time it was made.

Disclosure is required unless the transaction or arrangement was not entered into during the financial year and did not subsist at any time during it.

The Act does not define a loan, but a definition which has received judicial approval is 'a sum of money lent for a time to be returned in money or money's worth'. Thus an essential ingredient of a loan is that there should be an intention of the parties that it should be repaid at some future time. On this basis an amount drawn by a director on account of remuneration (e.g. of a bonus which only becomes payable when approved at the annual meeting) would not be classified as a loan. Similarly advances of sums which are intended to meet expenses to be incurred on the company's business are not loans. However every case must be considered on its merits and regard had to the substance of the transaction. If a sum advanced to a director purports to be on account of remuneration, then PAYE ought to be applied at the time of payment, and if this is not done then the payment may assume the characteristics of a loan. Similarly advances made on account of expenses which are clearly in excess of any amount which a director could reasonably be expected to incur within a reasonable time, are probably entered into in order to give the director concerned the benefit of the use of the money and should therefore be classified as loans. In any case amounts advanced may require the approval of shareholders (see Section 18.050).

Any transaction with a director or with a person connected with him is treated as a transaction in which that director is interested. But disclosure is not required if:

- a director is interested in a contract only by virtue of being a director of the other company (this would not apply if he was also a shareholder of that company),

- it is in respect of a director's contract of service.

A loan from a director to his company or to a subsidiary company is a 'transaction or arrangement' which must be disclosed, unless it can be excluded as not material as discussed below.

Transactions and arrangements which must be disclosed under (vi) above are restricted to those contracts in which the director's interest is 'material', but there are some differences of view as to how materiality should be judged in this context.

It is suggested that the best way to approach the matter is to consider whether the knowledge of the director's interest in the transaction is likely to be significant to the readers of the financial statements. What is required is the disclosure of significant information concerning the existing relationship between the company and its directors and of matters which might affect this relationship in the future. On this basis it is not necessary to disclose a director's interest in a transaction on the grounds that the interest is material to the transaction as a whole if the transaction itself is insignificant; on the other hand an item should not be excluded from disclosure merely because the amount involved is small in relation to the amounts included in the accounts.

The Act specifically provides that if the directors, or a majority of them (but excluding the director whose interest is under consideration) resolve that an interest in a particular transaction or arrangement is not material, then that is conclusive and the interest need not be disclosed under (vi) above.

Other transactions exempt from disclosure under (vi) above are:

(i) transactions entered into by a company in the ordinary course of business and on an arm's length basis (i.e. on terms not less favourable to the company and the group than would have been obtained if there had been no director's interest) [Sch 6: 7]; and

(ii) transactions in which any director was interested if the aggregate value of the transactions for that director made after the commencement of the financial year together with any liability outstanding in respect of transactions entered into before the beginning of that year did not exceed £1,000 or if they did exceed £1,000, did not exceed the lower of £5,000 or one per cent of the net assets of the company at the year end. [Sch 6: 12]

There is also an exemption from disclosure of credit transactions, guarantees of credit transactions, and agreements to enter into credit transactions in respect of any individual director if the aggregate outstanding of such transactions entered into for that director and persons connected with him did not exceed £5,000 at any one time during the financial year. [Sch 6: 11]

(c) Particulars to be disclosed

The particulars to be disclosed [Sch 6: 9] are:

(i) the principal terms of the transaction;

(ii) a statement that the loan, guarantee, transaction etc. was made or subsisted during the financial year;

(iii) the name of the person for whom it was made (if the person is a connected person, the name of the director with whom he is connected must also be given);

(iv) in the case of a loan made or to be made, the amount of the liability in respect of principal and interest at the beginning and end of the financial year, the maximum amount of the liability during the financial year, any interest due which has not been paid, and the amount of any provision made against the loan or accrued interest;

(v) where a company has guaranteed, or provided security for a loan, the amount for which the company was liable at the beginning and end of the financial year, the maximum potential liability, and the amount of any actual liability incurred;

(vi) in the case of quasi-loans and credit transactions, the value of the transaction;

(vii) in the case of any other transaction or arrangement in which a director had a material interest, the name of the director concerned and the nature of the interest, and the value of the transaction or arrangement.

The value of a transaction or arrangement is the value which would be attached on an arm's length basis in the ordinary course of business to the goods or services which are the subject of the transaction. If the transaction is a loan or guarantee it is the principal of the loan or the amount guaranteed or secured. [s 340]

Appendix 4 of this manual summarises the above rules.

An example of good disclosure of a transaction in which a director has a material interest is given below:

EXAMPLE

C.P. Plastics Ltd. (a member of the group) has during the year contracted to purchase its plastic raw material requirements over the next three years from Plastic Products Ltd. Mr. J. Docker, a director of Tramp Holdings p.l.c., owns a significant proportion of the equity share capital of Plastics Products Ltd. Based on forecast production schedules and prices agreed for the year ending 31 December 1985, the company will purchase materials valued at approximately £1.2 million in 1985. The value of the contract for the years 1986 and 1987 will depend on a price formula tied to the direct production costs incurred by Plastic Products Ltd.

11.082 DISCLOSURE OF TRANSACTIONS WITH OFFICERS OTHER THAN DIRECTORS

The notes to the accounts must disclose information in respect of arrangements made by the company or any of its subsidiaries for persons who were officers of the company at any time during the financial year, but who were not directors. [s 233]

The information to be disclosed [Sch 6: 15,16] is the aggregate amount outstanding at the end of the financial year under each of the following headings:

(i) loans;

(ii) quasi-loans; and

(iii) credit transactions.

In each case guarantees and securities for these items and agreements to enter into such arrangements are to be included under the appropriate head.

The number of officers for whom they were made must also be stated.

If the aggregate of such arrangements outstanding at the end of the financial year in respect of any individual officers does not exceed £2,500 then they may be excluded from the amounts disclosed.

11.083 STOCK EXCHANGE REQUIREMENTS

The Stock Exchange requires listed companies to disclose the following:

(i) particulars of any contracts of significance (see definition below) subsisting during or at the end of the financial year to which a company in the group was a party and in which a director of the company was materially interested; if there are no such contracts this fact must be specifically stated;

(ii) particulars of any contracts of significance between the company or one of its subsidiaries and a corporate substantial shareholder; (both 'contract of significance' and 'corporate substantial shareholder' are defined below); and

(iii) particulars of any contract for the provision of services to the company or any of its subsidiaries by a corporate substantial shareholder; an exception is allowed if the services provided are those which it is the principal business of the shareholder to provide and the contract is not a 'contract of significance'.

A 'contract of significance' is defined as:

- a capital transaction or a transaction whose principal purpose is the granting of credit where the contract represents an amount or value equal to 1% or more of the consolidated net assets of the group; and

- a revenue transaction where the contract represents an amount or value equal to 1% or more of the consolidated group purchases, sales, payments or receipts as appropriate.

A 'corporate substantial shareholder' is defined as:

- any body corporate entitled to exercise or control the exercise of 30% or more of the voting power at general meetings of the company; and

- any corporate body which is in a position to control the composition of a majority of the board of directors of the company.

The Stock Exchange does not specify how this information is to be given but it is usual to comply with Stock Exchange requirements in the directors' report. However, if a 'contract of significance' requires disclosure as a material contract under the statutory rules, it should be disclosed only in the financial statements.

12 GROUP ACCOUNTS

12.010 REQUIREMENT TO PRODUCE GROUP ACCOUNTS

The Act places an obligation on a company, which at the end of the year has subsidiaries, to produce group accounts dealing with the company and its subsidiaries. [s 229]

The principal exception given in s 229(2) to the requirement to produce group accounts relates to a holding company which at the end of its financial year is itself a wholly owned subsidiary of another company incorporated in Great Britain. A company which, although a subsidiary of another, has minority shareholders and a company whose shares are held by an overseas company are not excluded from the requirement to produce group accounts.

12.020 DEFINITION OF HOLDING COMPANY/SUBSIDIARY COMPANY RELATIONSHIP

12.021 DEFINITION

The Act [s 736(1)] states that one company is a subsidiary of another if but only if:

(i) the other company is a member of it and controls the composition of its board of directors; or

(ii) the other company holds more than half in nominal value of its issued equity share capital; shares held by a nominee for the other company or beneficially by another subsidiary of it are treated as being held by it; or

(iii) where it is a subsidiary of a company which is itself a subsidiary of the other company.

A company is a holding company of another if that other is its subsidiary.

These definitions are adopted in SSAP 14.

12.022 EXPLANATION OF SECTION 736(1)

The composition of a company's board of directors is deemed to be controlled by another company only if that company can appoint or remove all or a majority of the directors without the consent or concurrence of any other person (e.g. through holding shares giving sufficient voting rights).

The holding company is deemed to have the power to appoint a director:

(i) if a person cannot be appointed a director without the exercise in his favour of a power by the company; or

(ii) if a person's appointment follows automatically from his appointment as a director of the holding company; or

(iii) the directorship is held by the other company itself or by one of its subsidiaries.

Equity share capital is any issued share capital other than that whose rights to specific amounts in the distribution of both dividends and capital are restricted. (This means that participating preference shares are equity capital.)

In determining whether a company is a holding company, any shares held or power exercisable by the company's nominee (or by a nominee for its subsidiary) are treated as being held or exercisable by the company.

Any shares held or power exercisable by one company in a fiduciary capacity or by virtue of the provisions of any debentures of another or of a trust deed for securing such debentures, are disregarded for the purpose of determining whether that other company is a subsidiary of the first. Shares held by the company (or any subsidiary or nominee) are also disregarded if the business of the company (or its subsidiary) includes the lending of money and the shares are held as security for a transaction entered into in the ordinary course of that business.

12.023 EXAMPLES

These definitions can lead to some unexpected results.

(i) A company can be the subsidiary of two holding companies, one with voting control, the other with more than 50% of the equity capital. However, SSAP 14 specifically excludes from consolidation those companies which are subsidiaries under the Act by virtue of ownership, but are not in fact controlled by the holding company. It should be noted that the Act still requires the inclusion of such subsidiaries in group accounts in some other way.

(ii) A company may have an effective interest in more than half of the equity capital of a company but still not be its holding company, e.g.

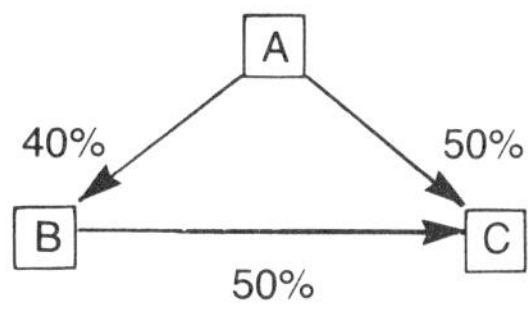

A holds an effective interest of 70% of C (50% directly and 40% x 50% = 20% indirectly). C, however, is not a subsidiary of A because as B is not a subsidiary of A its holding in C is ignored.

(iii) However in the following situation:

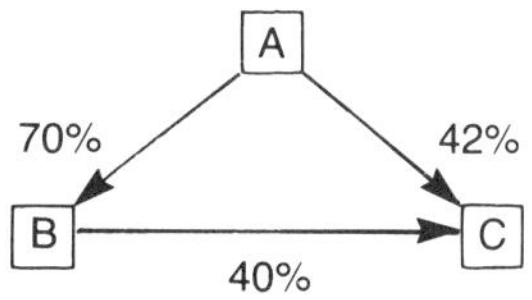

A's effective interest in C is again 70% (70% x 40% = 28% plus 42% direct) but in this case C is a subsidiary of A, since B is a subsidiary of A and therefore its holding in C is taken into account.

(iv) Whereas in the following example:

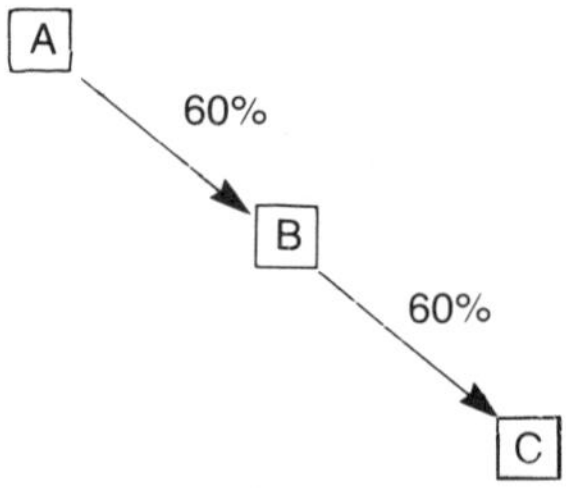

although A's effective interest in C is only 36% of the equity capital (i.e. 60% x 60%) C, nevertheless, is a subsidiary of A. This is because C is a subsidiary of B which is, in turn, a subsidiary of A.

Similarly in:

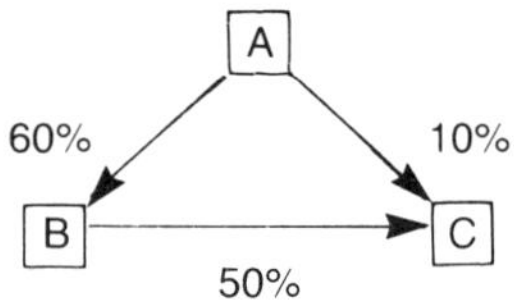

although A's effective interest in C is only 40%, C is a subsidiary of A because the holding of A's subsidiary B together with A's direct holding is more than 50%.

12.030 OMISSION OF SUBSIDIARIES FROM GROUP ACCOUNTS

The Act [s 229(3)] allows the omission of one or more subsidiaries from group accounts if, in the opinion of the directors, its inclusion:

(i) is impracticable; or

(ii) would be of no real value to members in view of the insignificant amounts involved; or

(iii) would involve expense or delay out of proportion to the value to members of the company; or

(iv) would be misleading; or

(v) would be harmful to the business of the company or any of its subsidiaries; or

(vi) the business of the holding company and that of the subsidiary are so different that they cannot reasonably be treated as a single undertaking.

The approval of the Secretary of State is required in cases (v) and (vi).

Where subsidiaries are excluded from group accounts, the additional information in respect of the subsidiaries required by Sch 4: 69 must be given in the holding company's financial statements (see Section 12.031 below).

12.031 DISCLOSURE IN RESPECT OF SUBSIDIARIES EXCLUDED FROM GROUP ACCOUNTS

Where group accounts are not submitted or where any subsidiaries are excluded from group accounts, the following additional information must be given in the notes to the accounts [Sch 4: 69]:

(i) the reasons why the subsidiaries are not dealt with in group accounts;

(ii) a statement showing any qualifications in the reports of the auditors on the financial statements of the excluded subsidiary companies, which are material to the members of the holding company and are not otherwise dealt with in its financial statements;

(iii) the aggregate amount of the total investment of the holding company in the shares of the excluded subsidiaries determined by way of the equity method of valuation. (This is not required if group accounts are not prepared because the company is a wholly owned subsidiary of another UK company.)

The Act also requires a statement showing 'any note or saving' contained in the subsidiary's accounts to draw attention to a matter which apart from that note would have been the subject of an audit qualification. It is not known how to interpret this requirement since presumably it is not intended that all material notes to the accounts of omitted subsidiaries should be reproduced, and no examples of such a disclosure have been identified. It is suggested that the only matters which require to be disclosed are those which are in any case necessary to show a true and fair view.

If any of the above information is unobtainable, this fact must be stated in a note. Application can be made to the Secretary of State for exemption from any of the above requirements.

In addition, balances with and interests in any unconsolidated subsidiaries must be disclosed separately in the group financial statements. [Sch 4: 67]

12.040 FORM OF GROUP ACCOUNTS

The Act provides that group accounts shall be consolidated accounts, comprising a consolidated balance sheet and a consolidated profit and loss account (extended by SSAP 14 to include a consolidated statement of source and application of funds) unless the directors are of the opinion that the required information may be better or more clearly presented in another form. [s 229]

It is generally accepted that consolidated financial statements provide, except in special circumstances, the best way of presenting a true and fair view of a group's state of affairs and results.

12.041 OTHER FORMS OF GROUP ACCOUNTS

The following possible alternative forms of group accounts are specifically referred to as being acceptable [s 229(6)]:

(i) *More than one set of consolidated financial statements*

One set will deal with the holding company and one group of subsidiaries, the other set with the remaining subsidiaries. This form of presentation may be suitable where the companies in a group are involved in totally different types of operations (e.g. manufacturing operations as against mining operations). In such circumstances the information given in a single set of consolidated financial statements might well be misleading or confusing.

(ii) *Separate financial statements for each subsidiary and holding company*

In this case the financial statements of the holding company would be accompanied by the financial statements of each of the subsidiaries in the group. This method might be appropriate where the principal activity of each company in the group is significantly different from that of the other companies in the group. This form of presentation would be feasible only where there were very few subsidiaries. Otherwise it could hardly be contended that the information was in a form to be readily appreciated by members of the holding company.

(iii) *Statements expanding the information about the subsidiaries in the holding company's own financial statements*

A situation in which this method might be appropriate would be an investment by the holding company in an insolvent subsidiary where the holding company is not committed to and does not intend to bear the losses and liabilities of this subsidiary. In this case the information regarding the investment shown in the holding company's balance sheet could be expanded by a statement giving details of the net deficit, the reasons for making the investment, etc.

(iv) *Any combination of the foregoing*

Other forms of group accounts must give the same or equivalent information as that required to be given by consolidated financial statements. [Sch 4: 68]

SSAP 14 states that group accounts should be in the form of a single set of consolidated financial statements covering the holding company and its subsidiaries (except those subsidiaries which should be excluded from consolidation under the circumstances discussed in Section 12.061 below). If group accounts are prepared in any other form the onus is on the directors to justify and state the reasons for reaching the conclusion that the resulting group accounts give a fairer view of the financial position of the group as a whole.

12.050 CONSOLIDATED FINANCIAL STATEMENTS

Consolidated financial statements must combine the financial information contained in the separate financial statements of a holding company and its subsidiaries as if they were the accounts of an actual company (with such adjustments as the directors of the holding company think necessary). [Sch 4: 61, 62]

The consolidated financial statements must also comply with all the requirements of Sch 4, giving information for the group as if it was a single company, except for the following [Sch 4: 63]:

(i) particulars of directors' emoluments [Sch 5: Part V] should deal with directors of the holding company only (see Section 5.152);

(ii) loans to, and transactions with, directors and officers [Sch 6] should deal with holding company directors and officers only (see Section 11.080);

(iii) emoluments of senior employees [Sch 5: Part VI] should deal with senior employees of the holding company only (see Section 5.151(c));

(iv) information required about investments other than subsidiaries [Sch 5: Part II] should be given in respect of investments of the holding company only (see Section 6.041(f)).

The other major difference is that consolidated financial statements may deal with an investment by way of the equity method of accounting in appropriate circumstances. Some such circumstances are referred to in Section 12.061 below in relation to subsidiaries excluded from consolidation; other appropriate circumstances and the application of the method are discussed in Section 12.080.

The Act requires disclosure in the notes in respect of each principal subsidiary, of the name, country of incorporation and proportion of shares held. [Sch 5: 1] Stock Exchange companies must also disclose the country of operation. In addition, SSAP 14 requires an indication of the nature of the business of each principal subsidiary. (See Section 6.041(f) which discusses these requirements in more detail.)

12.051 HOLDING COMPANY ACCOUNTS

A holding company preparing consolidated accounts must also prepare its own balance sheet and related notes in accordance with the Act but it is not required to prepare its own profit and loss account provided that the consolidated profit and loss account shows how much of the consolidated profit or loss for the financial year (after tax and extraordinary items) is dealt with in the accounts of the holding company. The notes to the group accounts must disclose that the company has taken advantage of this subsection. [s 228(7)]

An example of the information required to be given is contained in note 10 to the model financial statements on page 34.

The amount of the consolidated profit or loss for the financial year dealt with in the accounts of the holding company should be the amount which would have been disclosed in the holding company's own profit and loss account as 'profit or loss for the financial year' if such an account had been produced. Thus dividends received and receivable from subsidiaries in respect of the financial year should normally be included. If an amount is charged against profits to reflect a permanent diminution in value of a subsidiary below cost, this should also be taken into account. The only adjustment necessary to the holding company's profit arises if it includes any adjustments which are not part of the group profit of the year. Thus if a dividend declared by a subsidiary exceeds that subsidiary's profit for the year, the excess cannot be regarded as part of the group profit for the year. Similarly a provision for permanent diminution in value can only be treated as part of the group profit or loss for the year to the extent that it reflects the loss incurred by the particular subsidiary in the year. A revaluation of investments in subsidiaries under the alternative accounting rules, such as is referred to in Section 6.043 does not constitute dealing with the group profits in the holding company accounts.

12.060 EXCLUSION FROM CONSOLIDATION

12.061 BASIS FOR EXCLUSION

Section 12.030 sets out the circumstances where subsidiaries may legally be excluded from group accounts. SSAP 14 deals with the circumstances where it is appropriate to exclude subsidiaries from consolidated financial statements. Unless subsidiaries are excluded from consolidated financial statements on grounds which also justify exclusion from group accounts, they must be dealt with in the group accounts in some other way (see Section 12.041).

The circumstances which justify exclusion from consolidation and the appropriate accounting treatment in each case are discussed below.

(a) Dissimilar activities

> *The activities of the subsidiary are so dissimilar from the rest of the group that consolidated financial statements would be misleading and information would be better provided by presenting separate financial statements of the subsidiary.*

There should be very few instances where subsidiaries will be excluded for this reason. It must be shown that the consolidation of the financial statements of such subsidiaries distorts the true and fair view of the group's financial position (e.g. a bank or insurance company in the context of a manufacturing group).

Group accounts must include the separate financial statements of that subsidiary or the combined financial statements of the subsidiary and others with similar operations. In the consolidated financial statements the group's investment in the excluded subsidiary(ies) should be accounted for using the equity method of accounting.

The separate financial statements should disclose:

(i) the holding company's interest;

(ii) particulars of intra-group balances;

(iii) the nature of transactions with the rest of the group;

(iv) a reconciliation with the amount included in the consolidated financial statements for the group's investment in the subsidiary.

(b) Lack of effective control

> *The holding company although owning directly or indirectly through its subsidiaries more than 50% of the equity share capital, either:*
>
> *(a) does not own share capital carrying more than 50% of the votes, or*
>
> *(b) has contractual or other restrictions imposed on its ability to appoint a majority of the board of directors.*

A subsidiary which has been excluded for this reason should be accounted for in the consolidated financial statements using the equity method of accounting if it meets the criteria for an associated company under SSAP 1 (see Section 12.083). If it does not meet these criteria, the investment in the subsidiary should be included in the consolidated balance sheet at cost less any provision for permanent diminution in value or at an appropriate alternative valuation. If the equity method of accounting is not used, the consolidated profit and loss account should reflect only dividends received or receivable from the subsidiary and any provision made for diminution in value of the investment.

Unless omission from group accounts is justified by one of the reasons discussed in Section 12.030 above, the separate financial statements of a subsidiary excluded from consolidation for this reason should be included as part of the group accounts.

(c) Severe restrictions

> *The subsidiary operates under severe restrictions which significantly impair control by the holding company over its assets and operations for the foreseeable future.*

Examples of circumstances which might be viewed as significantly impairing control include:

(i) long term currency restrictions on the transfer of funds;

(ii) trade embargoes imposed by the home country;

(iii) pending nationalisation or expropriation.

A subsidiary which is excluded from consolidation because of severe restrictions should be stated in the consolidated balance sheet at the amount at which it would have been included under the equity method at the date the restrictions came into force. No accrual should be made for the subsequent earnings or losses of the subsidiary; however, if the value of the investment has been permanently impaired, provision for the loss must be made in the consolidated profit and loss account.

The severe restrictions which justify exclusion from consolidation would probably justify omission from the group accounts (see Section 12.030), but if not, the separate financial statements of the subsidiaries excluded from consolidation for this reason should be included as part of the group accounts.

(d) Temporary control

Control over a subsidiary is intended to be temporary.

A subsidiary should only be excluded from consolidation on the grounds that control is intended to be temporary if the temporary nature of the control is apparent at the time when the interest that gives control is acquired. A subsidiary which has previously been consolidated should not be excluded from consolidation on the grounds that a decision to dispose of it has been taken and therefore control is temporary. Elsewhere in SSAP 14 it is made clear that a subsidiary's results should be included in the profit and loss account up to the date of disposal.

A subsidiary which is excluded from consolidation on the grounds that control is temporary should be included in the consolidated balance sheet as a current asset and stated at the lower of cost and net realisable value. It is probable that exclusion from consolidation for this reason will also justify omission from the group accounts on the grounds that inclusion would be misleading.

12.062 DISCLOSURE REQUIREMENTS ABOUT EXCLUDED SUBSIDIARIES

The following additional information is required by SSAP 14 to be disclosed in respect of subsidiaries excluded from consolidation:

(i) the names of the principal subsidiaries excluded;

(ii) any premium or discount on acquisition (goodwill or negative goodwill) to the extent not written off;

(iii) in respect of a subsidiary excluded by reason of severe restrictions: its net assets; its profit or loss for the period; and any amounts included in the consolidated profit and loss account in respect of dividends received or writing down of the investment. (Clearly this information is not necessary if the separate financial statements of the subsidiary are included as part of the group accounts.)

12.063 EXAMPLE OF NOTE DEALING WITH EXCLUDED SUBSIDIARY

An example of disclosure which meets the requirements of SSAP 14 regarding the exclusion from consolidation on the grounds of severe restrictions and of the Act in respect of exclusion from group accounts is given below:

EXAMPLE

The financial statements of Utopia Incorporated, a subsidiary company operating in Ruritania, have been omitted from group accounts since in the opinion of the directors, it would be misleading to include them in view of the trading sanctions imposed on that country by the international community and the consequent impairment of control over its assets and operations. The value of the company's 80% interest in the share capital of Utopia Incorporated determined under the equity method of accounting was £506,000 at 31 December 1984. The audited financial statements of Utopia Incorporated at that date disclosed net assets of R$5,230,000 (£632,000) and a profit for the financial year of R$369,000 (£44,600). This investment is included in the group balance sheet at £428,000, being the amount attributable under the equity method of accounting in 1982 when trading sanctions were first imposed.

The auditors of Utopia Incorporated have included the following statement in their report on the financial statements.

'We were unable to agree the amount provided in the financial statements for slow moving and obsolete stock. In our opinion an additional amount of approximately R$400,000 should have been provided and to this extent profits before taxation are overstated.'

12.070 CONSOLIDATION ADJUSTMENTS

The basic consolidation process consists of the aggregating of the assets, liabilities, income and expenditure of the holding company and its subsidiaries while setting off the book value of the investment in each subsidiary against the appropriate proportion of its issued capital and reserves. What is the 'appropriate proportion' and the other important adjustments that arise when shares in a subsidiary company are acquired depend on whether acquisition or merger accounting is employed and these are discussed in Section 12.090 and 12.100 below. In order to produce group accounts which achieve the objective of showing a true and fair view of the state of affairs and profit of the group as though it was a single company, certain other adjustments are usually necessary. In particular the effect of transactions between group companies must be eliminated: liabilities due to one group company by another should be set off against the corresponding asset in the other company's accounts: sales made by one group company to another should be excluded both from turnover and from cost of sales or appropriate expense heading in the group profit and loss account. Some other consolidation adjustments that are frequently required are discussed below (but the list is not exhaustive).

12.071 UNIFORM ACCOUNTING POLICIES

It is desirable that all companies in the group should follow uniform accounting policies, but circumstances may arise which may make this impracticable or inappropriate, for example:

(i) the policy is prohibited by legislation in another country;

(ii) the policy is contrary to generally accepted accounting principles in the relevant country (e.g. deferred taxation calculated under SSAP 15 rules is not allowed in the U.S.A.);

(iii) the policy would result in serious adverse tax consequences.

Where group accounting policies are not adopted in the financial statements of a subsidiary, appropriate adjustments must be made in the consolidated financial statements to achieve uniformity. In exceptional cases where this is impracticable, different accounting policies may be used provided they are generally accepted and disclosure is made of:

(i) the different accounting policies used;

(ii) an indication of the amounts of assets and liabilities involved and, where practicable, of the effect on results and net assets of the adoption of the differing policies;

(iii) the reasons for the different treatment.

12.072 GROUP ACCOUNTING PERIODS

Both the Act and SSAP 14 require the financial years of the holding company and its subsidiaries to be identical unless there is good reason for having different dates. If one or more subsidiaries have different accounting dates, some distortion in the consolidated accounts is unavoidable and it is important to ensure that this distortion is not so significant as to result in the consolidated accounts as a whole not showing a true and fair view.

(a) Reasons for differing dates

There are sometimes circumstances which make it impracticable to have identical dates. Some reasons which may be justifable are:

(i) companies in remote territories may be unable to comply with the parent company's time table for preparing annual financial statements which will usually be framed with a view to avoiding undue delay in publication;

(ii) legislation in certain countries require financial statements to be prepared to a specified date;

(iii) the normal trading cycle in certain trades (e.g. agriculture) may make it desirable for subsidiaries to have financial year ends which coincide with it (e.g. when crops have been harvested);

(iv) a change in accounting date may have serious adverse tax consequences, or significant tax advantages may arise from having a different accounting date.

Where the financial year of a subsidiary does not coincide with that of the holding company, the group accounts must deal with the financial statements of the subsidiary for its last financial year (ending with or before that of the holding company), unless the consent of the Secretary of State is obtained. [s 230(7)]

(b) Use of special financial statements

Where the financial year of a subsidiary differs from that of the holding company, SSAP 14 envisages, where practicable, the use of special financial statements made up to the same date as the holding company's financial year end. These statements are often interim management financial statements for the period subsequent to the end of the last audited financial statements of the subsidiary. Thus, where the group's financial year end is 31 December 1984 and a subsidiary's financial year end is 31 October, that subsidiary's results would be based on the interim results for the two months ended 31 December 1984, plus the results for the financial year ended 31 October 1984, less the interim results for the two months ended 31 December 1983. The use of interim statements might be appropriate in circumstances (ii) to (iv) cited above but is unlikely to be practicable due to time constraints in circumstance (i).

The consent of the Secretary of State is required for the use of such special financial statements. [s 230(7)]

(c) Disclosure requirements

SSAP 14 requires the following information to be disclosed for each principal subsidiary whose accounting date differs from that of the holding company:

(i) its name;

(ii) its accounting date (also required by Sch 4: 70);

(iii) the reason for using a different accounting date (also required by Sch 4: 70);

(iv) where the length of the accounting period is different from that of the holdings company, the accounting period involved should be stated.

EXAMPLE

The group financial statements consolidate the financial statements of the Company and 37 subsidiaries. Owing to seasonal trade or local conditions and because of the need to avoid undue delay in the presentation of group financial statements, it is impracticable for six subsidiaries to make up financial statements to 31st December. The names of these subsidiaries and their accounting dates are disclosed in the listing of subsidiaries on page 15.

(d) Adjustments for abnormal intervening transactions

In practice the use of such special financial statements is rare and the general approach is to consolidate the financial statements of the subsidiary for its financial year ending immediately before the holding company's year end. When this is done appropriate adjustments need to be made in the consolidated financial statements for any abnormal transactions in the intervening period. The necessary adjustments would not reflect normal trading results but would include such events as:

(i) major trading losses;

(ii) extraordinary losses arising from disposal or discontinuance of business;

(iii) intercompany transactions which result in omission or double counting of significant balance sheet items.

12.073 ELIMINATION OF UNREALISED INTRA-GROUP PROFITS

Current assets should be recorded in historical cost financial statements at cost (or net realisable value if this is lower than cost). Any unrealised profit arising from trading transactions between group companies should therefore be eliminated from the consolidated financial statements. Similarly, unrealised inter-company profits arising from intra-group construction of fixed assets and transfers of assets should be eliminated.

When the process of manufacturing involves the transfer of goods between group companies, the transfer values may be based on arms-length prices. This may be done to compare profitability of various companies or for the purpose of bonus incentives, etc. or may be necessary in the interests of minority shareholders. To the extent that goods bought from a group company remain in stock in another group company at the balance sheet date, this results in an unrealised profit as far as the group is concerned. All such unrealised profits should be eliminated for financial statement purposes.

The elimination is made as a consolidation adjustment and not in the financial statements of any individual company. Since U.K. tax is charged on the results of individual companies and not on the group, the elimination will probably result in a timing difference as far as the group is concerned between income recognised for financial accounts purposes and income recognised for taxation purposes. This may require an adjustment to deferred tax in the consolidated accounts. The subject of deferred tax is dealt with in Section 14.080.

Special considerations must be borne in mind if a construction or contracting company is a member of a group and carries out work for other group companies.

(i) If the building or other asset being constructed will on completion be a fixed asset of another group company (e.g. a new factory or an investment property) then, as indicated above, any profit made by the construction company must be eliminated on consolidation. However if the asset being constructed will become a current asset of the other group company (e.g. a property for resale) then any profit made by the construction company need not be eliminated provided it is measured in accordance with the rules governing the recognition of profit on long-term contract work in progress (see Section 7.016).

(ii) If the construction company includes interest in the cost of construction, any interest must be a genuine charge as far as the group is concerned. This point is significant if finance for the project is being provided by another group company which is charging interest, since the interest charged may not represent interest paid by the group on money borrowed to finance the project.

There are two generally accepted methods of dealing with the elimination of unrealised profits or losses where there is a minority interest. These are:

(i) the elimination of all inter-company profit or loss on the theory that the group of companies should be regarded as a single trading entity.

(ii) the elimination of only that proportion of the inter-company profit or loss which concerns members of the holding company, based on the percentage holding in either the selling company, or the company holding the inventory.

Since the profit or loss to be eliminated is included in the financial statements of the selling company, the soundest approach would be to follow the first alternative of method (ii) above. Thus, where parent P holds an 80 percent interest in subsidiary A and 70 percent in subsidiary B, 80 percent of the gross profit would be eliminated on all 'unrealised' sales made by A to P and B. In this case the remaining 20% of the profit, less tax, will be shown as minority interest. However, method (i) has the merit of simplicity and is probably more common in practice. Whichever method is used, it is important that it be followed consistently from year to year.

The measurement of unrealised profits on intra-group transactions often involves difficult practical problems in identifying intra-group purchases held as stock and complex calculations to determine the amount of unrealised profit involved and the amount involved is often not large. Consequently it is common for such adjustments not to be made other than in circumstances where the large volume of assets purchased intra-group and held at the balance sheet date is likely to cause a need for a material consolidation adjustment.

12.074 MINORITY INTERESTS

As indicated above the basic consolidation process involves the aggregation of the assets, liabilities, income and expenditure of the individual group companies. Therefore where the group does not hold the whole of the share capital of a subsidiary, an adjustment is necessary to take account of the interests of the outside shareholders. Their interests in the capital and reserves of the subsidiary need to be recognised in the group balance sheet and their share of the subsidiary's profit or loss for the year needs to be taken into account in arriving at the group profit or loss. The presentation of these matters is discussed below.

(a) Balance sheet presentation

Although the balance sheet formats do not provide a heading for minority interests, this heading should appear as a separate item in the consolidated balance sheet, unless the amount is immaterial, when it might be combined with 'Other creditors'. Minority interests should not be shown as part of capital and reserves as the consolidated balance sheet is intended to show the financial position of the group so far as concerns members of the holding company only. The most appropriate position in Format 1 is immediately after 'Provisions for liabilities and charges'.

Dividends payable to the minority should be included under 'Other creditors including taxation and social security'.

It sometimes happens that the minority interest in a subsidiary is a debit balance (because the accumulated deficit on reserves exceeds the nominal value of the issued share capital). A debit balance on minority interests should be recognised in a consolidated balance sheet only under the exceptional circumstances where the minority shareholders have accepted a binding obligation which they are able to meet to make good their share of the losses incurred. In other circumstances the accumulated deficit attributable to the minority beyond the nominal value of their share capital should be treated as losses attributable to the holding company.

(b) Profit and loss account presentation

SSAP 14 states that the minority's share of profits and losses should be shown separately after arriving at the group profit or loss after tax and before extraordinary items and that the minority's interest in extraordinary items should be deducted from the related amounts in the consolidated profit and loss account.

12.075 RESTRICTION ON DISTRIBUTIONS

The group profit and loss account discloses the group profit for the year, the dividends paid and proposed, and the retained profits for the year. The group balance sheet discloses the aggregated retained profits of the group. The retained profits disclosed are generally assumed to be available for distribution but there may in fact be significant restrictions on the ability of the holding company to distribute them. Such restrictions can arise in many ways, e.g.:

(i) as a result of contractual undertakings, such as sometimes arise in loan agreements or agreements for the acquisition of a subsidiary;

(ii) statutory or exchange control restrictions in a foreign country;

(iii) additions to consolidated reserves arising from the adjustment of a subsidiary's accounts to group accounting policies;

(iv) post-acquisition profits of a subsidiary company which have to be applied against pre-acquisition losses;

(v) post-acquisition profits of a subsidiary which have been capitalised.

The existence of such restrictions is clearly of importance to shareholders and others and should therefore be disclosed in a note to the accounts. The most significant matter which should be disclosed is the extent to which the retained profits of the year cannot be distributed. Readers of financial statements are interested in the extent to which the profits after tax cover the dividends and will be misled if a significant proportion of the retained profits are not available for payment of dividends and this fact is not clearly disclosed. Although restrictions on the group's ability to distribute the retained profits of prior years are usually of less significance, SSAP 14 requires that where there are significant restrictions on the ability of the holding company to distribute the retained profits of the group because of statutory, contractual or exchange control restrictions the extent of the restrictions should be indicated. Accordingly disclosure should be made if a large proportion of the accumulated retained profits cannot be distributed for such reasons. A general indication of the extent of the restrictions is sufficient; it is usually unnecessary and often impracticable to define precisely the amount of past profits affected.

Although SSAP 14 applies to group accounts only, similar information should obviously be given if a comparable situation arises in relation to the retained profits of an individual company (e.g. because of significant exchange control restrictions in a country where the company has a major branch).

12.080 EQUITY METHOD OF ACCOUNTING

12.081 DEFINITION

SSAP 14 defines the equity method of accounting as a method 'under which the investment in a company is shown in the consolidated balance sheet at:

(i) the cost of the investment; and

(ii) the investing company's or group's share of the post-acquisition retained profits and reserves of the company;

(iii) less any amounts written off in respect of (i) and (ii) above;

and under which the investing company accounts separately in its profit and loss account for its share of the profits before tax, taxation and extraordinary items of the company.'

The equity method has sometimes been described as a mini-consolidation since it produces the same result on the consolidated profit and loss account and reserves as the normal consolidation process; the difference lies in the details shown in the financial statements. In consolidation, a company's assets, liabilities, turnover and other profit and loss information are included in the group totals with the minority's share of the net assets being shown as one item; under the equity method, the group's share of the net assets of the company is reflected in the investment account and the shares of operating profit or loss and taxation are shown separately in the profit and loss account.

12.082 APPLICABILITY OF METHOD

The Act [Sch 4: 65] permits an investment to be dealt with in consolidated accounts by the equity method if the directors consider that the investee company is so closely associated with the group as to justify the use of the method. Investments to which the method should be applied are:

(i) investments in associated companies as defined by SSAP 1, and

(ii) investments in subsidiaries which are not consolidated because of dissimilar activities, lack of effective control, or severe operating restrictions (see Section 12.061 above).

Proportionate consolidation techniques, as described in Section 12.083(g)(iv), may be more appropriate than the equity method in dealing with investments in partnerships and non-corporate joint ventures.

12.083 EQUITY METHOD APPLIED TO ASSOCIATED COMPANIES

(a) Definition

An associated company is a company which is not a subsidiary but in which the interest of the investing company or group:

(i) is effectively that of a partner in a joint venture or consortium, or

(ii) is for the long term and is substantial.

In both cases the investing company or group must be in a position to exercise a significant influence over the company. This essentially involves participation in the financial and operating policy decisions of the company, including dividend policy but not necessarily control of those policies. The most usual way of participating in policy decisions is by representation on the board of directors, but SSAP 1 makes it clear that such representation is not conclusive evidence of participation and also that an investing company may participate in policy decisions without board representation.

No specific size test is applied where the interest is effectively that of a partner in a joint venture or consortium. In other cases an interest which amounts to 20% or more of the equity voting rights of a company is presumed to carry the ability to exercise significant influence and an interest of less than 20% of such rights is presumed not to do so. Both these presumptions may be rebutted if it can be clearly demonstrated that they are not true. For example, an interest which exceeds 20% of the voting rights may not carry significant influence if there are other large shareholders which prevent it. However, unless there are special circumstances, demonstration that an interest of less than 20% carries significant influence should include an acknowledgement from the investee company that the investor is able to exercise significant influence over it. In determining the size of the group's investment, the investments of the holding company and all its subsidiaries should be aggregated but the holdings of other associated companies should be ignored.

It should be noted that the definition of associated companies is not restricted to corporate enterprises; it can include investments in non-corporate joint ventures and consortia.

Where an investment consisting of 20% or more of the equity voting rights of a company (subsidiaries and holdings which are effectively that of a partner in a joint venture or consortium are excluded) is not accounted for by the equity method, details of the accounting treatment adopted and the reasons for doing so should be disclosed by way of note. But where such disclosure would be harmful to the company, the information may be omitted if the auditors concur with the reasons given by the directors. Where the investment is less than 20% and is accounted for by the equity method, a note should disclose the basis on which significant influence is exercised.

(b) Treatment in consolidated profit and loss account

The investing group's share of the pre-tax profits less losses of associated companies should be shown separately in the consolidated profit and loss account as a single item. Other income and expense headings should not include any amounts relating to the associated companies. The tax attributable to this share of profits is included in the group tax charge and disclosed separately.

The group's share of any extraordinary items of associated companies should be included in the group's extraordinary items to the extent that such items would be classified under the criteria of SSAP 6 as an extraordinary item in the context of the investing group's financial statements, and if these are material they should be disclosed separately from other extraordinary items of the group.

The group's share of the profits less losses retained by associated companies should also be disclosed. This is often done by sub-dividing the group retained profit for the year between that retained by the holding company, by subsidiary companies, and by associated companies.

(c) Treatment in consolidated balance sheet

The amount of the investing group's interest in associated companies shown in the consolidated balance sheet should be the total of:

(i) the group's share of the net assets other than goodwill of the associated companies, and

(ii) the group's share of any goodwill in the associated companies' own financial statements, and

(iii) the premium (or discount) on acquisition of the investment in the associated companies in so far as it has not already been written off or amortised.

Item (i) should be shown separately but items (ii) and (iii) may be combined in one amount.

SSAP 1 suggests that for the purpose of determining the amount of the net assets other than goodwill, where possible fair values should be attributed to these assets at the time the acquisition is made. In practice this approach is seldom taken since the consequent adjustments in the annual financial statements are likely to be complex and unlikely to be material. Further it is normally not possible except in those rare circumstances where the associate agrees to co-operate in making a revaluation at the time when the investment is made.

Goodwill arising on the acquisition of an associated company should either be written off immediately against reserves or amortised, according to the same policy as is adopted for other goodwill by the investing company.

The group's share of the post-acquisition accumulated reserves of associated companies (and any movements therein) should be disclosed separately from the other group reserves. The reserves to be disclosed are those which arose during the period in which the investment met the definition of an investment in an associated company. The dates of acquisition and disposal for this purpose are the same as for a subsidiary company, i.e. the earlier of the date on which consideration passes or that on which an offer becomes unconditional.

(d) Accounting adjustments

SSAP 1 indicates that, where material, adjustments which are required when consolidating subsidiaries (such as the elimination of intra-group profits on stocks and to achieve consistency of accounting policies within the group) should also be made when accounting for associated companies in group accounts. In practice difficulty may be encountered in obtaining the information necessary to evaluate any adjustments necessary and only in rare cases are they likely to be material.

(e) Financial statements to be used

The financial statements used for the purpose of including associated company results should be financial statements either co-terminous with those of the investing company or made up to a date which is either not more than six months before, or shortly after, the date of the investing group or company's financial statements. In the case of listed companies, only published financial information should be disclosed.

(f) Additional disclosure requirements

(i) Where the results of an associated company are so material to the investing group that more information about them would assist in giving a true and fair view, this should be provided in a note, disclosing for the associate concerned its total turnover, depreciation charges, profit before taxation and the amount of this profit attributable to the investing group. Similarly more detailed information should be given by way of note about associated companies' assets and liabilities if the interests in such companies are so material that such additional information would assist in giving a true and fair view.

(ii) The names of the principal associated companies, the proportion of the issued shares of each class held and the nature of their businesses should be disclosed.

(iii) If the accumulated reserves of associated companies overseas which are included as reserves in the group balance sheet would be subject to further taxation on distribution, this should be made clear.

(iv) Any significant restrictions on the ability of an associated company to distribute its retained profits because of statutory, contractual or exchange control restrictions should be indicated.

(g) Special situations

(i) Investing company which does not prepare consolidated accounts

Equity accounting is only permitted in consolidated accounts. As indicated earlier investments must be shown in company balance sheets either at a valuation or at cost less provision for diminution in value, while income from investments should be restricted to dividends received and receivable.

When a company does not prepare consolidated accounts, the information concerning associated companies required under equity accounting should be provided either by preparing a separate balance sheet and profit and loss account (additional to the statutory accounts) in which associates are dealt with on an equity accounting basis, or by adding the necessary information in supplementary form to its own balance sheet and profit and loss account.

(ii) Investment trusts

The Association of Investment Trust Companies has advised its members that in respect of their holdings which fall into the definition of associated companies, only those which are themselves investment trusts should be treated in accordance with SSAP 1.

There appear to be three types of associated companies in which investment trusts may have an interest:

(i) other investment trusts;

(ii) companies which carry on a business which is akin to an investment trust (e.g. an investment dealing company or an investment management company);

(iii) other companies.

In the absence of special circumstances there would normally be no reason to depart from SSAP 1 in the case of either (i) or (ii).

In the case of (iii) there would be justification for the results being omitted if their inclusion would be misleading. The reason for the omission should then be stated and if significant, the figures of profit and dividend received should be given by way of note.

It should be noted that in some cases the investment is being held on a short-term basis only (e.g. there may be an intention to float the undertaking by way of an offer of shares to the public). The investment would not come within the definition of an associated company in such circumstances.

(iii) Associate with deficiency of net assets

Where an associated company has a deficiency of net assets, the appropriate accounting treatment depends on the intentions of the investing company in regard to its associate. If the investing company intends to continue to support the company, then its share of the deficiency should be recorded as a liability in the consolidated balance sheet. If the company does not intend to continue support, then it is effectively abandoning its investment which should be written off both in the company's balance sheet and in the consolidated accounts; any loans to the associate should also be written off except to the extent that they can prudently be regarded as recoverable. After these amounts have been written off in the profit and loss account, no further entries should be made in respect of the profits or losses of the associated company.

(iv) Investments in unincorporated entities

Investments in partnerships and unincorporated joint ventures may expose the investing company to losses in excess of the investment made in such entities. This arises from the joint and several liability undertaken by each member of a partnership. Consideration will need to be given to providing for losses in excess of the amount of the investment where it is likely that the investing company will be required to meet its share of losses of defaulted members, or to disclose as a contingent liability the amount of potential losses.

In certain limited circumstances it may be appropriate to account for an investment in non-corporate joint ventures and partnerships in a manner which is sometimes referred to as 'proportionate consolidation'. Under this approach, the investing group's share of the individual assets and liabilities as well as income and expenses of the entity would be included in the amounts shown for the group. Although SSAP 1 recognises that non-corporate joint ventures and partnerships may have features which justify adopting this method, it does not offer any guidance on what these features might be. It is seldom used in practice.

(v) Loss of status as associated company

An investment in a company which no longer meets the definition of an associated company should be included in the consolidated balance sheet at the carrying amount under the equity method at the date of change in status. This amount should be adjusted for dividends subsequently paid out of profits earned before that date and for any provision for impairment in value that is necessary.

12.084 EQUITY METHOD APPLIED TO UNCONSOLIDATED SUBSIDIARIES

SSAP 14 states that the investment in unconsolidated subsidiaries should be accounted for in the consolidated financial statements using the equity method of accounting where exclusion from consolidation is justified for the following reasons:

(i) *Dissimilar activities*

The same method as applied to associated companies (see above) should be applied to subsidiaries which are excluded for this reason. The method will achieve the same consolidated profit for the financial year and the same consolidated share capital and reserves as would have been shown in the consolidated accounts if these subsidiaries had been consolidated.

(ii) *Lack of effective control*

The equity method should be used in these circumstances only if the investment meets the criteria for an associated company under SSAP 1 (i.e. while the holding company may have lost 'effective control', it still exercises significant influence) (see Section 12.061(b)).

(iii) *Severe restrictions*

In these circumstances, the investment should be stated in the consolidated balance sheet at the amount at which it would have been included under the equity method at the date the restrictions came into force (see Section 12.061(c)). During the period of the restrictions, the investment should remain unchanged unless there is a need to make provision for a permanent diminution in value.

12.090 ACQUISITION OR DISPOSAL OF GROUP COMPANIES

The objective of consolidated accounts is to present the financial position and results of the holding company and its subsidiaries as if they were those of a single company from the point of view of the members of the holding company. This generally implies that when a new subsidiary company is purchased by the group, for the purpose of the consolidated financial statements the holding company is treated as having acquired the assets and liabilities as they existed at the date of acquisition at their fair values at that date; consequently any profits earned by the subsidiary prior to the date of acquisition are included in the value of the net assets acquired and cannot be treated as profits of the group in the consolidated profit and loss account. This approach is known as 'acquisition accounting'. There is an alternative approach known as 'merger accounting' which is available under certain circumstances and which is discussed in Section 12.100 below. The sections which follow relate only to acquisition accounting.

12.091 EFFECTIVE DATE OF ACQUISITION OR DISPOSAL

SSAP 14 states that the effective date for both acquisitions and disposals of subsidiaries should be the earlier of:

(i) the date on which consideration passes; or

(ii) the date on which an offer becomes or is declared unconditional.

The consolidated profit and loss account should include the results of subsidiaries, beginning with the effective date of their acquisition and ending with the effective date of their disposal, even though the buyer under the purchase agreement may share in the profits of the acquired business from an earlier date.

Normally financial statements drawn up to the effective date are not available and for practical reasons it will be necessary to apportion the results on a time, turnover, or other appropriate basis, based on the audited financial statements issued after the effective date. Where reliable interim financial statements or latest audited financial statements are drawn up to a date sufficiently near the effective date, these may be used.

Some companies follow the practice of including the full year's results of a subsidiary acquired during the year in the group profit on ordinary activities before taxation, the pre-acquisition portion being shown as a single line deduction after 'profit after taxation' to arrive at the profit attributable to shareholders of the holding company. This practice should be discouraged except where the acquired subsidiary has a seasonal trading pattern and the effect of including only the post-acquisition results in the consolidated profit and loss account would distort the true and fair view. In this case, the financial statements or notes should disclose the amounts included in turnover, profit on ordinary activities before tax, taxation and other profit and loss information which relate to pre-acquisition trading.

12.092 ALLOCATION OF PURCHASE CONSIDERATION

When a group of assets is acquired for a single consideration, it is necessary to apportion the total cost to each of the separate assets in the group. Similarly, in the consolidation process it is necessary to apportion the cost of the investment in a subsidiary to the relevant assets and liabilities at the date of acquisition. SSAP 14 requires the purchase consideration to be allocated between the underlying net tangible and intangible assets other than goodwill on the basis of the fair value to the acquiring company. The difference between the fair value of the net tangible and intangible assets of the acquired subsidiary and the purchase consideration represents a premium or discount on acquisition (i.e. goodwill or negative goodwill). The various methods of dealing with goodwill are discussed in Section 6.024.

(a) Determination of purchase price

When assets other than cash are given as part of the consideration for the purchase of shares it is necessary to ascertain the value of these assets in order to determine the value of the total consideration given.

The most usual consideration other than cash consists of new shares in the acquiring company and if the new shares are to be equivalent to existing listed shares, a common practice is to value them by reference to the price of the listed shares at the effective date of purchase. However this may not always be a fair measure of the value of the consideration since the price at the date of acquisition will take account of the anticipated effect of the acquisition. The price of the listed shares when the proposed acquisition is first announced is often a fairer measure of the value of the consideration given.

(b) Fair value of acquired company

No guidance is given in any SSAP as to what constitutes the fair value of the net tangible and intangible assets of the acquired company. Values attached to specific assets and liabilities in a vending agreement or in negotiating positions are not necessarily conclusive as to the fair value. It is recommended that the following valuation bases should be applied to the specific balance sheet items:

Debtors	– the expected cash recoverable.
Stocks	– the lower of replacement cost or net realisable value. (In most situations, the value shown in the books of the acquired company will closely approximate this value).
Marketable assets such as investments	– current market value.
Fixed tangible assets	– existing use basis, which normally will be the depreciated replacement cost of the asset. No consideration should be given to any change in use of the asset unless the change in use was contemplated at the time of purchase. Any assets which are not intended to continue in use should be valued at net realisable value.
Intangible assets other than goodwill	– current market value or director's valuation of those assets which can be separately identified, i.e. patents, concession, franchises, favourable leases.
Liabilities	– the amounts payable for all outstanding liabilities and required provisions, including unfavourable leases, plant closure and other reorganisation costs expected to arise as a result of the acquisition.

The explanatory note to SSAP 22 includes anticipated future losses amongst the items for which provision should be made but this should be interpreted with caution. The anticipation of substantial future losses over a significant period is inconsistent with a material payment for goodwill; it is suggested that where the consideration includes any significant element of goodwill any provision for anticipated future losses should be restricted to clearly identifiable amounts arising over a short period which can be expected with reasonable confidence to occur. On the other hand if the purchase consideration is less than the fair values of the net assets, this may well be due to the anticipation of future losses over a rather longer period.

In determining the acquisition price, the purchasing company may take account of liabilities or potential liabilities which under its accounting policies are not reflected in the balance sheet, such as potential liabilities for redundancy pay, the total potential liability for deferred tax, or contingent liabilities. Such items should be taken into account only to the extent that it is appropriate to recognise them in the consolidated balance sheet, e.g. liabilities for redundancy pay should be recognised only to the extent that payment can be foreseen and contingencies should only be included if it is probable that a loss will arise.

Where the initial determination of fair values of the separable net assets gives rise to negative goodwill, the values should be reviewed carefully to ensure that assets have not been overstated and liabilities have not been overlooked. Further consideration should also be given to the basis used to determine fair value; in particular, depreciated replacement cost may not provide a fair value for fixed assets being used in a business which is presently insufficiently profitable. Net realisable value may be a more appropriate basis in such circumstances.

(c) Contingent purchase consideration

Some agreements provide for the payment of additional purchase consideration contingent upon the occurrence of some future event. For example, an agreement might provide for the payment of an agreed sum upon signing of the agreement plus an additional amount if the future earnings of the acquired company exceed a stipulated amount.

The best estimate of the additional purchase consideration which is likely to be payable should be recorded at the effective date of acquisition of the subsidiary. Any remaining portion of the purchase consideration which cannot be determined with reasonable certainty should be recorded at the time the uncertainty is removed. A note should disclose the contingent liability under the agreement and it should quantify the maximum additional payment, if possible, and the effect on goodwill.

If the additional consideration is to be satisfied by the issue of additional shares at some future date, the best estimate of the value of the number of shares to be issued (using the market value of such shares at that time) should be recorded as a non-current liability, with a note explaining that the liability is to be satisfied by the issue of shares giving rise to additional share capital and share premium account indicating also the contingent factors surrounding the number of shares to be issued and the effect on goodwill. The number of such shares which it is expected will be issued should be taken into account in calculating fully diluted earnings per share.

12.093 DETERMINATION OF GAIN OR LOSS ON DISPOSAL

SSAP 14 states that the gain or loss on sale of a subsidiary should be the difference at the time of sale between the proceeds of sale and the holding company's share of its net assets together with any premium (less any amounts written off) or discount on acquisition.

In the accounts of the investing company the profit or loss on sale will be the difference between the cost of the investment and the proceeds of sale. Part of this difference represents the profit or loss of the subsidiary which is already reflected in the last consolidated balance sheet, part represents the profit or loss from the beginning of the current financial year to the date of sale which is included as a trading item in the group profit and loss account, and the balance represents the profit or loss on sale of the subsidiary to be disclosed in the group profit and loss account. If any assets of the subsidiary have been revalued, then any balance on the group revaluation reserve in respect of the subsidiary must be released at the date of sale; the amount released should be added to the profit on sale of the subsidiary in the group profit and loss account.

For example, assume the following:

	£
A purchased the whole of the issued capital of B for	*100,000*
The undistributed post-acquisition profits of B at 31 December 1983 amounted to	*120,000*
The profit after tax of B for the six months to 30 June 1984 is estimated at	*30,000*
A sold the whole share capital of B on 30 June 1984 for	*300,000*

In A's own accounts the transaction results in a profit of £200,000 (sale price of £300,000 less cost of £100,000). Of this amount:

- £120,000, being the undistributed post-acquisition profit, is already included in the group accounts as part of the balance of group profit and loss account;
- £30,000 represents the trading profit to the date of sale which should be included in the group profit and loss account in the current year; and
- £50,000 is the balance to be recognised in the group profit and loss account as the profit on sale of the subsidiary.

12.094 ACQUISITION OF A SUBSIDIARY OVER A PERIOD OF TIME

Where one company becomes a subsidiary of another as a result of a number of separate acquisitions of shares over a period of time, there are two alternative methods of determining the amount to be regarded as pre-acquisition reserves for the purpose of consolidation. These are:

(i) to calculate the pre-acquisition reserve separately in respect of each separate purchase, and

(ii) to calculate the pre-acquisition reserve by reference only to the position on the date the company became a subsidiary.

These alternative methods are illustrated in the following example:

Assume the financial year end is 31 December.

Date of purchase	*Portion acquired*	*Reserves of subsidiary*	*Pre-acquisition reserves (Method (i))*
		£	*£*
31/12/82	*20%*	*100,000*	*20,000*
31/12/83	*25%*	*120,000*	*30,000*
31/12/84	*25%*	*200,000*	*50,000*
			100,000

Under the first method the pre-acquisition reserves are £100,000, calculated as shown in the last column.

Under the second method the pre-acquisition reserves are 70% of £200,000, i.e. £140,000.

It is suggested that the choice of method depends on whether equity accounting has been applied to the investment before the holding/subsidiary relationship was established. The first method should be used starting from the date on which equity accounting was first used since from that date the group's share of the post-acquisition reserves will already have been reflected in the consolidated profit and loss account. The second method is more appropriate for purchases before equity accounting is adopted.

In the example given, if equity accounting had been applied from the date of the first purchase on 31/12/82 then the first method is the correct approach and the pre-acquisition reserves should be set at £100,000. The effect of applying the second method would be to convert £40,000 which had previously been recognised as post-acquisition profit into pre-acquisition. On the other hand if for any reason equity accounting had not previously been applied, then the second method is preferable, since the first method would result in an immediate addition to post-acquisition reserves of £40,000 in respect of prior year's profits which had not been previously recognised in the accounts.

12.095 NEW ISSUE OF SHARES BY SUBSIDIARY

If a subsidiary issues new shares in circumstances whereby the holding company acquires more or less than its pro-rata share of the new issue, and the consideration is other than exactly equal to the net asset value per share as shown in the subsidiary's accounts, then the holding company's share of the book value of the net assets of the subsidiary will rise or fall by an amount different from the consideration which it paid for any new shares acquired.

It is suggested that this difference is best regarded as representing an adjustment to the value of the goodwill of the subsidiary which is not recorded in its books and it should be carried direct to reserves in accordance with the principles of SSAP 22.

If the effect of the transaction is to change the status of the investment from that of a subsidiary to that of an associated company, then the consolidated balance sheet should be adjusted to eliminate the assets and liabilities of the subsidiary, the equivalent net asset amount being shown as an investment in an associated company.

12.100 MERGER ACCOUNTING

The following is a brief description of the theory underlying merger accounting:

(i) When two companies are combined in one group on terms that the equity shareholders in each company become the equity shareholders in the combined entity, the substance of the transaction is that the two sets of shareholders have pooled their interests in their respective companies even though the form may be an acquisition of one by the other.

(ii) An essential feature of a pooling of interests is that the net assets of the combined company should be substantially the same as the net assets of the individual companies prior to the merger, i.e. no significant resources should leave the group, in cash or otherwise, incidentally to the merger.

(iii) The best way of accounting for a pooling of interests under such circumstances is to prepare accounts as if the two companies had always been one.

The practical effects of this approach are that the net assets of the two companies are combined using existing book values, the new shares issued as consideration for the merger are entered at their nominal amount (their fair value being ignored), no amount is recognised as consideration for goodwill or negative goodwill, and substantially all the distributable reserves of each company remain available for distribution by the combined group. The consolidated profit and loss account includes the profits of each company for the entire period regardless of the date of the merger, and the corresponding amounts in the consolidated accounts are restated to the aggregate of the amounts recorded by the two companies. The only exception is the disclosure of the emoluments of directors and higher paid employees (see Section 12.103(d) below).

The only adjustment that may be necessary for consolidation is to eliminate any difference between the carrying amount of the investment shown in the acquiring company's balance sheet and the nominal value of the shares acquired; this amount is added to or deducted from group reserves. The carrying amount of the investment is equal to the nominal value of the shares issued as consideration, subject to a possible small adjustment if cash or any other consideration was also involved.

A merger usually takes the form of an issue by one company of its own equity shares, as consideration for the acquisition of the equity capital of the other, but it may also take other forms, such as the creation of a new holding company which issues its own equity shares in exchange for the equity capital of two or more other companies.

12.101 COMPARISON OF MERGER VS ACQUISITION ACCOUNTING

The difference between merger accounting and acquisition accounting is best illustrated by an example.

Upper Ltd, makes an offer for the shares of Lower Ltd., which is accepted as at 31 December 1984, the year end of both companies. At that date, the summarised accounts of the two companies were as follows:

	Upper Ltd. £'000	**Lower Ltd.** £'000
Balance sheets at 31 December 1984		
Sundry net assets	*350*	*300*
Share capital (shares of £1 each)	*150*	*50*
Distributable reserves	*200*	*250*
	350	*300*
Profit for the financial year		
1984	*70*	*30*
1983	*60*	*80*

Under the offer, Upper issues 100,000 shares in exchange for all of the 50,000 shares of Lower. Assume a fair value of £3.50 for each Upper share and a fair value of the net tangible assets of Lower of £320,000.

Merger accounting

Using merger accounting, Upper would record the investment in subsidiary in its books at £100,000 (i.e. the nominal value of the 100,000 shares issued by Upper) and the only difference to be eliminated on consolidation is the difference between the nominal value of the issued capital of Lower Limited of £50,000 and the nominal value of the shares in Upper Limited issued to acquire it. This difference is adjusted on the group reserves. With this exception the consolidated accounts are simply the aggregation of the accounts of the two separate companies.

Acquisition accounting

Under acquisition accounting, Upper would record the investment in subsidiary (i.e. the 100,000 shares of Lower acquired) in its books at £350,000 (100,000 x £3.50). The excess of £350,000 over the £100,000 nominal value of the shares issued must be credited to a separate reserve. On consolidation, the excess of the investment (£350,000) over the fair value of the tangible net assets of Lower (£320,000) would be treated as goodwill on consolidation.

The effects

The respective consolidated balance sheets at 31 December 1984 would be as follows:

	Merger Accounting	**Acquisition Accounting**
	£'000	*£'000*
Sundry net assets	*650*	*670 (1)*
Share capital	*250*	*250*
Merger reserve	*–*	*220 (2)*
Distributable reserves	*400 (3)*	*200*
	650	*670*
Group profit for 1984	*100*	*70 (4)*
Corresponding amount for 1983	*140 (5)*	*60*

Notes:

(1) Under acquisition accounting the net assets of Lower are included at their fair value at date of acquisition (£320,000). Under merger accounting, they are included at their book amount of £300,000.

(2) The merger reserve represents the excess of the fair value of the shares issued over their par value (£250,000) less the goodwill arising on consolidation (£30,000) which is written off to reserves immediately. If relief had not been available under the Act (see below) the excess of fair value over par value of £250,000 would have had to be treated as Share Premium Account and goodwill would have been written off the distributable reserves.

(3) The distributable reserve under merger accounting is the aggregate of the distributable reserves of the individual companies (£450,000) less the difference between the nominal value of the shares issued and the nominal value of the shares acquired (£50,000).

(4) Since the acquisition took place at 31 December 1984, all the profits of Lower prior to that date are pre-acquisition and are not available under acquisition accounting.

(5) Under merger accounting, corresponding amounts are restated to include the profits of Lower for 1983.

12.102 RESTRICTIONS ON USE OF MERGER ACCOUNTING

(a) The legal position

The Act contains measures to facilitate merger accounting. [s 131] Briefly it gives relief from the requirement to transfer a premium arising on the issue of shares to the share premium account in specified circumstances. These are that the issuing company has secured at least a 90% equity holding in another company, and that the consideration for the new shares allotted is provided by the issue or transfer to the issuing company of equity shares in the other company (or by the cancellation of shares not held by the issuing company). The amount of the premium that would otherwise have to be transferred to share premium account may also be disregarded for the purpose of determining the carrying amount of the investment in the company's balance sheet.

The Act also gives relief from any statutory restrictions on the availability for distribution of the pre-acquisition profits of the subsidiary under these circumstances.

(b) SSAP 23 – Accounting for acquisitions and mergers

This statement defines the criteria which must be met before merger accounting may be used to account for a business combination. It should be noted that acquisition accounting may always be used to account for any business combination. The statement indicates that a business combination may be, but is not required to be, accounted for as a merger if all of the following conditions are met:

(i) the business combination results from an offer to holders of all equity shares and all voting shares not already held by the offeror;

(ii) the offeror has secured, as a result of the offer, at least 90% of all equity shares (taking each class of equity separately) and shares carrying at least 90% of all votes of the offeree company;

(iii) immediately prior to the offer, the offeror does not hold 20% or more of all equity shares of the offeree (taking each class of equity separately) or shares carrying at least 20% or more of the votes of the offeree company;

(iv) not less than 90% of the fair value of the total consideration given for the equity shares (including that given for shares already held) is in the form of equity shares; and not less than 90% of the fair value of the consideration given for voting non equity shares (including that given for shares already held) should be in equity and/or voting non-equity shares.

Any convertible stock outstanding is not to be regarded as equity except to the extent that it is converted into equity as a result of and at the time of the business combination.

Condition (iii) above will not permit merger accounting to be applied to any acquisition if the company already holds more than 20% of the equity or voting share capital of the offeree and condition (iv) limits the non-equity portion of the consideration to no more than 10% of the fair value of the total consideration.

Those business combinations which fail to meet all of the above conditions must be accounted for using acquisition accounting rules.

12.103 SPECIAL CONSIDERATIONS IN MERGER ACCOUNTING

(a) Uniform accounting policies

As indicated in Section 12.071 above, it is desirable that all companies in the group should follow uniform accounting policies, and where this is not done appropriate adjustments must be made in the consolidated financial statements to achieve uniformity. This requirement is equally applicable when merger accounting is adopted. Thus although book amounts rather than fair values of the net assets of the merged subsidiary are used for the purpose of consolidation, these book amounts should first be adjusted to the extent necessary to achieve uniformity in accounting policies.

(b) Restatement of comparative figures

As indicated above, the corresponding amounts in consolidated accounts should be restated as if the companies had been combined throughout the previous period and at the previous balance sheet date. This requires a restatement of the called up share capital at the preceding balance sheet date to reflect the nominal value of the new shares subsequently issued to acquire the merged company. If there is any cash or non-share element in the consideration, this must also be reflected in the preceding balance sheet as a reduction in cash at bank or increase in overdrafts or other liabilities, as appropriate.

(c) Statement of reserves

The reserves at the beginning of the year must be adjusted to indicate the reserves of the merged companies. A further adjustment is necessary to take account of any difference between the carrying value of the investment in the accounts of the holding company (i.e. the nominal value of the shares issued to acquire the subsidiary together with any cash consideration) and the nominal value of the shares acquired. This difference should be treated as a reserve arising on consolidation or as a reduction of reserves. There is no specific requirement in SSAP 23 to disclose this adjustment separately and there seems to be little merit in doing so.

SSAP 23 is silent on how the expenses in connection with the merger should be dealt with. The method which seems most appropriate to the concept of accounting as if the combining companies had always been one is to write off the expenses of the merger directly against the combined reserves in the group accounts and this method is therefore recommended. However ED 36 proposes that all profits and losses recognised in the financial statements for the year should be included in the profit and loss account except for those items which are specifically permitted by law or accounting standards to be taken direct to reserves. If it is adopted in its present form, it may therefore be interpreted as prohibiting the charging of merger expenses direct to reserves and it is to be hoped that this requirement will be modified or clarified following exposure.

An example of a suitable statement of reserves following a merger is given below.

EXAMPLE

	Profit and loss account £'000	*Revaluation reserves £'000*	*Other reserves £'000*
Balance, beginning of year			
As previously reported	*13,450*	*1,283*	–
Reserves of merged companies	*5,991*	*588*	*250*
As restated	*19,441*	*1,871*	*250*
Expenses of merger	*(175)*	–	–
Profit retained for the year	*2,770*	–	–
Balance, end of year	*22,036*	*1,871*	*250*

(d) Remuneration of directors and higher paid employees

In determining the disclosures to be made in relation to the emoluments of directors and higher paid employees [Sections 5.151(c) and 5.152], only directors and higher paid employees of the holding company, and only their emoluments during the period when they had that status should be considered. For example, if a director of the acquired company becomes a director of the acquiring company on the merger, the emoluments to be reported are restricted to those which he received following the merger. (The full emoluments for the financial year will of course be reported in the acquired company's own accounts.)

(e) Accounting period covered by a newly formed holding company

When a merger is effected by setting up a new holding company which acquires the issued shares of the merging company in exchange for the issue of its own, it frequently happens that the first accounting reference period of the new company is less than a year ending on the accounting reference date chosen for the group. This will normally be the existing accounting reference date of one or more of the merging companies.

In these circumstances, although the holding company is a new company and in consequence its own balance sheet will show no corresponding amounts, the group accounts will consolidate the accounts of the merging subsidiaries for the whole of the year (not merely for the post-incorporation period) and will also disclose corresponding amounts in respect of the previous year.

As indicated above however the disclosure required in respect of emoluments of directors and higher paid employees is only of the emoluments in the post merger period of those who were directors and higher paid employees of the holding company. Companies may however wish also to disclose on a voluntary basis the emoluments received for the full year by holding company directors who were also executives of one or more of the merged subsidiaries.

(f) Fair value of consideration given

A difficult problem on which no guidance is given in SSAP 23 is how to determine the fair value of shares given as part of the consideration for the shares to be acquired. This information is necessary if the consideration is not all in equity shares to establish whether the test specified in Section

12.102(b)(iv) above has been met, and in any case is required by SSAP 23 to be disclosed. In the absence of such guidance it is considered that the value can only be determined by the directors who must exercise their judgment on the basis of the information available to them. If the shares to be issued are identical with shares already listed on a stock exchange, then the market price of the listed shares at the time when the offer is made is clearly significant information to be taken into account, but is not necessarily conclusive evidence as to fair value. It is thought that the market price of the listed shares after the offer has been announced is not evidence as to the fair value of the consideration since at that time the market will be reacting to the news of the offer and may be attempting to place a value on the combined entity. An important advantage of this approach is that the directors know at the time when they make the offer whether or not merger accounting will be available to them if the offer is successful.

(g) Contingent purchase consideration

Where a business combination which has been treated as a merger provides for the issue of additional shares upon the occurrence of some future event (e.g. the achieving of profit goals in subsequent periods), the issue of additional shares will result in an increase in share capital and a corresponding decrease in reserves equal to the par value of such shares. No provision in respect of the contingent purchase consideration should be made in the accounts at the time of the merger, but the notes to the accounts should disclose the particulars of the contingency in sufficient detail to allow the potential impact on the share capital and reserves to be appreciated.

If the contingent purchase consideration also involves cash payments, the best estimate of the future cash payments will need to be considered when deciding on whether the combination qualifies to be treated as a merger (see Section 12.102(b) above). The approach in respect of the cash element of any contingent purchase consideration should follow the recommendations given in Section 12.092(c) above.

12.104 DISPOSALS OF ASSETS FOLLOWING A MERGER

Merger accounting results in the investment in the merged subsidiary being included in the balance sheet of the holding company at the nominal value of the shares issued to acquire it and the underlying assets being reflected in the group accounts at book values. If, as is common, the holding company's own shares command a substantial premium over their nominal value, both the investment and the underlying assets are brought into the accounts at an undervalue. In consequence it is possible in these circumstances for an acquiring company to create large profits by selling either shares in a subsidiary or significant assets of the subsidiary shortly after the merger has taken place.

To deal with this situation Sch 4: 75 requires disclosures in regard to certain sales of shares and assets (including indirect sales) of a subsidiary company if the subsidiary was acquired during the financial year or either of the two preceding financial years in circumstances that the relief provisions of s 131 (see Section 12.102(a)) applied in relation to the shares issued for the purpose of the acquisition. It should be noted that the disclosure is required if s 131 applied even if merger accounting was not used to account for the purchase. The matters to be disclosed are:

(i) any profit or loss realised on the disposal of shares in the acquired company or on the disposal of any assets which were fixed assets of the acquired company or its subsidiaries at the time of the allotment; and

(ii) any part of any profit or loss realised on disposal by the group of any shares in a company (not being shares in the acquired company) which was attributable to the fact that at the time of the disposal there were amongst the assets of that company or its subsidiaries such shares or assets mentioned in (i) above;

together with an explanation of the transactions. If consolidated financial statements are not prepared, this information is to be given in the issuing company's financial statements.

12.110 DISCLOSURES REQUIRED IN RESPECT OF SUBSIDIARIES ACQUIRED OR SOLD

(a) General

SSAP 23 requires the following information to be disclosed in respect of all material business combinations which have taken place during the financial year, whether accounted for as an acquisition or a merger:

(i) the names of the combining companies;

(ii) the number and class of securities issued in respect of the combination, and details of any other consideration given;

(iii) the accounting treatment adopted for the business combination (i.e. whether it has been accounted for as an acquisition or a merger);

(iv) the nature and amount of significant accounting adjustments by the combining companies to achieve consistency of accounting policies.

(b) Additional disclosures in respect of mergers

The following information must be given by way of note to the accounts where during the financial year the company allotted shares in consideration for the issue, transfer, or cancellation of shares in another company under an arrangement in which the merger relief provisions of s 131 apply [Sch 4: 75]:

(i) the name of the acquired company;

(ii) the number, nominal value and class of shares allotted;

(iii) the number, nominal value and class of shares in the acquired company so issued, transferred or cancelled;

(iv) particulars of the accounting treatment adopted in respect of the shares in the acquired company issued, transferred or cancelled; and

(v) particulars of the effect on the group profit and loss of the inclusion of pre-acquisition profit or loss of the acquired company or any of its subsidiaries.

It should be noted that this information must be provided whenever the relief provided by s 131 applies (see Section 12.102(a)) whether or not merger accounting is in fact used.

SSAP 23 also requires the following to be disclosed where an acquisition made during the financial year is accounted for as a merger:

(i) the fair value of the consideration given by the issuing company;

(ii) an analysis of the current year's attributable profit before extraordinary items between that before and after the effective date of merger;

(iii) an analysis of the attrributable profit before extraordinary items of the current year up to the effective date of the merger and of the previous year between that of the issuing company and that of the subsidiary; and

(iv) an analysis of each individual extraordinary item between pre- or post-merger events and indicating to which party to the merger the items relate.

(c) Additional disclosures in respect of acquisitions and disposals

SSAP 14 requires consolidated financial statements to contain sufficient information about the results of material subsidiaries acquired or disposed of in the period to enable the shareholders to appreciate the effect on the consolidated results. The statement gives no guidance as to what constitutes a material acquisition or disposal and what is sufficient information. The following guidance is offered.

If the profit on ordinary activities before taxation or turnover of the acquired or sold subsidiary exceeds 5% of the group's annual earnings, or turnover, the acquisition or disposal should be considered material. Also any transaction which would fall into The Stock Exchange's definition of a Class I or Class II acquisition, which will require disclosure to be made to The Stock Exchange and the press, should be considered material. The 5% criterion is consistent with the minimum percentage used to determine a Class II acquisition.

It is suggested that the information to be given should be the turnover and profit or loss on ordinary activities after taxation included in the consolidated profit and loss account and the corresponding amounts for the preceding financial year of the company being acquired or sold.

SSAP 23 requires the effective date of all major acquisitions to be disclosed. Although it is not specifically required, it also seems appropriate to disclose the effective date of major disposals.

13 ACCOUNTING FOR FOREIGN CURRENCY TRANSACTIONS

13.010 INTRODUCTION

A company may undertake foreign currency activities in two ways:

(i) it may enter directly into transactions denominated in a foreign currency; and

(ii) it may operate through an investment in a foreign enterprise which maintains its accounting records in a foreign currency.

The methods of accounting for foreign currency transactions under both sets of circumstances have been standardised by SSAP 20.

13.020 PREPARATION OF FINANCIAL STATEMENTS OF INDIVIDUAL COMPANIES

13.021 INITIAL RECORDING OF TRANSACTIONS

The initial recording in the accounting records of a transaction denominated in a foreign currency should normally be made in the entity's local currency by using the rate of exchange appropriate to the transaction.

(i) if the contract provides for the transaction to be settled at a specified rate of exchange, then that is the rate appropriate to the transaction;

(ii) if the rate at which the transaction will be settled has been fixed by entering into a matching forward contract to buy or sell the foreign currency concerned, then the rate established in the forward contract is the rate appropriate to the transaction;

(iii) in all other cases the rate appropriate to the transaction is the rate ruling at the date on which the transaction occurs.

It is a common practice among companies which engage in a large number of foreign currency transactions to fix for a period the rate of exchange at which they record those transactions in their accounting records and to disregard day to day fluctuations in exchange rates. Where this approach is used care must be taken to ensure that the carrying value of non-monetary assets, particularly stocks, is not materially different from what it would have been if actual rates had been used for translation. It is suggested that only the actual rate appropriate to the transaction should be used to record the acquisition of fixed assets.

13.022 NON-MONETARY ASSETS

Non-monetary assets, such as stocks, fixed tangible assets and equity investments, normally require no further translation as these balances reflect the historical cost of acquiring the assets. For the purpose of determining the net realisable value of current assets the rate ruling at the balance sheet date should normally be used. If any asset is valued in accordance with any of the alternative valuation rules, then the rate to be used for this purpose is that ruling at the date of the valuation.

The special considerations which apply where foreign equity investments are hedged by foreign currency borrowings are described in Section 13.040.

13.023 MONETARY ASSETS AND LIABILITIES

Amounts receivable or payable which represent the settlement of open transactions should be recorded at the rate appropriate to the transaction if this is fixed either by being specified in the contract or by a matching forward contract. With this exception all monetary assets and liabilities, such as cash and bank balances, debtors and creditors, which are denominated in foreign currencies should be translated into the local currency using the rates of exchange ruling at the balance sheet date.

13.024 EXCHANGE GAINS AND LOSSES

Exchange gains and losses arise from exchange rate movements between the time transactions are first recorded in the accounting records (or the beginning of the year in respect of unsettled balances) and when they are settled. They also arise on unsettled transactions when the exchange rate at the balance sheet date differs from the rates at which the transactions are recorded in the accounts.

EXAMPLE

Assume Company A with a year-end of 31 December purchased goods abroad on 1 December 1984 when the exchange rate was £1 = $1.60, payment of $24,000 to be made on 26 January 1985. The invoice should be recorded in the bought ledger at £15,000 ($24,000 ÷ 1.60). If the exchange rate at the year end was £1 = $1.58, the bought ledger balance must be translated into sterling using the year end rate, increasing the liability to £15,190 ($24,000 ÷ 1.58). The loss of £190 arising from the adverse movement of the US dollar between the purchase date and the year end date should be charged as an exchange loss in the profit and loss account. If at the settlement date of 26 January 1985 sterling had strengthened to £1 = $1.62, the liability would be settled for £14,815 and an exchange gain of £375 (being the difference between the previous translated amount and the settlement) should be credited to the profit and loss account in the year ending 31 December 1985.

Exchange gains and losses should be recognised as profits or losses from ordinary activities unless they arise from transactions which are themselves extraordinary, in which case they should be included as part of the relevant extraordinary item. Gains and losses arising from trading transactions should normally be included in the profit and loss account under 'Other operating income or expense' and those arising from financing arrangements should be included under 'Other interest receivable/payable and similar income/expense'.

In SSAP 20 a distinction is drawn between those monetary items which are short-term, i.e. which fall due within one year of the balance sheet date, and those which are long-term. In regard to long-term items only it is stated that it is necessary in exceptional circumstances to consider on the grounds of prudence whether 'the amount of the gain, or the amount by which exchange gains exceed past exchange losses on the same items to be recognised in the profit and loss account, should be restricted'. The exceptional circumstances arise 'where there are doubts as to the convertibility or marketability of the currency in question'. It is hard to understand what is intended by this requirement and in particular why it should apply to long-term items but not to short-term ones. If convertibility or marketability problems exist when the financial statements are being prepared, they affect all monetary items in that currency equally and restricting the recognition of apparent exchange gains is unlikely to be a sufficient response to the problem.

In SSAP 20 it is stated in the section dealing with legal requirements in the U.K. that exchange gains arising on unsettled long-term monetary items are unrealised. This statement is surprising in view of the definition of realised profits in Sch 4: 91. Its consequence is that the recognition of such gains in the profit and loss account (which is required by SSAP 20) must be regarded as a departure from one of the accounting principles prescribed by the Act. Therefore when material gains on unsettled long-term monetary items are included in the profit and loss account, it is necessary to disclose particulars of the departure from the accounting principle, the reasons for it, and its effect in a note to the accounts.

EXAMPLE

The profit and loss account includes unrealised exchange gains of £243,000 (1983, £156,000) arising from unsettled long-term monetary items. The directors consider this departure from the statutory requirement to include only realised profits in the profit and loss account necessary in order for the financial statements to give a true and fair view.

13.030 TRANSLATION OF FINANCIAL STATEMENTS OF FOREIGN ENTERPRISES

Once a foreign enterprise's own financial statements have been prepared in its local currency in accordance with the rules described in Section 13.021, they must then be translated into the reporting currency of the investing company or group before they can be incorporated into the investing company's own financial statements or the group's consolidated financial statements.

The translation rules for this purpose set out in SSAP 20 apply to financial statements of foreign subsidiaries, associated companies, and branches of the investing company. For this purpose a foreign branch can be either a legally constituted enterprise located overseas or simply a group of assets and liabilities which are accounted for in a foreign currency (e.g. a ship purchased in foreign currency with associated loans, revenue and expenses recorded in the foreign currency).

The standard requires one of two translation methods to be applied to each foreign enterprise, depending upon the economic environment in which that enterprise operates. The closing rate/net investment method (the 'net investment' method) of translation should be applied to the local currency financial statements of those foreign enterprises in the group which operate as separate or quasi-independent entities from that of the investing company. The temporal method should be applied to foreign enterprises whose affairs are so closely connected with those of the investing company as to constitute an extension of the economic environment of the investing company. Once adopted, these methods should be applied consistently from period to period unless the financial and other operational relationships between the enterprise and the investing company change. These methods are described in Sections 13.031 and 13.032 below.

13.031 CLOSING RATE/NET INVESTMENT METHOD

Under the net investment method, balance sheet assets and liabilities should be translated using the closing rate of exchange. The profit and loss account should be translated either at the closing rate or at an average rate for the period. The standard does not prescribe the method of calculating the average rate, but any method which appropriately weights the calculation to take account of the volume of transactions during the period will be acceptable. For example a foreign entity which translates monthly accounts into the reporting currency at each month end rate and accumulates these monthly results to produce the full year's results will have effectively used an appropriate weighted average rate.

Exchange differences will arise from the retranslation of:

(i) the opening net investment at the closing rate compared to the exchange rate ruling at the end of the previous year; and similarly any capital injections at the closing rate compared to the exchange rate ruling at the date of such injections; and

(ii) the profit or loss for the financial year at the closing rate compared to the average exchange rate where this rate was used to translate the profit and loss account.

These exchange differences are dealt with by direct transfer to or from reserves.

It is suggested that if foreign exchange translation differences dealt with through reserves constitute in the aggregate a material balance, they should be disclosed as a separate reserve entitled 'Foreign exchange translation'; otherwise they should be included in the balance of profit and loss account.

The net investment is defined by SSAP 20 as the company's effective equity stake in the foreign enterprise and comprises its share of the enterprise's net assets. The net investment will be the proportion of share capital and reserves of the enterprise attributable to the investor's holdings but in addition it may include long-term intra-group loans and other deferred balances where these are regarded as equivalent to a permanent equity stake.

Where loans or other deferred balances are regarded by an investing company as equivalent to a permanent equity stake then they should be so treated for all purposes. In particular the investing company should treat the loan or balance as a non-monetary item in its own balance sheet and retain it at historical cost, i.e. assuming that the balance is denominated in the foreign currency (which will normally be most convenient), it should be translated at the rate ruling when it was first recognised as constituting permanent equity.

If the loan is denominated in the currency of the investing company, it should be treated in the accounts of the enterprise receiving it as a non-monetary item and translated at the rate ruling when it was first recognised as constituting permanent equity. If it is necessary to adopt a different translation policy in order to comply with local regulations, then an adjustment should be made before the accounts are consolidated with those of the investing company.

13.032 TEMPORAL METHOD

The temporal method should be applied to financial statements of a foreign enterprise whose affairs 'are so closely interlinked with those of the investing company that its results may be regarded as being more dependent on the economic environment of the investing company's currency than that of its own reporting currency'. Some of the factors which need to be considered in determining whether the temporal method should be used are given in SSAP 20 as follows:

(i) the extent to which the cash flows of the enterprise have a direct impact upon those of the investing company;

(ii) the extent to which the functioning of the enterprise is dependent directly upon the investing company;

(iii) the currency in which the majority of the trading transactions are denominated;

(iv) the major currency to which the operation is exposed in its financing structure.

Situations where the temporal method is appropriate might include foreign enterprises whose principal activities include:

(i) selling of goods received from the investing company, the proceeds of which are remitted back to that company;

(ii) manufacturing of components or sub-assemblies to be included in the investing company's own products;

(iii) raising of finance for other companies in the group.

Under the temporal method, all transactions and balances are treated as if they were directly entered into by the investing company itself, i.e. as described in Section 13.021 above. Thus the translation procedures to be applied to the foreign entity's financial statements are as follows:

Items	***Exchange rate to be used***
Non-monetary items	
Fixed assets carried at:	
(i) historical cost	– historical rate, i.e. the rate ruling at the date the transaction was established.
(ii) valuation	– rate ruling at the date of the valuation.
Stocks and current asset investments carried at:	
(i) historical cost	– historical rates.
(ii) net realisable value	– closing rate.
Monetary items	
All other assets and liabilities	– closing rate.
Profit and loss account	
Cost of sales	
Opening and closing stocks	– at the rates used for balance sheet purposes.
Depreciation	– historical rates, i.e. the same rates as applied to the asset being depreciated.
All other income and expense items	– average rate.

All differences arising on translation are taken to profit and loss account.

13.033 FOREIGN ENTERPRISE EXPERIENCING HYPER-INFLATION

It is acknowledged in SSAP 20 that where a foreign enterprise operates in a country in which there is a very high rate of inflation, it may not be possible to present fairly the financial position of that foreign enterprise simply by applying a translation process to historical cost accounts. (A very high rate of inflation is not defined). It is suggested that in such circumstances the local currency financial statements should be adjusted where possible to reflect current price levels before the translation process is undertaken. This restatement should be made using the 'current purchasing power' concept rather than the 'current cost' concept.

No guidance is given as to the approach to be adopted if price level adjustments are not possible. Two alternative approaches might be considered depending on the circumstances, namely:

(i) to apply the temporal method which is the solution adopted by SFAS 52, the corresponding U.S. statement; or

(ii) if the temporal method is not practicable or does not result in a fair presentation, to exclude the enterprise from consolidation on the grounds that its inclusion is impracticable or would be misleading.

13.040 EQUITY INVESTMENTS FINANCED BY FOREIGN BORROWINGS

13.041 OFFSET RULES APPLICABLE TO INDIVIDUAL COMPANY

Normally, investments in foreign entities should be treated like other non-monetary items, i.e. they should be carried in the balance sheet at their historical cost which reflects the exchange rate at which they were purchased.

An exception to this rule is permitted where a company has borrowed foreign currencies to finance or provide a hedge against its foreign equity investments. In these circumstances the investments may be denominated in the appropriate foreign currency and the carrying amounts translated at each year end at the closing rates of exchange in the individual company's financial statements. Any exchange differences should be taken to reserves. Similarly the exchange gains or losses on translating the related foreign currency loans at the closing rates should be offset as a reserve movement against these exchange differences. SSAP 20 requires the following conditions to be met:

(i) in any accounting period, exchange gains and losses on the borrowings may be offset only to the extent of the exchange differences arising on the equity investments;

(ii) the foreign currency borrowings, whose exchange gains or losses are used in the offset process should not exceed, in the aggregate, the total amount of cash that the investments are expected to generate, whether from profits or otherwise; and

(iii) the accounting treatment adopted should be applied consistently from period to period.

Where this treatment is applied to a foreign equity investment which is neither a subsidiary nor an associated company, the same treatment may be applied in the consolidated financial statements.

13.042 OFFSET RULES APPLICABLE TO GROUP COMPANIES

Where foreign borrowings have been used to finance group investments in foreign enterprises or to provide a hedge against the exchange risk associated with such investments, the exchange gains or losses arising on the translation of the foreign borrowings may be offset as a reserve movement against the exchange differences arising on the retranslation of the net investments, subject to the following conditions:

(i) the relationships between the investing company and the foreign enterprises concerned justify the use of the closing rate method for consolidation purposes;

(ii) in any accounting period, exchange gains and losses arising on foreign currency borrowings may be offset only to the extent of the exchange differences arising on the net investments in foreign enterprises;

(iii) the foreign currency borrowings, whose exchange gains or losses are used in the offset process, should not exceed, in the aggregate, the total amount of cash that the net investments are expected to be able to generate, whether from profits or otherwise; and

(iv) the accounting treatment adopted should be applied consistently from period to period.

The offset procedures in Section 13.041 above which are available to the investing company, may also be applied on consolidation to those foreign equity investments which are neither subsidiaries nor associated companies.

13.043 IMPLEMENTATION OF OFFSET RULES

The implementation of the offset rules is discussed below. Although the examples given illustrate their application to an individual company, the approach in group situations is the same.

There are no restrictions on the application of these rules other than those specified in SSAP 20 and the overall requirement to show a true and fair view. Thus the period of the loans is not relevant and there is no requirement for them to be in the same currency as the investment. It appears that one loan can be replaced by another in a different currency without invalidating the offset treatment. In view of the flexibility permitted the requirement for consistency of treatment is extremely important if an unfair presentation is to be avoided.

(a) Determination of borrowings which constitute finance or a hedge, and measurement of cash generation

The following example illustrates the accounting treatment in the case where the borrowing made in the same currency exceeds the related investment.

EXAMPLE

Assume Company A acquired a 15% equity stake in a German company for DM800,000, borrowing DM1,000,000 to finance the purchase of this investment and also to provide funds for working capital and other purposes. The investment and borrowing would be initially recorded in the accounting records at the rate of exchange then prevailing, say £1 = DM4, at £200,000 and £250,000 respectively. If the investment and borrowings remained unchanged at the year end when the exchange rate was say £1 = DM3.95, the investment may be denominated in Deutschmarks and translated at the year end rate (£202,532) with the exchange difference of £2,532 (DM800,000 ÷ 3.95 – £200,000) being credited direct to reserves.

Of the exchange loss of £3,165 arising from translating the borrowings at the year end rate (DM1,000,000 ÷ 3.95 – £250,000), £2,532 can be offset against the credit arising from the retranslation of the investment and the balance should be charged to profit and loss account.

(b) Borrowings in different currencies

It is permissible to apply the offset principle to any foreign currency borrowings to the extent that such borrowings do not exceed the cash expected to be generated from the investment, either from profits or otherwise. Equally the standard permits the offset principle to be applied on a pooled basis to a group of investments financed by a variety of different currencies, including those currencies which may have moved in opposite directions during the period.

(c) Expected cash to be generated by investments

The extent to which foreign currency loans can be offset against net investments in foreign currency is restricted to 'the total amount of cash that the net investments are expected to be able to generate whether from profits or otherwise'. While this restriction seems reasonable in principle, it is hard to see when it will have any practical effect since no guidance is given either as to how the expectation of cash generation is to be measured or as to the period of profit earning that is to be taken into account.

The extent to which offset is possible is in any case restricted to the book value of the investment in the case of a single company and the group's share of the book value of the net assets of the enterprise where the net investment method is being used. Accordingly provided the foreign enterprise is profitable the additional restriction is unlikely to have any effect since the cash expected to be generated by future profits is virtually unlimited. If the foreign enterprise is unprofitable or earns negligible profits after taking account of the interest payable on the loan, the expected cash to be generated must be represented by the estimated net realisable value of the investment; if this amount is less than the book values used in the financial statements, then the restriction might apply.

If the foreign enterprise was subject to stringent exchange control restrictions so that the prospect of significant cash being generated outside the country was low, it would clearly not be appropriate to regard a loan in another freely marketable foreign currency as a hedge against that investment. However in these circumstances, consolidation by the net investment method would probably not be appropriate in any event.

(d) Borrowings subsequently reduced

Borrowings which may have been treated as finance for or a hedge against an equity investment in the preceding year may be substantially reduced or repaid in full during the current financial year. This does not give rise to any change in accounting treatment in group accounts, but if an equity investment held by an individual company has been translated at the closing rate, that treatment will no longer be appropriate unless a new foreign currency loan is obtained or there are other foreign currency borrowings available as a hedge for the investment. The investment (or the unhedged proportion of it) should be translated at the rate ruling when repayment of the hedging loan takes place. Thereafter it should be retained at that amount unless a new hedging loan is arranged.

EXAMPLE

Assume in the preceding example that the directors decided to take advantage of the strong pound by repaying the DM1,000,000 loan midway through the subsequent year when the exchange rate was £1 = DM4.80. The rate ruling at the year end was £1 = DM4.10.

The exchange gain arising on the settlement of the loan is the difference between the loan balance shown in the opening balance sheet (DM1,000,000 ÷ 3.95 = £253,165) and the loan repayment (DM1,000,000 ÷ 4.80 = £208,333), or £44,832.

The equity investment should be translated using the rate of exchange ruling on the date the borrowing cover ceased, i.e. £1 = DM4.80, giving rise to a translation debit of £35,865 (£166,667 (i.e. DM800,000 ÷ 4.80) – £202,532) to be shown as a reserve movement. Therefore the exchange gain of £44,832 arising on the loan settlement should be applied as to £35,865 direct to reserves and as to £8,967 credited to profit and loss account. At the year end the equity investment should continue to be valued at £166,667 (DM800,000 ÷ 4.80), subject to the need for any provision for diminution in value.

(e) Borrowings made before or after the investment

Sufficient freedom is contained in SSAP 20 to permit the cover approach to be applied to borrowings taken out either before or after the investment is made. However, the standard is not clear as to the appropriate exchange rate to be used in denominating the foreign currency investment where there is a time gap between the date the investment was made and the date of the loan. If the cover method is to make sense, it would appear that the offset of exchange gains or losses on the loans should only be made against the exchange differences arising on the equity investment during the cover period. Accordingly to achieve this matching, the exchange rates ruling on the first day in which both the investment and loan were held should be used to translate the investment as the starting point in the calculation of the exchange difference available for offset.

EXAMPLE

Assume Company B paid $240,000 for an equity investment in an overseas company when the exchange rate was £1 = $2.40, the investment being carried in books at £100,000. Several years later the directors considered the investment to be worth at least $600,000 and hedged the investment by obtaining a $600,000 loan the proceeds of which were invested in sterling deposits at £375,000 (£1 = $1.60). At the year end the exchange rate was £1 = $1.67.

If the purpose is to provide a hedge against the value of the investment, the directors of B should bring it into the accounts at directors' valuation (i.e. $600,000). The investment would be initially valued at £375,000 ($600,000 ÷ 1.60) and the surplus arising of £275,000 would be credited to revaluation reserve. As both the investment and loan would be carried at the same amount, the exchange difference arising from retranslating the investment at the closing rate would be fully covered by the opposite difference arising from the retranslation of the loan at the closing rate, leaving no exchange gain or loss to be included in the profit and loss account.

Where the directors of B are not prepared to revalue the investment as suggested above, an alternative approach is to use the historical cost of the investment in dollar terms (i.e. $240,000) as the starting point. This amount would then need to be translated first at the exchange rate at the date the loan was obtained (£1 = $1.60) giving £150,000 and then at the closing rate (£1 = $1.67) giving £143,713. The exchange difference of £50,000 arising from the movement in rates between the purchase of the investment and the date of the loan should be credited direct to reserves as this represents a revaluation surplus. The movement in rates to the year end produces a further exchange difference of £6,287 (£150,000 − £143,713) and it is this exchange difference which should be available to be covered by the exchange gain or loss arising on the loan. In this case an exchange gain on the loan of £15,719 ($600,000 ÷ 1.60 − $600,000 ÷ 1.67) arises but only £6,287 should be credited direct to reserves as an offset to the debit of similar amount arising from the retranslation of the investment and the balance should be credited to the profit and loss account.

13.050 DISCLOSURES

The methods used to translate the financial statements of foreign enterprises and the treatment accorded to exchange differences should be disclosed in the financial statements. Furthermore, Sch 4: 58(1) requires the basis on which sums originally denominated in foreign currencies have been translated into sterling to be disclosed in the notes. These disclosures are normally given in the accounting policies note.

An example of a suitable accounting policy note, which should be adapted to fit individual circumstances, might be:

EXAMPLE

Transactions of U.K. companies denominated in foreign currencies are translated into sterling at the rate ruling at the date of the transaction. Amounts receivable and payable in foreign currencies at the balance sheet date are translated at the rate ruling at that date.

The financial statements of overseas subsidiary and associated companies are translated into sterling at the closing rates of exchange and the difference arising from the translation of the opening net investment at the closing rate is taken direct to reserves. Differences arising on the translation of foreign currency loans taken to finance the group's foreign investments are also taken direct to reserves. All other translation differences are dealt with in the profit and loss account.

SSAP 20 requires all companies to disclose the net movement on reserves arising from exchange differences.

SSAP 20 also requires all companies, or group of companies, which are not exempt companies (i.e. bank, insurance and shipping companies and certain companies registered in Northern Ireland and the Republic of Ireland which take advantage of the exemptions from full disclosure given by their companies acts) to disclose the net amount of exchange gains and losses on foreign currency borrowings less deposits, identifying separately:

(i) the amount offset in reserves under the rules set out in Sections 13.041 and 13.042; and

(ii) the net amount charged/credited to the profit and loss account.

There is no further requirement to disclose the net amount of exchange gains or losses included in the profit and loss account unless the amount involved meets the criteria of an exceptional or extraordinary item.

13.060 FORWARD EXCHANGE CONTRACTS

Under a forward exchange contract a company enters into a binding agreement to buy or sell a specified amount of foreign currency at a specified rate on a given future date. This contract does not give rise to an entry in the accounting records until it is settled by the payment or receipt of sterling. The methods normally used to account for such transactions in year-end financial statements are discussed below.

Forward exchange contracts are normally entered into by trading companies to protect themselves against currency fluctuations (i.e. as hedges). For example a trader who sells goods for $1,000,000 receivable in 90 days might immediately enter into a forward contract to sell $1,000,000 in 90 days' time, thereby fixing the sterling value of his sale. In such a case the debt should be converted into sterling at the year end at the rate specified in the forward contract. Normally no further entries are necessary in respect of the contract.

An alternative method sometimes used is to record the debtor at the exchange rate ruling at the date of sale and amortise any difference between that rate and the forward contract rate over the period of the contract. If in the above example, the sale had been made on 1 November when the exchange rate was $2 = £1 and the three months forward contract rate was $1.95 = £1, then the debt would be recorded as £500,000 while the sterling amount receivable under the forward contract would be $1,000,000 ÷ 1.95, i.e. £512,820. At 31 December, two-thirds of the 'gain' on the forward contract of £12,820, i.e. £8,547, would be recognised as profit.

Where a forward exchange contract is not a hedge for a trading transaction but a speculation, then it will give rise to a profit or loss depending on the movement in the exchange rate over the period to maturity. For example, a company contracts to sell $1,000,000 90 days forward at $1.95 = £1. At the end of the 90 days it must buy $1,000,000 in order to meet its contract, and it will thus make a profit if £1 buys more than $1.95 at that time.

At the year end it is necessary to determine the profit or loss, if any, which should be recognised in respect of any such contracts which are open at that time. There are two generally accepted methods of doing this:

(i) to compare the forward rate in the contract with the corresponding forward rate to maturity at the year end; and

(ii) to compare the 'spot' rate (i.e. the rate for immediate conversion) with the spot rate at the year end and to amortise the contracted forward discount or premium over the period of the contract.

Method (i) is that approved by SFAS 52 and is to be preferred.

EXAMPLE

A company contracts on 1 November 1984 to sell $1,000,000 90 days forward at $1.95 = £1, i.e. at 30 January 1985 it must deliver $1,000,000 in exchange for £512,820. At 1 November 1984 the spot rate was $2 = £1 [$1,000,000 = £500,000]. At the year end on 31 December 1984 the 30 day forward was $1.96 = £1 [$1,000,000 = £510,204] while the spot rate was $1.97 = £1 [$1,000,000 = £507,614].

Method (i)

	£
Contracted price for delivery of $1,000,000 at 30 January 1985	*512,820*
Cost of '30 January 1985 dollars' at 31 December 1984 (i.e. 30 days forward)	*510,204*
Profit earned to 31 December 1984	*2,616*

Method (ii)

	£	
Spot price of $1,000,000 at 1 November 1984, date of contract		*500,000*
Spot price of $1,000,000 at 31 December 1984		*507,614*
		(7,614)
Contracted price at 1 November 1984	*512,820*	
Spot price of $1,000,000 at same date	*500,000*	
Premium on contract	*12,820*	
Proportion accrued to 31 December 1984 – 60/90 of £12,820		*8,547*
Profit earned at 31 December 1984		*933*

Another method, adopted by a number of banks, compares the forward rate in the contract with the spot rate at the balance sheet date, on the grounds that the company could crystallise its obligation by buying spot dollars immediately. Thus in the example above the profit to be recognised is the difference between the contract amount of £512,820 and the spot price of $1,000,000 at the year end of £507,614, i.e. £5,206. This treatment is not suitable for the majority of companies because it ignores the cost of holding the dollars for one month, but may be suitable for banks and similar institutions which maintain a level of liquid dollar balances with which to meet such obligations at any time.

13.061 DISCLOSURES

Where forward exchange contracts are material, the method adopted should be clearly explained in the accounting policies note. The particulars of significant speculative open forward contracts should be disclosed to comply with the requirements of Sch 4: 50(5) to disclose financial commitments which are relevant to assessing the company's state of affairs.

14 TAXATION

14.010 METHOD OF COMPANY TAXATION IN THE U.K.

The main features of company taxation in the U.K. (often referred to as the 'Imputation System') are:

(i) Corporation tax is levied on the company's taxable profit.

(ii) When a distribution is made to shareholders the company has to pay to the Inland Revenue an advance payment of corporation tax (ACT).

(iii) A tax credit at the basic rate of ACT is imputed to the shareholder. This tax credit discharges the liability to income tax at the basic tax rate of a U.K. resident.

(iv) ACT is available to be set off against the company's liability to corporation tax (except the tax on chargeable gains) for the period in which the dividend is paid. The set off is restricted to the imputed tax rate (the basic rate liability to income tax of a U.K. resident) on the company's taxable income. Any unrelieved ACT can be carried back for six years or carried forward indefinitely.

(v) The resultant net liability is known as 'mainstream' corporation tax.

In addition charges or credits can arise under the following headings of taxation:

Overseas tax
Double tax relief
Income tax
Tax on franked investment income
Deferred tax
Development land tax

14.020 PRESENTATION OF TAXATION IN FINANCIAL STATEMENTS

14.021 BALANCE SHEET

(a) Statutory format

The headings in the balance sheet formats which include taxation are:

(i) Creditors: other creditors including taxation and social security (sub-divided between amounts falling due within one year, and amounts falling due after more than one year).

(ii) Provisions for liabilities and charges: taxation including deferred taxation.

It is considered that all amounts due in respect of taxation on the results of the financial year or any previous financial year should be included under creditors, payable either within one year or after more than one year as appropriate. The rate of tax may not be known because it is fixed in arrear (as was the position with U.K. corporation tax prior to 1984) and therefore the exact liability cannot be computed with certainty. This is not a justification for treating the estimated amount payable as a provision rather than as a creditor.

Provisions should normally be restricted to deferred taxation. Provisions for taxation other than deferred taxation only arise on those rare occasions where there is doubt about the existence of a tax liability in respect of particular circumstances or transactions but it is considered advisable to provide for the possible liability.

Any amounts receivable in respect of repayments of tax should be treated as 'Other debtors'. If any deferred tax is carried forward as an asset, it should be included under 'Prepayments and accrued income'.

(b) Disclosures

The disclosure requirements of the Act are:

(i) the amount in respect of taxation and social security shall be shown separately from the amount of other creditors (note 9 to balance sheet format). This is interpreted as requiring one amount to be shown to include all liabilities in respect of taxation and social security, i.e. corporation tax, income tax, ACT, VAT, PAYE, N.I. contributions and any foreign equivalents.

(ii) the amount of any provisions for taxation other than deferred taxation must be stated [Sch 4: 47].

The treatment of deferred tax, including the disclosure requirements, is dealt with in Section 14.080.

14.022 PROFIT AND LOSS ACCOUNT

(a) Statutory format

All profit and loss account formats require the disclosure of the following items relating to taxation:

Tax on profit or loss on ordinary activities

Profit or loss on ordinary activities after taxation

Tax on extraordinary profit or loss

Other taxes not shown under the above items

(b) Disclosures

The separate elements of tax on the profit or loss on ordinary activities which should be disclosed, if material, either on the face of the profit and loss account or in the notes to the accounts are as follows:

Corporation tax
Less double taxation relief
Deferred taxation
Overseas taxation
Irrecoverable advance corporation tax
Tax on franked investment income
Income tax
Associated companies – tax attributable to group share of profits
Under/over provision for prior year(s)

Any tax which arises on extraordinary items must be included under the heading 'Tax on extraordinary profit or loss'. The notes should disclose the division of this heading into the same separate elements as above.

The basis on which the charge for U.K. corporation tax and U.K. income tax must be stated. [Sch 4: 54(1)]

Particulars must be given of any special circumstances affecting taxation liabilities in the current year and in future years. [Sch 4: 54(2)]

Under/over provisions for prior year liabilities are not normally material. If they are material, the amounts and reasons for the adjustments should be disclosed in the notes. If immaterial, the amounts may be combined with the current year's tax charge. These adjustments arise mainly from the correction of estimates inherent in the accounting process and therefore should not be treated as prior year adjustments.

14.030 CORPORATION TAX

The corporation tax charge should be computed using the best available estimate of the rate that will apply for the financial year. Normally this is the latest known rate when the financial statements are prepared, but on occasions (as in the Finance Act 1984) future rates may be fixed in advance. The rate used should be disclosed.

When the corporation tax charge is reduced by relief from double taxation, both the amount of the charge and the amount it would have been but for such relief must be stated. [Sch 4: 54(3)]

14.040 OVERSEAS TAXATION AND DOUBLE TAXATION RELIEF

The amount of overseas taxation to be disclosed separately is the amount or estimated amount of taxation payable by the company or the group in foreign countries in respect of the profits of the financial year. It should include any additional taxes on dividends or distributions.

Double taxation relief is the relief allowed against U.K. corporation tax on account of overseas taxes suffered.

An example of suitable disclosure of tax on profit on ordinary activities, including corporation tax, overseas taxation and double taxation relief, is as follows:

EXAMPLE - Note on tax on profit on ordinary activities

	1984	*1983*
	£	*£*
Corporation tax, based on the profit for the year at 46.25% (1983 – 50.5%)	*175,000*	*240,000*
Less double taxation relief	*23,000*	*2,000*
	152,000	*238,000*
Overseas tax	*68,000*	*52,000*
	220,000	*290,000*

14.050 ADVANCE CORPORATION TAX

The ACT on any dividend payable at the balance sheet date and on any proposed dividend should be recognised as a liability in the balance sheet, being included in 'Taxation and social security' falling due within one year. When those dividends are paid the ACT on them constitutes a payment in advance of the corporation tax liability of the year in which they are paid, i.e. of the year following the date of the balance sheet. The ACT should therefore be recognised as an asset, provided that it is foreseen that the following year's taxable profits together with any profits of previous years that are available will be sufficient to permit offset. The restrictions on offset are discussed below.

The ACT on dividends paid during the financial year is available as a deduction from the corporation tax liability for the year. Thus the amount to be included in the balance sheet in respect of the liability for corporation tax for the financial year is the amount charged in the profit and loss account less any ACT that is available for offset in respect of dividends paid in the year.

The amount of ACT that is available for offset in any year is restricted to 30% of the amount of the company's taxable income in that year (assuming that the basic rate of income tax is 30% and ACT is three-sevenths of the amount of any dividend). For example if the dividends paid were £7,000, ACT £3,000, and the profit assessable to corporation tax £8,000, then the ACT that can be offset is restricted to £8,000 at 30%, i.e. £2,400.

Any ACT on dividends paid in the year that cannot be offset against the corporation tax liability of that year may be offset against the corporation tax liability of the previous six years to the extent that there is taxable income in those years available to absorb the offset. Thus, if in the example above the previous year's profit assessable to corporation tax had been £12,000 and the distribution the same, i.e. dividend paid £7,000, ACT £3,000, then there would be £2,000 of taxable income available (£12,000 less dividend and ACT of £10,000); this would absorb £600 (£2,000 at 30%) and would therefore permit recovery of the unrelieved ACT of the current year.

ACT that cannot be set against the taxable income of the year in which it arises or any of the six previous years (unrelieved ACT) may be carried forward indefinitely to be set against the taxable income of future years. However unrelieved ACT should only be included in the balance sheet as an asset if it is regarded as recoverable.

14.051 RECOVERABLE ACT

As indicated above ACT on dividends unpaid at the balance sheet date should be recorded as a liability. It should also be regarded as recoverable and recognised as an asset provided it is foreseen that the following year's taxable profits together with any available profits of previous years will be sufficient to permit offset.

ACT on dividends paid prior to the balance sheet date and which cannot be offset against the corporation tax liabilities of the current or previous years can only be regarded as recoverable if:

(i) it can properly be set off against timing differences for which provision has been made for a deferred tax liability; or

(ii) future profits in excess of dividends to be paid are forecast with reasonable certainty to recover the unrelieved ACT. SSAP 8 suggests that the forecast period should normally be limited to the next accounting period.

ACT can properly be set off against a deferred tax liability except to the extent that deferred tax represents tax on deferred chargeable gains. However, the deferred tax liability will be calculated using the estimated corporation tax rate and the rate at which ACT is relieved is restricted to 30%. Consequently the amount of ACT which can properly be set against deferred tax will normally be significantly less than the deferred tax liability. Deferred tax is dealt with in Section 14.080 below.

If ACT is regarded as recoverable, it should be offset against the deferred tax liability to the extent that this can properly be done. Otherwise, it should be included in 'Prepayments and accrued income'. If 'Prepayments and accrued income' is included under debtors rather than as a separate main heading, then the recoverable ACT must be included in the amount falling due after more than one year which must be disclosed.

14.052 IRRECOVERABLE ACT

ACT not considered recoverable within the succeeding year or available to be set off against the provision for deferred tax should be written off and shown separately as part of the tax on profit on ordinary activities. Should it subsequently be recovered, the credit should be disclosed separately as a deduction in arriving at this amount.

The reasons for writing off or recovery through the profit and loss account should be explained in the notes and the accumulated amount of any ACT written off but available for recovery against future corporation tax liabilities should also be disclosed.

14.060 INCOME TAX

The amount of the charge for U.K. income tax and the basis on which that charge is computed must be disclosed. [Sch 4: 54(1)] It is rare for a company to incur a material liability to income tax. The most frequent circumstance in which this arises is where the investment income of a close company exceeds its distributions, there is an apportionment among its participators and the resultant liability falls on the company to the extent that it is not paid by the participators.

Stock Exchange companies are required to indicate whether, so far as the directors are aware, the company is a close company for taxation purposes, and this is usually done in the directors' report. If a close company has substantial investment income, it is desirable for a fair presentation to disclose in the notes to the accounts that the company is a close company.

14.070 TAX ON FRANKED INVESTMENT INCOME

Dividends received from U.K. companies are known as franked investment income, since they are not subject to further taxation as income in the hands of the receiving company. Instead a tax credit at the ACT rate is imputed to the shareholder. If the shareholder is a company, this credit can be set against ACT arising on dividends paid.

Franked investment income received should be grossed up by the amount of the tax credit before inclusion in the profit on ordinary activities before taxation. [SSAP 8] The tax on franked investment income (i.e. the tax credit) should be included with the tax charge in the profit and loss account. Where franked investment income represents a material source of income, the accounting policies note should disclose the manner in which the income and related tax credit has been treated.

EXAMPLE – accounting policy note

Franked investment income comprises the amount of qualifying distributions received from U.K. resident companies plus the related tax credit. The amount equivalent to the credit has been treated as part of the charge for taxation.

14.080 DEFERRED TAX

The formats require the provision for deferred taxation to be included in the sub-heading 'Taxation, including deferred taxation' under the main heading 'Provisions for liabilities and charges'.

The principles of, and methods of accounting for, deferred taxation are set out in SSAP 15 (revised 1985). The requirements of this standard together with guidance on financial statement presentation are discussed below.

14.081 DEFINITION AND PRINCIPLES

Deferred tax is defined as the tax attributable to timing differences. Timing differences are differences between profits or losses as computed for tax purposes and results as stated in financial statements which arise from the inclusion of items of income and expenditure in tax computations in periods different from those in which they are included in financial statements. Timing differences originate in one period and are capable of reversal in one or more subsequent periods.

SSAP 15 states that tax deferred or accelerated by the effect of timing differences should be accounted for to the extent that it is probable that an asset or liability will crystallise and should not be accounted for to the extent that it is probable that an asset or liability will not crystallise. An asset or liability crystallises when the reversal of a timing difference is not replaced by a new timing difference of at least the same tax effect with the result that there is a decrease or increase in the amount of the taxation liability.

14.082 METHOD OF CALCULATION

SSAP 15 specifies that deferred tax should be computed under the liability method, i.e. the tax is calculated using the corporation tax rate which is expected to apply when the timing differences reverse and a deferred tax asset or liability crystallises. Thus the amount of the provision for deferred tax must be changed if there is a change in the rate of corporation tax expected to apply.

The deferral method whereby the deferred tax is computed using the rate ruling when the provision is set up, and subsequent reversals are made at the same rate, is no longer acceptable.

14.083 TIMING DIFFERENCES

Timing differences arise from five main sources:

(i) Short-term timing differences

These arise from the use of the receipts and payments basis for tax purposes and the accruals basis in the financial statements and normally reverse in the next accounting period. Examples include non-specific bad debt provisions, provision for future losses on contract work in progress, interest receivable, provision for plant closure or re-organisation costs, and inter-company profits in stocks eliminated on consolidation.

(ii) Capital allowances

Timing differences arise when capital allowances exceed the corresponding depreciation charge in the financial statements or alternatively where the depreciation charge in the financial statements exceeds the corresponding capital allowances.

(iii) Revaluation of fixed assets

If a fixed asset on which capital allowances are claimed is revalued, then to the extent that the revaluation restores previously charged depreciation, a timing difference arises similar to the differences referred to in (ii) above of the amount by which capital allowances exceed the depreciation charged. If all depreciation has been restored, the timing difference will be the total of the capital allowances claimed in respect of that asset.

To the extent that the valuation exceeds original cost, there is a potential timing difference in that tax on a chargeable gain may be payable if the asset is sold at its revalued amount. However, no deferred tax should be provided at the time of the valuation. Provision should be made out of the revaluation surplus as soon as a liability is foreseen, which in the absence of rollover relief will be at the time the company decides in principle to dispose of the asset. Depreciation on the valuation in excess of cost will not have an effect on deferred tax as this is a permanent difference.

(iv) Disposal of fixed assets

Where a fixed asset has been disposed of and the proceeds invested in a replacement asset, tax on the gain may be deferred by the application of rollover relief. Where rollover relief is obtained the tax deferred will not crystallise until the replacement asset is sold and possibly not even then. Unless the sale of the replacement asset without further rollover relief is likely, crystallisation of the liability cannot be foreseen and it should not be provided.

(v) Losses

A loss for tax purposes which is available to relieve future profits from tax constitutes a timing difference.

14.084 ASSESSING THE EFFECT OF TIMING DIFFERENCES

In order to assess the extent to which assets or liabilities arising from timing differences will crystallise, it is necessary to make reasonable assumptions as to future events, in particular as to the new timing differences which are likely to arise to replace the reversal of existing differences. These assumptions should be based on all relevant information available including the intentions of management, and ideally will include financial plans and projections covering a future period of years. The appendix to SSAP 15 suggests that a period of three to five years may be sufficient where the pattern of timing differences is expected to be regular, but may need to be longer in other cases. There is little guidance provided for those cases probably the majority in number, where financial plans and projections for such a period are not available. However, it is stated that a prudent view should be taken, particularly where financial plans or projections are susceptible to a high degree of uncertainty or are not fully developed.

The combined effect of all timing differences should be considered when attempting to assess whether a tax liability will crystallise, rather than looking at each timing difference separately. This suggests that a potential liability arising from a short term timing difference such as the deferral of development costs, should not be provided if in the period of reversal substantial capital expenditure can be foreseen which will result in capital allowances in excess of depreciation being such that no net liability will arise. Similarly the effect of present and forecast future tax losses should be taken into account: clearly there can be no crystallisation of a deferred tax liability in a future year, if there will be no actual liability in that year.

(a) Short term timing differences

Generally assessment of the effect of short term timing differences should be relatively simple. Many will arise as a result of recurring annual payments and receipts being treated on an accruals basis for accounting purposes and on a payments basis for tax purposes; the reversing timing differences are replaced by equivalent new timing differences so that it is probable that a tax liability or asset will not crystallise. The same considerations apply to annual adjustments such as the elimination of intra-group profits on stocks, assuming that the level of such adjustments will not differ significantly between one year and another. Other short term timing differences are likely to be of the 'one-off' variety which arise in one period, reverse in one or more subsequent periods and for which replacement cannot be foreseen: most provisions made in advance of expenditure or losses being incurred (e.g. for non-specific bad debts, for future repairs or re-organisation costs), and deferrals of expenditure incurred to future periods are likely to fall into this category.

(b) Capital allowances

Assessment of the effect of capital allowances requires the making of assumptions as to future levels of capital expenditure and it is in this area that financial plans and projections for some years ahead are most significant. Where adequate plans and projections have been prepared, a comparison between projected depreciation charges and capital allowances will reveal the extent if any to which timing differences can be expected to reverse and result in the crystallisation of a liability or asset. Where such plans and projections are not prepared, an assumption must be made on the basis of the best information available, which will normally be restricted to the history of past expenditure and known needs. It is stressed that any assumption based on such limited evidence should be made with prudence, i.e. doubts as to the crystallisation of a deferred tax item should be resolved on the basis that liabilities will crystallise and assets will not.

(c) Losses

Trading losses constitute timing differences which can be expected to reverse when they are relieved against profits of future years. Therefore they can be set against other timing differences which are expected to reverse in future and which on reversal will form part of the trading profits against which the losses can be relieved. Care must be taken to ensure that the losses will be available for relief having regard to the timing of the expected reversal of the other differences. Although trading losses can generally be carried forward without limit in the U.K. an exception arises in respect of such losses which arose from stock relief under the Finance Act 1981 which are only available for carry forward for six years. The extent to which carry forward is permitted overseas is often more restricted. Capital losses may constitute timing differences but they are normally available only to be set off against future capital profits and therefore they can only be expected to crystallise if a future taxable gain against which the loss can be set is identified. They may be set against timing differences which need to be recognised arising from the revaluation of assets (see Section 14.087 below), but otherwise can only be recognised if the circumstances justify carrying forward a deferred tax debit balance. These circumstances are discussed below.

14.085 DEFERRED TAX DEBIT BALANCES

Deferred tax debit balances should not be carried forward as assets except to the extent to which they are expected to be recoverable without replacement. The Appendix to SSAP 15 uses the rather stronger phrase 'recovery is assured beyond reasonable doubt'.

With regard to debit balances, other than those arising from losses, it is suggested that they should be carried forward only to the extent that:

(i) their recovery without replacement in the following accounting period can be clearly foreseen, or

(ii) they are small in amount in relation to the past taxable profits of the company and to the forecast taxable profits in those periods when crystallisation is foreseen.

The tests which are suggested in the Appendix to SSAP 15 to establish that the recovery of deferred tax relating to current trading losses is assured beyond reasonable doubt are:

(i) the loss results from an identifiable and non-recurring cause; and

(ii) the enterprise has been consistently profitable over a considerable period, with any past losses being more than offset by income in subsequent periods; and

(iii) it is assured beyond reasonable doubt that future taxable profits will be sufficient to offset the current loss during the carry-forward period prescribed by tax legislation.

It is suggested as a general rule that sufficient future taxable profits can only be assured beyond reasonable doubt if they are foreseen to arise in the next accounting period. Only in exceptional circumstances can forecasts of profits for longer periods be assured beyond reasonable doubt.

A question which must be considered is whether the tax effect of losses of prior years, which has not previously been recognised as an asset because recovery was not assured beyond reasonable doubt may be recognised in the current year because as a result of improved profitability their recovery can now be foreseen. There is nothing in SSAP 15 to suggest that this is not permissible but the guidance in the appendix refers only to current trading losses. It is suggested that previous losses can properly be taken into account in determining whether or not it is necessary to recognise a deferred tax liability; but if the tax effect of a loss is not recognised as an asset in the period in which the loss is incurred, it should not be recognised subsequently until recovery in fact takes place.

The recovery of deferred tax relating to a capital loss is assured beyond reasonable doubt only if the taxable gain against which the capital loss will be relieved can be identified with reasonable certainty. This implies that there is an asset identified for sale on which a taxable gain can be anticipated; it is suggested that the sale of the asset should normally be expected to take place in the next accounting period.

14.086 GROUPS OF COMPANIES

Where a company is a member of a group, it should take account of any group relief which is expected to be available and of any charge that would be made for such relief. (Group relief is discussed in Section 14.090 below.)

The deferred tax position of each group company should thus be determined separately and the results aggregated to determine the group position. The only adjustments to the group deferred tax liability or asset which may be necessary are those which arise from consolidation adjustments, such as the elimination of intra-group profits. The practice previously adopted by some groups of making full provision for deferred tax in the financial statements of the subsidiaries and only assessing the probable deferred tax position on a group basis is no longer acceptable.

(a) Overseas companies

Where subsidiaries are incorporated overseas, it may not be possible to insist that deferred tax is dealt with in accordance with SSAP 15 in their financial statements. For example under U.S. accounting principles full provision for deferred tax must be made using the deferral method. If the effect is material, it will be necessary to restate such financial statements in accordance with SSAP 15 for the purpose of consolidation.

In many cases the remittance of earnings of overseas companies results in additional taxation liabilities on those earnings. Thus to the extent that earnings are not fully remitted, a timing difference may arise which should be dealt with like other timing differences, i.e. the liability should only be recognised to the extent that remittance of past earnings of the overseas subsidiary can be foreseen in the future. To the extent that remittance cannot be foreseen it may be reasonable to think that it will never take place and to regard the potential liability as a permanent rather than a timing difference.

The translation of the financial statements of overseas subsidiaries for the purpose of consolidation does not give rise to any timing differences.

14.087 REVALUATION

Timing differences which arise from the revaluation of fixed assets are discussed in Section 14.083(iii) above. To the extent that the revaluation results in previously charged depreciation being restored, it results in a timing difference which will reverse as depreciation is charged on the revalued amount while no corresponding capital allowances are available. Whether it is necessary to provide for deferred tax on this timing difference and the extent of any provision required depends on the extent to which its effect will be balanced by the effect of other timing differences. If provision is necessary, it should be made directly out of the revaluation surplus and not by a charge in the profit and loss account.

No provision is necessary for any deferred tax on any revaluation above cost until a liability can be foreseen, which will normally be at the time when the company decides in principle to dispose of the asset in circumstances in which rollover relief is unavailable. This position arises only if there is a significant delay between the decision in principle to sell and actual sale and in the meantime the asset continues in use in the company's business so that it is not reclassified as a current asset. If a provision does become necessary under such circumstances it should be made by means of a direct charge against the revaluation reserve.

As indicated in Section 9.025 if a fixed asset which has been revalued is sold or reclassified as a current asset, its book amount must be adjusted to its depreciated historical cost by a transfer from revaluation reserve. At the same time any amount in the deferred tax provision in respect of the reversal of timing differences arising from the revaluation of that asset should be eliminated by being transferred to revaluation reserve.

14.088 DISCLOSURE REQUIREMENTS IN RESPECT OF DEFERRED TAX

(a) Accounting policy

It is customary to disclose the accounting policy for dealing with deferred tax if it is material. An example of the appropriate policy note is as follows:

> ***EXAMPLE***
>
> *Deferred taxation is provided at the anticipated tax rates on timing differences arising from the inclusion of items of income and expenditure in taxation computations in periods different from those in which they are included in financial statements to the extent that it is probable that a liability or asset will crystallise in the future.*

(b) Profit and loss account

(i) Deferred tax relating to ordinary activities should be shown as a separate component of tax on ordinary activities (see Section 14.022 above).

(ii) Deferred tax relating to extraordinary items should be shown as a separate component of tax on extraordinary profit or loss.

(iii) The amount of any unprovided deferred tax in respect of the period should be shown, analysed into its major components. Presumably the intention is to require the disclosure of any timing differences which arise in the period to the extent that the tax effect is not recognised, but the wording would appear to require offsetting debit and credit items to be separately disclosed.

> ***EXAMPLE:***
>
> *The charge to U.K. corporation tax is reduced by £40,000 by the effect of capital allowances for tax purposes being in excess of depreciation charged in the profit and loss account, and by £30,000 in respect of development expenditure carried forward in the accounts but allowed for corporation tax when incurred.*

(iv) Adjustments of deferred tax caused by changes in tax rates and changes in rate of tax allowances should be included as part of the tax charge for the year, but disclosed separately if material. However, a material effect of a change in the basis of taxation or of a significant change in Government fiscal policy should be treated as an extraordinary item. What constitutes a 'significant change in Government fiscal policy' is not defined and is likely to prove a fruitful field for differences of opinion.

The following is an example of disclosure of the details of the tax charge where there has been a change in rate of tax:

EXAMPLE

	1984	*1983*
	£	*£*
Tax on profit on ordinary activities		
Corporation tax based on the profit for the year at 46.25% (1983 – 50.5%)	*175,000*	*240,000*
Deferred tax	*18,000*	*(37,000)*
Decrease in opening balance of deferred tax arising from changes in anticipated rates of tax)	*(14,000)*	*–*
	179,000	*203,000*

(c) Balance sheet

(i) The amount of the deferred tax account and its major components should be shown in a note.

(ii) The total amount of unprovided deferred tax should be disclosed in a note, analysed into its major components. It should be noted that this requirement is different from the original requirement in SSAP 15 which was to show the full potential deferred tax liability and the amount provided under each category.

It is convenient to combine the information required in (i) and (ii) above in a single note as in the following example:

EXAMPLE

The amounts of deferred tax provided and unprovided in the accounts are:

	Provided		*Unprovided*	
	1984	*1983*	*1984*	*1983*
	£'000	*£'000*	*£'000*	*£'000*
Capital allowances in excess of depreciation	*242*	*197*	*501*	*487*
Surplus on revaluation of fixed assets	*–*	*–*	*640*	*640*
Other	*20*	*18*	*–*	*–*
	262	*215*	*1,141*	*1,127*
Less: trading losses carried forward	*(112)*	*(70)*	*–*	*–*
Unrelieved advance corporation tax	*(129)*	*(84)*	*(21)*	*(76)*
	21	*61*	*1,120*	*1,051*

(iii) Where amounts of deferred tax arise which relate to movements on reserves (e.g. resulting from expected disposal of revalued assets), the amounts transferred to or from deferred tax should be shown separately as part of such movements.

(iv) If the potential amount of deferred tax arising on the revaluation of an asset or as a result of the receipt of rollover relief is not disclosed this fact should be stated. This requirement recognises the position where tax on a revaluation surplus is regarded as likely to be perpetually deferred (because even if the asset is sold rollover relief will be available in respect of its replacement and no tax liability is expected to arise on the disposal of the replacement asset). In these circumstances it may be treated as a permanent difference and not as a timing difference.

(v) If the value of an asset is disclosed in a note because it differs materially from its book amount, the note should also disclose the tax effects, if any, that would arise if the asset were realised at the balance sheet date at the noted value. It may be that, as outlined in (iv) above, the difference should be regarded as permanent and the tax effect as nil because of the availability of rollover relief. This requirement applies equally to disclosure of the value of an asset in the directors' report as to disclosure in a note to the accounts.

(vi) If deferred tax is not provided on earnings retained overseas and not disclosed as a potential deferred liability on the grounds that it is not a timing difference, this fact should be stated (see Section 14.086 above).

EXAMPLE

No provision has been made for taxation that would arise in the event of certain overseas subsidiaries and associated companies distributing the balance of their reserves.

(vii) If in assessing its deferred tax position a company which is a member of a group takes account of any group relief and any payment therefor, the assumptions made as to the availability of and payment for group relief should be stated. (see Section 14.086 above)

14.090 GROUP RELIEF

Within a U.K. group of companies trading losses of one company can be set against taxable income of another for the same accounting period provided that the surrendering and receiving companies are either the holding company or subsidiaries which are at least 75% owned and that other restrictions as to share of profits and assets in a winding-up are satisfied. Relief is also available where 75% of the share capital of a company with trading losses is owned by a consortium of companies, each of which owns at least 5% of the ordinary share capital.

The company which has incurred and surrendered the losses loses all right to any relief in respect of them. The surrender may be made for any consideration or none, provided due regard is paid to the interests of any minority shareholders or creditors who may be affected. The most usual arrangement is for the receiving company to make a payment equal to the tax that it will save, but alternative arrangements sometimes seen are for the loss to be surrendered for no consideration at all, and for a payment to be made equal to the full amount of the losses rather than just the tax saving.

A question that arises for subsidiary companies which have received or surrendered group relief is how the relevant transactions should be recorded in the profit and loss account. It should be noted that the matter does not arise for a holding company in the normal circumstance where it produces a consolidated profit and loss account only, since all the entries cancel out on consolidation.

It is suggested that the most satisfactory approach is to regard all group relief and payments therefore as extraordinary items, since they clearly derive from transactions that fall outside the ordinary activities of the company; they derive from the company's membership of a group and not from its activities at all. The following examples illustrate the presentation recommended and disclosure required. The examples assume that £100,000 of tax losses have been surrendered to a profit making company and that in case A, no payment (contribution) is made, in case B, payment equivalent to the tax relief is made and in case C, payment equivalent to the losses surrendered is made. A corporation tax rate of 45% is assumed.

EXAMPLE: Profit making company

	A	*B*	*C*
	£'000	*£'000*	*£'000*
Profit on ordinary activities before taxation	*300*	*300*	*300*
Tax on profit on ordinary activities	*135*	*135*	*135*
Profit on ordinary activities after taxation	*165*	*165*	*165*
Extraordinary items (note 4)	*45*	–	*55*
Profit for the financial year	*210*	*165*	*110*

Note 4 – Extraordinary items

Extraordinary charge – contribution made to another group company in respect of its loss of £100,000 surrendered	–	*(45)*	*(100)*
Extraordinary income – tax benefit of loss surrendered	*45*	*45*	*45*
Extraordinary profit (loss)	*45*	–	*(55)*

EXAMPLE: Loss making company

Loss on ordinary activities before taxation	*(100)*	*(100)*	*(100)*
Tax on loss on ordinary activities	*(45)*	*(45)*	*(45)*
Loss on ordinary activities after taxation	*(55)*	*(55)*	*(55)*
Extraordinary items (note 4)	*(45)*	–	*55*
Loss for the financial year	*(100)*	*(55)*	–

Note 4 – Extraordinary items

Extraordinary income – contribution received from another group company in respect of the loss of £100,000 surrendered	–	*45*	*100*
Extraordinary charge – tax benefit of loss surrendered	*(45)*	*(45)*	*(45)*
Extraordinary profit (loss)	*(45)*	–	*55*

In example B (which is the most common situation) it will be noted that there is no net extraordinary item since the payment or receipt and the related tax effect cancel out. A strict interpretation of the statutory rule that amounts in respect of items representing income may not be set off against amounts in respect of items representing expenditure nevertheless seems to require that both amounts are disclosed in the manner indicated. In practice an alternative approach which may be acceptable in these circumstances is to deal with the matter within the taxation note, thus:

EXAMPLE: in the financial statement of the profit making company

Of the tax on profit on ordinary activities of £135,000, £45,000 has been relieved by the surrender of losses by another group company in exchange for a payment of the same amount.

EXAMPLE: in the financial statements of the loss making company

The tax benefits of £45,000 arising from the losses incurred have been surrendered to another group company in exchange for a payment of the same amount.

14.100 DEVELOPMENT LAND TAX

Development land tax (DLT) is assessable when an interest in land in the U.K. is disposed of or a project of material development is started. It is a tax on the betterment gain which arises from the granting of planning permission for development. It has been abolished in respect of disposals and developments taking place after 18 March 1985. The following guidelines for accounting for DLT charges which arise in respect of occurrences before that date are suggested.

(i) Where DLT arises as a result of a disposal, the liability should be charged against the consideration received so as to reduce the profit on disposal (or increase the loss thereon). As the portion of the profit on disposal which forms the basis for assessment to DLT is not subject to corporation tax, the tax charge in the financial statements will be distorted. Where material, the amount of DLT charged in cost of sales and the amount by which the tax charge has been reduced should be disclosed.

Alternatively DLT can be treated as part of the tax charge in the profit and loss account, but if this treatment is adopted it should be disclosed in the accounting policies note and the amount of DLT charged should be separately disclosed in the notes to the accounts.

(ii) If DLT arises other than on a true disposal (e.g. on the commencement of a project of material development), then the DLT should be capitalised and added to the cost of the related asset.

14.110 SPECIAL CIRCUMSTANCES AFFECTING TAXATION

The Act requires particulars to be given of any special circumstances which affect liability in respect of taxation of profits, income or capital gains for the financial year or for succeeding financial years. [Sch 4: 54(2)] Generally circumstances which should be disclosed are those which result in the tax charge for the year being materially higher or lower than would normally be expected, and items such as losses carried forward or ACT written off as irrecoverable which are available to reduce the tax liabilities on the profits of future years. However, where there are two or more circumstances which all have a material effect on the liability for the year, they should all be disclosed even though the combined effect of them leaves the tax charge for the year at a normal level.

One specific circumstance which is referred to in SSAP 15 and which is discussed in Section 14.088(b)(iii) above is where timing differences have arisen in the period but deferred tax has not been provided because no asset or liability is expected to crystallise.

Examples of the more common taxation situations which require disclosure are given below.

(i) Current year's losses

Where a company has incurred a loss (as adjusted for tax purposes), it is appropriate to recognise a credit for tax in the profit and loss account to the extent that:

(a) repayment of tax can be obtained by carrying back the loss to reduce the taxable profit of the previous year; or

(b) the loss can be surrendered to another group company under the group relief arrangements; or

(c) the loss can be set against a liability arising in respect of an extraordinary credit or of a gain which has not passed through the profit and loss account; or

(d) the loss can be set against other timing differences to reduce a deferred tax liability that is expected to crystallise; or

(e) exceptionally, it can be foreseen with reasonable certainty that the loss can be set off against profits of the next accounting period.

If credit cannot be taken for tax on all the losses incurred in the foregoing ways then the difference should be disclosed as losses which are available to set against future profits since this is a special circumstance which will affect the liability of future financial years. The note should also explain why the tax credit is low.

EXAMPLE

The tax relief available in respect of the loss for the current year is restricted to the corporation tax paid in respect of the previous financial year. Unrelieved losses of £240,000 are carried forward and are available to reduce tax liability in respect of future profits.

(ii) Prior year's losses brought forward

Where a company's taxable profit is reduced by the application of losses brought forward for which credit has not been taken previously, the resulting low tax charge should be explained.

EXAMPLE

Tax on profit on ordinary activities has been reduced by tax relief of £18,000 in respect of prior years' losses brought forward.

(iii) Significant disallowable items

Although some items which are properly treated as revenue expenditure are disallowable for tax purposes (e.g. entertaining expenses) it is rare for their effect on the tax liability to be sufficiently large to require disclosure. A problem which is likely to be more significant is that losses incurred by a company operating in one country cannot normally be set off against profits earned by other group companies elsewhere.

EXAMPLE

The tax liability is unduly high in relation to the group profit on ordinary activities before tax because of losses of £179,000 incurred by a foreign subsidiary for which no tax relief is immediately available. Unrelieved losses of the foreign subsidiary totalling US$520,000 (approximately £430,000) may be set against its future profits but will cease to be available for this purpose at various dates over the next five years.

(iv) Irrecoverable ACT

ACT which has not been recovered otherwise may be carried forward indefinitely and set against future corporation tax liabilities. The amount of ACT written off as irrecoverable should be disclosed.

14.120 ALLOCATION OF TAX TO EXTRAORDINARY ITEMS

The Act requires that the tax charge for the year is divided between tax on profit or loss on ordinary activities and tax on extraordinary profit or loss. In practice the total tax charge will be based on the results of ordinary activities and extraordinary items combined and a number of different methods for allocating the charge between the two elements have been used. ED 36 (the proposed revision of SSAP 6) proposes a single method as standard. This is that the tax on the results of ordinary activities should be computed as if the extraordinary item did not exist. This amount should be compared with the actual tax charge on the profit or loss for the financial year and the difference ascribed to extraordinary items.

EXAMPLE

	£
Profit on ordinary activities before tax	*1,900,000*
Extraordinary item; costs of factory closure	*(2,400,000)*
Accounts loss	*(500,000)*
Disallowable ordinary expenses	*150,000*
Capital allowances in excess of depreciation (no deferred tax required)	*(300,000)*
Disallowable closure costs	*250,000*
Adjusted loss for tax purposes	*(400,000)*
The loss can be relieved by set-off against the profits for the previous years so the tax credit to be recognised is: £400,000 at 50%, i.e.	*(200,000)*
If there had been no extraordinary items the tax charge would have been:	
£1,900,000 + £150,000 − £300,000, or £1,750,000 at 45%, i.e.	*787,500*
Therefore the tax credit should be shown as:	
Tax on profit on ordinary activities	*787,500*
Tax credit in respect of extraordinary loss	*(987,500)*

EXAMPLE

The facts are the same as in the above example except that the tax loss cannot be set against the profit of previous years and the circumstances do not justify it being carried forward as an asset. Therefore the tax credit to be recognised in the profit and loss account is:	*nil*
The tax position should be shown as:	
Tax on profit on ordinary activities	*787,500*
Tax credit in respect of extraordinary loss	*(787,500)*

If the method described in ED 36 is followed strictly it can produce some strange results if there is a loss on ordinary activities and an extraordinary profit. Consider the following example:

EXAMPLE

	£
Loss on ordinary activities (as adjusted for taxation purposes)	*(800,000)*
Extraordinary profit (as adjusted for taxation purposes)	*1,800,000*
Adjusted profit for tax purposes	*1,000,000*
Tax payable at 50%	*500,000*

In theory the extent to which any credit may be taken for the tax effect of the loss on ordinary activities depends on whether or not there exist other reasons for recognising the credit, such as prior years' profits or a deferred tax liability available for set off.

Thus if there are such reasons for recognising the tax credit arising from the loss, then, assuming tax at 50% throughout, the tax position should be shown as:

Tax credit on loss on ordinary activities	*(400,000)*
Tax on extraordinary profit	*900,000*

Whereas if there was no justification for believing that recovery of the tax on the loss was reasonably assured, the position would be:

Tax on loss on ordinary activities	*nil*
Tax on extraordinary profit	*500,000*

In fact recovery of the tax on the loss is assured in these circumstances since it will be recovered by being set against the tax on the extraordinary profit. Therefore the treatment seems illogical and it is to be hoped that the position will be clarified before ED 36 becomes a SSAP. In the meantime it is suggested that the tax on any loss on ordinary activities should always be regarded as fully recoverable to the extent of tax on any extraordinary profit against which it may be offset.

14.130 TAX CHARGE IN INTERIM STATEMENTS

Listed companies are required to prepare a half-yearly or interim report reflecting a charge for U.K. and overseas taxation in arriving at the half-year profit (or loss) on ordinary activities after taxation. Questions arise as to how this tax charge should be calculated. It is generally considered that interim results should be regarded as an integral part of an annual period and therefore the tax rate to be applied to the interim profit or loss on ordinary activities should be based so far as practicable on the effective annual tax rate. If group profits are being reported, the effective annual tax rate of the group should be applied to the interim profits of the group.

The application of this principle is dealt with below.

(a) Calculation of effective annual tax rate

The calculation of the effective annual tax rate is based on the formula (expressed as a %):

$$\frac{\text{Estimated annual tax charge or credit} \times 100}{\text{Estimated annual profit or loss on ordinary activities before taxation}}$$

In applying this formula, the following should be taken into account:

(i) The estimated annual tax charge or credit should be calculated using the same degree of prudence as would be applied in the annual financial statements and should follow the rules laid down in SSAP 8 (e.g. treatment of irrecoverable ACT and availability of trading losses).

(ii) Where material capital expenditure is to take place during the year which will give rise to timing differences that will not be provided in the financial statements, the estimated annual tax charge should be estimated by projecting the total of unprovided timing differences on the basis of the entire year's capital expenditure.

(iii) Extraordinary items and the related tax should be excluded from the calculations. Extraordinary gains or losses in the second half of the year should not be anticipated unless the events which give rise to such gains or losses are virtually certain to occur.

The effective tax rate thus calculated should then be applied to the interim profit or loss on ordinary activities (subject to the restrictions mentioned in (b) below arising from trading losses or losses brought forward).

(b) Treatment of losses

Difficult questions sometimes arise in regard to the treatment of losses.

The company may accumulate tax losses or suffer a trading loss in one or both halves of a year. If the tax losses can be used (e.g. by applying them against profits of the previous year) or it is estimated with reasonable certainty that there will be sufficient profits in the full year to absorb the losses, then the estimated effective annual tax charge (or the amount recoverable) should be apportioned over the two half years by reference to accounting profits or losses. No credit should be taken for tax to be recovered if sufficient profits are neither available nor predictable.

The following chart gives guidance on the availability of losses in calculating the interim period's tax charge.

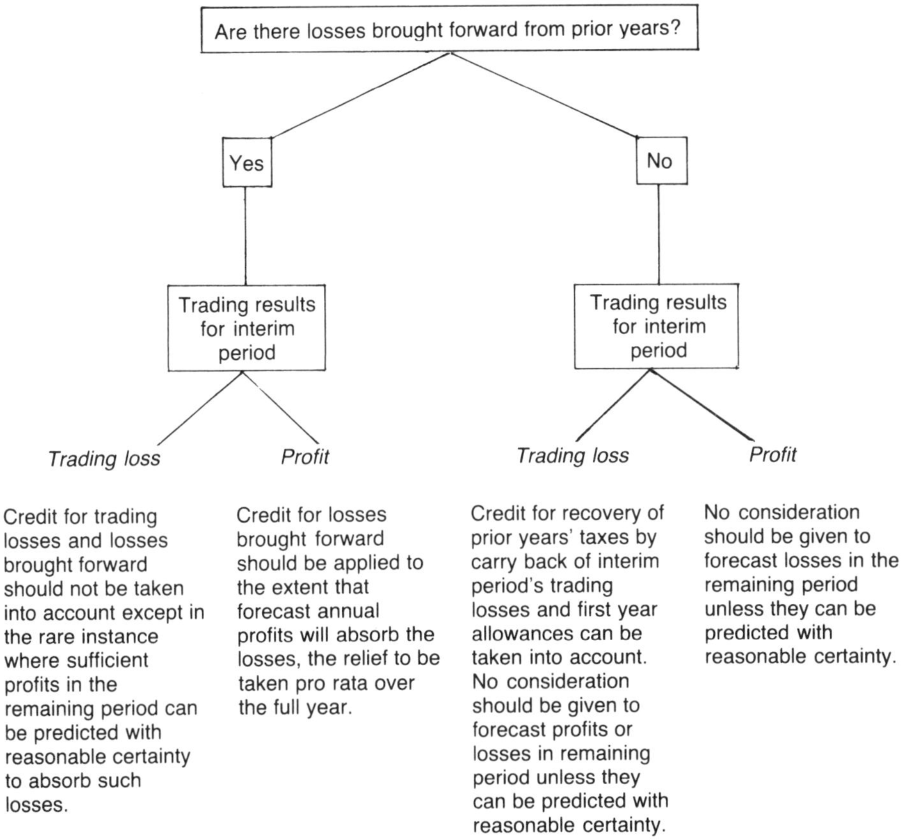

(c) Example of tax calculation using above rules

The following example illustrates the application of the above rules to a routine set of circumstances.

EXAMPLE:

	£
The profit before taxation for the interim period is	*500,000*
The estimated results for the full year are as follows:	
Profit before tax	*1,500,000*
Capital allowances in excess of depreciation (assuming no deferred tax is required)	*(400,000)*
Disallowed expenses	*100,000*
Taxable profit	*1,200,000*
Tax payable at 46.25% of £1,200,000 is	*555,000*
The effective annual tax rate is: £555,000 ÷ £1,500,000, i.e.	*37%*
The tax charge to be included in the interim statement is: £500,000 at 37%, i.e.	*185,000*

Note that it is not necessary (and not practicable) to estimate the capital allowances available for the interim period.

If in the above example the company had trading losses brought forward of £400,000, this would have the effect of reducing the estimated taxable profit for the year to £800,000, which at 46.25% gives a liability of £370,000. The effective annual rate becomes £370,000 ÷ £1,500,000, i.e. 24.7%, and the tax liability on the interim period is £500,000 at 24.7%, i.e. £123,000.

(d) Comparative figures

The comparative figures should be based on the actual tax rate for the previous full year. Companies may not wish to alter previously published figures. However, where the actual tax rate is significantly different from the rate used in last year's interim statement, restatement using the actual rate should be encouraged.

15 LEASING

15.010 INTRODUCTION

The accounting treatment of leases, both by lessors and lessees, is dealt with in SSAP 21, 'Accounting for leases and hire purchase contracts'. In some cases the accounting requirements and disclosures are complex and for this reason the ASC has issued guidance notes on SSAP 21 which give guidance on how the statement might be applied but which do not have mandatory status. The requirements of SSAP 21 affect the financial statements of accounting periods beginning on or after 1 July 1984 but, because of the transitional arrangements, only become fully effective in relation to accounting periods beginning on or after 1 July 1987 in the case of lessees and 1 July 1989 in the case of lessors.

15.020 DEFINITIONS

(i) A lease is defined as a contract for the hire of a specific asset whereby the lessor retains ownership of the asset and conveys the right to the use of the asset to the lessee for an agreed period of time in return for the payment of specified rentals. A lease may be either a finance lease or an operating lease.

(ii) A finance lease is defined as a lease that transfers substantially all of the risks and rewards of ownership to the lessee.

(iii) An operating lease is defined as any lease which is not a finance lease.

(iv) A hire purchase contract is defined as a contract for the hire of an asset which contains a provision giving the hirer an option to acquire legal title to the asset upon the fulfilment of certain conditions stated in the contract.

15.030 ACCOUNTING BY LESSEES

The approach required by SSAP 21 is that a finance lease should be capitalised by the lessee; when the lease is entered into, the continuing right to the use and enjoyment of the asset should be recognised in the balance sheet along with the obligation to make future payments. If the lease is an operating lease the rental payable is taken into account only as it arises. As with all statements of standard accounting practice, SSAP 21 need not be applied to immaterial items, and in many cases this consideration may justify accounting for finance leases as operating leases. The guidance notes suggest that the relevant criterion is the size of the leases in aggregate in the context of the size of the lessee and that regard should be had to the effect which capitalisation would have on the financial statements as a whole. Thus consideration should be given to the effect on total fixed assets, total borrowings, the gearing ratio and the profit or loss for the year. If capitalisation of finance leases would not have a material effect on any of these items, then the leases need not be capitalised.

Where leases entered into by a lessee are material the most difficult problem is to determine whether or not a lease falls within the definition of a finance lease. This problem is discussed in the following section.

15.031 IDENTIFICATION OF FINANCE LEASES

As stated above a finance lease is defined as one which transfers substantially all of the risks and rewards of ownership of the asset to the lessee. SSAP 21 indicates that such a transfer of risks and rewards of ownership should be presumed to take place if at the inception of the lease the present value of the minimum lease payments, including any initial payment, amounts to substantially all (normally 90% or more) of the fair value of the leased asset.

The fair value of the leased asset is normally its purchase cost on a cash basis, but any grants that would be receivable towards its purchase should be deducted. If the fair value cannot be determined accurately, it must be estimated.

The minimum lease payments are the minimum payments over the lease term (excluding charges for services and taxes) together with any residual amounts guaranteed by the lessee or a party related to him. The lease term is the initial lease period plus any further periods for which the lessee has the option to continue the lease which it is reasonably certain at the inception of the lease that he will exercise.

Where a lease gives the lessee an option for early termination, any calculation of the minimum lease payments which assumes the exercise of that option should include any penalties associated with the termination.

The present value of the minimum lease payments should be calculated using the interest rate 'implicit in the lease'. The interest rate implicit in the lease is defined as the discount rate which when applied at the inception of the lease to the amounts which the lessor expects to receive and retain, produces a present value equal to the fair value of the leased asset. Since the amounts which the lessor expects to receive and retain include any residual value of the asset even though that value is not guaranteed, calculation of the interest rate implicit in the lease requires a knowledge on the part of the lessee of the lessor's estimate of that residual value. If, as is likely, this information is not available to the lessee, it is not possible to determine the interest rate implicit in the lease. If the rate is not determinable then the rate which the lessee would be expected to pay on a similar lease should be used.

The Guidance Notes on SSAP 21 suggest alternative ways of determining whether a lease is a finance lease. One suggested approach is to consider whether the present value of any amounts which the lessor expects to receive but which do not form part of the minimum lease payments of the lessee exceeds 10% of the fair value of the leased asset. Most commonly, the only amount to be considered for this purpose will be the estimated residual value of the asset at the end of the lease term (less any amounts which, because they are guaranteed by the lessee, are included as part of the minimum lease payments); if the present value of this residual value is less than 10% of the fair value of the asset it will usually imply that the lease is a finance lease. However this approach does not solve the problem that the amount to be taken into account is the amount the lessor expects to receive, i.e. the lessor's estimate of the residual value; this will generally not be known to the lessee and therefore it will only be possible to estimate residual value reasonably where the asset is one, such as a motor vehicle, in which there is a ready market throughout its life. Another approach that is suggested, is to determine if the lessee has the use of the asset for a period over which substantially all of the economic benefits can be derived from the asset, in which case the lease is likely to be a finance lease.

The requirement to include in the lease term any periods for which the lessee has an option to renew which he is reasonably certain to exercise is one which is likely to cause difficulty in interpretation. It is suggested that the phrase 'reasonably certain' should be interpreted strictly. It is not sufficient that the optional renewal terms should appear advantageous to the lessee at the time of the inception of the lease since uncertainties relating to rates of interest, technological developments, and economic circumstances must be taken into account. Clearly these uncertainties become more significant the longer the period before the option is exercisable. Unless the initial lease period is very short, it is unlikely that reasonable certainty of renewal will exist other than on the payment of a nominal rental only. Thus in practice the determination of whether or not a lease is a finance lease will normally be made by reference only to the lease period for which the lessee is irrevocably committed at the inception of the lease.

SSAP 21 stresses that the presumption that substantially all the risks and rewards of ownership have been transferred in the circumstances indicated above may be rebutted if it can clearly be demonstrated that this is not the case. Equally the presumption that a lease which does not meet those conditions is not a finance lease may be rebutted. Clearly the intention is to look at the substance of the transaction rather than to lay down strict rules; if the substance is that substantially all the risks and rewards of ownership are transferred by a lease then it should be accounted for as a finance lease.

It must be recognised however that as far as possible, lessees will prefer to enter into operating leases rather than finance leases, since an important effect of SSAP 21 is that finance leases have to be recognised as liabilities and therefore are no longer a source of 'off balance sheet finance'. It is clear that in order to meet this preference, many leasing companies are offering contracts structured in such a way that they do not meet the conditions which are specified as giving rise to the presumption that substantially all the risks and rewards of ownership are transferred by the lease, while at the same time keeping to a minimum the risks accepted by the leasing company. It seems probable therefore that in practice the requirements for recognition as a finance lease will be strictly interpreted and that the presumption that a lease which does not meet the specified conditions is not a finance lease will very rarely be rebutted.

15.032 ACCOUNTING FOR FINANCE LEASES

At the inception of a finance lease, both the leased asset and the related lease obligation should be recorded in the balance sheet at the present value of the minimum lease payments. In most cases the fair value of the asset is a close approximation of the present value of the minimum lease payments; where the leased asset is also offered on a cash sale basis, the cash price might be a suitable measure of the present value. Alternatively, the contract terms or rates quoted by finance houses may indicate a suitable discount rate.

Leased assets should be described as such in the balance sheet to distinguish them from owned assets. They should be depreciated over the shorter of the lease term or their estimated useful lives.

The difference between the total minimum lease payments and their present value at the inception of the lease represents a finance charge. This should be allocated to accounting periods over the term of the lease so as to produce a constant rate of interest (or a reasonable approximation thereto) on the remaining balance of the lease obligation. This is achieved by apportioning each rental payment between a finance charge and a reduction of the lease obligation. SSAP 21 does not specify particular methods which are to be used for this purpose; however the Guidance Notes do set out three methods which are often used in practice. These are:

(i) Actuarial method

This method achieves an accurate apportionment of interest cost over the term of the lease. Often the information necessary to adopt this basis is provided to the lessee by the lessor. Otherwise the method requires access to a computer and a suitable computer program and is seldom used in practice.

(ii) Sum of digits method

This is also referred to as the 'Rule of 78'. In most cases the method produces an acceptable approximation of the results obtained by the actuarial method, but is simpler to apply. It is probably most frequently used in practice. The following is an example of the calculation.

EXAMPLE – Sum of digits method

Asset leased under a finance lease for a three year period, twelve quarterly rental payments; total finance charge £10,000.

(i) If rentals are paid quarterly in arrears

The digit assigned for the first period will be twelve and for the last period, one.

Period	*Quarter*	*Digit*	*Finance charge allocation*			*£*
Year 1	*1*	*12*	*£10,000*	×	*12/78*	*1,539*
	2	*11*	*£10,000*	×	*11/78*	*1,410*
	3	*10*	*£10,000*	×	*10/78*	*1,282*
	4	*9*	*£10,000*	×	*9/78*	*1,154*
Year 2	*1*	*8*	*£10,000*	×	*8/78*	*1,026*
	2	*7*	*£10,000*	×	*7/78*	*897*
	3	*6*	*£10,000*	×	*6/78*	*769*
	4	*5*	*£10,000*	×	*5/78*	*641*
Year 3	*1*	*4*	*£10,000*	×	*4/78*	*513*
	2	*3*	*£10,000*	×	*3/78*	*385*
	3	*2*	*£10,000*	×	*2/78*	*256*
	4	*1*	*£10,000*	×	*1/78*	*128*
		78				*10,000*

(ii) If rentals are paid in advance

Since there is no capital outstanding during the final quarter of the last year, there is no finance charge allocation. Consequently, the digit for the last period will be zero; and for the first period, eleven. The sum of the digits becomes sixty-six.

(iii) Straight-line method

The finance charge is spread equally over the period of the lease. Thus, if it were applied in the circumstances of the above example, the finance charge would be £833 in each quarter. This method does not attempt to produce a constant periodic rate of charge and does not, therefore, comply with SSAP 21. It is only appropriate to apply this method if the difference between the figures thus produced and those which would be produced by one of the above methods would not be material to the financial statements. It is not usually acceptable if the aggregate amount of finance leases is large relative to the size of the company.

In some circumstances the availability of grants and capital allowances to the lessor will mean that an asset can be offered on a finance lease at a rental which gives a total for the minimum lease payments which is actually less than the fair value of the asset. In such a case recording the lease obligation at the fair value of the leased asset would give rise to a negative finance charge which is specifically prohibited by SSAP 21. Consequently, the leased asset and the obligations under the lease should be recorded at the start of the lease at the total of the minimum lease payments. This will result in no finance charge being suffered by the lessee.

The Guidance Notes suggest that where a lease contains variation clauses which adjust the rentals to take account of movements in base rates of interest or changes in taxation, no adjustment need normally be made to the calculations which are carried out at the start of the lease. Any increase or reduction in rentals should be accounted for as an increase or reduction in finance charges in the period in which it arises. Where the reduction in rentals exceeds the future finance charges the excess should be applied to reduce future depreciation charges. Thus in most cases any difference between the rental assessed at the start of the lease and the actual amount payable may be dealt with in the profit and loss account for the period covered by the particular payment. In exceptional circumstances where a very large change in rental for a significant period is involved it may be thought necessary to spread the aggregate difference over the remainder of the lease period by the same method as was used to allocate the finance charges initially (e.g. by the sum of the digits method).

15.033 ACCOUNTING FOR OPERATING LEASES

Rentals payable under an operating lease should be charged on a straight-line basis over the lease term even though the payments are not made on that basis unless another systematic and rational basis is more appropriate. For example, where the rentals of an asset are based on the actual usage of that asset, or are revised periodically to reflect the efficiency of the asset or current market rates, the rentals actually payable may be an appropriate measure.

This requirement seems to imply that, where a lease grants a 'rent holiday' during which no payments are required, the total rental payments should be spread equally over the holiday period as well as the period during which payments are actually made. Rent holidays often arise at the beginning of a lease to provide the lessee with time to install the asset and bring it into operation, or in the case of a property to fit out and furnish it. In these circumstances it seems unreasonable to make an apportionment of rent to a period in which the lessee derives no benefit from his possession of the asset and that a rational basis which is more appropriate is to charge the rentals payable over a period which begins on the earlier of the date on which the lessee begins to derive benefit from the asset and the date on which the holiday ends and rent begins to be charged.

15.034 ACCOUNTING FOR HIRE PURCHASE CONTRACTS

Generally hire purchase contracts have all the characteristics of finance leases and should be accounted for as such. They should be accounted for as operating leases only if the contract is such that substantially all the risks and rewards of ownership do not pass to the hirer at the inception of the contract. Such a situation might arise if at the conclusion of the lease period the hirer's right to acquire legal title to the asset was on condition that he paid an amount equal to the then market value of the asset which was not insignificant in relation to its original cost. Contracts of this nature are very rare.

15.035 ACCOUNTING FOR SALE AND LEASEBACK TRANSACTIONS

A sale and leaseback transaction is a linked arrangement whereby the owner of an asset sells that asset and immediately leases it back from the purchaser. The subject of the sale and leaseback is usually a property but may be another fixed asset.

The lease may be a finance lease if it meets the criterion that substantially all the risks and rewards of ownership remain with the lessee or it may be an operating lease. A long lease of a property at a fixed annual rental may be a finance lease since the present value of the reversion of the property at the end of the lease term is likely to be very small. On the other hand a short lease or one which incorporates provision for regular rent reviews would be an operating lease. The lease should be accounted for as a finance lease or as an operating lease in the manner described above.

In order to account for the sale part of the transaction, the book value of the asset should be adjusted to its appropriate historical cost amount; if it has been revalued it must be adjusted to depreciated historical cost by a transfer from revaluation reserve (see Section 9.025(d)); if the book value is above the fair value of the asset at the date of sale, then a permanent diminution in value has taken place and the book value must be reduced accordingly by a charge to profit and loss account.

If the related lease is a finance lease the substance of the transaction is that no disposal of property has taken place and therefore no gain or loss on disposal should be recognised. The difference between the sale price and the book value should be carried forward and amortised over the same period as that in which the leased asset is depreciated (i.e. the shorter of the lease term and the estimated useful life of the asset).

If the related lease is an operating lease, it is necessary to determine the fair value of the asset and compare this with the contract sale price. Because the sale and lease transactions are connected the sale may be arranged at other than fair value, the effect of any difference being recognised in the rentals payable. The appropriate accounting is as follows:

(i) if the sale price is equal to fair value, any profit on sale should be recognised in the profit and loss account immediately;

(ii) if the sale price is above fair value, the profit to be recognised immediately should be restricted to any excess of the fair value over book value; the excess of sale price over fair value will be reflected in higher rental charges and should therefore be carried forward and amortised over the period to the first rent review or over the period of the lease if there is no rent review;

(iii) if the sale price is below fair value, then fair value may be ignored; any excess of the sale price over book value should be recognised immediately; but if the sale price is below book value the shortfall will be compensated by lower rentals in the lease agreement and it may therefore be carried forward and charged to profits over the period to the first rent review or over the period of the lease if there is no rent review. (It should be noted that the fair value cannot be below book value since the book value of the asset must first be adjusted as indicated above.)

The following examples illustrate these rules:

EXAMPLES

(i) Sale price above fair value

	£
Book value	*100*
Fair value	*110*
Sale price	*125*
Profit to be recognised	*10*
Profit to be deferred	*15*

(ii) Sale price below fair value

	Asset A £	*Asset B* £
Book value	*100*	*100*
Sale price	*110*	*95*
Fair value	*125*	*110*
Profit to be recognised	*10*	–
Apparent loss to be deferred if compensated by below market rentals	–	*5*

15.036 DISCLOSURE REQUIREMENTS

The disclosure requirements of SSAP 21 for lessees are summarised below.

(a) Accounting policies

The policies adopted for accounting for operating leases and finance leases must be stated. An example of an appropriate note is included in the financial statements of Tramp Holdings p.l.c. on page 30.

(b) Finance leases

(i) The gross amount, related accumulated depreciation and total depreciation allocated for the period in respect of assets held under finance leases, by each major class of asset should be shown. A suggested description for capitalised leased assets is 'assets held under finance leases and hire purchase contracts'. Alternatively, these amounts may be included in similar items in respect of owned fixed assets, in which case the net amount of assets held under finance leases, and the depreciation allocated for the period in respect of such leased assets included in the overall totals should be disclosed.

The alternative treatment is illustrated in Notes 7 and 14 in the model financial statements of Tramp Holdings p.l.c.

(ii) The amount of lease obligations (net of future finance charges) should be disclosed separately either on the face of the balance sheet or in the notes, analysed between amounts payable within one year, in two to five years inclusive, and amounts payable thereafter. Where the analysis is shown separately from amounts shown for other liabilities, it may be presented as an analysis of the gross obligations, with the future finance charges being separately deducted from the total. A suggested description of the net lease obligations is 'obligations under finance leases and hire purchase contracts'. In the model financial statements of Tramp Holdings p.l.c. the information is included with amounts for other borrowings. An example of the alternative presentation is as follows:

EXAMPLE

Obligations under finance leases and hire purchase contracts.

	1984	*1983*
	£'000	*£'000*
Minimum lease payments payable		
Within one year	*22*	*19*
Within two to five years	*104*	*101*
After five years	*16*	*14*
	142	*134*
Finance charges allocated to future periods	*(18)*	*(16)*
	124	*118*

(iii) The aggregate finance charges for the period must be disclosed.

(iv) The amount of any commitments for finance leases entered into at the balance sheet date but whose inception occurs after the year end must be shown.

EXAMPLE

The group has entered into a contract to lease an asset under a finance lease whereby the asset will be delivered and rental obligations commence in February 1985. The minimum payments under the lease total £25,000 payable over five years.

(c) Operating leases

(i) The lease payments which the lessee is committed to make during the next year should be disclosed. These commitments should be analysed between those relating to lease terms which expire within that year, those which expire within two to five years inclusive, and those which continue for over five years from the balance sheet date; commitments in respect of leases of land and buildings should be shown separately from other operating leases. An example of an appropriate note is shown as Note 26 in the model financial statements of Tramp Holdings p.l.c.

(ii) The total operating lease rentals charged to profit and loss during the period should be disclosed, analysed between (i) hire of plant and machinery and (ii) other operating leases.

The statutory disclosure requirements which are relevant to obligations under leases are as follows:

(i) Sch 4: 50(5) requires particulars to be given of any other financial commitments which have not been provided for and are relevant to assessing the company's state of affairs;

(ii) Sch 4: 53(6) requires disclosure of the amount charged to revenue in respect of hire of plant and machinery.

The first of these requirements is met by requirements (b)(iv) and (c)(i) above, and the second by requirements (b)(iii), (c)(ii) and the disclosure of the annual depreciation of leased assets included under (b)(i).

15.037 TRANSITIONAL PROVISIONS

SSAP 21 should be adopted as soon as possible but for lessees is to be regarded as standard only in respect of accounting periods beginning on or after 1 July 1987. In earlier years therefore it will not be necessary to capitalise finance leases in balance sheets, although the practice is encouraged.

However the disclosure requirements detailed in Section 15.036, with the exception of those specified in paragraph (b)(i) (i.e. the disclosures relating to leased assets capitalised), are standard in respect of accounting periods beginning on or after 1 July 1984. This appears to imply that finance leases must be distinguished from operating leases in the notes to the accounts even though the accounting treatment of both is identical. In practice the disclosures required in respect of each type of lease are so similar that it seems unnecessary to distinguish between the two during the transitional period.

15.040 ACCOUNTING BY LESSORS

The approach required by SSAP 21 to finance leases is to recognise the substance of the transaction, namely that the lessor is providing finance to the lessee to enable him to obtain the use of a specific asset. Consequently the asset recognised by the lessor under a finance lease is the amount receivable from the lessee rather than the asset which is the subject of the lease. Under an operating lease, the lessor treats the leased asset as a fixed asset and the rentals received as income.

Although SSAP 21 does not apply to immaterial items, most lessors carry out leasing business as a significant activity and it is therefore unlikely that the standard will not apply on the grounds of immateriality.

15.041 IDENTIFICATION OF FINANCE LEASES

The circumstances under which a lease is presumed to be a finance lease are the same for a lessor as for a lessee (see Section 15.031 above). However there are certain differences in circumstances, including differences in the cash flows arising, which may result in the lessor treating a lease in a different manner from the lessee; in particular leases which are regarded as finance leases by lessors may be operating leases as far as lessees are concerned. The principal matters which give rise to these differences are summarised below:

(i) In determining the minimum lease payments a lessee takes account only of payments to be made by him or by a party related to him, whereas the lessor also takes account of amounts to be received from independent third parties. A lessor may be able to arrange at or before the commencement of the lease that at its conclusion the asset will be sold to a third party at a guaranteed minimum price; he would take account of any such guaranteed residual value in determining the minimum lease payments.

(ii) While the interest rate implicit in the lease and the fair value of the leased asset may not be known to the lessee, they will certainly be known to the lessor. In determining the interest rate implicit in the lease the lessor will take account of amounts receivable from all sources including grants receivable and the incidence of tax relief.

15.042 ACCOUNTING FOR FINANCE LEASES

The net investment in the lease should be recorded in the balance sheet as a debtor. Initially the net investment is normally the cost to the lessor of the leased asset less any grant receivable. As with any other debtor balance consideration should be given to its collectibility and provision made for any anticipated losses. In considering collectibility regard should be had not only to amounts expected to be received from the lessee but also to amounts which may be recovered by sale of the leased asset. The net investment in the lease is reduced over the lease period by the proportion of rental income which is treated as repayment of the debtor balance.

The rentals (net of any charges for services etc) received by the lessor should be apportioned between finance income to the lessor and repayment of the debtor balance. Over the whole period of the lease the finance income equals the gross earnings from the lease, i.e. the amount by which the total of the receipts expected by the lessor exceeds the cost of the leased asset. The receipts expected by the lessor consist of the total rentals payable by the lessee together with any residual value of the asset which is receivable by the lessor, whether or not that residual value is guaranteed. The cost of the asset is the net cost after deducting any grants receivable by the lessor.

The gross earnings should normally be allocated to accounting periods over the term of the lease so as to produce a constant rate of return (or a reasonable approximation thereto) on the lessor's net cash investment in the lease. This allocation should take account not only of the cost of the asset and the rentals received but also of all cash flows associated with the lease (such as tax cash flows arising from capital allowances claimed by the lessor). The net cash investment at any given time is:

(i) the net investment at the start of the lease (i.e. cost of the asset less related grants); *plus*

(ii) the following related payments:

(a) taxation payments on the rental income;

(b) interest payments on related borrowings; and

(iii) profit taken out of the lease; *less*

(iv) the following related receipts:

(a) rentals received (excluding charges for services etc.);

(b) interest received on any cash surplus;

(c) taxation receipts including reductions in taxation liabilities as a result of capital allowances on the leased asset; and

(d) any amount received for the sale of the asset at the end of the lease term, or if no amount is received, its residual value (if any) at that time.

The Guidance Notes set out two methods which are commonly used to allocate gross earnings so as to give a constant rate of return on the net cash investment:

(i) *Actuarial method after tax*

Under this method a rate is calculated which when applied to the net cash invested in the lease, makes the total return over the whole period during which cash flows occur in respect of the lease, equal to the gross earnings determined as above.

(ii) *Investment period method*

Under this method the net cash invested is calculated as for the actuarial method. The gross earnings are then allocated to those periods in which the lessor has positive cash invested. This allocation is made in proportion to the net cash invested in each period.

The two methods will generally lead to very similar results. The main difference will occur where the net cash invested becomes negative at some stage. In these circumstances the investment period method gives a more prudent result. In both cases the calculations are complex. Examples of calculations using each method are given in the Guidance Notes.

Hire purchase contracts which are considered to be finance leases, will not normally give rise to cash flows for the lessor as a result of such items as capital allowances. Consequently, an allocation of gross earnings so as to give a constant rate of return on the net investment (that is, the balance sheet carrying value of the debtor before any provision for bad and doubtful debts) will usually be an acceptable approximation to an allocation based on net cash investment. The Guidance Notes contain examples of two methods, the actuarial method before tax and the sum of digits method, which may be appropriate for hire purchase contracts.

Initial direct costs, such as commission, legal fees, selling costs etc. which are incurred by the lessor in arranging a lease may be deferred and apportioned over the period of the lease on a systematic and rational basis, or they may be written off as incurred. Apportionment may be achieved by treating the costs as a deduction from gross earnings before the earnings are allocated to accounting periods.

Where grants are received against the purchase price of assets acquired for leasing they should be credited to income over the period of the lease. This will occur automatically by applying the methods of allocating finance income set out above. In most cases some or all of the benefit of receipt of a grant will be passed on to the lessee in the form of reduced rentals. Where a grant is tax free, this may result in the lessor's profit and loss account showing a loss before tax and a profit after tax in respect of that lease. Consequently, SSAP 21 allows, as an option to treating the grant as tax free income, the grossing up of the grant at the appropriate tax rate by adding the appropriate amount both to pre-tax profits and to the tax charge for the period. Where this treatment is adopted the lessor should disclose the amount by which the profit before tax and the tax charge have been increased as a result of the grossing up. An example of the grossing up process is set out in the Guidance Notes.

As a consequence of the progressive reduction in corporation tax rates introduced by the Finance Act 1984, lessors will frequently obtain tax relief for the purchase of an item at a rate of corporation tax which is higher than that at which they will pay tax on the rental income, giving rise to a 'tax gift'. In many cases the benefits of such tax gifts will be passed on to the lessee either under the terms of the lease contract or as an ex gratia adjustment. This may also give rise to pre-tax losses but post-tax profits for the lessor. The Equipment Leasing Association has issued a guidance note which sets out a method of adjusting the results so as to show a pre-tax profit. This method is comparable to the grossing up method for tax-free grants. Appropriate adjustments are also required to the deferred tax account. In view of the artificiality of the adjustments, the accounting methods set out in the Equipment Leasing Association paper should not be regarded as best practice. However, as the method is not in contravention of SSAP 21, it must be regarded as acceptable provided the treatment is clearly explained in the notes.

15.043 ACCOUNTING FOR OPERATING LEASES

Assets leased under operating leases should be recorded as fixed assets and depreciated over their useful lives.

Rental income, excluding charges for services such as insurance and maintenance, should be recognised on a straight-line basis over the lease term even though the payments are not made on that basis, unless another systematic and rational basis is more representative of the way in which the benefit of the leased asset is receivable (for example where rentals are based on usage).

Initial direct costs in arranging the lease may either be written off immediately or deferred and amortised over the lease term.

15.044 ACCOUNTING BY MANUFACTURER/DEALER

Where a manufacturer or dealer offers leasing terms as an option to normal selling terms, whether or not a selling profit should be recognised when the asset is first leased, will depend on whether there has, in effect, been a disposal of that asset. In the case of an operating lease, the manufacturer or dealer has retained the asset with a view to using it to generate rental income. Consequently, no selling profit should be recognised and the asset should be included in the balance sheet initially at its purchase price or production cost. In the case of a finance lease, there are two types of income associated with the contract, a profit on the 'sale' of the asset and finance income over the period of the lease. The selling profit should be recognised at the commencement of the lease. However, the amount of selling profit should be restricted to the excess of the fair value of the asset (that is its normal selling price reflecting appropriate discounts and current market conditions) over its cost to the lessor (net of grants receivable by the lessor). As the lessor will often allow some degree of discount on the normal selling price in order to obtain the overall deal, the assessment of the fair value of the asset should be calculated to ensure that the finance income under the lease is based on a normal rate of interest.

15.045 DISCLOSURE REQUIREMENTS

The disclosure requirements of SSAP 21 for lessors are summarised below.

(a) Accounting policies

The policies adopted for accounting for operating leases and finance leases and, in detail, the policy for recognising finance lease income, must be disclosed.

(b) Finance leases

The following should be disclosed:

(i) the net investment in finance leases (sub-divided between finance leases and hire-purchase contracts) at the balance sheet date; this amount should be included under debtors and a suitable description is 'Amounts receivable under finance leases (and hire-purchase contracts)';

(ii) the cost of assets acquired for the purpose of letting under finance leases;

(iii) the aggregate rentals receivable in the accounting period in respect of finance leases.

(c) Operating leases

The following should be disclosed:

(i) the gross amount and related accumulated depreciation charges of assets held for use in operating leases; and

(ii) the aggregate rentals receivable in the accounting period in respect of operating leases.

15.046 TRANSITIONAL PROVISIONS

SSAP 21 is to be regarded as standard by lessors for financial statements relating to accounting periods beginning on or after 1 July 1984. It should be applied to all leases and hire purchase contracts entered into after 1 July 1984 and to all those which had five years or more to run on that date.

It need not be applied retroactively to contracts existing at 1 July 1984 which had less than five years to run, but if advantage is taken of this transitional arrangement then there must be disclosed the amounts of gross earnings from finance leases and hire purchase contracts which have arisen under each of the principal bases used. This information should be disclosed both for the current year and for the comparative period.

16 ACCOUNTING FOR THE EFFECTS OF CHANGING PRICES

16.010 INTRODUCTION

SSAP 16 'Current Cost Accounting' which was first introduced in March 1980 has been the subject of substantial criticism. The exposure draft of a proposed new simplified standard to replace SSAP 16 (ED 35) provoked much unfavourable comment and has now been withdrawn. The CCAB has suspended the mandatory status of SSAP 16. The ASC is currently considering a new initiative on the requirements for accounting for the effects of changing prices and, in consequence, future developments are uncertain. It is certain, however, that in spite of the clear reluctance on the part of many preparers of financial statements to deal with the problems of accounting for the effects of changing prices, these problems are not going to go away, and that acceptable solutions will have to be developed. In their statement suspending the mandatory status of SSAP 16, the CCAB states that the standard is being retained as an authoritative reference on accounting under the current cost convention and that companies are still encouraged to provide information on the effects of changing prices. Accordingly guidance on the requirements of SSAP 16 is retained in this manual.

16.020 FORM AND CONTENT OF FINANCIAL STATEMENTS UNDER SSAP 16

Entities should include in their annual financial statements a current cost profit and loss account, balance sheet and explanatory notes incorporating specified minimum disclosures. This data may be supplementary to the historical cost financial statements, or the statutory financial statements may be presented on the current cost basis, with either supplementary historical cost financial statements or sufficient historical cost information to satisfy company law requirements. This chapter describes compliance by means of a supplementary current cost statement.

An example of a recommended format for current cost financial statements presented as supplementary information is contained in the model financial statements of Tramp Holdings p.l.c.

The ASC issued guidance notes on SSAP 16 at the same time as the standard was published. These notes which are described as for guidance only and not forming part of the statement of standard accounting practice contain advice on the practical application of the standard. They should be referred to in cases of difficulty.

16.021 PROFIT AND LOSS ACCOUNT

SSAP 16 requires certain adjustments to the historical cost profit and loss account to be made and disclosed to arrive at current cost operating profit and current cost profit attributable to shareholders.

(a) Current cost operating profit

This figure must be disclosed separately and is arrived at by making three specified adjustments to historical cost operating profit before interest:

(i) *Depreciation Adjustment* – the difference between the proportion of the value to the business of fixed assets consumed in the period and the depreciation calculated on the historical cost basis. Value to the business will usually be the net current replacement cost, and will generally be established by determining an appropriate index of price changes for each class of asset and then applying index factors to original cost to arrive at a gross replacement cost, from which an appropriate depreciation charge may be calculated (using the same depreciation rate as that used in the historical cost accounts). In the case of non-specialised buildings, the value to the business will normally be determined by reference to a recent professional valuation at open market value.

(ii) *Cost of Sales Adjustment* – the difference between the value to the business and the historical cost of stock consumed in the period.

(iii) *Monetary Working Capital Adjustment* – the extent to which changes in input prices have affected monetary working capital. This is defined in SSAP 16 as the aggregate of trade debtors, prepayments, trade bills receivable and stocks not subject to a cost of sales adjustment, less trade creditors, accruals and trade bills payable. Monetary working capital may also include an element of either cash or bank overdraft.

If monetary working capital includes any element of cash or bank overdraft, then a further adjustment is required to take account of interest on that element in arriving at current cost operating profit. In addition, certain other adjustments may be required to adjust the historical cost figures for profits or losses of associated companies, gains or losses on foreign currency translation or sales of fixed assets, on to a basis consistent with the definition of current cost operating profit.

The adjustments referred to above need not be disclosed on the face of the profit and loss account. However, the notes must contain a reconciliation between current cost operating profit and historical cost profit, before interest and tax. This should show each of these adjustments separately, (except that the cost of sales and monetary working capital adjustments may be combined).

(b) Current cost profit attributable to shareholders

This figure must be disclosed and, in order to derive it from current cost operating profit, it is necessary to adjust for interest payable or receivable (excluding any relating to monetary working capital), taxation, extraordinary items and minority interests. (Extraordinary items and minority interest may each need adjusting to a current cost basis.) In addition, a gearing adjustment must be made.

The gearing adjustment is based on the company or group's gearing ratio (ratio of average net borrowings to average net current cost operating assets). It is applied to the adjustments to operating profit described above, to arrive at an abatement or write-back of the proportion of those adjustments which is effectively borne by the providers of loan capital to the company.

SSAP 16 states that Nationalised Industries should not make a gearing adjustment in their profit and loss accounts and that interest on their net borrowings should be shown after taxation and extraordinary items.

(c) Disclosures

The disclosures which are required by SSAP 16 to be made in the profit and loss account or the notes are:

(i) In the profit and loss account:

- current cost operating profit,
- interest/income relating to the net borrowing on which the gearing adjustment has been based,
- the gearing adjustment,

- taxation,
- extraordinary items,
- current cost profit after taxation attributable to shareholders.

(ii) Corresponding amounts for the preceding period.

(iii) In the notes, a description of the bases and methods adopted in relation to the depreciation, cost of sales, monetary working capital and gearing adjustments, foreign currency translation and any other material adjustments to the historical cost profit and corresponding amounts.

(iv) The reconciliation between historical and current cost operating profit, already referred to.

(v) For listed companies, current cost earnings per share, based on current cost profit attributable to equity shareholders before extraordinary items.

(vi) The treatment that has been adopted where it has proved impracticable to calculate, in a way consistent with the standard's definition of profit, gains/losses on asset disposals, extraordinary and exceptional items, prior year items, income from associates, group consolidation adjustments, minority interests and translation of foreign currencies.

Additionally, where related companies do not themselves prepare current cost financial statements and as a result the investing group includes information based on the directors' best estimates, SSAP 1 requires that this fact be disclosed.

Where an extraordinary item has to be adjusted from historical to current cost, that adjustment will require abating by the gearing ratio in the same way as the current cost adjustments to operating profit. It is logical that that abatement should appear in the same section of the profit and loss account as the extraordinary item itself and this is illustrated in the model financial statements of Tramp Holdings p.l.c.

16.022 BALANCE SHEET

(a) Bases of valuation

The current cost balance sheet may be presented in summarised form, provided that a full historical cost balance sheet is given. All fixed assets, stock subject to a cost of sales adjustment and investments other than those treated as current assets are to be included at the appropriate value to the business. Current assets, other than stock subject to a cost of sales adjustment, and all liabilities remain unchanged at their historical cost figures. Goodwill should normally remain unchanged.

(b) Reserves

Reserves should include revaluation surpluses or deficits and the cumulative adjustments made to allow for price changes in arriving at current cost profit attributable to shareholders. Although there is reference, in the explanatory notes and in the appendix to the standard, to a current cost reserve which would include these balances, the standard itself is silent on the need for a separate reserve for this purpose.

It is recommended that all transfers to and from reserves required as a result of the application of current cost principles during the accounting period should be summarised in the analysis of movements on reserves, under the heading 'Transfer to/from current cost reserve'. However, it is also recommended that the current cost reserve should not be shown as a separate, cumulative total. Instead, the current cost movement on reserves should open and close with an unanalysed total reserve figure. The reason for this recommendation is that any current cost reserve total must be an arbitrary number, which is dependent upon the point at which the company commenced producing current cost financial statements and upon the company's individual view on when items may be released from that reserve.

(c) Disclosures

The disclosures which are required by SSAP 16 to be made in the balance sheet or the notes are:

(i) Summaries of fixed asset accounts and of movements on reserves.

(ii) Totals of net operating assets and net borrowing and their main elements.

(iii) Corresponding amounts for the previous period.

(iv) A description in the notes of the bases and methods adopted in determining the value to the business of fixed assets and stock and work in progress, and the amount of any other material adjustments to historical cost balances, and in arriving at corresponding amounts and the translation of foreign currencies.

(v) Where directors choose to value listed investments (other than those treated as current assets) at other than mid-market value, the basis of valuation and the reasons for the difference.

16.023 GROUP FINANCIAL STATEMENTS

A company which is the parent company of a group should produce group financial statements in accordance with the principles set out in SSAP16. It need not however produce current cost financial statements for itself as a single company. There is a requirement to treat group consolidation adjustments in a manner consistent with the definitions of current cost profit.

16.024 RELATIONSHIP WITH OTHER STANDARDS

Current cost financial statements produced to comply with SSAP 16 must also comply with all existing standards relating to historical cost financial statements, 'except where a conflict exists caused by the conceptual difference between the systems'. Conceptual differences will not often arise in this context.

One apparent conceptual difference is in the treatment of depreciation following the reassessment of asset lives. Current cost principles suggest that depreciation should be recalculated on the basis of the new assessment of total useful life and gross current replacement cost, whereas SSAP 12 requires that the undepreciated balance is depreciated over the remaining useful life of the asset as reassessed.

16.025 ENCOURAGED BUT NON-MANDATORY DISCLOSURES

The explanatory notes to the standard contain a number of suggestions for disclosure of additional information. They include:

(i) Excess monetary assets – information on any changes in the value to the business and effective purchasing power of any excess of monetary assets over borrowings. (This 'negative gearing adjustment' is not to be charged in the profit and loss account, but should be disclosed in the notes to the financial statements).

(ii) A statement of change in shareholders' equity interest after allowing for change in the general purchasing power of money.

(iii) Corresponding amounts (and any 5/10 year statements) adjusted to a common price basis.

(iv) Explanations of the operating and attributable profit figures and of assets employed, to assist user's understanding.

The explanatory notes suggest that a current cost source and application of funds statement could also be shown. This is not recommended where the main accounts already include a funds statement in compliance with SSAP 10, in view of the large amount of duplication of information which would be involved.

17 COMPANY REQUIREMENTS TO PRODUCE, PUBLISH, AND FILE FINANCIAL STATEMENTS

17.010 RULES FOR PREPARING AND FILING FINANCIAL STATEMENTS

Every U.K. company registered under the Companies Acts is required to prepare a balance sheet and profit and loss account in respect of each accounting reference period. The directors must lay these documents, together with the auditors' report and directors' report, before the company in general meeting. A copy of these documents must be sent to every member and debenture holder not less than 21 days before the date of the annual general meeting.

In addition, every such company (except an unlimited company which is not a subsidiary or holding company of a limited company) must deliver a copy of these documents to the Registrar of Companies within seven months, if a public company, or ten months if a private company, of the end of the accounting reference period. [ss 241 and 242] Companies which have businesses or interests outside the U.K., Channel Islands and the Isle of Man can claim a three months extension. These documents may take the form of modified accounts in the case of small and medium-sized companies who qualify for this exemption (see Section 17.020 below).

Stock Exchange requirement

Stock Exchange companies are required to issue their annual reports and financial statements within six months following the date of the end of the financial period. Companies with significant overseas interests may apply for an extension.

17.020 MODIFIED ACCOUNTS

17.021 EXEMPTION GIVEN TO SMALL AND MEDIUM-SIZED COMPANIES

In most cases, the accounts to be delivered to the Registrar of Companies will be the same as those required under s 241 to be laid before the company in a general meeting. Certain companies, however, which qualify as small or medium-sized companies may take advantage of some or all of the exemptions given under ss 247 to 250 and file 'modified accounts' with the Registrar. This will require the preparation of another set of financial statements solely for this purpose and companies may therefore not consider it worthwhile to take advantage of the exemption.

The qualifying conditions for a company to be treated as a small or medium-sized company for purposes of filing modified accounts are:

(i) The company, or any company in the group of which it is a member, must not be a public company, a banking, insurance or shipping company. In addition a company must not be a member of a group which includes a body corporate not registered under the Companies Acts (e.g. a foreign company) if that body corporate has power to offer its shares or debentures to the public or is a recognised bank or insurance company. [s 247]

(ii) The company, or the holding company and its subsidiaries in the case of groups, must not exceed two or more of the following criteria [s 248]:

	Small company	**Medium-sized company**
1. Turnover (1)	£1,400,000	£5,750,000
2. Balance sheet total (2)	£700,000	£2,800,000
3. Average number of employees in year (3)	50	250

(1) If the financial year is not a year, the turnover figure is to be proportionately adjusted.

(2) Total of all assets without any deduction for liabilities.

(3) Average to be determined on a weekly basis using the method stated in Sch 4: 56(2)(3) (see page 56).

A dormant company which otherwise would be ineligible because it does not meet the conditions in (i) above may avail itself of the filing exemptions of a small company if it is exempt from the obligation to appoint auditors (see Section 17.030 below). [s 247(4)]

A newly incorporated company will qualify as small or medium-sized in its first financial year if it meets the appropriate criteria in (ii) above in that year. For any other company, the conditions in (ii) above must have been satisfied for at least two consecutive years. However, a company which is qualified as small or medium-sized does not cease to be so qualified if it fails to meet the appropriate criteria in one year. If it fails to meet the criteria in two consecutive years, it ceases to be qualified and must then meet the criteria for a further two consecutive years before it can regain its status as small or medium-sized. [s 249]

The following example illustrates the application of the above rules to a company whose first financial year ends on 31 December 1985:

EXAMPLE

Year	*Size criteria*	*Permitted to file modified accounts as:*	*Explanation*
1985	*Small*	*Small*	*Initial year of incorporation.*
1986	*Medium-sized*	*Small*	*Having qualified as small in 1985, it does not cease to qualify as a result of one year's failure to meet the criteria.*
1987	*Large*	*Medium-sized*	*Even though it failed to meet the criteria in 1987, it has met the criteria as medium-sized in each of the preceding two years, and thus continues to qualify.*
1988	*Large*	*Not permitted*	*It has failed to meet the criteria in two consecutive years.*
1989	*Medium-sized*	*Not permitted*	*Having ceased to qualify as medium-sized, it must now meet the criteria for two consecutive years to be reinstated.*
1990	*Medium-sized*	*Medium-sized*	*It has met the criteria for two consecutive years.*

17.022 FORM AND CONTENT OF MODIFIED ACCOUNTS

The modified accounts must be an abbreviated version of the financial statements required to be laid before the company in a general meeting. The documents and information required by Sch 8: Part I are as follows:

	Small company	Medium-sized company
Auditors' report	Not to be published.	
Special auditors' report	This report, to be prepared by the auditors, must state that in their opinion the requirements for exemption have been met. The full text of the auditors' report on the main financial statements must be reproduced. (See page 290).	
Directors' report	Not required.	Copy required without modification.
Balance sheet	An abbreviated version. (See (a) below)	Copy required without modification.
Statement of directors on balance sheet	A statement of the directors that they have relied on the exemptions for individual or group accounts is to be placed immediately above the directors' signatures on the balance sheet. (See (b) below for example)	
Profit and loss account	Not required.	An abbreviated version. (See (c) below)
Accounting policies	Required to be disclosed including basis of translation of foreign currency amounts into sterling.	
Other disclosures in notes	Only the following information is required to be given: 1. Share capital [Sch 4: 38] 2. Particulars of allotments [Sch 4: 39] 3. Particulars of debts [Sch 4: 48(1)(4)] 4. Corresponding amounts [Sch 4: 58(2)] 5. Transactions with directors and officers [Sch 6] 6. Subsidiaries, related companies, and other investments [Sch 5: Parts I, II and III] 7. Ultimate holding company [Sch 5: Part IV]	Required to be disclosed without modification with the exception that particulars of turnover and profit or loss before taxation by class of business and geographical markets need not be given.

(a) Modified balance sheet

The modified balance sheet must be a version of the company's balance sheet prepared under s 228, abbreviated to show at least those items to which a letter or Roman numeral is assigned in the balance sheet formats. (See Appendix 5). The balance sheet or the notes to the accounts must disclose separately the amounts of debtors falling due after one year and where format 2 is used the amounts of creditors falling due within one year and after more than one year.

(b) Statement of the directors

A statement by the directors is required to be placed immediately above the directors' signature on the balance sheet, indicating that they have relied on the exemptions provided by ss 247 to 249. [Sch 8: 9] An example of such a statement follows:

> ***EXAMPLE***
>
> *The directors rely on Sections 247 to 249 of the Companies Act 1985 entitling them to deliver modified accounts to the Registrar of Companies on the ground that the company is entitled to the benefits of those sections as a (small/medium-sized) company.*

Where the holding company delivers copies of modified group accounts to the registrar, the directors' statement to be shown on the balance sheet of the holding company shall include a statement that the documents delivered include copies of modified group accounts. [Sch 8: 21] No statement is required to be made on the group balance sheet. An example of this statement, which should follow the wording given in the example above, is as follows:

> ***EXAMPLE***
>
> *The documents delivered to the Registrar of Companies include modified group accounts as permitted by Section 250 of the Companies Act 1985.*

(c) Modified profit and loss account

The modified profit and loss account must correspond to the company's profit and loss account prepared under s 228, with the exception that the items listed below may be combined as one item under the heading 'Gross profit or loss'.

Formats 1 and 3: turnover, cost of sales, other operating income.

Formats 2 and 4: turnover, changes in stocks, own work capitalised, raw materials and consumables, other external charges and other operating income.

17.023 HOLDING COMPANY AND GROUP ACCOUNTS

For a holding company and its subsidiaries to be classified as a small or medium-sized company, the total of all their turnover (excluding intra-company turnover), assets and employees must be included in the calculation as if the group were one company. If the consolidated accounts exclude the accounts of any subsidiary, the relevant figures of the omitted subsidiaries must be included in the consolidated figures except where the subsidiary is omitted by virtue of s 229(3)(a) on the grounds that it is impracticable to deal with that subsidiary in the accounts. [s 250(3)]

The holding company can only be entitled to the benefits of the exemption if it and all its subsidiaries would qualify as a small or medium-sized company. Thus if a holding company qualifies as a small company but the group qualifies as a medium-sized company, then the holding company must be treated as a medium-sized company. Similarly if the group does not qualify for exemption, the holding company cannot qualify even if it fulfils the criteria for a small or medium-sized company. [s 250]

17.030 DORMANT COMPANIES EXEMPTION FROM AUDITS

A company may pass a special resolution making itself exempt from the obligation to appoint auditors, subject to the following conditions [s 252]:

(i) the resolution must be passed at a general meeting at which the accounts for a financial year are laid before the company;

(ii) the directors must be entitled to deliver modified accounts as for a small company to the Registrar of Companies in respect of the financial year dealt with in the accounts being laid at the general meeting (see Section 17.021 above) or that directors would have been so entitled but for the company being at some time during the financial year a member of an ineligible group (i.e. a group which includes a public company, a bank or an insurance company);

(iii) the directors are not required to lay group accounts in respect of that financial year; and

(iv) since the end of the financial year dealt with in the accounts being laid at the general meeting the company has been dormant.

For a company to be dormant during any period it must have no transactions during that period which are required by s 221 to be entered in the company's accounting records, other than the taking up of shares by the subscribers to the memorandum. Thus a company is not dormant during a period in which it makes any payment, however small.

It should be noted that a company cannot pass a special resolution making itself exempt from the obligation to appoint auditors if its articles contain a specific requirement to appoint auditors. This is likely to be the position of most companies incorporated before December 1981. In these circumstances the company's articles must be suitably amended before the special resolution can validly be passed.

It is emphasised that the test in (ii) above is whether modified accounts as a small company may be lodged with the Registrar in respect of the last financial year. Thus if Company A was a small company which became dormant in 1984, it could pass a resolution dispensing with the requirement to appoint auditors at the annual general meeting in 1985. If it was not a small company in 1984, the earliest date at which it would be able to pass the resolution would be 1987 since 1986 would be the first year for which modified accounts would be lodged with the Registrar. If the company met the criteria to be classed as small in 1984 (the year in which it became dormant) but had not done so previously, it would first become entitled to file modified accounts in respect of the year 1985 and could pass the resolution to dispense with the requirement to appoint auditors at the annual general meeting in 1986.

If a dormant company which has passed the special resolution making itself exempt from appointing auditors subsequently ceases to be dormant (as a result of entering into a transaction which must be recorded in the accounting records), or ceases to qualify for exemption for any other reason, auditors must be appointed before the next general meeting at which accounts are laid before the company. The auditors will then be required to audit the accounts for the financial year in which the company ceased to be dormant.

If a dormant company's accounts are not audited then the balance sheet delivered to the Registrar of

Companies must include a statement by the directors, placed immediately above their signatures on the balance sheet, that the company was dormant throughout the financial year.

17.040 PUBLICATION OF FINANCIAL STATEMENTS

The Act [ss 254 and 255] requires that where a company or group:

(i) publishes (e.g. in a newspaper) full individual accounts, comprising the statutory financial statements and directors' report, it shall publish with them the auditors' report thereon; if the company is a holding company it may not publish its own accounts without also publishing the group accounts;

(ii) publishes modified accounts which have been filed with the Registrar of Companies by small and medium-sized companies (see Section 17.020), it must publish the related special auditors' report; if it is a holding company it must also include the modified group accounts;

(iii) publishes abridged accounts (e.g. any balance sheet or profit and loss account relating to any financial year of the company, such as preliminary announcement of annual results or employee reports which contain information which can be regarded as a balance sheet or profit and loss account), it shall publish with them a statement indicating:

 (a) that the accounts are not full accounts;

 (b) whether full accounts have been delivered to the Registrar of Companies;

 (c) whether the auditors have made a report in respect of the full accounts and, if so, whether the report was an unqualified report.

 The company must not publish the auditors' report with the abridged accounts.

The publication of statements covering interim periods, such as an interim profit announcement, is not covered by the above requirements. Some interim profit announcements contain comparable information covering the preceding financial year and these figures may be regarded as constituting abridged accounts. In these circumstances a statement along the following lines should be made:

EXAMPLE

The accounts for the year ended (date) are not full accounts. A copy of the full accounts for that year, on which the auditors have issued an unqualified report, has been delivered to the Registrar of Companies.

17.050 NOTICE OF MEETING

At least 21 days' notice of the annual general meeting must be given in writing. [s 369] Timetables for the publication of financial statements must take into consideration this statutory requirement, particularly where the notice of meeting is contained in the annual report and financial statements.

17.060 RULES REGARDING COMPANY YEAR ENDS

The Act requires the directors to prepare a profit and loss account in respect of each accounting reference period and a balance sheet as at the last day of the financial year. [s 227] The following sections summarise the rules regarding accounting periods and gives guidance as to the procedures for varying the statutorily determined length of accounting reference periods.

17.061 DEFINITIONS

Accounting reference period (ARP): the period by reference to which financial statements have to be prepared and presented to members. [s 224]

Accounting reference date (ARD): the date on which the accounting reference period ends. [s 224(2)]

Financial year: the period covered by the statutory profit and loss account, whether this is a year or not. [s 742(d)]

17.062 ACCOUNTING REFERENCE DATE

A newly incorporated company must notify the Registrar of Companies of its ARD within six months of the date of incorporation. If an ARD has not been notified, its ARD will be 31st March. [s 224(3)]

17.063 ACCOUNTING REFERENCE PERIODS

The first ARP begins on the date of incorporation and ends on the accounting reference date and is a period of more than six months and not more than eighteen months. [s 224(4)]

Succeeding ARPs will be for twelve months unless valid notice is given of an alteration in ARD. [s 225] They start on the day after that on which the preceding ARP ends.

17.064 FINANCIAL YEAR

The financial year of a company will normally be the same as its ARP. However to accommodate fifty two week accounting, the financial year may begin or end on dates which are not more than seven days before or after the ARD. [s 227(2)]

17.065 CHANGES IN ACCOUNTING REFERENCE PERIODS

To change an accounting reference period, notice must be given in the prescribed form to the Registrar of Companies specifying (i) the new accounting reference date on which the accounting reference periods are to end and (ii) whether the accounting reference period to which the notice relates is to be treated as being shortened or lengthened. Subject to the restrictions that are summarised in the table below, notice may be given to change either the accounting reference period current at the date when notice is given or the immediately previous period.

CHANGE	CHANGE NOTIFIED IN RESPECT OF:	
	PREVIOUS PERIOD	CURRENT PERIOD
1. Which lengthens the period	Only if the new ARD is that of its holding company or its subsidiary company and the time limit for filing the previous financial statements has not expired. [s 225(2)(3)] The ARP must not exceed eighteen months. [s 225(5)]	Only if: (a) no earlier extension of an ARP has been made by the company; or (b) at least five years have passed from the end of any earlier ARP which itself had been extended; or (c) the new ARD is that of its holding company or its subsidiary company. [s 225(6)] The ARP must not exceed eighteen months. [s 225(5)]
2. Which shortens the period	Only if the new ARD is that of its holding company or its subsidiary company and the time limit for filing the previous financial statements has not expired. [s 225(2)(3)]	No restrictions.

It will be noticed that certain changes can only be made if the new ARD is that of the holding company or subsidiary company. There appears to be nothing to prevent the formation of a subsidiary company for this purpose even if the new company is formed after the end of the ARP which is to be changed.

It appears that there is nothing to prevent notice being given to change the accounting reference date and to shorten the accounting reference period before the end of the first accounting reference period of the company and thus to circumvent the requirement that the first accounting period must be for a minimum of six months.

18 COMPANY REQUIREMENTS CONCERNING SHARE CAPITAL, DISTRIBUTIONS AND DIRECTORS' LOANS

INTRODUCTION

The provisions of the Act relating to share capital, distributions and directors' loans are complex and include various exemptions and relaxations which are not dealt with here. The following is a summary only and where necessary reference should be made to the Act.

18.010 ISSUE OF SHARE CAPITAL

The Act contains regulations regarding the issue of share capital. [ss 80 to 116] A summary of the major provisions is as follows:

(i) Shares may not be allotted at a discount. [s 100]

(ii) Ordinary shares (or securities convertible into ordinary shares) to be allotted for cash must first be offered pro-rata to existing holders of shares or securities of the same class on terms similar to or more favourable than those on which they are to be offered to others (pre-emption rights). [s 89]

(iii) No share of a public company can be allotted unless one quarter of its nominal value and the whole of any premium is paid up. [s 101]

(iv) A public company cannot allot shares otherwise than for cash (except in connection with a take-over or merger) unless the consideration has been valued within the previous six months. The valuation report required for this purpose will usually be given by the auditor who may rely on the valuation of an expert. [s 103]

(v) The board of directors may not allot shares unless it is given authority to do so by the company's articles or by an ordinary resolution of the company. [s 80]

18.020 PURCHASE OR REDEMPTION OF OWN SHARES

The Act contains provisions which permit limited companies to redeem or purchase their own shares. [ss 159 to 181] The relevant sections may be summarised as follows:

(i) A company may redeem or purchase its own shares only if so authorised by its articles. Shareholder approval is required for the purchase as follows:

Off-market purchase: the terms of the proposed contract must be authorised by a special resolution before the contract is entered into; for a public company this resolution must specify the date on which the authority expires, which must not be more than 18 months from the date of the resolution.

Market purchase: authority must be obtained from the company in general meeting; the authority

(a) may be restricted to a specific class of share capital or may be a general authority to purchase its own shares;

(b) may be conditional or unconditional;

(c) must state the maximum number of shares to be acquired;

(d) must state the maximum and minimum prices to be paid;

(e) must specify the date on which it expires, which must not be more than 18 months from the date of the resolution.

(ii) The power to issue redeemable shares or to purchase a company's own shares is limited by the requirement that there must always be a member of the company who holds non-redeemable shares.

(iii) The shares may not be redeemed or purchased unless they are fully paid.

(iv) Shares redeemed or purchased must be cancelled; such cancellation does not reduce the authorised share capital.

(v) Except in the case of private companies (see viii below), shares may only be redeemed or purchased out of distributable profits or out of the proceeds of a new issue made for that purpose. To the extent that the redemption or purchase is made out of distributable profits or exceeds the proceeds of a new issue of shares, a transfer must be made to the capital redemption reserve.

(vi) With the exceptions given in (vii) and (viii) below, any premium payable on the redemption or purchase of shares must be paid out of the distributable profits of the company.

(vii) Where shares which have been redeemed or purchased were issued at a premium, any premium payable on their redemption or purchase may be paid out of the proceeds of a fresh issue of shares made for the purpose up to the lesser of:

(a) the amount of the premium originally received by the company on the issue of the shares redeemed or purchased, and

(b) the current balance on share premium account (including any premium on the new shares).

(viii) If authorised by its articles to do so, a private company may redeem or purchase its shares out of capital. [s 171] The capital portion, referred to as the permissible capital payment, is defined as the price of redemption or purchase less the sum of any distributable profits and the proceeds of any new issue of shares made for that purpose. Where the aggregate of the permissible capital payment plus the proceeds of a new issue is greater than the nominal amount of the shares redeemed or purchased, the excess may be applied to reduce the amount of any capital redemption reserve, share premium account, fully paid share capital of the company or revaluation reserve.

The following safeguards must be met before a payment out of capital can lawfully be made [ss 173 to 175]:

- the payment must be approved by a special resolution;
- the directors must make a statutory declaration (see Section 19.405);
- a report by the company's auditors must be annexed to the directors' declaration (see Section 19.405);

- a notice of the proposed capital payment, giving the information specified in s 175, must be published in the Gazette and either in a national newspaper or by written notice to each creditor within a week of the date of the resolution. Creditors and members may apply to the court within five weeks of the date of the resolution for the resolution to be cancelled. The payment must not be made less than five weeks or more than seven weeks after the date of the resolution.

18.021 CAPITAL REDEMPTION RESERVE

Where shares are redeemed or purchased wholly or partly out of distributable profits, the Act requires a transfer to be made to the capital redemption reserve.

EXAMPLE

Shares having a nominal value of £100,000 are redeemed or purchased for £130,000.

	Debit	*Credit*
	£	*£*
Profit and loss account (distributable reserves)	*130,000*	
Called up share capital	*100,000*	
Cash		*130,000*
Capital redemption reserve		*100,000*

To record redemption (purchase) of 100,000 £1 shares at £1.30 per share and to transfer the nominal value of such shares to capital redemption reserve.

Note: The capital redemption reserve would be the same even if the shares were purchased at a discount from nominal value.

Where the redemption or purchase is financed partly by a new issue of shares, the transfer required is reduced by the proceeds of the new issue.

18.030 FINANCIAL ASSISTANCE FOR ACQUISITION OF OWN SHARES

With the exceptions outlined below, s 151 makes it unlawful for a company to give financial assistance directly or indirectly (i.e., loan, gift, guarantee, indemnity or security, etc.) for the purpose of the acquisition of its shares or those of its holding company or for the purpose of reducing or discharging any liability incurred in the acquisition of such shares.

This prohibition does not apply where:

(i) the lending of money is part of the ordinary business of the company and the money is lent in the ordinary course of business; or

(ii) the provision of money is made in accordance with an employee's share scheme for the acquisition of fully paid shares; or

(iii) the loan is made to bona fide employees (not directors) to enable them to purchase shares in the company or its holding company to be held by them by way of beneficial ownership; or

(iv) the principal purpose of the transaction is not to give financial assistance for the purpose of the acquisition of shares, or is incidental to some larger purpose, and the assistance is given in good faith in the interest of the company. [s 153]

However, a public company may only give this financial assistance if its net assets are not thereby reduced or to the extent the net assets are reduced the assistance is provided out of distributable profits. [s 154]

The prohibition on the giving of financial assistance imposed by s 151 does not apply to a private company provided the company fulfills certain requirements for safeguarding the interests of creditors and shareholders (as set out in ss 156 and 157). The principal limitation imposed on any financial assistance given which does not fall into categories (i) to (iii) above is that the company's net assets shall not be reduced by the financial assistance or to the extent that the net assets are reduced the assistance shall be made out of distributable profits. The safeguards which must be met before the financial assistance can lawfully be given include:

- approval of the assistance by special resolution in general meeting;
- a statutory declaration by the directors (see Section 19.404);
- a report by the auditors on the directors' statutory declaration (see Section 19.404).

Loans and other financial assistance which may be made by a company under the above rules must not include any loans, etc. to directors which are prohibited by s 330 (see Section 18.050).

18.040 PROFITS AVAILABLE FOR DISTRIBUTION

The provisions of the Act regarding the payment of dividends and other distributions relate to individual companies only and not to groups.

The Act defines which profits are distributable and the circumstances in which they may be legally distributed. [ss 263 to 281] A distribution for these purposes is defined as any distribution of a company's assets to members except by way of:

- an issue of fully or partly paid bonus shares;
- redemption or purchase of company's own shares out of capital (including the proceeds of any fresh issue of shares) or out of unrealised profits;
- certain reductions of capital;
- distribution of assets in a winding-up.

(a) Rules regarding the payment of dividends

The rules vary as between four classes of companies.

A *private* company can, subject to any other restriction imposed by law, distribute the whole of its accumulated realised profits (not previously distributed or capitalised) less its accumulated realised losses (not previously written off in a reduction or reorganisation of capital). It is not required to take account of unrealised losses. However, as indicated below a provision is usually to be treated as a realised loss. [s 263(3)]

A *public* company cannot distribute its realised profits without first making good any excess of unrealised losses over unrealised profits. It can make a distribution only if the distribution does not reduce the company's net assets below the aggregate of the called up share capital and undistributable reserves. [s 264]

An *investment* company (as defined in s 266) is subject to special rules which, in general, allow it to make distributions out of the accumulated realised revenue profits less revenue losses, both realised and unrealised provided that the distribution does not reduce its assets to less than one and a half times its liabilities. Liabilities include provisions for liabilities and charges. These rules allow an investment company to ignore capital losses whether realised or unrealised when making a distribution. [s 265]

An *insurance* company is subject to the same restrictions as any other company, and there is an additional proviso that an amount properly transferred to the profit and loss account from a surplus on its long term business fund shall be treated as a realised profit, any deficit in that fund shall be treated as a realised loss, and any other profit or loss in that business shall be disregarded. [s 268]

(b) Relevant accounts

To determine whether a distribution contravenes the provisions of ss 263 to 265 and whether there are sufficient profits available to make a distribution, reference must be made to 'the relevant accounts'. [s 270] These will normally be the last annual accounts, but if a distribution would contravene the relevant section if reference were made only to the last annual accounts, a company may produce interim accounts to demonstrate the availability of distributable profits. If the company is a public company, these interim accounts must be 'properly prepared' but need not be audited and a copy must be sent to the Registrar of Companies.

Where a company proposes to make a distribution during its first accounting reference period, or before any financial statements are laid or filed in respect of that period, initial accounts must be prepared. Where such accounts are prepared by a public company the auditors must report whether, in their opinion, the accounts have been 'properly prepared', and the accounts together with the auditors' report must be filed with the Registrar of Companies.

In the case of initial or interim accounts, 'properly prepared' means that the financial statements comply with s 228 (form and content of individual accounts), the balance sheet has been signed by the directors and the profit and loss account and balance sheet show a true and fair view.

If the audit report on the annual or initial accounts contains a qualification, the auditors must state in writing, either at the time of their report or subsequently, whether in their opinion the matter in respect of which the report is qualified is material for determining whether the distribution would be in contravention of the relevant section (see Section 19.402). [ss 271(4), 273(5)]

If the qualification concerns annual accounts, the auditors' statement must be laid before the company in general meeting. If the qualification concerns initial accounts, the statement must be sent to the registrar.

Where a company has already made a distribution or has otherwise entered into an arrangement (e.g. the purchase or redemption of shares or the giving of financial assistance for the purchase of its shares) which reduces its distributable reserves shown in the relevant accounts, appropriate account must be taken of the reduction in the reserves when determining the amount of any remaining reserves which are available for distribution.

(c) Definition of realised profits and losses

Realised profits in relation to a company's accounts are defined in Sch 4: 91 as those profits which fall to be treated as realised in accordance with principles generally accepted at the time those accounts are prepared. In addition the Act specifically provides that certain items are to be treated as realised or unrealised.

The following guidance may be helpful in distinguishing between realised or unrealised profits.

(i) When determining whether an item is realised, particular regard should be had to the prudence concept – profits should not be anticipated and should only be recognised in the profit and loss account when realised in the form either of cash or of other assets the ultimate cash realisation of which can be assessed with reasonable certainty, and that losses are provided for whether the amount is known with certainty or is a best estimate in the light of the information available.

(ii) The CCAB in its guidance statement on realised profits states:

- a profit which is required by SSAPs to be recognised in the profit and loss account should normally be treated as a realised profit, unless the SSAP indicates otherwise.

- a profit will normally be a realised profit if the accounting policy adopted is not the subject of a SSAP, or, exceptionally, is contrary to a SSAP (in order to give a true and fair view) and if that policy is consistent with the accounting principles stated in the Act and with the accruals and prudence concepts set out in SSAP 2.

(iii) The CCAB in its guidance statement on distributable profits states:

- valuations or contingencies included in the notes to the accounts but not incorporated therein have no effect on the amount of distributable profits.

- there is no requirement that distributions can only be made out of distributable profits described as such in the accounts.

(iv) On the basis of the prudence concept and the rules laid down in Sch 4, a surplus arising from a revaluation of any fixed asset should be regarded as unrealised. Sch 4: 34 requires the measure of the surplus to be the difference between the revalued amount and the historical cost amount after provisions for depreciation and diminution in value.

(v) Any provision for liabilities or charges and any provision for depreciation or diminution in value of assets other than a write down in value of a fixed asset appearing on a revaluation of all fixed assets (other than goodwill) of the company, are realised losses. [s 275(1)]

In order that companies can avail themselves of the exception given in this section in circumstances where only certain assets (e.g. properties) have been revalued, assets which have not been revalued can be treated as being revalued for the purposes of this section if the directors are satisfied that their aggregate value is not less than the aggregate amount at which they are stated in the accounts. If the directors are so satisfied, the effect of this extension is to permit a provision for diminution in value of a fixed asset to be treated as an unrealised loss provided there is appropriate disclosure in the relevant accounts. [s 275(4)(5)(6)]

(vi) Depreciation of a revalued asset in excess of the depreciation of that asset based on original cost is a realised profit. Thus it will be appropriate to make a transfer annually from undistributable to distributable reserves (i.e. from revaluation reserve to the profit and loss account). [s 275(2)]

(vii) If the directors cannot determine whether a particular profit or loss made before 22 December 1980 is realised or unrealised, they may treat any profit as realised and any loss as unrealised. [s 263(5)]

(viii) Development costs shown as an asset in the balance sheet shall be treated as a realised loss unless the directors can justify the costs carried forward not being so treated and a note to the accounts explains the circumstances relied upon to justify the decision of the directors. [s 269] The CCAB advises, in its statement on distributable profits, that development costs carried forward in accordance with SSAP 13 will normally provide the directors with such justification.

(ix) If a distribution is made of a non-cash asset, any unrealised profit relating to that asset is treated as a realised profit for the purpose of determining the lawfulness of the distribution and that amount may be transferred from the revaluation reserve to the profit and loss account. [s 276]

(x) SSAP 20 advises that all exchange gains taken through the profit and loss account, are realised, although the foreword to the SSAP does state that it does not deal specifically with the determination of distributable profits. The decision of the House of Lords in the Marine Midland case in 1983 has put into doubt whether any translation gain can be construed as a profit before a foreign currency balance is actually converted into a local currency. Consequently legal advice should be taken wherever translation gains or losses are crucial to the distributability of reserves.

18.050 RESTRICTIONS ON LOANS TO DIRECTORS

The legislation concerning restrictions on loans to and similar transactions with or on behalf of directors and persons connected with them is contained in ss 330 to 347. The relevant definitions are discussed in Section 11.081 which sets out the disclosure requirements for such transactions. One further item requires definition:

Relevant company: [s 331(6)]	A company which is either (a) a public limited company or (b) a member of a group which includes a public limited company.

S 330 provides that:

(i) A company shall not make a loan to a director or to a director of its holding company or guarantee or provide security in connection with a loan made by any person to such a director.

(ii) A 'relevant' company shall not make a loan or quasi-loan, or enter into a credit transaction or guarantee or provide security in connection with a loan, quasi-loan or credit transaction to its director or director of its holding company, or to a person 'connected' with such a director.

(iii) A company shall not arrange for the assignment to it or the assumption by it of any rights, obligations or liabilities under a transaction which, if the company has entered into it, would have been prohibited by (i) and (ii) above.

(iv) A company shall not take part in any arrangement whereby another person enters into a transaction described in (i) and (ii) above and in return that person obtains some benefit from the company or another company in the group.

The following are excepted from the above rules:

(i) loans to directors if the aggregate amount to any director does not exceed £2,500; [s 334]

(ii) loans and guarantees between group companies; [ss 333 and 336]

(iii) credit transactions up to £5,000 or where entered into in the normal course of business and on normal commercial arms-length terms; [s 335]

(iv) provision to a director (but not to a director of its holding company) of funds to meet expenditure for the purposes of the company or to enable him to perform his duties as an officer of the company. The provision must either be approved in advance at a general meeting or made on conditions that unless it is approved at the next general meeting it will be repaid within the six months thereafter. In a relevant company the provision must not exceed £10,000. [s 337]

(v) loans made to an employee before he is appointed to the Board;

(vi) quasi-loans aggregating not more than £1,000 which are required to be repaid within two months. [s 332]

There are additional exemptions for money lending companies.

There are civil remedies and criminal penalties (including up to two years imprisonment) for breaches of these requirements.

Appendix 3 of this manual summarises the above rules.

19 AUDITORS' AND ACCOUNTANTS' REPORTS

19.010 INTRODUCTION

The various types of reports issued by accountants are discussed below under the following headings:

- Reports on audited financial statements

  (i) unqualified audit reports

  (ii) qualified audit reports

- Special reports
- Reports on unaudited financial statements
- Additional information reports

19.020 REPORTS ON AUDITED FINANCIAL STATEMENTS

19.021 THE AUDITING STANDARD – 'THE AUDIT REPORT'

This standard, which was issued by the Councils of the UK Accountancy Bodies in April 1980, prescribes the matters to be dealt with in all reports in which the auditor expresses an opinion on financial statements intended to give a true and fair view.

The audit report should identify those to whom it is addressed and the financial statements to which it relates and should state:

(i) whether the financial statements have been audited in accordance with approved Auditing Standards; and

(ii) whether in the auditor's opinion the financial statements give a true and fair view of the state of affairs, profit or loss, and, where applicable, source and application of funds.

It must also refer expressly to any matters prescribed by relevant legislation or other requirements.

Approved Auditing Standards are defined as those Statements of Auditing Standards which are approved for issue by the three United Kingdom Institutes of Chartered Accountants and by the Chartered Association of Certified Accountants and which are effective for the period covered by the financial statements on which the auditor is reporting.

The standard is not intended to override the statutory exemptions granted in respect of certain types of enterprise (e.g. banks and insurance companies) but is intended to apply to the audit reports on such enterprises in other respects.

19.022 COMPANIES ACT REQUIREMENTS

The majority of audit reports issued are reports on companies incorporated under the Companies Acts and the relevant legislation is contained in the Act.

Auditors are required to report to the members of the company on every balance sheet and profit and loss account and on all group accounts laid before the company in general meeting during their terms of office. [s 236]

The requirement to state whether in the auditors' opinion the balance sheet, profit and loss account and group accounts show a true and fair view is included in the Act as well as in the auditing standard, and the Act imposes an additional requirement for the auditors to state whether in their opinion the accounts have been properly prepared in accordance with the Act.

The auditor has a duty under s 237 to carry out such investigations as will enable him to form an opinion as to whether or not:

(i) proper accounting records have been kept by the company and proper returns adequate for their audit have been received from branches which they did not visit;

(ii) the balance sheet and profit and loss account are in agreement with the accounting records (and returns); and

(iii) the information given in the directors' report is consistent with the financial statements.

The auditor must report specifically on these matters only if in his opinion the requirements have not been complied with. He must also report if he has not obtained all the information and explanations he requires. The absence of any comment in his report is therefore equivalent to an assurance that he has investigated and satisfied himself on these matters.

19.030 FORM AND POSITION OF AUDIT REPORTS

The audit report should include a heading, reporting paragraphs, signature, address of issuing office and date.

19.031 HEADING

Reports issued on the statutory financial statements of companies should be addressed to the members of the company concerned, as follows:

EXAMPLE

Auditors' Report to the Members
of
Tramp Holdings p.l.c.

A change in the company's name during the period will require a mention of the former name in the heading of the report, as follows:

EXAMPLE

Auditors' Report to the Members
of
C.P. Plastics Limited
(formerly C.P. (Birmingham) Limited)

It is usually appropriate in reports on non-statutory financial statements to address the report to the individuals or bodies who have engaged the auditor.

19.032 REPORTING PARAGRAPHS

The reporting paragraphs must deal with all the matters required by the auditing standard. As a general rule, the first paragraph should refer to the scope of audit, followed by a paragraph expressing an opinion or disclaiming an opinion on the true and fair view and compliance with relevant legislation.

If the opinion is qualified, disclosure of the reasons for qualifying and the effect of the qualification on the financial statements should be contained in an explanatory paragraph preceding the opinion paragraph. In such cases, the opinion paragraph will refer to the qualifying matter.

Additional considerations affecting the reporting paragraphs are dealt with below:

(a) Use of term 'financial statements'

In accordance with the policy adopted by ASC and supported by APC, the opinion should normally refer to 'financial statements' instead of the 'accounts and notes'. (See Section 2.011) Reference in the directors' report should also be to financial statements. However, consistency of terminology is desirable and if the directors insist on using a term like 'accounts and notes', then the audit report should do the same.

(b) Reference to page numbers

It is important that the scope paragraph clearly defines the financial statements to which it refers and this is best done by identifying by numbers the pages which contain these financial statements.

(c) Reporting periods

If the period reported upon is other than a year, it is preferable to refer to the precise period, e.g. 'for the six months then ended' and not 'for the period then ended'.

(d) Reporting on 'profit or loss'

The Act requires the auditor to report whether the profit and loss account shows a true and fair view of the profit or loss for the financial year. The report should refer to a profit for the year or to a loss for the year depending on whether the item in the profit and loss formats entitled 'profit or loss for the financial year' (i.e. after tax and extraordinary items) is a profit or a loss.

(e) Reference to accounting convention

The explanatory notes to the Auditing Standard state that reference should be made in the audit report to the accounting convention used in the preparation of the financial statements if the auditor considers it necessary in order to avoid misunderstanding. It is likely that no misunderstanding will arise at present where only historical cost information is given. As indicated in Section 11.011, the accounting convention used should be stated in the financial statements in the description of accounting policies. It is normally only where this is not done that the auditor should consider the need for a reference to the accounting convention in his report. An example of appropriate wording in such cases is:

> ***EXAMPLE***
>
> *In our opinion the financial statements give, under the historical cost convention as modified by the revaluation of land and buildings, a true and fair view. . . .*

19.033 SIGNATURE

In principle the report should be signed only after the directors have signed the balance sheet. If in exceptional circumstances and for reasons of expediency the auditor agrees to sign his report before the balance sheet has been signed by two directors, it is important that he ensures that the financial statements have been approved by the board and that a fully signed copy will be supplied to him at an early date. For his own protection it is advisable that he should record the circumstances in a letter to the board.

Where printed financial statements are prepared, steps should be taken to ensure that the printers do not insert the printed signature until the auditor has approved and manually signed his report.

19.034 DATE

The date of the audit report, which should be the actual date of signing (or the nearest possible estimate), should be subsequent to or identical to the date of the directors' report. Under no circumstances should the audit report be dated before the directors' report or the date of approval of the financial statements by the directors.

It is important that any delay between the date on which the directors approve the financial statements and the date of the audit report should be as short as possible. The auditor must take account of all events occurring up to the date on which he gives his opinion. If this date is after the date of approval of the financial statements by the directors and a significant event occurs in the intervening period, the auditor may need to persuade the directors to reconsider these financial statements or to issue a qualified report.

Delay sometimes arises between the completion of the audit field work and the signing of the report. It is therefore important that the auditor should remain alert to the possibility of events occurring subsequent to the completion of the audit which should be reflected in the financial statements. (See Section 11.070)

Where the delay is one month or more it will be necessary for the post balance sheet review to be updated. In cases where the client may be affected by rapidly changing political, economic or industrial developments or is under threat of or party to material adverse litigation, the situation should be kept under close review up to the date of signing the report.

19.100 UNQUALIFIED REPORTS

19.101 DEFINITION

An unqualified report is one in which the auditor can report affirmatively in respect of all the matters specified in the Auditing Standard 'The Audit Report'. (See Section 19.021)

19.102 APPROPRIATE ACCOUNTING POLICIES

When the auditor expresses his opinion that the financial statements give a true and fair view, the Auditing Standard require that he be satisfied that:

(i) all relevant SSAP's have been complied with, except in situations in which for justifiable reasons they are impracticable or, exceptionally, having regard to the circumstances, would be inappropriate or give a misleading view; and

(ii) any significant accounting policies which are not the subject of SSAPs are appropriate to the circumstances of the business.

19.103 REFERENCE TO IMPORTANT MATTERS

The auditing standard 'The Audit Report' suggests that in rare circumstances the auditor may wish to draw the reader's attention to important matters shown in the financial statements (e.g. a significant post balance sheet event, and an unusual accounting policy) in order that the reader may have a better understanding of the financial statements. These matters should be stated in a separate paragraph introduced by the phrase 'we draw attention to'. As they do not affect the auditors' opinion, no reference to such matters should be made in the opinion paragraph. It is emphasised that it is only appropriate in rare circumstances to add anything to the audit report which is not a qualification, and that such an 'emphasis of matter' should never be used as a substitute for a qualification.

19.110 UNQUALIFIED REPORT – SINGLE COMPANY

An example of the wording of an unqualified report to the members of a single company incorporated under the Companies Acts is as follows:

> ***EXAMPLE***
>
> *We have audited the financial statements on pages 9 to 22 in accordance with approved Auditing Standards.*
>
> *In our opinion the financial statements give a true and fair view of the state of the company's affairs at 31 December 1984 and of its profit and source and application of funds for the year then ended and comply with the Companies Act 1985.*

19.111 NON-TRADING COMPANIES

Where a company has not traded during the year and the preceding year, a profit and loss account should not be prepared but a note to the balance sheet should indicate that the company has not traded and has made neither profit nor loss in the financial year. In these circumstances the unqualified audit report should be as follows:

> ***EXAMPLE***
>
> *We have audited the balance sheet on pages 2 and 3 in accordance with approved Auditing Standards.*
>
> *In our opinion the balance sheet gives a true and fair view of the state of the company's affairs at 31 December 1984 and complies with the Companies Act 1985.*

It should be noted that a profit and loss account is necessary for the first year in which a company does not trade since the corresponding amounts for the preceding year must be disclosed.

A non-trading company may qualify as a dormant company and resolve not to appoint auditors (see Section 17.030).

19.120 UNQUALIFIED REPORT – GROUP OF COMPANIES

An example of the wording of an unqualified report in circumstances where group financial statements comprise consolidated financial statements of the group and the balance sheet of the holding company, is as follows:

EXAMPLE

We have audited the financial statements on pages 9 to 22 in accordance with approved Auditing Standards.

In our opinion the financial statements give a true and fair view of the state of affairs of the company and the group at 31 December 1984 and of the profit and source and application of funds of the group for the year then ended and comply with the Companies Act 1985.

19.121 REFERENCE TO OTHER AUDITORS

It is not uncommon for auditors to refer in their reports to returns or financial statements of subsidiary or associated companies being audited by other firms. It seems clear from the legal opinion obtained by the English Institute that such references in no way affect the responsibility of the reporting firm to ensure that the financial statements show a true and fair view.

The Institute's Statement on Auditing U 21 recommends that the significance to the group of those companies which have been audited by other auditors should be indicated in the schedule of principal subsidiaries and associated companies (or in the directors' report or in the note to the accounts) by referring to the amount of their assets, sales or profits or losses on ordinary activities before taxation. Statement U 21 also suggests that where the financial statements do not contain this information the auditor should consider whether or not he should give it in his report. Many auditors consider that reference to other auditors in audit reports can only serve to create doubts in the minds of readers of the financial statements as to their credibility while affording no legal protection.

Where the client provides such information, it is recommended that the term 'assets' be interpreted as 'total assets' and not as 'net assets'. Where profits are used as a yardstick, care must be taken in the circumstances where some subsidiaries have incurred losses that a misleading impression is not given of the proportion of the group which is not audited by the auditor of the holding company.

19.122 SUBSIDIARIES WITH DIFFERENT ACCOUNTING DATES

No reference need be made in the report where subsidiaries use different accounting dates from that of the holding company as long as appropriate disclosures are made in the notes to the accounts (see Section 12.072(c)).

19.130 UNQUALIFIED REPORT – UNINCORPORATED CONCERNS

An example of an unqualified report suitable for financial statements of unincorporated concerns which are intended to show a true and fair view of profit or loss and financial position is as follows:

EXAMPLE

We have audited the financial statements on pages 2 to 10 in accordance with approved Auditing Standards.

*In our opinion the financial statements give a true and fair view of the state of the * affairs at 31 December 1984 and of its profit (or net income, net revenue, results, excess of income over expenditure, etc. as appropriate) and source and application of funds for the year then ended.*

* Here will be inserted 'Club's', 'Trust's', 'Partnership's', etc. as appropriate.

In addition the terms of appointment of the auditor may sometimes require him to confirm that the form and content of the financial statements comply with rules contained in the statute or other regulations which govern the concern. An example is as follows:

EXAMPLE

. . . for the year then ended and comply with the requirements relating to the financial statements as laid down in the Trust Deed.

19.140 REPORTS ON CURRENT COST STATEMENTS

As indicated in Chapter 16 the preparation of supplementary current cost statements under SSAP 16 is no longer mandatory, and until the position is changed, auditors will only rarely be asked to deal with such statements in audit reports. If they are asked to report on financial statements which include supplementary current cost information prepared in accordance with SSAP 16, a suitable form of audit report is as follows:

EXAMPLE

We have audited the financial statements on pages 9 to 31 in accordance with approved Auditing Standards.

In our opinion the financial statements on pages 9 to 22 give, under the historical cost convention, a true and fair view of the state of the company's affairs at 31 December 1984 and of its profit and source and application of funds for the year then ended and comply with the Companies Act 1985.

In our opinion the abridged supplementary current cost statements on pages 23 to 31 have been properly prepared, in accordance with the policies and methods described in notes 1 and 2, to give the information required by Statement of Standard Accounting Practice No. 16.

It should be noted that the first paragraph of the audit report refers to all pages comprising the financial statements, CCA as well as historical. The audit will, of course, cover fully both sets of statements regardless of the form of the opinion.

Because the report deals with accounts prepared under two different accounting conventions it helps to avoid misunderstanding if the conventions used are referred to in the audit report. Where the historical cost convention has been modified (e.g. by revaluation) and this has been stated in the notes to the accounts, the audit report should refer to 'the historical cost convention as described in Note 1'.

19.200 QUALIFIED REPORTS

19.201 INTRODUCTION

Where circumstances arise which result in the auditor being unable to express an unqualified opinion, the report must be qualified. His judgment should not be influenced by the nature of the ownership of a company (e.g. the fact that it is wholly owned by another company or by the directors).

Before giving a qualified report, he should discuss the financial statements with the directors and make his position clear so that they may, where possible, take steps to provide any information which he may require to form an unqualified opinion or to amend the financial statements so that they will present a true and fair view and comply with the Act.

Since qualifications must be stated in terms chosen to fit the circumstances of each case, it is impracticable to suggest standard wording. The examples which are cited in this manual are for illustrative purposes only.

19.202 DRAFTING QUALIFYING STATEMENTS

The audit report should disclose the reasons for qualification and the effects on the financial statements where this is relevant and practicable. Qualifying statements should:

(i) cover all material matters on which the auditor has reservations,

(ii) be briefly worded without loss of meaning,

(iii) be specific as to items and facts and as far as possible state the amounts involved,

(iv) within the limits of the information available, indicate their effect on the financial statements, including where appropriate the effect on earnings per share, and

(v) state, where the auditor disagrees with the facts or treatment shown in the financial statements, his opinion as to the facts or treatment.

For greater clarity the reasons for qualifying will normally be disclosed in a separate paragraph(s) before the opinion.

Where a note to the accounts explains the problem in detail, the qualifying paragraph may include a reference to the note in order to minimise repetition; nevertheless, the reservations and the financial effects must be stated in the audit report.

19.203 MATERIALITY

It is not appropriate to qualify an audit report unless the matters involved are material in relation to the financial statements. The exceptions to this principle are in respect of certain disclosure requirements under the Act, which if not made in the financial statements, require mention in the audit report, regardless of the size of the amounts involved (see page 276).

Materiality can be defined as follows: an item, or group of items, is material to a set of financial statements if there is a reasonable prospect that the qualitative or quantitative nature of the item(s) would be significant to the decisions of (i.e. likely to influence) the user of the financial statements.

19.204 TYPES OF QUALIFICATIONS

The Auditing Standard 'Qualifications in Audit Reports' classifies the circumstances which give rise to qualifications into two categories:

(i) uncertainty – where there is an uncertainty which prevents the auditor from forming an opinion on a matter; and

(ii) disagreement – where the auditor is able to form an opinion on a matter but this opinion conflicts with the view given by the financial statements.

The wording of the opinion paragraph will depend upon whether the subject matter of the uncertainty or disagreement is or is not considered fundamental to the view shown by the financial statements. The types of opinions which are appropriate in different circumstances are diagrammatically shown in the Auditing Standard as follows:

Nature of circumstances	Material but not fundamental	Fundamental
Uncertainty	'SUBJECT TO' OPINION	DISCLAIMER OF OPINION
Disagreement	'EXCEPT FOR' OPINION	ADVERSE OPINION

(a) Fundamental matters

The Auditing Standard 'Qualifications in audit reports' states:

'Where the auditor has decided that a matter is sufficiently material to warrant a qualification in his audit report, a further decision is required as to whether or not the matter is fundamental, so as to require either an adverse opinion or a disclaimer of opinion on the financial statements as a whole. An uncertainty becomes fundamental when its impact on the financial statements is so great as to render the financial statements as a whole meaningless. A disagreement becomes fundamental when its impact on the financial statements is so great as to render them totally misleading. The combined effect of all uncertainties and disagreements must be considered.

'It is emphasised that the adverse opinion and the disclaimer of opinion are the extreme forms of the two main categories of qualification of opinion arising from disagreement and uncertainty. In most situations the 'except for' or 'subject to' form of opinion will be the appropriate form to use; the adverse opinion and the disclaimer should be regarded as measures of last resort.'

A more detailed interpretation as to the circumstances which give rise to a fundamental uncertainty or disagreement, and hence a disclaimer or adverse opinion, follows:

A disclaimer should be given only where:

(i) the nature of the uncertainty is such that it is probable that, as a result of its resolution, the company will be unable to continue in business; or

(ii) there are pervasive deficiencies in the accounting records such that it is not practicable to prepare meaningful financial statements; or

(iii) there are serious deficiencies in audit evidence, other than the accounting records affecting so many important parts of the financial statements that the auditor is unable to express any meaningful opinion on them; or

(iv) management representations are an essential element in the auditor's ability to express an opinion on the financial statements and he has strong reasons to doubt management's integrity.

Where there is a disagreement, the reader of the financial statements will be able to obtain readily a proper appreciation of the results of operations, financial position and source and application of funds by reading the statements in conjunction with the information in the audit report. Where the disagreements are such that this is not the case, the auditor should express an adverse opinion. However, it should be noted that the circumstances in which such an opinion is appropriate are rare.

(b) 'Subject to' opinion

A 'subject to' opinion arises where, as a result of material uncertainty, the auditor is unable to form an opinion on one or more matters which together are not considered fundamental to the financial statements as a whole. The qualification of his opinion should be introduced by the phrase 'subject to' followed by wording which should explain the implications of the uncertainty. Use of the phrase 'subject to the above matter' is insufficiently precise.

EXAMPLE

(Audit scope paragraph referring to limit in scope of audit)

(Qualifying paragraph)

Subject to the effect of any adjustments which might have been required had (explain omitted procedure) been carried out, in our opinion the financial statements give a true and fair view of the state of the company's affairs at 31 December 1984 and of its profit and source and application of funds for the year then ended and comply with the Companies Act 1985.

(c) Disclaimer of opinion

A disclaimer of opinion is only appropriate in very exceptional circumstances where the uncertainty(ies) is considered fundamental and the auditor cannot therefore form an opinion as to whether the financial statements show a true and fair view and comply with the relevant legislation. It is possible that a number of matters taken individually may not be considered fundamental but taken together may cause the financial statements to be meaningless and in such circumstances a disclaimer is required.

EXAMPLE

(Audit scope paragraph)

(Qualifying paragraph)

Because of the significance of the matters referred to in the preceding paragraph, we are unable to form an opinion as to whether the financial statements give a true and fair view of the state of the company's affairs at 31 December 1984 and of its profit and source and application of funds for the year then ended or whether the financial statements comply in all respects with the Companies Act 1985.

(d) 'Except for' opinion

An 'except for' opinion is appropriate where the auditor disagrees with the treatment or disclosure in the financial statements of one or more matters. The qualifying paragraph should make clear the matters to which the auditor takes exception and where possible indicate the financial effect on the financial statements. The qualification of the opinion should be introduced by the phrase 'except for' followed by wording which explains the implications of the exception. Use of the phrase 'except for the above' is often insufficiently precise.

> ***EXAMPLE***
>
> *(Audit scope paragraph)*
>
> *(Qualifying paragraph)*
>
> *Except for the failure to provide for the amount described above, in our opinion the financial statements give a true and fair view of the state of the company's affairs at 31 December 1984 and of its profit and source and application of funds for the year then ended and comply with the Companies Act 1985.*

For listed companies, the qualifying paragraph should disclose the effect on earnings per share of the disagreed amounts.

(e) Adverse opinion

An adverse opinion arises in exceptional circumstances where the auditor disagrees on matters (very exceptionally on a single matter) which in his opinion are fundamental and therefore destroy the true and fair view shown by the financial statements as a whole. In such a case he will have obtained sufficient information to arrive at an opinion but he will have concluded that the financial statements do not give a true and fair view.

> ***EXAMPLE***
>
> *(Audit scope paragraph)*
>
> *(Qualifying paragraph)*
>
> *In view of the significance of the various matters referred to in the preceding paragraph, in our opinion the financial statements do not give a true and fair view of the state of the company's affairs at 31 December 1984 and of its profit and source and application of funds for the year then ended and accordingly do not comply with the Companies Act 1985.*

(f) Other forms of qualification

A qualified opinion on the balance sheet will usually result in a similar opinion being given on the remainder of the financial statements.

There may however be circumstances where although the auditor has to give a qualified opinion on the profit and loss account and statement of source and application of funds, he can still give an affirmative opinion on the balance sheet (e.g. where there is an uncertainty or disagreement as to the financial position at the beginning of the year).

19.205 OMISSION OF SOURCE AND APPLICATION OF FUNDS STATEMENT

Since the omission of the source and application of funds statement does not affect the auditor's view of the historical cost balance sheet and profit and loss account, his opinion on these financial statements should be unaffected. A concluding paragraph dealing with the omission should be worded as follows:

EXAMPLE

The financial statements do not include a statement of source and application of funds as required by Statement of Standard Accounting Practice No. 10.

19.210 EXAMPLES OF QUALIFIED REPORTS ARISING FROM UNCERTAINTIES

Circumstances which give rise to uncertainty include:

(i) Limitation in scope of audit

- inability to carry out audit procedures
- proper accounting records have not been kept

(ii) Uncertainty inherent in the circumstances

- valuation of assets and liabilities
- doubts about going concern

In the subsections which follow, each of the categories of circumstances which can give rise to a material uncertainty is discussed in detail and examples of audit reports are given.

Where the uncertainty arises from a limitation in the scope of the audit, the auditor will not be able to make a positive assertion that he has conducted his audit in accordance with approved Auditing Standards and he will need to modify the scope paragraph accordingly.

19.211 INABILITY TO CARRY OUT AUDIT PROCEDURES

(a) Imposed restrictions

Companies which are subject to the Act are prohibited from imposing restrictions on the scope of the audit. Where the auditor is prevented from carrying out the procedures he considers necessary and is unable to carry out acceptable alternative procedures, he must qualify his report appropriately. It is not sufficient merely to state in the report that he has not obtained all the information and explanations he requires but he must state the restrictions imposed and the effect on the audit.

Organisations such as sole traders, partnerships, clubs, trusts, etc. which are not required by law to have an audit, sometimes wish to restrict the normal audit scope. If the restrictions are so extensive as to prevent the auditor from forming an opinion on the financial statements as a whole, he should not accept the audit engagement and should follow the procedures stated in Section 19.500 for reporting on unaudited statements.

EXAMPLE – Subject to opinion; stocks not observed or confirmed

We have audited the financial statements on pages 9 to 22. Our audit was conducted in accordance with approved Auditing Standards except that the scope of our work was limited in the following respect.

As instructed by the partners, we did not observe or confirm stocks held by subcontractors included in stocks in the balance sheet at £117,500 and there were no practical alternative auditing procedures that we could apply to verify stock quantities. Accordingly, we have not received all the information and explanations we require as to the existence of such stocks.

Subject to the effect of any adjustments which might have been shown to be necessary had the omitted procedures been carried out on stocks held by subcontractors, in our opinion. . . .

(b) Information not made available to auditors

The Act requires the officers of the company to give the auditors such information and explanations as the auditors consider necessary for the performance of their duties. [s 237] An officer of a company who knowingly or recklessly gives information to an auditor which is misleading, false or deceptive is guilty of a criminal offence.

The Act also imposes a duty on a U.K. subsidiary and its auditors to give to the auditors of the holding company such information and explanations as they may reasonably require to carry out their duties. [s 392] If the subsidiary is incorporated outside Great Britain the holding company auditors may request the holding company to take such steps as are reasonably open to it to obtain from that subsidiary the information and explanations required by the auditor.

Where such information and explanations are not forthcoming the auditor is required to so report. [s 237(4)]

In order to form an opinion on the consolidated financial statements the auditor of the holding company needs to be satisfied with all material information included in these statements which relates to subsidiaries which he has not audited. If he is not satisfied that an adequate audit has been performed in respect of any material subsidiaries not audited by him, and if he has not been given sufficient information and explanations to overcome his reservations, he will need to qualify his opinion in respect of such amounts included in the consolidated financial statements. These should be disclosed, preferably by way of reference to a note identifying the assets, liabilities and profits or losses of the subsidiaries concerned.

EXAMPLE – Subject to opinion; foreign subsidiary not audited

We have audited the financial statements on pages 9 to 22. Our audit was conducted in accordance with approved Auditing Standards except that the scope of our audit was limited in the following respect.

Note 10 to the financial statements summarises the amounts included in the consolidated financial statements in respect of Trampois, S.A., a wholly owned French subsidiary. These amounts are derived from management financial statements which have not been audited for the reasons set out in the note. Accordingly we have not been able to satisfy ourselves as to the amounts included in the consolidated financial statements in respect of this subsidiary.

Subject to the effect of any adjustments which might have been indicated as required if the above subsidiary had been audited, in our opinion. . . .

Where the auditor is not able to satisfy himself that the financial statements of a consolidated subsidiary have been audited in accordance with U.K. auditing standards, he should review the extent to which, on the basis of the work done by the other auditor, together with any supplementary procedures performed by him, he is satisfied with each item in that subsidiary's financial statements. He may decide that some items have been adequately audited. He should then consider the effect on his opinion on the consolidated financial statements of the remaining items about which he still has reservations.

(c) Limitations arising in the first year of appointment as auditors

Where the auditor has not audited the financial statements of the previous year, he cannot rely on them for the assurance that he requires regarding the opening balances without making further enquiries. The most efficient way of obtaining the necessary assurance will often be by consultation with the outgoing auditors and review of their working papers. Where he cannot obtain assurance in this way he may not be able to carry out all the necessary verification work since he will usually have been appointed after the start of the financial year. In such circumstances he may have reservations as to the fairness of the profit and loss account and statement of source and application of funds but should be satisfied that the balance sheet is fairly stated.

EXAMPLE – Qualified opinion; opening stocks not audited

We have audited the financial statements on pages 8 to 21. Our audit was conducted in accordance with approved Auditing Standards except that the scope of our work was limited by the matter referred to below.

We were not appointed auditors of the company until 3 March 1984 and therefore could not be present to observe the physical stocktaking at the beginning of the year, nor were we able to verify stock quantities by other means. The valuation of opening stocks is material in determining the trading results of the year ended 31 December 1984.

In our opinion the financial statements give a true and fair view of the state of the company's affairs at 31 December 1984 and, subject to the effect of any adjustment which might have been shown to be necessary had we been present at the physical stocktaking at the beginning of the year, a true and fair view of its profit and source and application of funds for the year then ended and comply with the Companies Act 1985.

(d) Small companies

The Auditing Standards and Guidelines deal specifically with the problem of auditing small enterprises and suggest that in many cases in such enterprises there will be insufficient evidence to support an audit opinion, particularly on the matter of completeness of records. They include a specific example (Example 6) of an audit report which is suitable for such circumstances: the audit report reads as follows:

'We have audited the financial statements on pages .... to .... Our audit was conducted in accordance with approved Auditing Standards having regard to the matters referred to in the following paragraph.

In common with many businesses of similar size and organisation the company's system of control is dependent upon the close involvement of the directors/managing director, [who are major shareholders]. Where independent confirmation of the completeness of the accounting records was therefore not available we have accepted assurances from the directors/managing director that all the company's transactions have been reflected in the records.

Subject to the foregoing, in our opinion . . . .'

The very widespread use of this form of report since the auditing guideline on audit reports was published suggests that many auditors regard it as the standard report to be used on small company audits. It is thought that this report is unhelpful and that in most circumstances where its use is permissible it should be possible to give the normal unqualified report.

Before issuing this form of report the auditor should be satisfied:

(i) that steps have been taken to obtain all the evidence which can reasonably be obtained; thus this form of report cannot be used as a justification for restricting the scope of the audit;

(ii) that the evidence obtained is insufficient to support an opinion that the accounting records are materially complete; profit margin reviews coupled with extensive substantive tests on purchases, costs and inventories will often give sufficient evidence for this purpose;

(iii) that there is no evidence to suggest that the assurances may be inaccurate; for example if margin reviews produced unexplained unsatisfactory results, this would be evidence that the assurances may be inaccurate and the appropriate report would include a qualification as to uncertainty about the inclusion of income, without reference to management assurances (an example of such a qualification is given below);

(iv) that the system of accounting and control is reasonable having regard to the size and type of the enterprise's operations; if the business is one which in the auditor's view should have controls which can be tested and relied upon, but these are not present, then again the report should be qualified on the grounds of uncertainty; this should refer to the inadequacy of control and not to management assurances;

(v) that management is actually in a position to know that the assurances it gives are accurate; for example a manager of one shop who is present throughout its opening hours might be able to give assurance that all sales are accounted for, but he cannot do so if he manages two or more shops; in such cases a system of control is essential and it should be possible to assess its reliability.

If it is decided that it is appropriate to use this form of opinion, careful consideration should be given to the precise wording to be used. It is obviously more helpful if the auditor can specify precisely the area or areas where independent confirmation of completeness is not available (unless they are very wide), e.g. 'Independent confirmation of the completeness of the sales records was therefore not available and we have accepted assurances from the directors that all the company's sales have been reflected in the records.'

Where adequate assurance cannot be obtained and the requirements outlined above are not met, qualification without reference to management assurances is appropriate.

EXAMPLE – Subject to opinion; inability to substantiate cash sales

We have audited the financial statements on pages 9 to 22. Our audit was conducted in accordance with approved Auditing Standards except that the scope of our work was limited by the matter referred to below.

A substantial part of the company's turnover comprises cash sales. There was no system of control over such sales on which we could rely and no practical auditing procedures were available to determine the completeness or otherwise of the recorded cash sales. We were, therefore, unable to obtain all the information and explanations which we considered necessary.

Subject to the whole of the cash sales being properly recorded, in our opinion. . . .

19.212 PROPER ACCOUNTING RECORDS NOT KEPT

Accounting records must:

(i) be sufficient to show and explain the company's transactions,

(ii) disclose the company's financial position at any time, and

(iii) be such as to enable the directors to ensure that any balance sheets and profit and loss accounts which they are required to prepare comply with the Act. [s 221]

In particular accounting records must contain:

(i) entries from day to day of all sums of money received and expended and the matters in respect of which the receipts and expenditure take place;

(ii) a record of the assets and liabilities of the company; and

(iii) where the company's business involves dealing in goods,

(a) statements of stock held at the end of each financial year;

(b) all statements of stocktakings from which any statements in (a) above have been prepared; and

(c) except in the case of goods sold by way of ordinary retail trade, statements of all goods sold and purchased in sufficient detail to identify the goods and the buyers and sellers.

For an interpretation of these requirements reference should be made to Appendix 6 of this manual.

The failure of a company to maintain proper accounting records will usually result in the auditor not obtaining all the information and explanations which he requires. S 237 will then require him to report his opinion that proper accounting records have not been kept and that he has not obtained all the information and explanations he required. If the deficiencies are so pervasive and wide-ranging that it is not practicable to prepare meaningful financial statements, then a disclaimer of opinion may be required, but normally a 'subject to' opinion is appropriate.

EXAMPLE – Disclaimer; missing records

We have audited the financial statements on pages 9 to 22. Our audit was conducted in accordance with approved Auditing Standards except that the scope of our work was limited by the matters referred to below.

As a consequence of a fire on 7 January 1985 at the company's computer centre, accounting records concerning the company's debtors, creditors and stocks were destroyed. The financial statements therefore include significant amounts based on estimates. In these circumstances we were unable to carry out all the auditing procedures or to obtain all the information and explanations we consider necessary.

Because of the significance of the matters referred to in the preceding paragraph, we are unable to form an opinion as to whether the financial statements give a true and fair view of the state of the company's affairs at 31 December 1984 and of its profit and source and application of funds for the year then ended, or whether the financial statements comply in all respects with the Companies Act 1985. In our opinion, proper accounting records have not been kept.

The Act also requires the auditor to report where in his opinion proper returns adequate for his audit have not been received from branches not visited by him. [s 237] Such returns will be deemed adequate where the whole of the bookkeeping applicable to such branch is centralised at another office which has been visited and audited. It will not be necessary to report on those returns of branches not visited where the branches are considered immaterial.

(a) Financial statements not in agreement with accounting records

When the balance sheet and profit and loss account are not in agreement with the accounting records and returns, the auditor is required to state that fact in his audit report. [s 237]

Usually the company records all approved audit adjustments so that the books agree with the financial statements. However, care should be taken to ensure that all adjustments made at the consolidation level, except those normal consolidating adjustments necessary to eliminate intercompany investments, balances and profits, are recorded in the books of the applicable companies.

19.213 INHERENT UNCERTAINTY AFFECTING VALUATION OF ASSETS AND LIABILITIES

The auditing standard 'Qualifications in audit reports' indicates that inherent uncertainties result from circumstances in which it is not possible to reach an objective conclusion due to the circumstances themselves rather than to any limitation of the scope of audit procedures. It also indicates that they do not normally includes instances where the auditor is able to obtain adequate evidence to support estimates and use his experience to reach an opinion as to their reasonableness.

This distinction is unhelpful particularly as 'adequate evidence' is not defined. It is axiomatic that the evidence available to support an estimate or a probable future outcome can only be persuasive and never conclusive. The evidence available to an auditor to support an opinion on the reasonableness of an accounting estimate is often far from conclusive. Unless what constitutes adequate evidence is clearly defined, there is an obvious danger that evidence will be regarded as inadequate in any case where an estimate which was regarded as reasonable by the auditor is subsequently proved to have been wrong.

It is very difficult for the auditor to determine which of the many uncertainties that are inherent in all financial statements are sufficiently significant to require him to issue a qualified opinion and it is inevitable that the judgments of different auditors will differ widely in this respect. Consequently readers of audit reports must interpret such a qualification with care and should not assume that its absence indicates that there are no uncertainties in the financial statements.

It is suggested that as far as possible qualifications on the grounds of inherent uncertainties should be avoided. They should be restricted to circumstances which are unusual to the company, where the amounts involved are large and where such evidence as exists is not at all persuasive. Examples of circumstances which might justify qualification include major litigation where the outcome cannot reasonably be foreseen, major contracts likely to give rise to large unquantifiable losses due to unsolved technical problems, uncertain political or economic circumstances in countries where the company has substantial assets. Since the directors are required to produce financial statements which show a true and fair view, all such circumstances will normally be disclosed in the notes to the accounts in any event. However as indicated in 19.222 below it is normal practice to qualify on the grounds of uncertainty where the auditor reaches a different opinion from the directors on the basis of inconclusive evidence.

The following are examples of suitable qualifications on the grounds of inherent uncertainty.

EXAMPLE – Subject to opinion; valuation of assets

We have audited the financial statements on pages 8 to 21 in accordance with approved Auditing Standards.

Contract work in progress includes a provision of £2,000,000 for the estimated loss on completion of a contract, the details of which are stated in note 15 to the accounts. We are unable to determine the adequacy or otherwise of the provision in view of the unresolved technical problems and delays which have arisen.

Subject to any adjustment that may be required to reflect the total loss to completion of the above contract, in our opinion. . . .

EXAMPLE – Subject to opinion; litigation

We have audited the financial statements on pages 8 to 21 in accordance with approved Auditing Standards.

As more fully explained in note 3 to the accounts a claim has been lodged against the company in respect of one of its major contracts. The claim calls for rectification and for substantial compensation for alleged damage to the customer's business. The directors have made provision for the estimated cost of rectification but no provision for compensation as that part of the claim is being strongly resisted. It is not possible to determine with reasonable accuracy the ultimate cost of rectification and compensation, if any, which may become payable.

Subject to the adjustment, if any, that may be required when the claim referred to above is determined, in our opinion . . . .

19.214 INHERENT UNCERTAINTY ABOUT GOING CONCERN

It is one of the fundamental accounting principles prescribed by the Act that a company shall be presumed to be carrying on business as a going concern. SSAP 2 defines the going concern concept as being that the company will continue in operational existence for the foreseeable future, and indicates that this implies that the profit and loss account and balance sheet assume no intention to liquidate or curtail significantly the scale of operation. A departure from this principle is only permissible for special reasons which would presumably only arise if the directors concluded that the company was not a going concern.

Amongst the inherent uncertainties that might give rise to a necessity for qualification which are listed in the auditing standard 'Qualifications in audit reports' is 'doubts about the ability of the enterprise to continue as a going concern'. Since there must always be some degree of doubt as to the ability of any enterprise to continue in business, the requirement to qualify on the grounds of uncertainty as to the appropriateness of the going concern concept is a matter of extreme difficulty to the auditor. On the one hand it may be argued that the presumption of going concern should be accepted by the auditor without qualification unless there is very persuasive evidence that the presumption is inappropriate; on the other hand it is suggested that the absence of a going concern qualification is equivalent to an assurance by the auditor that the company will continue in operational existence for a reasonable period following the date of his report. Between these two extremes no guidance is available as to what degree of doubt or uncertainty requires the auditor to qualify about the appropriateness of the going concern principle. The APC has issued an exposure draft of a proposed auditing guideline entitled 'The auditor's considerations in respect of going concern' but this draft provides no useful guidance on this point.

In these circumstances it is inevitable that the judgments of different auditors will vary very widely as to the circumstances in which a going concern qualification is appropriate. Consequently readers of audit reports need to interpret going concern qualifications with particular care, and they learn nothing from the absence of such qualifications.

It is suggested that going concern qualifications should be restricted to cases where there are special circumstances which give rise to a substantially higher than normal risk that the company may be unable to continue as a going concern. Examples of such circumstances are:

- an excess of liabilities over assets
- significant liquidity or cash flow problems
- major losses or cash flow problems which have arisen since the balance sheet date and which threaten the enterprise's continued existence
- major litigation in which an adverse judgment would imperil the company's continued existence
- major debt repayment falling due where re-financing is necessary to the company's continued existence

The following is an example of an audit report containing a going concern qualification.

EXAMPLE – Subject to opinion; going concern

We have audited the financial statements on pages 8 to 21 in accordance with approved Auditing Standards.

As stated in note 2 the company is currently negotiating for long-term facilities to replace the loan of £1,400,000 which becomes repayable on 15 May 1985; continuation of the company's activities is dependent upon a successful outcome to these negotiations. The financial statements have been drawn up on a going concern basis which assumes that adequate facilities will be obtained.

Subject to a satisfactory outcome of the negotiations referred to above, in our opinion the financial statements give a true and fair view of the state of the company's affairs at 31 December 1984 and of its profit and source and application of funds for the year then ended and comply with the Companies Act 1985.

The foregoing example follows closely the example included in the auditing guideline 'Audit report examples'. The exposure draft of the guideline 'The auditor's considerations in respect of going concern' includes an alternative form of report which emphasises the adjustments to amounts and classifications which would arise if the financial statements were not prepared on a going concern basis. This seems an unhelpful form of report since what is significant to the reader is the nature and extent of the uncertainty; the adjustments which are necessary if the going concern basis is not adopted are generally of little interest to the reader particularly as they are usually unquantifiable. The amounts involved are likely to be so significant as to require a disclaimer of opinion rather than a 'subject to' opinion. It is suggested that, unless the example in the guideline 'Audit report examples' is formally withdrawn by the APC, it should continue to be used as a model for uncertainty qualifications.

Whether the auditor considers it necessary to qualify his opinion or not, it is very important that all circumstances which give rise to a higher than normal risk that the enterprise may not continue as a going concern are fully and fairly disclosed in the financial statements, so that the reader of these statements can make his own assessment of the risks involved. If any relevant financial information has not been fairly disclosed, then the financial statements do not show a true and fair view and the auditor should qualify his opinion on the grounds of disagreement. He should issue an 'except for' opinion which should clearly disclose any omitted information or correct any unfairness in the information disclosed.

In exceptional circumstances financial statements may be prepared on a going concern basis when the auditor considers that the evidence that the enterprise is not a going concern is so persuasive as to rebut the presumption of going concern. In this situation he should also qualify on the grounds of disagreement but an adverse opinion is likely to be appropriate.

19.220 EXAMPLES OF QUALIFIED REPORTS ARISING FROM DISAGREEMENT

Circumstances which give rise to disagreement include:

(i) disagreement as to accounting policies followed.

(ii) disagreement as to facts or amounts shown in the financial statements.

(iii) disagreement as to manner or extent of disclosure in the financial statements.

(iv) non-compliance with relevant legislation.

In the subsections which follow, each of these categories are discussed in detail and examples of audit reports are given.

19.221 DISAGREEMENT AS TO ACCOUNTING POLICIES FOLLOWED

The Auditing Standard cites three situations in which departures from acceptable accounting practice should lead the auditor to consider qualifying his report. Sch 4 prescribes certain accounting practices, some of which are also dealt with by SSAPs. Where there is a departure from such a practice, the auditor must consider the matter with reference to both the requirements of the Act and those of the SSAP. He must qualify his report unless he is satisfied not only that the conditions which justify departure from a SSAP are met (see Section 19.102 above) but also that the departure from the Companies Act requirement is justified on the grounds that to follow the requirement would prevent the financial statements from showing a true and fair view. Each of these situations is discussed below.

(a) *Failure to comply with a relevant SSAP or accounting policies contained in the Act and the auditor does not agree*

If a company's accounting policy does not comply with a relevant SSAP, it is unlikely that the auditor will be able to agree with the departure. His concurrence with a material departure from a SSAP is permissible only where (i) for justifiable reasons it would be impractical to apply the SSAP or, in exceptional circumstances, the application of the SSAP would be inappropriate or give a misleading view and (ii) he is satisfied that the alternative treatment gives a true and fair view.

The notes to the accounts should disclose all significant departures from SSAPs and from the requirements of Sch 4 and the justification for these departures. The audit report need not make reference to departures with which the auditor agrees provided that the notes to the accounts disclose the departure. Where he disagrees with the departure, his report should make reference to the noncompliance and quantify, if possible, the financial effect of the departure (or refer to any note which gives this information), indicating also for listed companies the effect on earnings per share.

EXAMPLE – Departure from SSAP

We have audited the financial statements on pages 8 to 21 in accordance with approved Auditing Standards.

The company follows the policy of including in the financial statements only the dividends received from X Limited, its associated company. This is not in accordance with Statement of Standard Accounting Practice No. 1 (Accounting for the results of associated companies). If the company had recorded its share of the increase in the net assets of X Limited, in accordance with that accounting standard, the group profit on ordinary activities after taxation shown in the consolidated profit and loss account would have been increased by £290,000 (equivalent to 6 pence per share), and the group's interest in X Limited and the group reserves, as shown in the consolidated balance sheet, would have been increased by £1,830,000.

Except for the effects of accounting for the associated company in the manner stated above, in our opinion . . . .

There may be exceptional cases where a combination of departures from SSAPs renders the financial statements totally misleading. In such rare instances, an adverse opinion is appropriate.

(b) *Accounting policy not covered by a SSAP is adopted and the auditor does not concur*

The development of accounting in the U.K. has resulted in a diversity of accounting practices with varying degrees of acceptability. While the issue of SSAPs has done much to reduce the number of acceptable accounting practices, there still remain some areas where a number of different accounting practices are generally accepted.

Guidance as to the acceptability of accounting policies can be found by reference to the sources of information described in Section 1.030 of this manual.

If a company follows an accounting policy which is not the subject of a SSAP and which the auditor considers is not appropriate to the circumstances of the business, his report should refer to the policy with which he disagrees and should indicate the treatment he considers appropriate. He should quantify, if possible, the financial effect in a manner similar to the examples given above.

(c) SSAP has been followed with the result that the financial statements do not show a true and fair view.

While the possibility of this situation arising is recognised in the Auditing Standard, it is almost never encountered and for practical purposes can probably be disregarded.

19.222 DISAGREEMENT AS TO FACTS OR AMOUNTS INCLUDED IN THE FINANCIAL STATEMENTS

During the course of an audit, information may be obtained which the auditor concludes conflicts with the facts or amounts shown in the financial statements. Where the discrepancy is due to an error, there should be no disagreement since the company will normally alter the financial statements if the facts or amounts are material. There are however other instances where evaluation of the evidence leads the auditor to a conclusion which is different from that of the company. These often relate to the valuation of assets or liabilities. It is the auditor's duty to exercise his independent judgment and where a disagreement is considered material to an appreciation of the financial statements, his opinion must be qualified.

> ***EXAMPLE – no provision against investment***
>
> *We have audited the financial statements on pages 8 to 21 in accordance with approved Auditing Standards.*
>
> *The shares in Tramp Limited, which is in liquidation, are shown in the balance sheet at cost of £123,000. The liquidator has stated that it is unlikely that the company will be able to pay its debts in full and in our opinion full provision should be made against this investment.*
>
> *Except for the failure to make this provision, in our opinion . . . .*

As already indicated the evidence available to support an estimate can only be persuasive and never conclusive, and the Auditing Standard indicates that inherent uncertainties do not normally include instances where the auditor is able to obtain adequate evidence to support estimates and use his experience to reach an opinion as to their reasonableness. This implies that unless the evidence available is significantly less than the auditor is entitled to expect (in which case he should qualify on the grounds that he has not obtained all the information and explanations which he requires), the auditor must exercise his judgment on the basis of the information available. If on that evidence he reaches a conclusion which is different from that of the directors, he should qualify on the grounds of disagreement.

In practice it is not uncommon for the available evidence to lead the auditor to a conclusion different from that of the directors although he acknowledges that the conclusion reached by the directors is not unreasonable. In these circumstances it is normal for the auditor to give a 'subject to' opinion on the grounds that the evidence is not sufficiently conclusive to eliminate significant uncertainty.

(a) Information in notes which alters the view shown by the accounts

The notes form part of the financial statements for the purposes of the Act, but disclosures in the notes cannot correct or amend accounts which show a differing view. Therefore, if a note materially alters the view otherwise given by the accounts, it will be necessary to qualify the audit report.

For example, if a note to the accounts indicates that investments include £38,000 which is not expected to be recovered but that pending the final report of the liquidators, no provision has been made, the audit report might read:

> ***EXAMPLE***
>
> *We have audited the financial statements on pages 8 to 21 in accordance with approved Auditing Standards.*
>
> *As stated in Note 5 to the accounts an investment included in the balance sheet at £38,000 is not expected to be recovered and in our opinion provision should be made to write off this investment in full.*
>
> *Except for the failure to provide in full for the value of the above investment, in our opinion . . . .*

19.223 DISAGREEMENT AS TO THE ADEQUACY OF DISCLOSURE OF FACTS OR AMOUNTS IN THE FINANCIAL STATEMENTS

If the financial statements fail to disclose information which is required to be disclosed by SSAPs or significant information which the auditor believes is essential to a true and fair view, his report should be suitably qualified. The qualification will be 'except for', should clearly indicate the nature of the omitted information and should provide the omitted information if it is practicable and reasonable to do so.

19.224 FAILURE TO COMPLY WITH RELEVANT LEGISLATION OR OTHER REQUIREMENTS

(a) Companies Act disclosures concerning directors, officers, and higher paid employees

The Act requires certain information concerning directors, officers and higher paid employees of the company to be disclosed in a note to the accounts, and in addition provides that if it is not so given the auditor must give it in his report so far as he is reasonably able to do so.

The information covered by this requirement is that required by Sch 5: Parts V and VI and Sch 6, namely:

(i) details of directors' emoluments, pensions and compensation for loss of office (Section 5.152);

(ii) numbers of employees remunerated at higher rates (Section 5.151(c));

(iii) particulars of loans to directors and officers (Sections 11.081 and 11.082);

(iv) particulars of transactions and arrangements with directors (Section 11.081).

Qualification on these grounds is unlikely to be necessary since in most cases directors will agree to the necessary disclosure being included in the notes to the accounts when they appreciate that the alternative is disclosure in the audit report.

(b) Other Companies Act disclosures

Sch 4 and Sch 5: Parts I–IV require many items to be separately disclosed either in the accounts or in the notes. In some circumstances the auditor may consider that the financial statements show a true and fair view in spite of the omission of certain statutory disclosures, but will still require to indicate that the financial statements do not comply with the Act. In these circumstances there is no statutory requirement to provide the omitted information in the audit report. However the auditing standard 'Qualifications in Audit Reports' requires in respect of each qualification quantification of its effect on the financial statements if this is both relevant and practicable. Thus wherever practicable the omitted information should be included in the audit report. Often however, precise quantification will not be possible, as in the following example.

EXAMPLE – information not disclosed

We have audited the financial statements on pages 8 to 21 in accordance with approved Auditing Standards.

The comparable cost and accumulated depreciation determined under the historical cost accounting rules in respect of revalued fixed tangible assets or the differences between those amounts and the corresponding amounts shown in the balance sheet have not been disclosed as required by Schedule 4, paragraph 33(3) of the Companies Act 1985. This information has not been made available to us and accordingly we have not received all the information and explanations we require.

In our opinion, the financial statements give a true and fair view of the state of the company's affairs at 31 December 1984 and of its profit and source and application of funds for the year then ended and, except for the omission of the information referred to above, comply with the Companies Act 1985.

Exceptional circumstances may arise when the company declines to give the required information on the grounds that it is likely to be harmful to its business. If there are reasonable grounds for this view, the auditor may decide that it is not appropriate for him to disclose the omitted information. A particular example arises where the company has applied or intends to apply to the Secretary of State for exemption in accordance with the Act.

EXAMPLE – information not disclosed

We have audited the financial statements on pages 8 to 21 in accordance with approved Auditing Standards.

As explained in note 12 the information concerning overseas investments acquired during the year has not been disclosed as required by Schedule 5, paragraph 7 of the Companies Act 1985.

In our opinion the financial statements give a true and fair view of the state of the company's affairs at 31 December 1984 and of its profit and source and application of funds for the year then ended and, except for the omission of the disclosure concerning overseas investments referred to above, comply with the Companies Act 1985.

Note: Note 12 should explain the reason why the information is not given (i.e. it would be harmful to the company's business) and that application is being made to the Secretary of State for exemption under the 1985 Act. In this case, the opinion on the true and fair view shown by the financial statements is not impaired by omission of this required disclosure.

(c) Directors' report not consistent with the financial statements

The Act imposes a duty on the auditor to consider whether the information given in the directors' report relating to the financial year is consistent with the financial statements and, if there is an inconsistency, to state that fact in the audit report. [s 237(6)]

It is rare for there to be a straightforward difference between figures appearing in the audited financial statements and corresponding figures quoted in the directors' report. Sometimes however inconsistency arises from loose or ambiguous wording in the directors' report: for example a reference in the directors' report to the profit for the financial year of £A, where £A is in fact the profit on ordinary activities (either before or after tax) and the profit for the financial year disclosed in the profit and loss account is significantly lower because of a large extraordinary item, would result in an inconsistency between the report and the profit and loss account.

The most difficult area of possible inconsistency arises from the narrative content of the directors' report, in particular the fair review of the development of the business of the company and of its position at the year end. The auditor must distinguish between purportedly factual statements which are inconsistent with the information in the financial statements on the one hand, and expressions of opinion which place an interpretation on the financial statements with which he disagrees on the other. While he will try to get both changed, he should only refer to the matter in his report when he is satisfied that there is inconsistency. However, he should consider carefully the need to draw to the directors' attention in writing his disagreement with what he considers unfounded interpretations of the financial statements.

It is seldom necessary to qualify the audit report on these grounds since the directors will usually agree to amend their report to remove the inconsistency. When qualification is necessary the audit report should explain the nature of the inconsistency and the resulting difference. Since the truth and fairness of the financial statements is unaffected, the inconsistency should be reported in the audit report in a final paragraph following the opinion paragraph.

EXAMPLE

(Audit scope paragraph)

(Opinion paragraph)

In our opinion the directors' report is inconsistent with the financial statements in the following respect. The information on net asset value per share given on page 2 of the directors' report exceeds by 20.6p per share the net asset value calculated by reference to the consolidated balance sheet figure of share capital and reserves, the increase being attributed to the directors' assessment of the excess of market value over book value of undeveloped land which is not reflected in the financial statements in accordance with the accounting principles adopted by the company.

(d) Statutory financial statements not drawn up by reference to a valid accounting reference date

Companies sometimes prepare financial statements to a date which is not a valid accounting reference date under s 224, and the directors may ask the auditor to report on such statements. His attitude to this request will depend on the purpose for which the statements are required. If they are required for any purpose other than to lay before the members in general meeting (e.g. for the information of bankers), he should carry out his audit and report in the normal way with the exceptions that the report should be addressed to the directors and not to the members of the company and should not refer to compliance with the Companies Act 1985.

If the financial statements are intended to be laid before the members in general meeting, the auditor should point out to the directors that they are not acceptable as statutory accounts under s 227. If the directors are unable or unwilling to correct the position and insist on presenting such financial statements as statutory accounts, then the accounts cannot be said to comply with the Companies Act 1985 and the auditor must report accordingly.

EXAMPLE – invalid accounting reference date

We have audited the financial statements on pages 8 to 21 in accordance with approved Auditing Standards.

The financial statements are drawn up to a date other than the company's accounting reference date and in this respect do not comply with the Companies Act 1985.

In our opinion, the financial statements give a true and fair view of the state of the company's affairs at 31 December 1984 and of its profit and source and application of funds for the twenty months then ended and, except that they are not drawn up to the company's accounting reference date, comply with the Companies Act 1985.

(e) Corresponding amounts

The auditor's opinion as to the truth and fairness of the financial statements relates only to amounts reported in relation to the period covered by those statements and does not extend to the corresponding amounts. However the Act requires the disclosure of corresponding amounts for all items in a company's balance sheet and profit and loss account and that these amounts must be adjusted if necessary to be comparable with the amounts for the current financial year. The auditor's responsibility under the Act in respect of corresponding amounts [Sch 4: 4(2)] is therefore to ensure that the amounts disclosed as corresponding amounts are the amounts which appeared in the previous year's financial statements, or have been properly restated to be comparable with the amounts for the current year. Restatement will normally be appropriate only in the circumstances outlined in SSAP 6, i.e. to reflect a change in accounting policy or the correction of a fundamental error. Where corresponding amounts have been adjusted, particulars of the adjustments and the reasons for them must be shown in the notes to the accounts.

The auditor must qualify his opinion if he is not satisfied that the corresponding amounts are comparable. This might arise either:

(i) when he considers that the corresponding amounts should have been restated (e.g. to reflect a change in accounting policy) but this has not been done, or that the corresponding amounts have been restated in an unjustifiable manner, or

(ii) when the previous financial statements were qualified and he considers that the corresponding amounts are not, or may not be, comparable with those of the current period.

EXAMPLE

We have audited the financial statements on pages 8 to 21 in accordance with approved Auditing Standards.

As stated in note 5 to the accounts, the company has changed its accounting policy in respect of stocks to include appropriate production overheads which had previously been excluded. The stock records at 31 December 1982 were not prepared in sufficient detail to enable the stocks at that date to be restated in accordance with the new policy. Accordingly the corresponding amounts shown in the profit and loss account and statement of source and application of funds in respect of cost of sales, gross profit, profit before and after taxation and changes in stock and work in progress are not comparable with the figures for the current period.

In our opinion the financial statements give a true and fair view of the state of the company's affairs at 31 December 1984 and of its profit and source and application of funds for the year then ended and, except for the effects of the matter set out above, comply with the Companies Act 1985.

As with other qualifications the auditor should quantify the effects of the misstatement on the previous year's financial statements if this is relevant and practicable. It is sometimes not practicable to quantify these effects because it is not possible to determine the correct re-stated amount for the previous year following a change in accounting policy. When this situation occurs, it may be helpful to the reader of the financial statements to disclose in a note what the current year's result would have been under the old accounting policy. If the company is unwilling to do this, the auditor should consider providing the information in his report.

It should not be assumed that a qualified audit report in one year automatically results in a qualification of the corresponding amounts in the following year. If the matters which caused the qualification in the previous year have been resolved during the current year and properly reflected in the financial statements, no reference to the previous qualification is normally necessary. The most common circumstances are discussed below.

(i) The auditor disagreed with an accounting policy adopted by the client. The report will be qualified in the current year also unless the policy has been changed to meet the auditor's view, in which case the corresponding amounts should be restated.

(ii) The auditor disagreed with a treatment which had the effect of transferring profit between the previous period and the one now being audited (e.g. as to the valuation of closing stocks of raw materials). The report must be qualified because the auditor's disagreement affects the profit of the current year; the qualification should make clear the effect on the corresponding amounts also.

(iii) The auditor disagreed as to the amount to be included in respect of a material asset or liability. In the following year the disagreement may be resolved either because the matter has been determined or because the auditor or the client has changed his view in the light of current information. In the circumstances no qualification of the corresponding amounts is appropriate but if the resolution has a material effect on the results of the year and the preceding one, the auditor will need to be satisfied that suitable disclosure is made. In exceptional circumstances it might be necessary to deal with the matter as a correction of a fundamental error. If the matter has not been determined and both auditor and client adhere to their original views, the qualification must be repeated, but it is desirable to refer to the previous qualification so as to make it clear that the problem did not arise in the current period.

(iv) The auditor qualified on the grounds of uncertainty as to the amount to be included in respect of a material asset or liability. In these circumstances the considerations are identical to those in (iii) above: if the uncertainty has been resolved in the current period and properly reflected in the financial statements, no qualification of the corresponding amounts is necessary; if the matter remains unresolved, the qualification must be repeated but it is desirable to make clear that the problem did not arise in the current period.

EXAMPLE – continuing litigation

We have audited the financial statements on pages 8 to 21 in accordance with approved Auditing Standards.

As indicated in note 5 to the accounts, the company is contesting a claim for patent infringement calling for payment of substantial damages. The directors consider it inappropriate to make any provision in the accounts as the claim is being strongly resisted. At present it is not possible to determine the ultimate cost, if any, which may become payable. We qualified our audit report on the financial statements for the preceding year with regard to this same uncertainty.

Subject to the adjustment, if any, that may be required when the litigation is resolved, in our opinion . . .

(v) The auditor qualified on the grounds of uncertainty regarding the profit and source and application of funds but gave an unqualified opinion on the balance sheet. In this case it may be that the auditor is uncertain as to whether the comparable amounts in the profit and loss account and statement of source and application of funds are comparable and he may therefore require to qualify his report. The qualification relates to compliance with the Act only, since the true and fair view in respect of the current year is unaffected.

EXAMPLE

We have audited the financial statements on pages 9 to 21 in accordance with approved Auditing Standards.

The corresponding amounts in the current period's financial statements are derived from the financial statements for the year ended 31 December 1983. In our report on those financial statements we stated that we were unable to express an opinion on the profit and source and application of funds for the year ended on that date because we were unable to substantiate the amount of stock at 1 January 1983. Accordingly the corresponding amounts shown for the profit and source and application of funds may not be comparable with the figures for the current period.

In our opinion the financial statements give a true and fair view of the state of the company's affairs at 31 December 1984 and of its profit and source and application of funds for the year then ended and, subject to any effects of the matter set out above, comply with Companies Act 1985.

The foregoing example is included in the Auditing Guideline 'Amounts derived from the preceding financial statements'. Strictly speaking the statement of source and application of funds is not required by the Act and therefore it seems unnecessary to refer to it. It would seem acceptable (and possibly clearer) if the last sentence of the second paragraph read:

Accordingly the corresponding amounts shown for cost of sales and profit may not be comparable with the figures for the current period.

(f) Stock Exchange requirements

Stock Exchange companies are required to include additional information specified in Chapter 5 of the Yellow Book for listed companies and in the General Undertaking for USM companies. As a matter of client service the auditor will wish to bring to the attention of the directors their obligation to fulfil these requirements. However, he should not make any reference in his audit report to any failure to comply with them.

19.300 OTHER AUDIT REPORTS

19.301 INTERIM AUDITED FINANCIAL STATEMENTS

There may be special circumstances where the auditor is engaged to audit the financial statements of a company at a date other than the financial year end. These audited interim financial statements are usually prepared at the request of the directors for external purposes, e.g. financing arrangements. The audit report therefore should be addressed to the directors, or other persons who engaged the auditor, rather than to the members of the company.

An unqualified audit report on interim financial statements should be worded as follows:

EXAMPLE

We have audited the financial statements on pages 2 to 10 in accordance with approved Auditing Standards.

In our opinion the financial statements give a true and fair view of the state of the company's affairs at 31 December 1984 and of its profit and source and application of funds for the six months then ended.

No mention is made in the above report of compliance with the Act since the statements are not prepared for statutory purposes. However, care must be exercised to ensure that the financial statements give adequate disclosures and comply with SSAPs so as to present a true and fair view. If any disclosures required by the Companies Act are omitted, the auditor must consider whether the omitted information is necessary for a true and fair view, and if it is, he should qualify his report. For example, information regarding the remuneration of directors and senior employees may not be necessary for a true and fair view whereas information about fixed asset movements probably is.

19.302 BANKING, INSURANCE AND SHIPPING COMPANIES

Special category companies (i.e. banking, insurance and shipping companies) are required to prepare accounts in accordance with Sch 9 rather than Sch 4. Sch 9: Part III provides significant exceptions to the detailed requirements for the different categories of company. Although the Act requires that the accounts of special category companies must show a true and fair view, it is specifically provided that such accounts shall not be deemed not to show a true and fair view only because advantage has been taken of these exemptions.

Where a company has properly taken advantage of any of the exemptions in Sch 9: Part III, the audit report should state whether in the auditor's opinion the accounts have been properly prepared in accordance with the Act. An example of an audit report applicable to a special category company is as follows:

EXAMPLE

We have audited the financial statements on pages 8 to 21 in accordance with approved Auditing Standards.

In our opinion the financial statements comply with the provisions of the Companies Act 1985 applicable to insurance companies (banking companies, shipping companies).

If the financial statements do not show a true and fair view for any reason other than that advantage has been taken of the exemptions in Sch 9: Part III (e.g. if assets are materially overstated) then they have not been properly prepared in accordance with the Act and the auditor will be required to give a qualified report.

Difficult problems can arise where a group has one or more subsidiaries which are banks or insurance companies which take advantage of the provisions of Sch 9, while the other group companies are subject to the full requirements of Sch 4. In these circumstances there is a strong case for excluding the accounts of the banking or insurance subsidiaries from consolidation on the grounds that their activities are so dissimilar that it would be misleading to include them (see Section 12.061(a)).

The group financial statements would then comprise consolidated accounts for the parent company and those of its subsidiaries which are not banks or insurance companies, together with the separate financial statements of the banking and insurance companies. The auditor of the parent company is required to report on the group financial statements as a whole. The following is an example of a possible form of audit report assuming that the group auditor has also audited the financial statements of the insurance subsidiary:

EXAMPLE – Group which includes an insurance subsidiary

We have audited the financial statements on pages 8 to 21 in accordance with approved Auditing Standards.

In our opinion the financial statements insofar as they relate to the insurance subsidiary comply with the provisions of the Companies Act 1985 applicable to insurance companies. In our opinion, the financial statements insofar as they relate to other companies in the group give a true and fair view of the state of affairs of the company and the group at 31 December 1984 and of the profit and source and application of funds of the group for the year then ended and comply with the Companies Act 1985.

19.303 PENSION SCHEMES

Current best practice in accounting for pension schemes is set out in ED 34, a draft SORP on pension scheme accounts. ED 34 proposes that pension scheme accounts should include a revenue account recording the financial inflows and outflows of the fund, a statement of net assets which discloses the disposition and make-up of the net assets of the scheme, and a statement of the movement in total value of the fund, together with notes disclosing any additional information which is necessary to give true and fair view of the transactions of the scheme for the period and of the disposition of the net assets of the scheme at the accounting date. It is envisaged that the annual report of a pension scheme would include in addition to these accounts, a trustee's report, an actuarial report, and an investment report.

In these circumstances the auditor's unqualified report should normally be in the terms shown in the following example. Unless the constitution of the scheme specifically requires his report to be addressed to the scheme members, it should be addressed to the trustees.

EXAMPLE

We have examined the financial statements on pages 2 to 10 in accordance with approved Auditing Standards.

In our opinion, the financial statements give a true and fair view of the disposition of the net assets of the scheme at 31 December 1984 and of its transactions for the year then ended.

The auditor is not required to make any reference to the actuary's report and should not do so.

It should be noted that the consultative document issued by the Department of Health and Social Security includes proposals for statutory requirements for accounts and audit of pension schemes which are substantially the same as those of ED 34. Therefore if the financial statements are prepared in a different form from that described above, the auditor should recommend that form to the trustees. If he is unable to persuade them to change, he may need to agree the wording of his report with the trustees in the light of the objectives and form of the financial statements. If possible he should avoid expressing an opinion on the 'state of affairs of the scheme'.

Exceptionally, circumstances may arise where the auditor's terms of engagement require him to report whether the financial statements show a true and fair view of the state of affairs of the scheme, e.g. where this form of report is specifically required by the rules and constitution of the scheme. The most significant matter in regard to the state of affairs of the scheme is its ability to meet its commitments to present and future pensioners as they arise. Therefore the financial statements must include sufficient actuarial information to deal with this matter, probably in a note to the accounts. The information provided will invariably be based on an actuarial report.

If the auditor accepts an engagement which requires him to report in this way and he is satisfied that he can give an unqualified opinion, a possible form for such an opinion is as follows:

> ***EXAMPLE***
>
> *We have audited the financial statements on pages 2 to 10 in accordance with approved Auditing Standards.*
>
> *In our opinion, based on our audit and on the valuation dated 5 May 1985 by an independent actuary (if the actuary is not independent this should be explained e.g. 'by the company's actuary'), the financial statements give a true and fair view of the state of the scheme's affairs at 31 December 1984 and of its net revenue for the year then ended.*

The foregoing form of opinion is appropriate where a current actuarial report is available. It is, however, common for full actuarial valuations to be prepared at relatively long intervals, e.g. every three or four years. In the intervening years the auditor needs to obtain additional information from the actuary to ensure that his earlier valuation is not misleading. In these circumstances the unqualified opinion above would be amended to read '. . . based on our audit and on the valuation dated (date) by an independent actuary supplemented by subsequent information obtained from him, . . .'

19.304 NON-COMMERCIAL ORGANISATIONS

(a) Reporting on results

Financial statements of organisations which do not trade for profit include an income (or revenue) and expenditure account instead of a profit and loss account. In reporting on the income and expenditure account, the auditor should report on the nearest equivalent to the 'profit' or 'loss' on which he is required to report for profit making bodies: e.g. surplus/deficit, the excess of income over expenditure for the year, net income, net revenue, results, as appropriate.

(b) Applicability of accounting standards

The relevant sentence in the auditing guideline 'Charities' dealing with the applicability of SSAPs to the financial statements of non-profit organisations is as follows:

'In considering the appropriateness of particular SSAPs to charities, it must be remembered that SSAPs have been prepared primarily with business enterprises in mind, whereas charities are not-for-profit organisations. As a result it is important for the auditor to use his judgment as to the appropriateness or otherwise of an SSAP to the individual circumstances of the charity concerned.'

Although this statement is made with particular reference to charities, it is equally relevant to the accounts of all non-profit organisations. The departures from SSAPs which are most usually encountered in the financial statements of charities and other non-commercial organisations are as follows:

SSAP 2 : departure from the 'accruals concept'

SSAP 6 : accounting for income and expenditure through reserves or fund accounts

SSAP 12 : writing off fixed assets immediately on acquisition (or not depreciating them at all).

The auditor must use his judgment to determine whether these and other departures from SSAPs destroy the true and fair view in the particular circumstances, or whether the extent and nature of the disclosure is sufficient to overcome the problem. Apart from the circumstances specifically referred to below, it is suggested that financial statements intended to give a true and fair view ought to comply with all SSAPs save in exceptional circumstances.

A particular practice which is sometimes met is for transfers to be made from income and expenditure account to provisions of a general nature, such as buildings replacement provision. Unless these provisions are for existing liabilities or committed or planned expenditure, they are likely to be misleading and unacceptable. Where such transfers occur to a material extent, the auditor must consider qualifying his report.

(c) Alternative to 'true and fair' report

It is sometimes suggested that, by using alternative wording such as 'fairly present' instead of 'give a true and fair view of', the auditor can avoid the necessity to qualify his report on the grounds of non-compliance with SSAPs. This view seems unjustified.

An acceptable alternative to the 'true and fair' report would be wording which simply states that the financial statements are drawn up on the basis described in the accounting policy note.

EXAMPLE

We have audited the financial statements on pages 2 to 10 in accordance with approved Auditing Standards.

In our opinion the financial statements have been properly drawn up in accordance with the accounting policies set out on page 5 (and comply with the rules/constitution/trust deed etc. of the organisation).

The accounting policy note must be comprehensive. In particular it would need to give details of any departures from any of the fundamental accounting concepts (particularly the accruals concept), any items of income or expenditure that are dealt with through reserves, and other significant departures from SSAPs.

19.305 CHARITIES

The appropriate wording for an audit report on a charity depends on the constitution of the charity concerned and the terms of the audit engagement. Reports on the financial statements of charities incorporated under the Companies Acts should be addressed to the members of the company and should indicate whether the statements give a true and fair view of the state of affairs and surplus or deficit for the year of the charity. If the charity is registered under the Acts governing friendly, industrial or provident societies, the audit report will be addressed to the charity itself and will indicate whether the statements give a true and fair view of the state of affairs and income and expenditure of the charity. Audit reports on friendly, industrial and provident societies are further discussed in Section

19.306 below. Where charities are not governed by statute the audit report will be addressed to the persons appointing the auditor (usually the trustees) and the form and content of the report will be determined by the auditor's terms of engagement. The terms of engagement may be specified in the deed constituting the charity or may be fixed by the persons appointing the auditor. For example, an appropriate report might be simple that in the auditor's opinion the financial statements have been prepared in compliance with the regulations governing the charity's operations.

(a) Unqualified 'true and fair' opinion

An example of an unqualified opinion is as follows:

> ***EXAMPLE***
>
> *We have audited the financial statements on pages 2 to 8 in accordance with approved Auditing Standards.*
>
> *In our opinion the financial statements give a true and fair view of the state of the charity's affairs at 31 December 1984 and of its surplus/deficit (or, its income and expenditure) and source and application of funds for the year then ended and comply with (insert relevant statute or constitutional authority).*

The problem of whether an auditor can give an unqualified 'true and fair' opinion on the financial statements of charities where there are significant departures from SSAPs is discussed in general terms in Section 19.304 above. A particular problem which affects charities is that of accounting for specific funds.

It is not uncommon for charities to launch appeals for funds to be applied for specific purposes with the implication that monies received will be applied for the purpose mentioned and not used to defray the normal running costs of the organisation. In these circumstances it is usually appropriate to deal with the income and expenditure of such a fund separately from the general income and expenditure account, and it is suggested that an auditor would not think it necessary to qualify his report on the grounds of non-compliance with SSAP 6. Some charities deal with such expenditure and income within the general income and expenditure account, and then make a separate transfer of the unexpended balance of monies received to a separate fund in the balance sheet before the surplus or deficit on the general administration is arrived at. This also seems an accepted practice which should be distinguished from unsubstantiated transfers to general provisions referred to in Section 19.304. The difference in the case of specific appeals is that the unexpended funds are not available to meet general expenses and should be clearly indicated in the financial statements as being held to meet further expenditure related to the specific purpose in question.

(b) Qualified opinion

If the auditor considers that there is a material and unacceptable departure from SSAPs in financial statements intended to show a true and fair view, he should qualify his audit report. He may also have to qualify his opinion on the grounds of disagreement or uncertainty as discussed in Section 19.200 above.

The auditing guideline 'Charities' deals with a particular problem faced by many small charities in applying proper control over voluntary donations prior to the time they are entered in the accounting records. Where the auditor has carried out all reasonable procedures to obtain evidence, he may still be unable to give an unqualified opinion as to the completeness of income. Provided he is satisfied that the system of accounting and control is reasonable in the circumstances of the charity's operations and has no reason to believe that there is a material omission of income, his report should be qualified along the following lines:

EXAMPLE

We have audited the financial statements on pages 2 to 8. Our audit was conducted in accordance with approved Auditing Standards having regard to the matters referred to in the following paragraph.

This charity, in common with many others of similar size and organisation, derives a substantial proportion of its income from voluntary donations which cannot be fully controlled until they are entered in the accounting records, and are not therefore susceptible to independent audit verification.

Subject to the foregoing, in our opinion the financial statements give a true and fair view of the state of the charity's affairs at 31 December 1984 and of its surplus/ deficit and source and application of funds for the year then ended and comply with (insert relevant statute or constitutional authority).

19.306 FRIENDLY AND INDUSTRIAL AND PROVIDENT SOCIETIES

The auditor's responsibilities and reporting requirements relating to Friendly Societies are governed by the Friendly Societies Act 1974 and those relating to Industrial and Provident Societies which are registered under the Industrial and Provident Societies Act 1965 are governed by the Friendly and Industrial and Provident Societies Act 1968. Guidance on the requirements of these Acts is contained in a statement by the U.K. accountancy bodies (issued by the English Institute as U 26).

The report should state whether the revenue account(s) and balance sheet comply with the requirements of the 1974 Act (for Friendly Societies) or of the 1968 Act and the appropriate registration Act (for Industrial and Provident Societies) and whether in the auditor's opinion:

(i) the revenue account(s) gives a true and fair view of the income and expenditure of the society or branch as a whole and, in the case of each account which deals with a particular business, a true and fair view of the income and expenditure of that business, and

(ii) the balance sheet gives a true and fair view of the state of affairs of the society or branch. However, for societies to which Section 41 of the 1974 Act applies (i.e. the insurance-type of society where the auditors are not required to deal with long-term liabilities which can only be determined actuarially), the auditor must report whether the balance sheet gives a true and fair view of the assets and current liabilities and resulting balances of its funds.

EXAMPLE – Unqualified opinion

We have audited the financial statements on pages 8 to 21 in accordance with approved Auditing Standards.

In our opinion the financial statements give a true and fair view of the state of the society's affairs at 31 December 1984 and of the income and expenditure and source and application of funds of the society for the year then ended and comply with the requirements of the Friendly Societies Act 1974 (or the Friendly and Industrial and Provident Societies Act 1968 and the Industrial and Provident Societies Act 1965).

Suitable amendment to the above opinion would be required where there are separate revenue accounts which deal with particular businesses conducted by the society by adding the words 'as a whole and of the particular businesses dealt with thereby' after the words 'of the society'.

The 1974 Act further provides that where the audit report relates to any accounts other than the revenue account or accounts for the year in respect of which the auditor is appointed, the report shall state whether those financial statements give a true and fair view of any matter to which they relate. For example, if the financial statements include statements other than the balance sheet and revenue account(s), the report will cover this by adding the words 'and the other matters to which they relate' after the words 'year then ended'.

As with audits under the Companies Act, the auditor will have to carry out such investigations as will enable him to form an opinion as to whether the society has kept proper accounting records and whether the financial statements are in agreement therewith. An important additional legal requirement which goes beyond those of the Companies Act is to determine whether the society has maintained a satisfactory system of control over its transactions. If the auditor forms a negative opinion on any of these matters he must so state in his report.

19.307 BUILDING SOCIETIES, HOUSING ASSOCIATIONS, TRADE UNIONS

Reference should be made to the auditing guidelines on these subjects for a discussion of the reporting problems and for examples of appropriate forms of reports.

19.308 REPORTS ON U.K. FINANCIAL STATEMENTS STATED IN FOREIGN CURRENCY

A U.K. form of audit report on financial statements expressed in sterling will normally be the only report issued in respect of U.K. subsidiaries of foreign companies. In the exceptional circumstances, the auditor may be called upon to report on a second set of financial statements expressed in the currency of the country of the foreign parent. This version should contain both the sterling figures and the translated foreign currency figures. (Alternatively the separate foreign currency financial statements should be attached to the sterling financial statements). The auditor's report should express an opinion on the truth and fairness of the sterling financial statements only but should contain assurances as to the translation. The opening paragraph of the report should identify the approved auditing standards as being those of the U.K.

The example of an unqualified audit report shown below assumes the use of U.S. dollars as the foreign currency:

> ***EXAMPLE***
>
> *We have audited the financial statements on pages 8 to 21 in accordance with approved Auditing Standards of the United Kingdom.*
>
> *In our opinion the financial statements expressed in pounds sterling give a true and fair view of the state of the company's affairs at 31 December 1984 and of its profit and source and application of funds for the year then ended and comply with the Companies Act 1985.*
>
> *In our opinion the financial statements expressed in U.S. dollars have been properly translated on the bases described in note 2.*

Such financial statements should contain an accounting policy note on foreign currency translation along the following lines:

EXAMPLE – Policy note

The translation of the financial statements into U.S. dollars is included solely for convenience and they are stated, as a matter of arithmetical computation only, on the following bases:

(State bases)

This translation should not be construed as meaning that the sterling amounts actually represent, or have been or could be converted into, U.S. dollars.

19.309 REPORTS ON FINANCIAL STATEMENTS USING STANDARDS OF OTHER COUNTRIES

Special attention is required in cases where the needs of the engagement are not met by the statutory financial statements and the auditor is requested by the client to issue a second version in a format normally used in another country or in accordance with another country's accounting standards. In order to avoid the confusion which could arise from the existence of two versions of the financial statements (possibly even showing different profit figures), any second version should comply with U.K. accounting standards and only be modified in respect of format and the inclusion of a translation of the sterling amounts into the currency of the other country.

In very exceptional circumstances (e.g. because they are required to be filed with regulatory or governmental agencies of a foreign country, such as the SEC) it may be appropriate to report on a second version prepared in accordance with another country's accounting standards. In such limited circumstances, the secondary financial statements should disclose in a note the existence of the U.K. statutory financial statements and reconcile the differences between the two. The reconciliation should disclose the individual and combined effects on:

(i) net operating results for the year, and

(ii) shareholders' interests.

Where the reserves as shown by the secondary statements which are apparently available for distribution to shareholders by way of dividend exceed those shown as legally distributable as shown in the U.K. statutory financial statements, attention should be drawn to this fact in the notes to the secondary statements.

Where there are no differences between the secondary and U.K. statements other than language or format, the secondary financial statements should disclose the existence of the U.K. statutory financial statements and explain that there are no other differences of substance.

The example of an unqualified audit report in U.S. form given below assumes that the secondary financial statements contain both sterling and U.S. dollar amounts and comply with the SEC requirement to provide three year statements of earnings, stockholders' equity, and changes in financial position.

EXAMPLE

We have examined the balance sheet of Plastics Ltd. as of December 31, 1984 and 1983 and the related statements of earnings, stockholders' equity and changes in financial position for each of the three years in the period ended December 31, 1984, all expressed in pounds sterling. Our examination was made in accordance with generally accepted auditing standards of the United States of America and accordingly included such tests of the accounting records and such other auditing procedures as we considered necessary in the circumstances. We have also reviewed the translation of these statements into U.S. dollars on the bases described in note 2.

In our opinion, the aforementioned financial statements, expressed in pounds sterling, present fairly the financial position of Plastics Ltd. at December 31, 1984 and 1983 and the results of its operations and changes in financial position for each of the three years in the period ended December 31, 1984, in conformity with generally accepted accounting principles of the United States of America consistently applied in the periods. In our opinion, the financial statements expressed in U.S. dollars have been properly translated on the bases described in note 2.

19.400 SPECIAL REPORTS

19.401 SPECIAL REPORT ON MODIFIED ACCOUNTS

Section 17.020 explains the circumstances under which the directors may deliver modified accounts to the Registrar of Companies. Modified accounts so delivered must be accompanied by a copy of a special auditors' report instead of a copy of the auditors' report made in respect of the financial statements to be laid before the company in general meeting. [Sch 8: 10 and 22] An example of such a special report follows:

EXAMPLE

Special auditors' report to the directors of XYZ Ltd.
under Schedule 8 of the Companies Act 1985

In our opinion:

*(i) the directors of XYZ Ltd. are entitled, as claimed in their statement in the attached balance sheet, to deliver modified accounts * to the Registrar of Companies; and*

(ii) the accounts on pages 3 and 4 have been properly prepared in accordance with Schedule 8 of the Companies Act 1985.

The full text of our report dated 20 July 1985 issued under Section 236 of the Companies Act 1985 on the company's financial statements for the year ended 31 December 1984 is as follows:

'We have audited the financial statements on pages 5 to 13 in accordance with approved Auditing Standards.

In our opinion, the financial statements give a true and fair view of the state of the company's affairs at 31 December 1984 and of its profit and source and application of funds for the year then ended and comply with the Companies Act 1985.'

* For modified group accounts it will be necessary to insert the words 'and modified group accounts'.

19.402 AUDITORS' STATEMENT IN CONNECTION WITH A DISTRIBUTION

The rules regarding what amounts are legally available for distribution are dealt with in Section 18.040. The distributable amount is to be determined by reference to the relevant accounts, which are normally the last annual accounts prior to the distribution. If the audit report on these accounts was qualified and a distribution is envisaged, the auditor must state in writing whether in his opinion the matter giving rise to the qualification is material for determining whether the distribution would contravene the legislation. [s 271(4)]

The statement may be made either at the time of the audit report or subsequently, but a copy of it must be laid before the company in general meeting. It may therefore be convenient to make the necessary statement as a final paragraph in the audit report as in the following example:

EXAMPLE

In our opinion, the matter referred to in the second paragraph above is not material for determining by reference to these financial statements whether dividends totalling not more than £...... would contravene Sections 263 and 264 of the Companies Act 1985.

An example of a statement made separate from the audit report is as follows:

EXAMPLE

Auditors' statement
to the members of
Tramp Holdings p.l.c.

In our audit report to the members dated 1 July 1985 we expressed a qualified opinion on the financial statements of Tramp Holdings p.l.c. for the year ended 31 December 1984.

In our opinion the matter(s) in respect of which our report was qualified is (are) not material for determining by reference to the financial statements whether dividends totalling not more than £..... would contravene Sections 263 and 264 of the Companies Act 1985.

The suggested wording 'dividends totalling not more than £.....' would enable not only the proposed final dividend but also an interim dividend for the following year to be paid, provided that the amount specified was sufficient to cover both. If the statement refers specifically to the dividend proposed in the accounts, then it seems that before an interim dividend can be paid for the following year, the auditor must make a further statement and it must be laid before the company in general meeting.

For this purpose 'material' means that the effect of the matter which is the subject of the qualification is or may be such as to reduce the amount of distributable profits below that legally required to make a distribution of the sum under consideration. Where the qualification relates to an uncertainty which is not fundamental, the auditor may be able to form a view as to the maximum amount by which distributable profits might be reduced by the effects of the uncertainty. In this case he should use this criterion for determining whether or not the qualification is material in the context of the distribution. In all other cases of uncertainty he will have to report that the subject matter of the qualification is material. In practice, it is most unlikely that he will be asked to report formally in such circumstances.

There is also a requirement for a statement by the auditor in the circumstances where a public company intends to make a distribution before the end of its first accounting reference period.

[s 273(5)] These circumstances are likely to be rare, and the auditor will need to consider the appropriate form of report and the scope of work necessary to support it in each case.

19.403 VALUATION REPORT ON NON-CASH ASSETS

There are two situations where the Act requires a public company to obtain a valuation report from a person qualified to act as auditor of the company as to the value placed on non-cash assets to be acquired by the company. The valuation reports required in these situations are dealt with under the headings below.

(a) Shares allotted in exchange for non-cash consideration

A public company may not allot shares for a non-cash consideration unless a report as to the value of the consideration has been made within 6 months prior to the share allotment by a person qualified to be the auditor of the company. [s 103] A copy of the report must be sent to the allottee. These restrictions do not apply to takeover and merger situations.

The Act [s 108] requires the valuer's report to state:

(i) the nominal value of the shares to be issued;

(ii) the amount of any premium payable on them;

(iii) the description of the consideration, the method used to value it and the date of the valuation;

(iv) the extent to which the nominal value of the shares and any premiums are to be treated as paid up:

a) by the consideration,
b) by cash;

(v) that it appears reasonable to him to accept the valuation by another person (if applicable);

(vi) that whoever made the valuation the method of valuation was reasonable in all the circumstances;

(vii) that it appears that there has been no material change in the value of the consideration since the date of valuation;

(viii) that on the basis of valuation, the value of the consideration together with any cash received by the company is not less than the aggregate of the nominal value and the premium on shares which are treated as paid up by the consideration and the cash.

The valuer may use an outside expert with the requisite knowledge and experience to value all or part of the consideration. Where this is done, the report must state that fact and

(i) state the name of the valuer and give details of his knowledge and experience to carry out the valuation;

(ii) describe that part of the consideration valued by him and the method used to value it and the date of the valuation.

While the Act does not require a person who has relied on an outside valuation to include a copy of that valuation in his report, it would be prudent for him to do so.

A suitable valuation report is given below. This report assumes the following facts. Tramp Holdings p.l.c. proposes to allot 250,000 ordinary shares of £1 each under a contract with XYZ Ltd to acquire vending machines, transport vehicles and customer routes in the Midlands. Tramp Holdings has ascribed a value of £4 to each ordinary share to be treated as fully paid up. The auditor has obtained a valuation report on the fixed assets from professional valuers and he has been able to place a value on the customer routes.

EXAMPLE

To the Directors of
Tramp Holdings p.l.c.

In connection with the proposed allotment of 250,000 ordinary shares of £1 each of Tramp Holdings p.l.c. under an agreement dated 13 July 1985 between Tramp Holdings p.l.c. and XYZ Ltd, we report under Section 108 of the Companies Act 1985 as follows:

a. *The nominal value of the shares to be issued is £250,000, comprising 250,000 ordinary shares of £1 each. The premium payable on these shares is £3 per share making a total premium of £750,000. The whole of the nominal value and share premium is to be treated as fully paid up by the consideration.*

b. *The consideration is as follows:*

(i) vending machines and transport vehicles as listed in Schedule A of said agreement.

(ii) customer routes as described in Schedule B of said agreement.

c. *We believe it reasonable for the valuation of that part of the consideration stated in paragraph b(i) above to be made by Worthmore & Co., professional valuers of industrial and retail equipment. They have valued this equipment as at 30 July 1985 at £850,000 on the basis of net current replacement cost taking into account the condition and remaining useful life of the equipment. A copy of the valuation report issued to us by Worthmore & Co. is attached to this report.*

d. *We value the rights to service customers, forming the remainder of the consideration as at 13 July 1985 at £200,000, based on a discounted value of income expected to be earned from the vending machines kept at customers' premises.*

e. *We consider the methods of valuation used in the above valuations to be reasonable in all the circumstances and it appears that there has been no material change in the value of the consideration since the dates of valuation.*

f. *In our opinion, on the basis of the valuations stated in c and d above, the value of the consideration is not less than the aggregate of the nominal value and premium on shares which are treated as paid up by the consideration.*

Yours faithfully,

(b) Non-cash assets acquired from subscribers or members

Where a public company is to acquire, within 2 years of its date of incorporation or re-registration as a public company, a non-cash asset from a subscriber to its Memorandum or from a member of the company at the date of re-registration, and the consideration to be given equals one-tenth or more of the nominal value of the company's share capital, s 104 requires:

(i) the assets to be transferred to the company and any consideration to be paid by the company other than in cash to be valued by someone qualified to be the auditor of the company;

(ii) a report on the valuation to be delivered to the company during the six months preceding the date of the agreement;

(iii) the terms of the agreement to be approved by an ordinary resolution of the company; and

(iv) copies of the resolution and report to be circulated to the members not later than the giving of the notice of the meeting at which the resolution is proposed.

The provisions concerning the use of outside experts' valuations are identical to those in s 108 described in the preceding section (a) and the auditor should include a copy of any such valuation as an integral part of his report.

The content of the report is the same as that required under s 108 (see preceding section (a)) with the following changes.

(i) provisions dealing with shares are replaced by a requirement to state the consideration to be received (describing the asset in question and the amount to be received in cash) and the consideration to be given by the company, specifiying the amount to be given in cash.

(ii) instead of the statement required in (viii) of the preceding section, a statement that on the basis of the valuation, the value of the consideration received by the company is not less than the value of the consideration to be given by it.

The report should be modelled along the lines of the example given in (a) above.

19.404 REPORT ON FINANCIAL ASSISTANCE FOR ACQUISITION OF OWN SHARES

Private companies are allowed to give financial assistance for the purchase of shares in the company provided certain conditions and procedures are complied with. [s 155] (see Section 18.030) These include a statutory declaration by the directors that they have formed the opinion that there will, immediately following the date on which the assistance is provided, be no ground on which the company could be found unable to pay its debts, and that the company will be able to pay its debts as they fall due during the year immediately following that date or, if it is intended to wind up the company within twelve months of that date, that the company will be able to pay all its debts in full. As a further safeguard, the Act requires that this declaration shall have annexed to it a report addressed to the directors by the auditors of the company stating that they have inquired into the state of affairs of the company and are not aware of anything to indicate that the opinion expressed by the directors is unreasonable in all the circumstances.

The following form of report is suggested:

EXAMPLE

Report of the auditors to
the directors of Tramp Limited
under s 156(4) of the Companies Act 1985

We have inquired into the company's state of affairs as at (date).

We are not aware of anything to indicate that the opinion expressed by the directors in Part 2 of the attached declaration is unreasonable in all the circumstances.

The Act requires the auditors to state that they have enquired into the state of affairs of the company, but it is suggested that to be meaningful such a statement must refer to the state of affairs of the company at a specified date. The date specified should be the latest practicable date prior to the date of the report.

19.405 REPORT ON PURCHASE OR REDEMPTION OF OWN SHARES OUT OF CAPITAL

Private companies are permitted to purchase or redeem their own shares, subject to certain conditions and procedures, out of capital. [s 171] (see Section 18.020) Where any part of the payment is to be made out of capital, s 173(3) requires a statutory declaration by the directors which must state the amount of the 'permissible capital payment' as defined by the Act (see Section 18.020(viii)) and that in their opinion there are no grounds on which the company could be found unable to pay its debts immediately following the date of the payment and that the company will be able to carry on business as a going concern (and accordingly pay its debts as they fall due) throughout the following year.

The directors' statutory declaration must have annexed to it a report by the company's auditors addressed to the directors, stating that the auditors have inquired into the company's state of affairs, that the amount specified as the permissible capital payment has in the auditors' opinion been properly determined, and that the auditors are not aware of anything to indicate that the opinion expressed by the directors in their declaration is unreasonable in all the circumstances. [s 173(5)] If the auditors are unable to issue such a report without qualification, the company cannot legally purchase or redeem any of its shares out of capital.

A form of report based on that suggested by the APC is as follows:

EXAMPLE

Report of the auditors to
the directors of Tramp Limited
under s 173(5) of the Companies Act 1985

We have inquired into the company's state of affairs as at (date).

In our opinion the amount of (£xxx) specified in the attached statutory declaration by the directors as being the permissible capital payment for the shares to be purchased/ redeemed has been properly determined in accordance with Sections 171 and 172 of the Companies Act 1985.

We are not aware of anything to indicate that the opinion expressed by the directors in Part 2 of the attached statutory declaration is unreasonable in all the circumstances.

19.406 REPORT ON TENANTS' SERVICE CHARGES

Schedule 19 of the 1980 Housing Act requires certain landlords, at the request of a tenant or tenants' association, to give tenant(s) a written summary of the costs which are relevant to the service charges payable by the tenant(s). If there are more than four flats in the building or the relevant costs relate also to another building, this summary must be 'certified by a qualified accountant' as being in his opinion:

(i) a fair summary of those costs set out in a way which shows how they are or will be reflected in demands for service charges, and

(ii) sufficiently supported by accounts, receipts and other documents which have been produced to the accountant.

It is recommended that the report should be as follows:

EXAMPLE

We have examined the (attached) statement (on pages . . . . .) of service costs and charges to the tenants of Utopian Courts for the year ended 31 December 1984.

In our opinion this statement is:

(i) a fair summary of the costs set out in a way which shows how they are (will be) reflected in demands for service charges, and

(ii) sufficiently supported by accounts, receipts and other documents which have been produced to us.

19.407 REPORTS REQUIRED BY OFFICIAL BODIES

Accountants are frequently asked to give reports to official or quasi-official bodies. Examples are reports on investment grants, insurance for consequential loss, circulation of periodicals, royalties, government contracts, and borrowing powers under a trust deed. Quite often the report is contained in a printed form. Occasionally the form of the report has been agreed between the Institutes and the body concerned. For example that for investment grants was agreed with the then Board of Trade. If the wording has been previously agreed by the Institutes it is likely to be acceptable to the auditor. In some other cases however the wording may not be acceptable and he must either amend the standard form or completely re-write the report in a form in which he is prepared to give it.

The following amendments should be considered:

(i) His opinion should be based on 'his examination' (e.g. of books and records) and should not extend to matters outside his professional function as an accountant.

(ii) In place of words like 'correct' he should use words such as 'properly computed', 'reasonable' or 'fairly stated'.

(iii) He should avoid 'certifying' anything as he gives a report, not a certificate.

His report should normally be sent to the client for dispatch to the official body.

(a) Insurance certificate

As a basis for setting consequential loss premiums, some insurance companies require the auditor to complete a certificate in which he is required to 'certify' the amount of gross profit and wages for the preceding financial year. The auditor should refuse to complete such a certificate and instead he should prepare a report, addressed to the client, giving the required information in the manner suggested in the following example:

EXAMPLE

Consequential Loss Policy No. 48666

We have examined the above policy and the books of the branch and the computations of gross profit of £450,118 and wages (other than service department wages) of £1,437,000 for the year ended 30 November 1984.

In our opinion, based upon our examination, the above figures have been properly computed in accordance with the terms of the policy.

Yours faithfully,

(b) Government grant certificates

Regional development and other Government aid schemes require the auditor to express an opinion on various matters, in particular the amount of expenditure 'defrayed' (or in certain cases 'incurred') during the period of the grant claim. Before giving his opinion, the auditor must understand the definitions of the terms 'defrayed' and 'incurred' which are usually contained in the Government leaflet or offer document. The Government leaflet on Regional Development Grants defines these terms as follows:

'defrayed' means discharged by payment or otherwise settled, e.g. by trade-in allowance or other contra item to the contractor's account in the applicant's books; where payment is made by cheque or similar payable instrument, the expenditure is defrayed when the cheque or payable instrument is honoured by the bank; and

expenditure is regarded as 'incurred' when the applicant is under an obligation to pay (e.g. having been invoiced) whether the asset was purchased outright or provided under a hire purchase agreement or any other deferred payment terms.

(c) Lloyd's statement of means

The Committee of Lloyd's requires applicants for underwriting membership of Lloyd's to submit a statement of the applicant's net means. This statement must be signed by the applicant's banker, solicitor or accountant, with the applicant confirming that the statement is accurate.

It is unlikely that the accountant can sign such a statement without qualification for the following reasons:

(i) he is required to report on net means, which clearly implies the deduction of liabilities; there is no independent evidence available to him as to the total of the client's liabilities; and

(ii) he is required to state that the applicant 'has possessed for the past twelve months, the assets stated, or assets of an equivalent value', and that they (the assets) 'have not been during that period in any way charged or encumbered'; under most circumstances there will be inadequate evidence to support these statements.

In view of the difficulties, the accountant must carefully consider whether he should undertake this work or should refer the applicant to his banker or solicitor.

19.500 UNAUDITED FINANCIAL STATEMENTS

In addition to acting as auditors, professional accountants are also frequently called on to act in different capacities in relation to financial information. Typically they may be called on to prepare or review financial statements without carrying out an audit. It is important that whenever financial information with which a professional accountant is associated is made available to third parties, they should be left in no doubt as to the extent to which the accountant is responsible for the quality of the information provided. Therefore it is best practice for every set of financial statements made available to third parties to be accompanied by an accountant's report which clearly defines the scope of the accountant's engagement. An exception might be made if an accountant prepares on behalf of the directors the financial statements of a dormant company which has resolved not to appoint auditors.

Although most engagements involving unaudited financial statements are undertaken for sole traders and partnerships, the considerations set out below also apply to other unincorporated concerns and to unaudited interim financial statements of limited companies.

Where the accountant has been instructed to prepare financial statements but not to audit them, his report should be so worded that the association of his name with these statements cannot be misunderstood. The accountants' report should not therefore be extended to include expressions of opinion or to disclaim responsibility for particular items.

EXAMPLE

Accountants' Report to . . .

In accordance with the instructions contained in your letter to us of (date) we have prepared, without carrying out an audit, the financial statements on pages 8 to 21 for the year ended 31 December 1984 from the accounting records of (the partnership) and from information and explanations supplied to us.

This report should not of course be described as an audit report and the word 'audit' should not be used to describe the assignment in the financial statements, or in correspondence or bills.

There may be situations where although he is not carrying out an audit, the accountant has been asked to do certain work of an auditing nature (e.g. to verify investments or count cash). To avoid any misunderstanding by a reader, he should not include any reference to these tests in his report but should describe the work done in a separate letter to the client.

There is no requirement for unaudited financial statements to comply with the Act. However, if they purport to show a true and fair view, they should conform with accepted accounting policies (including appropriate SSAPs) which should be properly disclosed. There may be circumstances where it would be appropriate to depart from accepted principles (e.g. the financial statements of a social club might be more meaningful to members if they were drawn up on a cash basis). Such departures should be clearly explained in the financial statements and referred to in the accountant's report. Similarly the accounting policies adopted should be made clear either in the accounts or in the notes. This should include disclosure of the accounting convention followed. If the notes do not make this disclosure the accountant's report should do so.

If the client will not accept adjustments which the accountant wishes to make (e.g. a provision for bad debts) and these are significant to a fair presentation of the financial statements, he should set out the facts in his report.

EXAMPLE

Accountants' Report to . . .

In accordance with instructions contained in your letter to us of (date) we have prepared, without carrying out an audit, the financial statements on pages 2 to 10 for the year ended 31 December 1984 from the accounting records of (the partnership) and from information and explanations supplied to us.

A debt of £50,000 is, in our opinion, unlikely to be collected. No provision has been made in the financial statements to cover any loss on this debt.

The accountant should not allow himself to become associated with financial statements which he believes give a misleading view without giving a full explanation of the facts in his report. If during his work he has obtained knowledge of significant information which, if not disclosed, would make the financial statements materially misleading, he should insist that such information be disclosed. Failing this, he should not allow his name to be associated with the financial statements.

19.501 PROFIT ANNOUNCEMENTS

Stock Exchange companies must issue a preliminary announcement of their annual results. The announcement is to be issued as soon as possible after draft accounts have been agreed with the auditor as a basis for completing the annual report. Thus although the information is routinely described as unaudited any significant difference between the preliminary announcement and the audited financial statements would be a matter for concern. The auditor should therefore request the opportunity to examine the announcement before it is issued in order to ensure that it reflects fairly the relevant information that will be included in the financial statements; if for any reason he is not given this opportunity, he should examine the published announcement as soon as it is available.

The auditor has no statutory right or duties in regard to these preliminary announcements, but clearly The Stock Exchange will assume that he agrees with the information published. He is therefore in a difficult position in the rare circumstance where an announcement is made with which he does not agree or which he thinks is misleading. If this occurs, he should seek legal advice.

A Stock Exchange company is also required to issue a report on the results of its first six months. This report which contains similar information to that included in preliminary announcements of annual results is normally unaudited. The fact that it is unaudited must be stated. However if the accounting information contained in a half-yearly report has been audited, the audit report (including any qualifications) must be set out in the half-yearly report. This situation is only likely to arise where the figures for the half-yearly report are extracted from a complete set of financial statements which have been audited as outlined in Section 19.301 above, in which case the audit report on these financial statements must be published.

Although there is no requirement for half-yearly reports to be audited, the auditor is frequently asked by the directors to examine these statements before they are issued. It is important in such circumstances that the scope of the examination, which will probably be some form of limited review, should be agreed with the client in advance and be the subject of a letter of engagement. Although the auditor may be asked to report his findings orally in the first instance, he should confirm these findings in a letter to the directors.

19.600 ADDITIONAL INFORMATION

It is quite common for companies to ask for the preparation of financial statements which are in more detailed form than the statutory financial statements and which may include supporting schedules. The auditor is unlikely to have verified the allocation of revenue and expenses in detail although he will have carried out the tests necessary for his audit of the statutory financial statements.

It is advisable not to issue detailed statements and schedules separately from the statutory financial statements but there is of course no reason why the statutory financial statements should not be issued without detailed additional information being attached.

The combined financial statements should contain two audit reports. That referring to the detailed additional statements and supporting schedules will immediately precede this additional information while the statutory report will precede the statutory financial statements. Examples of recommended standard wording are illustrated below. If the report on the statutory financial statements is qualified, the report on the detailed additional statements and schedules must incorporate the qualification if it is relevant to this additional information.

The report on the additional information should be introduced by a heading 'ADDITIONAL INFORMATION' and be addressed to the person(s) who requested the information (e.g. the directors).

No reference need be made to the accounting convention adopted since reference to the statutory financial statements will give this information as well as other accounting policy disclosures.

19.601 COMPLETE AUDIT

Where a complete audit has been carried out on the additional information as well as on the statutory financial statements (i.e. the detailed income and expenditure allocation and any supporting schedules have been verified), an example of a report on the detailed information is as follows:

EXAMPLE

In connection with our examination of the statutory financial statements of Tramp Holdings p.l.c. for the year ended 31 December 1984, we have also examined the additional information contained on pages 23 to 28. In our opinion this information is fairly presented.

19.602 NORMAL STATUTORY AUDIT

Where there has been a normal statutory audit, and therefore the auditor has done sufficient work with regard to the detailed figures and supporting schedules to be satisfied that there are no material errors (this would entail the knowledge that the accounting system produces accurate figures, intelligent scrutiny of the figures and satisfactory explanation for significant variances from the previous year and the budget), an example of a report on the detailed information is as follows:

EXAMPLE

The additional information contained on pages 23 to 28 has been prepared (by us) from the books and records of the company. This information has been subjected to the tests and other auditing procedures applied in our examination of the statutory financial statements of Tramp Holdings p.l.c. for the year ended 31 December 1984. In our opinion, in relation to the statutory financial statements taken as a whole, this information is fairly presented in all material respects.

19.603 QUALIFICATION IN STATUTORY FINANCIAL STATEMENTS

The auditor may be unable to report positively as in Section 19.602 above, for example because of a qualification in his report on the statutory financial statements. In these circumstances he might amend his report as follows:

EXAMPLE

The additional information contained on pages 23 to 28 has been prepared (by us) from the books and records of the company. This information has been subjected to the tests and other auditing procedures applied in our examination of the statutory financial statements of Tramp Holdings p.l.c. for the year ended 31 December 1984. As stated in our report on the statutory financial statements, we were unable to satisfy ourselves as to the physical existence of stocks at the beginning of the year. Subject to the effect on the cost of sales, gross margin and profit before tax of any adjustment to stocks which we might have considered necessary had we been present at the physical stocktaking, in our opinion, in relation to the statutory financial statements taken as a whole this information is fairly presented in all material respects.

GLOSSARY

the Act	– Companies Act 1985
ACT	– Advance Corporation Tax
APB	– The United States Accounting Principles Board (now replaced by Financial Accounting Standards Board) issued accounting standards, known as APB's.
APC	– Auditing Practices Committee, which formulates auditing standards and guidelines for approval by the councils of the accountancy bodies.
ASC	– Accounting Standards Committee, which formulates SSAP's for approval by the councils of the accountancy bodies.
CCA	– Current cost accounting is the system of current value accounting in the U.K.
CCAB	– Consultative Committee of Accountancy Bodies (consisting of the three Institutes of Chartered Accountants, and the Certified, Cost and Management, and Public Finance bodies) makes submissions to the Government and issues pronouncements on matters of common interest to the profession.
ED	– Exposure draft issued by the Accounting Standards Committee.
EEC	– European Economic Community
GU	– General Undertaking adopted by USM companies.
RICS	– Royal Institution of Chartered Surveyors
SEC	– Securities and Exchange Commission
SFAS	– The pronouncements of the United States Financial Accounting Standards Board are known as SFASs.
SI	– Statutory Instrument. The government order which amends legislation. In the context of this manual these will normally be amendments to the Companies Acts.
SORP	– Statement of Recommended Practice issued by the ASC, which gives guidance on current best practice on topics which are not of major or fundamental importance.
SSAP	– Statement of Standard Accounting Practice issued by the CCAB.
Stock Exchange Companies	– Companies listed on The Stock Exchange and companies dealt with on the USM.
USM	– Unlisted Securities Market
VAT	– Value Added Tax
Yellow Book	– The publication of The Stock Exchange entitled 'Admission of Securities to Listing'.

CHECK-LIST OF DISCLOSURE REQUIREMENTS

INTRODUCTION

The purpose of this check-list is to give the disclosures required in the financial statements of companies in the United Kingdom. The list does not include exemptions given by the Act to special category companies, i.e. banking, insurance and shipping companies and some other minor exceptions allowed by the Act.

References in the check-list are as follows:

1. References to the Companies Act 1985 are given without reference to the year 1985, followed in parentheses by the corresponding legislation in the former Companies Acts.

EXAMPLE	***Reference***
Schedule 7, paragraph 6(b) of the 1985 Act, *(corresponding Section 13 of the 1981 Act)*	*Sch 7: 6(b)* *[1981 s 13]*

2. Statutory amendments are designated by 'SI' followed by the date and number of the statutory instrument.

3. Accounting standards of the CCAB are given the designation 'SSAP'.

4. Requirements of The Stock Exchange for listed companies are given the designation SE, followed by the paragraph reference of the 'Admission of Securities to Listing', Section 5, Chapter 2 (the Yellow Book). These disclosures must be included in the company's annual report and accounts and the directors may decide on the most appropriate location for the disclosures. This check-list places these disclosures in the directors' report section or under the relevant account heading as considered appropriate.

5. Requirements of The Stock Exchange for companies dealt with on the Unlisted Securities Market are given the designation GU, followed by the paragraph reference of the General Undertaking which is contained in 'The Stock Exchange Unlisted Securities Market' (the Green Book).

I DIRECTORS' REPORT

A. *ACTIVITIES AND RESULTS*

	Reference
1. The amounts recommended to be paid as dividends and transfers to reserves.	s 235(1) [1948 s 157]
2. The principal activities of the company and its subsidiaries during the year and any significant change in those activities in the year.	s 235(2) [1967 s 16]
3. A fair review of the development of the business of the company and its subsidiaries during the year and their position at the end of it.	s 235(1) [1981 s 13]
4. Particulars of any important events affecting the company or any of its subsidiaries which have occurred since the end of the year.	Sch 7: 6(a) [1981 s 13]
5. An indication of likely future developments in the business of the company and its subsidiaries.	Sch 7: 6(b) [1981 s 13]
6. An indication of the activities (if any) of the company and its subsidiaries in the field of research and development.	Sch 7: 6(c) [1981 s 13]
7. Stock Exchange companies are to give a geographical analysis of turnover and of contribution to trading results of those trading operations carried on by the company (or group) outside the UK and the Republic of Ireland.	SE 21(c) GU 10(c)
8. Stock Exchange companies are to give an explanation of any material difference between the trading results shown by the accounts and those given in any published forecast made by the company.	SE 21(b) GU 10(b)

B. *DIRECTORS*

1. Names of the persons who, at any time during the financial year, were directors of the company.	s 235(2) [1967 s 16]
2. Details of each director's interest (including nil interest) in shares or debentures of the company or group companies at the end of the financial year, and at the beginning of the financial year, or at the date during the year when he became a director. (This information may be given in the notes to the accounts).	Sch 7: 2(1) [1967 s 16] Sch 7: 2(3) [1981 s 13]
The interests to be disclosed are those recorded in the register of directors' interests maintained in accordance with Section 325 of the Act.	

I DIRECTORS' REPORT

	Reference
B. DIRECTORS (continued)	
3. Stock Exchange companies are to give details of directors' interests in share capital and options, distinguishing between beneficial and non-beneficial interests (companies dealt with on the USM need not give information on options).	SE 21(h) GU 10(h)
There should also be given details of any change in those interests or options which have occurred between the end of the financial year and a date not more than one month prior to the notice of AGM or, if there has been no change, disclosure of that fact.	
4. The unexpired period of any service contract of more than one year's duration of any director proposed for re-election at the forthcoming AGM of a listed company; if such director has no service contract of more than one year's duration, a negative statement is to be given.	SE 43(c)
5. Listed companies are to give particulars of any contract of significance subsisting during or at the end of the financial year in which a director of the company is or was materially interested, or, if there has been no such statement of that fact.	SE 21(k)
A 'contract of significance' for the purposes of the Stock Exchange requirements is one which represents in amount or value a sum equal to 1% or more of:	
(i) in the case of a capital transaction or a transaction of which the principal purpose is the granting of credit, the net assets of the company; or	
(ii) in other cases, the total purchases, sales, payments or receipts, as the case may be, of the company.	
C. CAPITAL	
1. Where a company purchases or otherwise acquires (e.g. by forfeiture or surrender) its own shares, the number and nominal value of the shares acquired and the percentage of the called up share capital which they represent: if the acquisition is by purchase, the consideration paid and the reasons for the purchase.	Sch 7: 7,8 [1981 s 14]
Disclosure is also required where a company's shares are acquired by its nominee or by another person with the company having a beneficial interest, or where shares are made subject to a lien or other charge taken by the company. Where these circumstances arise, reference should be made to Sch 7: 8 for the precise requirements.	

I DIRECTORS' REPORT

C. CAPITAL (continued)

	Reference
2. Listed companies are to give particulars of any shareholders' authority for the purchase by the company of its own shares existing at the end of the year. Where such purchases are made otherwise than through the market, or by tender or partial offer to all shareholders, particulars must be given of the names of the sellers of such shares purchased, or proposed to be purchased, by the company. In the case of any such purchases or options or contracts to make such purchases entered into since the year covered by the report, equivalent information must be given to that required under Sch 7: 7,8 (see above).	SE 21(p)
3. Stock Exchange companies are to give particulars, at a date not more than one month prior to the date of the notice of meeting, of an interest of any person, other than a director, in any substantial part of the share capital of the company and the amount of the interest, or if there is no such interest, statement of that fact. (A substantial holding is one which amounts to 5% or more of shares having full voting rights.)	SE 21(i) GU 10(i)

D. FIXED ASSETS

1. Any significant change in the fixed assets of the company or its subsidiaries during the financial year.	Sch 7: 1(1) [1967 s 16]
2. Any substantial difference between market value and balance sheet value of interests in land if the directors decide that this is significant for shareholders or debenture holders. To be indicated as precisely as practicable.	Sch 7: 1(2) [1967 s 16]

E. EMPLOYEES

1. Information concerning arrangements for securing the health, safety and welfare of employees. Regulations by statutory instrument to enact requirements have not yet been made.	Sch 7: 10 [1967 s 16]
2. A statement describing policy during financial year: (a) for giving full and fair consideration to applications for employment by disabled persons; (b) for continuing to employ and train employees who have become disabled; and (c) for training, career development and promotion of disabled persons employed by the company.	Sch 7: 9 [SI 1980-1160]

I DIRECTORS' REPORT

E. EMPLOYEES (continued)

	Reference
3. A statement describing action taken to introduce, maintain or develop arrangements to:	Sch 7: 11 [1967 s 16]
(a) provide employees with information on matters of concern to them as employees;	
(b) consult employees or their representatives so that their views can be taken into account when decisions are taken about their interests;	
(c) encourage employee involvement in company performance;	
(d) achieve employee awareness of the financial and economic factors affecting performance of the company.	
(Companies employing less than 251 people working wholly or mainly inside the UK are exempt from the requirements of 2 and 3 above. Companies within a group do not have to aggregate their employees for these purposes).	

F. POLITICAL AND CHARITABLE GIFTS

1. The amount (if in excess of £200) given by a company or group for political or charitable purposes. The amount for each is to be given and, if an individual payment given for political purposes exceeds £200, the name of the recipient and the amount are also to be given. If an individual payment given to a political party exceeds £200, the name of the party and the amount are to be given.	Sch 7: 3,4,5(3) [1967 s 19 SI 1980-1055]
A company which is the wholly owned subsidiary of a company incorporated in Great Britain does not have to give this information and payment for charitable purposes to non-residents of the UK are to be excluded.	

G. STANDARD ACCOUNTING PRACTICE

1. Stock Exchange companies are to give a statement as to the reason for any significant departure from standard accounting practices.	SE 21(a) GU 10(a)
(The Council of The Stock Exchange expect the financial statements of listed domestic companies to comply with UK accounting standards approved by the principal accounting bodies of the UK and Ireland.)	

II GENERAL DISCLOSURE RULES

A. TRUE AND FAIR VIEW

	Reference
1. The balance sheet and profit and loss account shall give a true and fair view of the state of affairs of the company as at the end of the financial year and of its profit or loss for the financial year. The same requirement applies to group financial statements.	s 228(2) s 230(2) [1981 s 1,2]
2. If the directors depart from any requirements of the Companies Act in order that the financial statements will give a true and fair view, particulars of the departure, the reasons for it and its effect shall be given in a note.	s 228(6) s 230(6) [1981 s 1,2]
3. If the financial statements drawn up in accordance with the Companies Act do not provide sufficient information to give a true and fair view, any necessary additional information must be provided in the accounts or in a note.	s 228(4) s 230(4) [1981 s 1,2]

B. EXEMPTION FROM REQUIREMENTS OF PART VII CHAPTER I

1. Banking, insurance and shipping companies may prepare their financial statements as previously and are entitled to the various exemptions contained in part VII Chapter II and their accounts shall comply with the requirements of Sch 9.	ss 257-262 [1981 s 17, 1981 Sch 2: 1,2]

C. ACCOUNTS FORMATS

1. The balance sheet and profit and loss account shall show the items listed in the formats in the order and under the headings and sub-headings given in the format adopted. (see appendix 5) The letters and numbers assigned to items in the formats need not be shown.	Sch 4: 1 [1981 Sch 1: 1]
2. In respect of items to which Arabic numbers have been assigned in the formats:	
(a) the directors shall adapt the arrangement and headings and sub-headings were the special nature of the company's business requires such adaptation.	Sch 4: 3(3) [1981 Sch 1: 3(3)]
(b) where these items are combined to facilitate the assessment of the state of affairs or profit and loss, the individual amounts of any items so combined shall be disclosed in a note.	Sch 4: 3(4) [1981 Sch 1: 3(4)]
3. Greater detail and additional items than required or covered by the format adopted may be shown.	Sch 4: 3 [1981 Sch 1: 3]
4. If a new format is adopted, particulars of the change, together with reasons for the change, shall be disclosed in a note.	Sch 4: 2 [1981 Sch 1: 2]

II GENERAL DISCLOSURE RULES

	Reference

D. CORRESPONDING AMOUNTS

1. Corresponding amounts are to be given for each item in the balance sheet and profit and loss account and notes to the accounts (adjusted if necessary to make them comparable: particulars and reasons for such adjustments must be given).	Sch 4: 4 Sch 4: 58(2) [1981 Sch 1: 4, 58(2)]
2. Exceptions to this rule are given under the appropriate disclosure sections which follow.	Sch 4: 58(3) [1981 Sch 1: 58(3)]

E. IMMATERIAL AMOUNTS

1. Amounts which in the particular context of any provision of Schedule 4 are not material may be disregarded for the purposes of that provision.	Sch 4: 86 [1981 Sch 1: 85]

F. NIL AMOUNTS

1. A heading or sub-heading shall not be included if there is a nil amount for both the current and immediately preceding financial year.	Sch 4: 3(5) [1981 Sch 1: 3(5)]

G. SIGNING AND APPROVAL OF FINANCIAL STATEMENTS

1. The balance sheet is to be signed on behalf of the Board by two directors (or by the sole director).	s 238(1) [1948 s 155]
2. The date on which the financial statements are approved by the Board should be given.	SSAP 17

III ACCOUNTING POLICIES

1. The accounting policies used to determine the amounts to be included in the balance sheet and profit and loss account shall be stated in the notes if not given in the accounts. These must include the policies used in respect of depreciation and diminution in value of assets.	Sch 4: 36 [1981 Sch 1: 36] SSAP 2
2. Where the principles followed in the preparation of the accounts depart from any of the first five principles stated in Sch 4 (i.e. going concern, consistency, prudence, accruals, separate determination of amounts), particulars of the departure, the reasons for it and its effect shall be given in a note.	Sch 4: 15 [1981 Sch 1: 15] SSAP 2

III ACCOUNTING POLICIES

	Reference
3. Methods used to translate accounts of foreign enterprises and treatment accorded to exchange differences should be disclosed.	SSAP 20
The basis on which amounts denominated in foreign currencies have been translated into sterling shall be stated.	Sch 4: 58(1) [1981 Sch 1: 58(1)]
4. The policies adopted for accounting for operating and finance leases. Lessors should disclose in detail the policy for accounting for finance lease income.	SSAP 21

IV BALANCE SHEET

A. CALLED UP SHARE CAPITAL NOT PAID

1. This heading may be shown in the alternative position on the balance sheet under debtors.

B. FIXED ASSETS – Intangible assets

1. The following must be shown separately:	
(a) Development costs There must be disclosed in the notes: (i) the reasons for capitalising the costs, and (ii) the period over which the amount is being written off.	Sch 4: 20 [1981 Sch 1: 20]
(b) Concessions, patents, licences, trademarks and similar rights and assets (if acquired for valuable consideration and are not goodwill, or created by the company itself)	
(c) Goodwill (if acquired for valuable consideration).	
The period chosen for writing off goodwill and the reasons for the choice shall be disclosed in a note.	Sch 4: 21 [1981 Sch 1: 21]
The accounting policy followed, including period selected for amortising the goodwill relating to each major acquisition. Where policy followed in respect of goodwill existing at date SSAP 22 is introduced is different from that followed for other goodwill, that treatment and the amounts involved should be disclosed.	SSAP 22
(d) Payments on account	

Note: Unless otherwise indicated by a reference, all the requirements listed above derive from the accounts formats (and accompanying notes) included in Sch 4.

IV BALANCE SHEET

	Reference
B. FIXED ASSETS – Intangible assets (continued)	
2. Full details must be shown of the movement during the year of: (a) each asset, and (b) accumulated depreciation thereon. Corresponding figures are not required.	Sch 4: 42, 58(3) [1981 Sch 1: 42,58(3)] SSAP 22
3. Where alternative valuation basis is used there must be disclosed: (a) year of valuation and the values; (b) in the year of valuation the name of the valuers (or particulars of their qualifications) and bases of valuation; (c) historical cost amounts or difference between these amounts and alternative values (for cost and depreciation).	Sch 4: 33,43 [1981 Sch 1: 33,43]
C. FIXED ASSETS – Tangible assets	
1. The following must be shown separately: (a) Land and buildings subdivided between freehold and leasehold and between long (not less than 50 years unexpired) and short leases (b) Plant and machinery (c) Fixtures and fittings, tools and equipment (d) Payments on account	Sch 4: 44,83 [1981 Sch 1: 44,82]
The carrying value of investment properties should be prominently displayed.	SSAP 19
2. Full details must be shown of the movement during the year of: (a) each asset and (b) accumulated depreciation thereon. Corresponding figures are not required.	Sch 4: 42,58(3) [1981 Sch 1: 42, 58(3)]
3. Where alternative valuation basis is used there must be disclosed: (a) year of valuation and the values; (b) in the year of valuation the name of the valuers (or particulars of their qualifications) and bases of valuation; (c) historical cost amounts or difference between these amounts and alternative values (for cost and depreciation).	Sch 4: 33,43 [1981 Sch 1: 33,43]
If the valuer of investment properties is an employee or officer of the company, this fact should be disclosed.	SSAP 19
4. For each major class of depreciable asset, the following is to be disclosed: (a) the depreciation methods used; (b) the useful lives or the depreciation rates used; (c) the gross amount of depreciable assets and the related accumulated depreciation; and (d) depreciation charged in the financial year.	SSAP 12

IV BALANCE SHEET

	Reference
C. FIXED ASSETS – Tangible assets (continued)	
5. In respect of assets held under finance lease and hire purchase contracts, give the gross amount and related accumulated depreciation; or if this information is combined with owned fixed assets, give the net amount.	SSAP 21
6. Lessors to give the gross amount of assets, and related accumulated depreciation, which are held for use in operating leases.	SSAP 21
D. FIXED ASSETS – Investments	
1. The following must be shown separately: (a) Shares in group companies (b) Loans to group companies (c) Shares in related companies (d) Loans to related companies (e) Other investments other than loans (f) Other loans (g) Own shares (nominal value to be shown separately)	
2. Movement of each category during the year must be shown. Corresponding figures are not required.	Sch 4: 42,58(3) [1981 Sch 1: 42,58(3)]
3. Listed investments to be subdivided between those listed on a recognised Stock Exchange and those otherwise listed.	Sch 4: 45 [1981 Sch 1: 45]
Aggregate market value to be given.	
4. Where the nominal value of a holding exceeds 10% of the allotted share capital or exceeds 10% of any class of equity or exceeds 10% of the investing company's assets, there must be disclosed: (a) name of company, and country of incorporation if other than Great Britain. (b) if incorporated in Great Britain, the country of registration unless this is the same as that of the investor company; and (c) the identity and proportion of the nominal value of each class of shares held. Holdings in subsidiaries to be distinguished between direct holdings of the company and those of its subsidiaries.	Sch 5: 1,2,7,8,9 [1967 ss 3,4] SSAP 14
This information may not be required in certain circumstances (eg, companies incorporated abroad, too numerous, or exempt from certain filing requirements).	Sch 5: 3,4,10,11 [1967 ss 3,4]
Corresponding information is not required.	Sch 4: 58(3) [1981 Sch 1: 58(3)]

Note: Unless otherwise indicated by a reference, all the requirements listed above derive from the accounts formats (and accompanying notes) included in Sch 4.

IV BALANCE SHEET

D. FIXED ASSETS – Investments (continued)

	Reference
5. In respect of each principal subsidiary and associated company, the nature of its business is to be given.	SSAP 1 SSAP 14
6. Stock Exchange companies must give the name of the principal country of operation of each subsidiary or company in which 20% or more of the equity capital is held by the group; and in the case of the latter company the particulars of its issued capital and debt securities and the percentage of each class of debt security held (directly or indirectly) is to be given.	SE 21(d)(e) GU 10(d)(e)
7. Unless unconsolidated subsidiaries and companies in which more than 20% of allotted capital is held have been accounted for by the equity method then, if material, additional information regarding underlying share capital, reserves and profits is to be given in respect of each investment.	Sch 5: 14,15,16,17 [1981 s 4]
8. Where alternative valuation basis is used there must be disclosed for unlisted securities: (a) year of valuation and the values; (b) in the year of valuation the name of the valuers (or particulars of their qualifications) and bases of valuation; and for listed and unlisted securities, (c) historical cost amounts or difference between these amounts and alternative values (for cost and depreciation).	Sch 4: 33,43 [1981 Sch 1: 33,43]
9. Where the alternative valuation is determined on a basis other than market value, disclose the details of the method of valuation and reasons for adopting it.	Sch 4: 31(3) [1981 Sch 1: 31(3)]
10. If the accounts of an associated company are not co-terminous with those of the investing company and are material, the facts and the date of year-ends should be disclosed.	SSAP 1

E. CURRENT ASSETS – Stocks

1. The following must be shown separately: (a) Raw materials and consumables (b) Work in progress (c) Finished goods and goods for resale (d) Payments on account	
2. The accounting policies which have been used in calculating cost, net realisable value, attributable profit and foreseeable losses (as appropriate) should be stated.	SSAP 9

Note: Unless otherwise indicated by a reference, all the requirements listed above derive from the accounts formats (and accompanying notes) included in Sch 4.

IV BALANCE SHEET

	Reference
E. CURRENT ASSETS – Stocks (continued)	
3. In relation to long term contracts there should be stated: (a) the amount of work in progress at cost plus attributable profit, less foreseeable losses; and (b) cash received and receivable as progress payments on account of contracts in progress.	SSAP 9
4. Any material difference between amount stated and replacement cost or most recent actual cost (if this latter comparison is considered appropriate by the directors) is to be disclosed. This applies where stocks are valued by one of the valuation methods other than the specific identification of actual costs.	Sch 4: 27(3) [1981 Sch 1: 27(3)]
F. CURRENT ASSETS – Debtors	
1. The following must be shown separately; (a) Trade debtors (b) Amounts owed by group companies (differentiating between subsidiaries and other group companies). (c) Amounts owed by related companies (d) Other debtors (e) Called up share capital not paid (may instead be shown as item A above) (f) Prepayments and accrued income (may instead be shown as item I below) Amounts falling due after more than one year shall be shown separately for each of the above items.	Sch 4: 59 [1981 Sch 1: 59]
2. Particulars of loans to directors (see Appendix 4).	s 232,Sch 6, Part I [1980 ss 54-59]
3. Loans given in respect of financial assistance for purchase of own shares are to be disclosed.	Sch 4: 51(2) [1981 Sch 1: 51(2)]
4. The aggregate amount of loans, guarantees and securities, quasi loans or credit transactions made by the company or its subsidiaries to officers (other than directors) which were outstanding at the year end. An amount not exceeding £2,500 in respect of any officer may be ignored. Also give the number of officers for whom the different types of transactions were made.	Sch 6: 13 [1980 s 56]
(If the financial statements do not give this information the auditors must give it in their report.)	s 237(5) [1980 s 59]
5. The net investment in finance leases and hire purchase contracts; also give cost of assets acquired for purposes of letting under finance leases.	SSAP 21

Note: Unless otherwise indicated by a reference, all the requirements listed above derive from the accounts formats (and accompanying notes) included in Sch 4.

IV BALANCE SHEET

	Reference
G. CURRENT ASSETS – Investments	
1. The following must be shown separately: (a) Shares in group companies (b) Own shares (nominal value to be shown separately) (c) Other investments	
2. Also the same disclosure (except movements) as for Fixed Asset – Investments to be given.	Sch 4: 45 [1981 Sch 1: 45]
H. CURRENT ASSETS – Cash at bank and in hand	
I. PREPAYMENTS AND ACCRUED INCOME	
1. This heading may be disclosed under debtors (see above).	
J. CREDITORS: AMOUNTS FALLING DUE WITHIN ONE YEAR	
1. The following must be shown separately: (a) Debenture loans (convertible loans to be shown separately) (b) Bank loans and overdrafts (c) Payments received on account (if not deducted from stocks) (d) Trade creditors (e) Bills of exchange payable (f) Amounts owed to group companies (differentiating between subsidiaries and other group companies)	 Sch 4: 59 [1981 Sch 1: 59]
(g) Amounts owed to related companies (h) Other creditors including taxation and social security (The amount for taxation and social security is to be shown separately) (i) Accruals and deferred income (may instead be shown under O below)	
2. Show aggregate dividend proposed (excluding ACT).	Sch 4: 51(3) [1981 Sch 1: 51(3)] SSAP 8
3. Aggregate amount of debts for which security has been given by the company and nature of security.	Sch 4: 48(4) [1981 Sch 1: 48(4)]
K. NET CURRENT ASSETS (LIABILITIES) [Format 1 only]	
1. This heading must include prepayments and accrued income wherever these are shown.	
L. TOTAL ASSETS LESS CURRENT LIABILITIES [Format 1 only]	

Note: Unless otherwise indicated by a reference, all the requirements listed above derive from the accounts formats (and accompanying notes) included in Sch 4.

IV BALANCE SHEET

	Reference
M. CREDITORS: AMOUNTS FALLING DUE AFTER MORE THAN ONE YEAR	
1. The following must be shown separately: (a) Debenture loans (convertible loans to be shown separately) (b) Bank loans and overdrafts (c) Payments received on account (if not deducted from stocks) (d) Trade creditors (e) Bills of exchange payable	
(f) Amounts owed to group companies (differentiating between subsidiaries and other group companies)	Sch 4: 59 [1981 Sch 1: 59]
(g) Amounts owed to related companies (h) Other creditors including taxation and social security (The amount for taxation and social security to be shown separately) (i) Accruals and deferred income (may instead be shown under O below)	
2. If debentures have been allotted during the year, give consideration received, amount and description of each class of debentures issued and reason for making the allotment.	Sch 4: 41(1) [1981 Sch 1: 41(1)]
3. Disclose particulars of debentures of the company held by its subsidiaries.	Sch 4: 60(1) [1981 Sch 1: 60(1)]
4. Aggregate amount of debts for which security has been given by the company and nature of security.	Sch 4: 48(4) [1981 Sch 1: 48(4)]
5. Give aggregate amount of creditors payable or repayable otherwise than by instalments and which fall due for payment or repayment after 5 years and the aggregate amount of creditors payable or repayable by instalments any of which fall due for payment after 5 years. In the latter case give also the aggregate amount of instalments falling due after 5 years. In respect of each of these debts, give the terms of payment and rates of interest payable (a general indication only is required where the number of creditors is excessive).	Sch 4: 48 [1981 Sch 1: 48]
6. Give details of redeemed debentures which the company has power to reissue.	Sch 4: 41(2) [1981 Sch 1: 41(2)]
7. Stock Exchange companies are to show in respect of: (a) bank loans and overdrafts and (b) other loans, the aggregate amounts repayable: (i) in one year or less or on demand; (ii) between one and two years; (iii) between two and five years; and (iv) in five years or more.	SE 21(f) GU 10(f)

Note: Unless otherwise indicated by a reference, all the requirements listed above derive from the accounts formats (and accompanying notes) included in Sch 4.

IV BALANCE SHEET

M. CREDITORS: AMOUNTS FALLING DUE AFTER MORE THAN ONE YEAR (continued)

	Reference
8. Lease obligations (net of future finance charges) to be shown separately, analysed between those payable within one year, second to fifth years inclusive, and amounts payable thereafter. Alternatively, the gross obligation may be analysed with the future finance charge being deducted from total.	SSAP 21

N. PROVISIONS FOR LIABILITIES AND CHARGES

1. To be shown separately: (a) Pensions and similar obligations (b) Taxation, including deferred taxation (c) Other provisions (Particulars of any material provision included in other provisions is to be given)	Sch 4: 46(3) [1981 Sch 1: 46(3)]
2. The provision for taxation other than deferred taxation is to be stated.	Sch 4: 47 [1981 Sch 1: 47]
3. The deferred tax balance and its major components, and transfers to or from deferred tax.	SSAP 15
4. Recoverable ACT to be deducted from the deferred tax account as appropriate. If there is no deferred taxation account, show as a deferred asset.	SSAP 8
5. In respect of the potential amounts of deferred tax, give: (i) the total amount of any unprovided deferred tax, analysed into its major components; (ii) where the potential amount on a revalued asset is not shown because the revaluation does not constitute a timing difference, a statement to this effect; (iii) where the value of an asset is shown in a note because it differs materially from its book amount, the tax effect, if any, that would arise if the asset were realised at the noted value; (iv) a statement that no deferred tax is provided on earnings retained overseas, if this is the case.	SSAP 15
6. If in assessing its deferred tax position a company which is a member of a group takes account of any group relief and any payment therefor, the assumptions made as to the availability of and payment for group relief should be stated.	SSAP 15
7. Transfers to provisions and, for a purpose otherwise than for which the provision was established, from provisions, are to be disclosed. Opening and closing balances to be given. Corresponding figures are not required.	Sch 4: 46, 58(3) [1981 Sch 1: 46,58(3)]

Note: Unless otherwise indicated by a reference, all the requirements listed above derive from the accounts formats (and accompanying notes) included in Sch 4.

IV BALANCE SHEET

N. PROVISIONS FOR LIABILITIES AND CHARGES (continued)

	Reference
8. If anticipated losses on individual contracts exceed cost incurred to date less progress payments received and receivable, such excess should be shown separately as provisions.	SSAP 9

O. ACCRUALS AND DEFERRED INCOME

1. Alternative positions are allowed: see J and M above.

P. CAPITAL AND RESERVES – Called up share capital

	Reference
1. To be shown separately: (a) allotted share capital (including number and aggregate nominal value of each class of shares allotted). (b) called up share capital which has been paid up.	Sch 4: 38(1) [1981 Sch 1: 38(1)]
2. Authorised share capital is to be given.	Sch 4: 38(1) [1981 Sch 1: 38(1)]
3. Earliest and latest redemption dates of redeemable shares, whether redemption is compulsory or at the option of the company or of the shareholder; also amount of any premium payable on redemption.	Sch 4: 38(2) [1981 Sch 1: 38(2)]
4. If shares have been allotted during the financial year, give consideration received and number, class, aggregate nominal value, for each class of shares and reason for allotment.	Sch 4: 39 [1981 Sch 1: 39]
5. Options (including convertible securities) to subscribe for shares, giving number, description and amount of shares, period exercisable and price to be paid.	Sch 4: 40 [1981 Sch 1: 40]
6. Arrears of cumulative dividends, giving the amount and period in arrears for each class.	Sch 4: 49 [1981 Sch 1: 49]
7. Disclose particulars of share capital of the company held by its subsidiaries.	Sch 4: 60 [1981 Sch 1: 60]
8. Where title of preference shares issued before 6 April 1973 includes a fixed rate of dividend, the new rate arising from the tax imputation system should be incorporated in the description.	SSAP 8
9. A listed company which is a subsidiary is to give particulars of the participation by the parent company in any vendor consideration placing (in respect of shares issued by the listed subsidiary) made during the year.	SE 22

Q. CAPITAL AND RESERVES – Share premium account

Note: Unless otherwise indicated by a reference, all the requirements listed above derive from the accounts formats (and accompanying notes) included in Sch 4.

IV BALANCE SHEET

	Reference
R. CAPITAL AND RESERVES – Revaluation reserve	
1. A title other than 'revaluation reserve' may be used.	Sch 4: 34(2) [1981 Sch 1: 34(3)]
2. There must be disclosed in a note the treatment for tax purposes of amounts credited or debited to revaluation reserve.	Sch 4: 34(4) [1981 Sch 1: 34(5)]
3. Changes in value of investment properties should be disclosed as a movement on investment revaluation reserve.	SSAP 19
S. CAPITAL AND RESERVES – Other reserves	
1. The following must be shown separately: (a) Capital redemption reserve (b) Reserve for own shares (c) Reserves provided for by the Articles of Association. (d) Other reserves.	
T. CAPITAL AND RESERVES – Profit and loss account	
U. RESERVES (the following apply to all reserves)	
1. Where any amount is transferred to or from any reserves, movements on reserves are to be given. Comparative figures are not required.	Sch 4: 46, 58(3) [1981 Sch 1: 46,58(3)]
2. Where amounts of deferred taxation arise which relate to movements on reserves, the amounts transferred to or from deferred taxation account should be shown separately as part of such movements.	SSAP 15
3. The group's share of the post-acquisition accumulated reserves of associated companies and any movements therein should be disclosed.	SSAP 1
4. The net movement on reserves arising from exchange differences.	SSAP 20
V. CONTINGENCIES	
1. Legal nature and amount of any contingent liability and, if secured, details of the security.	Sch 4: 50(2) [1981 Sch 1: 50(2)]
2. A material contingent loss not accrued should be disclosed except where the possibility of loss is remote. In respect of each contingency, the following should be disclosed: (a) the nature of the contingency and the uncertainties which are expected to affect the ultimate outcome; and (b) a prudent estimate of the financial effect, or a statement that it is not practicable to make such an estimate.	SSAP 18

Note: Unless otherwise indicated by a reference, all the requirements listed above derive from the accounts formats (and accompanying notes) included in Sch 4.

IV BALANCE SHEET

Reference

V. CONTINGENCIES (continued)

3. In the case of a contingent loss, the potential financial effect should be reduced by any amount accrued and the amounts of any components where the possibility of loss is remote; the net amount only need be disclosed.	SSAP 18
4. The estimate of the financial effect should be disclosed before taxation. The tax implication, in the event of a contingency crystallising, should be explained, if necessary, for a proper understanding of the financial position.	SSAP 18
5. Contingencies in respect of individual transactions common to a large number of similar transactions may be grouped for purposes of disclosure.	SSAP 18

W. POST BALANCE SHEET EVENTS

1. A material post balance sheet event should be disclosed where: (a) it is a non-adjusting event of such materiality that its non-disclosure would affect the ability of the users of financial statements to reach a proper understanding of the financial position; or (b) it is the reversal or maturity after the year end of transactions entered into before the year end, and the substance of which was primarily to alter the appearance of the company's balance sheet.	SSAP 17
2. The following information should be disclosed: (a) the nature of the event; and (b) an estimate of the financial effect, or a statement that it is not practicable to make such an estimate.	SSAP 17
3. The estimate of the financial effect should be disclosed before taking account of taxation. The taxation implications should be explained if explanation is necessary for a proper understanding of the financial position.	SSAP 17
4. It should be noted that the Act requires particulars of important post balance sheet events to be given in directors' report. It is suggested that the above information should be given in the notes to the accounts and referred to in the directors' report.	Sch 7: 6(a) [1981 s 13]

X. COMMITMENTS

1. Amount of capital expenditure contracted for; also amount authorised by directors but not yet contracted for.	Sch 4: 50(3) [1981 Sch 1: 50(3)]
2. Pension commitments both provided for and not provided for, giving separately details of commitments in respect of past directors.	Sch 4: 50(4) [1981 Sch 1: 50(4)]

IV BALANCE SHEET

X. COMMITMENTS (continued)

	Reference
3. Particulars of any other financial commitments which: (a) have not been provided for; and (b) are relevant to assessing the company's state of affairs.	Sch 4: 50(5) [1981 Sch 1: 50(5)]
4. Particulars of any charge on assets to secure another person's liabilities, including, where practicable, the amount secured.	Sch 4: 50(1) [1981 Sch 1: 50(1)]
5. For each of items 1 to 4 above, separate disclosure is required of commitments undertaken on behalf of or for the benefit of: (a) a holding company or fellow subsidiary company, and; (b) any subsidiary company.	Sch 4: 50(6) [1981 Sch 1: 50(6)]
6. Lease payments which lessee is committed to make during the next year under operating leases, analysed between commitments which expire within one year, within two to five years inclusive and over five years from balance sheet date; show separately commitments in respect of leases of land and buildings and other operating leases.	SSAP 21
7. Commitments under finance leases entered into but whose inception occurs after the year end.	SSAP 21

Y. CONTRACTS WITH DIRECTORS AND CORPORATE SUBSTANTIAL SHAREHOLDERS

1. Particulars of transactions and arrangements with directors (see Appendix 4)	s 232, Sch 6: Part I [1980 ss 54-59]
2. Listed companies are to give particulars of any contract of significance (see page 157) between the company, or one of its subsidiary companies, and a corporate substantial shareholder. Where a company has subsidiaries, comparison is to be made on a consolidated basis.	SE 21(l)
3. Listed companies are to give particulars of any contract for the provision of services to the company or any of its subsidiaries by a corporate substantial shareholder. Exceptionally, such a contract need not be disclosed, if it is a contract for the provision of services which it is the principal business of the shareholder to provide and it is not a contract of significance, for the purposes of paragraph (2) above.	SE 21(m)

Z. ULTIMATE HOLDING COMPANY

1. The name and (if known) the country of incorporation of the ultimate holding company of a subsidiary company are to be given in the notes. (Secretary of State may give exemption if the subsidiary is carrying on business outside the U.K.).	Sch 5: 20, 21 [1967 s 5]

IV BALANCE SHEET

	Reference
AA. CLOSE COMPANIES	
1. A Stock Exchange company is required to disclose whether the company is a close company for taxation purposes and any change in that status since the year end.	SE 21(j) GU 10(j)
BB. ASSET VALUES GIVEN IN NOTES	
1. Where the value of an asset is shown by way of note at an amount different from book value, material tax implications on realisation should be disclosed.	SSAP 15
CC. ASSET VALUES BASED ON EARLIEST AVAILABLE RECORD	
1. Where there is no record of purchase price or production cost, or this information cannot be obtained without unreasonable expense or delay, and the value given to any asset is the value ascribed to it in the earliest available record, particulars must be disclosed the first time this basis is used.	Sch 4: 51(1) [1981 Sch 1: 51(1)]
DD. INTEREST CAPITALISED	
1. The amount of interest included in determining the cost of an asset is to be disclosed in the notes.	Sch 4: 26(3) [1981 Sch 1: 26(3)]
2. Stock Exchange companies are also required to give the amount of interest capitalised in the year and the amount and treatment of any related tax relief.	SE 21(g) GU 10(g)

V PROFIT AND LOSS ACCOUNT

Reference

A. FORMATS

1. Four different formats are allowed for the profit and loss account. Whichever format is adopted the following items must be disclosed. Those items marked with an asterisk (*) must be disclosed in the profit and loss account itself; all other items can be disclosed either in the profit and loss account or in the notes.

(a) Turnover

(b) Other operating income

(c) Income from shares in group companies

(d) Income from shares in related companies

(e) Income from other fixed asset investments (show income from group companies separately)

(f) Other interest receivable and similar income (show interest from group companies separately)

(g) Amounts written off investments

(h) Interest payable and similar charges (show amount payable to group companies separately)

* (i) Profit or loss on ordinary activities before taxation — Sch 4: 3(6) [1981 Sch 1: 3(6)]

(j) Tax on profit or loss on ordinary activities

(k) Profit or loss on ordinary activities after taxation

(l) Extraordinary income

(m) Extraordinary charges

(n) Extraordinary profit or loss

(o) Tax on extraordinary profit or loss

(p) Other taxes not shown under the above items

(q) Profit or loss for the financial year

* (r) Aggregate amount of dividends — Sch 4: 3(7) [1981 Sch 1: 3(7)]

* (s) Amounts set aside to, or withdrawn from, reserves — Sch 4: 3(7) [1981 Sch 1: 3(7)]

2. The profit and loss account or notes must also disclose expenses and costs analysed either:

(a) by function as follows:

Cost of sales (include depreciation)
Gross profit or loss
Distribution costs (include depreciation)
Administration expenses (include depreciation)

Note: Unless otherwise indicated by a reference, all the requirements listed above derive from the accounts formats (and accompanying notes) included in Sch 4.

V PROFIT AND LOSS ACCOUNT

Reference

A. FORMATS (continued)

(b) by type of expenses as follows:

Change in stocks of finished goods and work in progress
Own work capitalised
Raw materials and consumables
Other external charges
Staff costs:
(i) wages and salaries
(ii) social security costs
(iii) other pension costs
Depreciation and other amounts written off tangible and intangible fixed assets
Exceptional amounts written off current assets
Other operating charges

B. TURNOVER

1. If the company has during the year carried on business of two or more classes that, in the opinion of the directors, differ substantially from each other, state for each class: (a) turnover and (b) profit or loss before tax. If sales have been made to geographical areas that in the opinion of the directors differ substantially from each other, the amount of turnover attributable to each market shall be stated. If the directors consider that the above disclosures would be seriously prejudicial to the interests of the company they need only say that the required information has not been given.	Sch 4: 55 [1981 Sch 1: 55]
2. For requirements of Stock Exchange companies to disclose geographical analysis of turnover and trading results, see item 7 page 304.	SE 21(c) GU 10(c)

C. ASSOCIATED COMPANIES

1. The investing group's consolidated profit and loss account should disclose the amounts attributable to associated companies of: (a) profit before taxation; (b) taxation; (c) extraordinary items (if material to group accounts); (d) net profit retained.	SSAP 1
2. Other items, if the associated company results are significant, should be shown separately, but should not be included in the group figure.	SSAP 1
3. The above also applies to an investing company which has no subsidiaries or which otherwise does not prepare consolidated accounts.	SSAP 1

Note: Unless otherwise indicated by a reference, all the requirements listed above derive from the accounts formats (and accompanying notes) included in Sch 4.

V PROFIT AND LOSS ACCOUNT

	Reference
D. TAXATION	
1. Give basis on which tax is computed and the rate of corporation tax used. Explain special circumstances which affect tax liabilities.	Sch 4: 54 [1981 Sch 1: 54]
2. State separately: (a) UK corporation tax (b) Double taxation relief (c) UK income tax (d) Foreign tax (e) Tax attributable to franked investment income (f) Irrecoverable ACT (g) Deferred tax (and separately as part of the tax charge adjustments to deferred tax arising from changes in tax rates and rates of tax allowances)	Sch 4: 54(3) [1981 Sch 1: 54(3)] SSAP 8 and 15
3. Deferred tax on extraordinary items should be included as part of 'Tax on extraordinary profit or loss' but disclosed separately.	SSAP 15
4. The amount of any unprovided deferred tax in respect of the period, analysed into its major components.	SSAP 15
5. Stock Exchange companies are to indicate the amount and treatment of any tax relief which relates to interest that has been capitalised.	SE 21(g) GU 10(g)
E. DIRECTORS' EMOLUMENTS	
1. Amounts received by directors and past directors as emoluments, pensions and compensation for loss of office, disclosing separately whether in respect of services as directors or as executives.	Sch 5: 22, 28, 29 [1948 s 196]
2. Emoluments of chairman, while chairman (unless his duties as chairman were wholly or mainly discharged outside the UK).	Sch 5: 24 [1967 s 6]
3. Emoluments of the highest paid director if they are greater than those of the chairman (ignoring anyone whose duties were wholly or mainly discharged outside the UK).	Sch 5: 25(3)(4) [1967 s 6]
4. Number of directors whose emoluments amounted to not more than £5,000, number of directors whose emoluments amounted to between £5,000 and £10,000 and so on in 'bands' of £5,000. Except directors who discharged their duties as directors wholly or mainly outside the UK.	Sch 5: 25 [1967 s 6, SI 1979-1618]
5. Number of directors who waived their emoluments and the aggregate amount waived.	Sch 5: 27 [1967 s 7]
Listed companies to give particulars of waivers, including waiver of future emoluments.	SE 21(n) GU 10(k)

V PROFIT AND LOSS ACCOUNT

	Reference
E. DIRECTORS' EMOLUMENTS (continued)	
Consolidated financial statements will only need to show details required in (1)-(5) for directors of holding company.	Sch 4: 63 [1981 Sch 1: 63]
Items (2)-(5) are not required if the company is not part of a group and the total emoluments do not exceed £60,000.	Sch 5: 23 [1967 s 6, SI 1982-1698]
Note: If this information is not given, the auditors are required to include the information in their report.	s 237(5) [1967 ss 6,8]
F. EMPLOYEE INFORMATION	
1. Staff costs	
Analysed as to wages and salaries, social security costs and other pension costs, unless these amounts are stated in the profit and loss account.	Sch 4: 56(4) [1981 Sch 1: 56(4)]
2. Emoluments of higher paid employees	
The number of employees whose emoluments exceeded £30,000 but were not more than £35,000, exceeded £35,000 but were not more than £40,000 and so on in bands of £5,000.	Sch 5: 35 [1967 s 8, SI 1982-1698]
This information is not required in respect of: (a) directors (b) employees who worked wholly or mainly outside the UK.	
Consolidated financial statements only need show the details for employees of holding company.	Sch 4: 63 [1981 Sch 1: 63]
Note: If this information is not given, the auditors are required to include the information in their report.	s 237(5) [1967 ss 6,8]
3. Number of employees	
Average number of persons employed in the year subdivided into categories selected by the directors.	Sch 4: 56 [1981 Sch 1: 56]
G. OTHER PROFIT AND LOSS DISCLOSURES	
1. Interest or similar charges in respect of: (a) bank loans and overdrafts and other loans repayable within 5 years; and (b) other loans. Exclude interest on loans with group companies.	Sch 4: 53(2) [1981 Sch 1: 53(2)]

V PROFIT AND LOSS ACCOUNT

G. OTHER PROFIT AND LOSS DISCLOSURES (continued)

	Reference
2. Aggregate financial charges under finance leases.	SSAP 21
3. Income from listed investments.	Sch 4: 53(4) [1981 Sch 1: 53(4)]
Dividends from UK companies should be grossed up for the tax credit.	SSAP 8
4. Rental income	
Rents from land (net of outgoings) if this is a substantial part of the company's revenue.	Sch 4: 53(5) [1981 Sch 1: 53(5)]
Aggregate rentals receivable in respect of (a) finance leases and (b) operating leases.	SSAP 21
5. Leasing charges	
Charges for hire of plant and machinery.	Sch 4: 53(6) [1981 Sch 1: 53(6)]
Charges for other operating leases.	SSAP 21
6. Remuneration (including expenses) of the auditors.	Sch 4: 53(7) [1981 Sch 1: 53(7)]
7. Exceptional items	
The effect of transactions falling within the ordinary activities that are exceptional in size or incidence	Sch 4: 57(3) [1981 Sch 1: 57(3)]
Their nature and size to be disclosed.	SSAP 6
8. Extraordinary items Particulars of extraordinary income or charges to be given.	Sch 4: 57(2) [1981 Sch 1: 57(2)] SSAP 6
9. Amounts set aside for redemption of share capital and redemption of loans.	Sch 4: 53(3) [1981 Sch 1: 53(3)]
10. Depreciation	
Provision for depreciation and diminution in value of tangible and intangible fixed assets to be disclosed in the notes where Formats 1 or 3 are used.	Sch 4 [1981 Sch 1] footnote 17 to P & L formats
Disclose effect of revaluation on annual depreciation.	SSAP 12
Total depreciation in respect of assets held under finance leases.	SSAP 21

V PROFIT AND LOSS ACCOUNT

G. OTHER PROFIT AND LOSS DISCLOSURES (continued)

	Reference
11. Provision for diminution in value of fixed assets and any such provision written back, which are not shown in the profit and loss account.	Sch 4: 19(3) [1981 Sch 1: 19(3)]
12. The effect of any amount relating to any preceding year which is included in any item in the profit and loss account.	Sch 4: 57(1) [1981 Sch 1: 57(1)]
Prior year adjustments are to be included in the statement of retained profits.	SSAP 6
13. Dividends waived	
Stock Exchange companies must give particulars of any arrangement under which a shareholder has waived, or agreed to waive, any dividends.	SE 21(o) GU 10(l)
14. The net amount of exchange gains and losses on foreign currency borrowings less deposits, identifying separately (i) the amount offset in reserves and (ii) the net amount charged/credited to the profit and loss account	SSAP 20
15. Listed companies to give on the face of the profit and loss account both basic and fully diluted (where the dilution is 5% or more of basic) net earnings per share for the financial year and the corresponding previous period. Basis of calculation, including amount of earnings and number of equity shares, also to be given.	SSAP 3
Note: A statement of retained profits/reserves should immediately follow the profit and loss account.	SSAP 6

VI CONSOLIDATED FINANCIAL STATEMENTS

A. GENERAL REQUIREMENTS

	Reference
1. Group financial statements are to be submitted if a company has subsidiary companies and is not a wholly owned subsidiary of another company incorporated in Great Britain. These should be consolidated financial statements, but the Act permits certain alternatives.	s 229(1)(2) [1948 ss 150, 151 1976 s 8]
The accounts of a listed group must be in consolidated form.	SE 20
2. Group financial statements shall give a true and fair view of the state of affairs and the profit or loss of the holding company and the subsidiaries, so far as concerns members of the company.	s 230(2) [1981 s 2]

VI CONSOLIDATED FINANCIAL STATEMENTS

	Reference
A. GENERAL REQUIREMENTS (continued)	
3. Consolidated financial statements (or 'group financial statements') are to comply with the requirements outlined for companies with respect to the form and contents of the accounts and additional information in the notes.	s 230(1) Sch 4: 62 [1981 Sch 1: 62] [1981 s 2]
4. Consolidated financial statements are to combine the information contained in the separate balance sheets and profit and loss accounts but with such adjustments as the directors of the holding company think necessary.	Sch 4: 61 [1981 Sch 1: 61]
The following items should be in respect of the holding company only: (a) Directors' and employees' emoluments [Sch 5: Parts V and VI) (b) Investments (Sch 5 Parts II and III) (c) Loans and transactions with directors (Sch 6)	Sch 4: 63 [1981 Sch 1:61]
5. Where a holding company is exempted by s 228 from preparing its own profit and loss account, it must disclose how much of the consolidated profit or loss has been dealt with in its accounts. It must also state that it has taken advantage of this exemption.	s 228(7) [1948 s 149(5)(6)]
6. A listed company's own accounts must be published in addition to consolidated accounts if they contain significant additional information.	SE 20
B. GROUP ACCOUNTS NOT PREPARED OR EXCLUDE SUBSIDIARIES	
1. Where group accounts are not submitted or where group accounts are prepared which do not deal with one or more of its subsidiaries, there shall be given in the notes (if this information is not obtainable, state this fact): (a) the reasons why subsidiaries are not dealt with in group accounts; (b) any qualifications in the reports of the auditors of the subsidiary companies, or any matter which would have been the subject of a qualification but has been dealt with in a note or other reference, unless immaterial or covered by the holding company's financial statements.	Sch 4: 69(2) [1981 Sch 1: 69(2)]
2. The total investment in unconsolidated subsidiaries shall be stated in a note by way of the equity method unless the company is a wholly owned subsidiary of another UK company and there is a note that in the opinion of the directors the aggregate value of investment in such unconsolidated subsidiaries (shares and amounts owing) is not less than the amount stated in the company's balance sheet.	Sch 4: 69(3)(4) [1981 Sch 1: 69(3)(4)]
The Secretary of State has power to grant exemption from these requirements.	

VI CONSOLIDATED FINANCIAL STATEMENTS

	Reference
C. ADDITIONAL DISCLOSURES IN RESPECT OF SUBSIDIARIES EXCLUDED FROM CONSOLIDATION	
1. In respect of subsidiaries excluded from consolidation, the following additional information should be disclosed in the consolidated financial statements:	SSAP 14
(a) the names of the principal subsidiaries excluded; and	
(b) any premium or discount on acquisition (in comparison with the fair value of assets acquired) to the extent not written off.	
2. Where a subsidiary is excluded from consolidation on the grounds of dissimilar activities, the group financial statements should include separate financial statements for that subsidiary. They may be combined with the financial statements of other subsidiaries with similar operations, if appropriate. The separate financial statements should include the following information:	SSAP 14
(a) a note of the holding company's interest;	
(b) particulars of intra-group balances;	
(c) the nature of transactions with the rest of the group; and	
(d) a reconciliation with the amount included in the consolidated financial statements for the group's investment in the subsidiary which should be stated under the equity method of accounting.	
3. Where a subsidiary is excluded from consolidation because of severe restrictions over control, the following information should be disclosed in the group financial statements:	SSAP 14
(a) its net assets;	
(b) its profits or losses for the period;	
(c) any amounts included in the consolidated profit and loss account in respect of dividends received and writing down of the investment.	

VI CONSOLIDATED FINANCIAL STATEMENTS

	Reference
D. DIFFERENT FINANCIAL YEARS	
1. Where the financial years of subsidiaries are not co-terminous with the financial year of the holding company, give:	Sch 4: 70 [1981 Sch 1: 70]
(a) the directors' reasons for this;	
(b) the dates of the subsidiaries' financial years or the earliest and latest of those dates;	
(c) the names of the principal subsidiaries; and	SSAP 14
(d) the accounting period involved where the accounting period of a principal subsidiary was of a different length from that of the holding company.	SSAP 14
E. RESTRICTIONS ON DISTRIBUTIONS	
1. If there are significant restrictions on the ability of the holding company to distribute the retained profits of the group (other than those shown as non-distributable) because of statutory, contractual or exchange control restrictions, the extent of the restrictions should be indicated.	SSAP 14
F. UNIFORM ACCOUNTING POLICIES	
1. Uniform group accounting policies should be followed by a holding company in preparing its consolidated financial statements. Where different accounting policies are followed there should be disclosed:	SSAP 14
(a) the different accounting policies used;	
(b) an indication of the amounts of the assets and liabilities involved, and where practicable an indication of the effect on results and net assets of the adoption of policies different from those of the group;	
(c) the reason for the different treatment.	
G. OUTSIDE OR MINORITY INTERESTS	
1. Outside or minority interests in the share capital and reserves of companies consolidated should be disclosed as a separate amount in the consolidated balance sheet and should not be shown as part of the shareholders' funds.	SSAP 14
2. Profits or losses of such companies attributable to outside interests should be shown separately in the consolidated profit and loss account after arriving at group profit or loss after tax but before extraordinary items. Minority interests in extraordinary items should be deducted from the related amounts in the consolidated profit and loss account.	SSAP 14

VI CONSOLIDATED FINANCIAL STATEMENTS

	Reference
H. ACQUISITIONS AND DISPOSALS OF GROUP COMPANIES	
1. In the case of material additions to or disposals from the group, the consolidated financial statements should contain sufficient information about the results of the subsidiaries acquired or sold to enable shareholders to appreciate the effect on the consolidated results.	SSAP 14
2. The date from which the results of major acquisitions have been brought into the accounts	SSAP 23
3. In respect of all material business combinations, the accounts of the acquiring company should disclose in the period in which the combination takes place:	SSAP 23
(a) the names of the combining companies;	
(b) the number and class of the securities issued in respect of the combination, and details of any other consideration given;	
(c) the accounting treatment adopted for the business combination (i.e. whether it has been accounted for as an acquisition or a merger);	
(d) the nature and amount of significant accounting adjustments by the combining companies to achieve consistency of accounting policies.	
I. MERGERS	
1. Where shares have been allotted during the financial year in consideration for the issue, transfer or cancellation of shares in another company where merger relief provisions of the Act apply, give:	Sch 4: 75(1) [SI 1982-1092]
(a) the name of acquired company;	
(b) the number, nominal value and class of shares allotted;	
(c) the number, nominal value and class of shares in the acquired company so issued, transferred or cancelled;	
(d) particulars of the accounting treatment adopted in respect of the shares in the acquired company issued, transferred or cancelled; and	
(e) particulars of the effect on the group profit or loss of the inclusion of pre-acquisition profit or loss of the acquired company.	

VI CONSOLIDATED FINANCIAL STATEMENTS

Reference

I. MERGERS (continued)

2. Where shares have been allotted during the financial year or the two preceding financial years to acquire a company and the merger relief provisions of the Act have been applied, disclose: — Sch 4: 75(2) [SI 1982-1092]

   (a) any profit or loss realised on disposal of

      (i) shares in the acquired company;
      (ii) any assets which were fixed assets of the acquired company at the time of the allotment; and

   (b) the part of any profit or loss realised on the sale of shares in a company (not being the acquired company) which is attributable to assets of that company or its subsidiaries which were shares or assets mentioned in (a) above;

   together with explanation of the transactions. If consolidated accounts are not prepared, this information is to be given in the issuing company's accounts.

3. In the year in which a merger takes place, the accounts of the acquiring company should disclose: — SSAP 23

   (a) the fair value of the consideration given by the issuing company;

   (b) an analysis of the current year's attributable profit before extraordinary items between that of before and that of after the effective date of the merger;

   (c) an analysis of the attributable profit before extraordinary items of the current year up to the effective date of the merger and of the previous year between that of the issuing company and that of the subsidiary; and

   (d) analysis of extraordinary items so as to indicate whether each individual extraordinary item relates to pre- or post-merger events, and to which party to the merger the item relates.

VII STATEMENT OF SOURCE AND APPLICATION OF FUNDS

	Reference
1. Audited financial statements should include a statement of source and application of funds both for the financial year and for the corresponding previous period. Where the financial statements are those of a group, this should reflect the operations of the group. This statement is not required for enterprises with turnover or gross income of less than £25,000 per annum.	SSAP 10
2. The statement should show the profit or loss for the period together with the adjustments required for items which did not use (or provide) funds.	SSAP 10
3. The following other sources and applications of funds should where material, also be shown: (a) Dividends paid. (b) Acquisitions and disposals of fixed and other non-current assets. (c) Funds raised by increasing, or expended in repaying or redeeming, medium or long-term loans or the issued capital of the company. (d) Increase or decrease in working capital subdivided into its components, and movements in net liquid funds.	SSAP 10
4. The statement should show purchases or disposals of subsidiaries either as a separate item or by reflecting the effects on the separate assets and liabilities. A summary of the transactions should generally be shown.	SSAP 10

VIII CURRENT COST ACCOUNTS

Reference

Although SSAP 16 is no longer mandatory, it remains in place. Its disclosure requirements are summarised below.

1. The current cost profit and loss account should show (not necessarily in this order): — SSAP 16

   (a) current cost operating profit or loss;

   (b) interest income relating to the net borrowings on which the gearing adjustment has been made;

   (c) the gearing adjustment;

   (d) taxation;

   (e) extraordinary items; and

   (f) current cost profit or loss (after tax) attributable to shareholders.

2. A reconciliation should be provided between the current cost operating profit and the profit or loss before charging interest and taxation calculated on the historical cost basis, giving the respective amounts of the following: — SSAP 16

   (a) depreciation adjustment;

   (b) cost of sales adjustment;

   (c) monetary working capital adjustment and where appropriate, interest relating to monetary working capital; and

   (d) other material adjustments made to profits calculated on the historical cost basis when determining current cost operating profit.

   The adjustments for cost of sales and monetary working capital may be combined.

3. The notes to the balance sheet should disclose the totals of net operating assets and net borrowings and their main elements. — SSAP 16

4. The balance sheet should be supported by summaries of the fixed asset account and the movement in reserves. — SSAP 16

VIII CURRENT COST ACCOUNTS

	Reference
5. The notes should describe the bases and methods adopted in preparing the current cost financial statements particularly in relation to:	
(a) the value to the business of fixed assets and the depreciation thereon;	
(b) the value to the business of stock and work in progress and the cost of sales adjustment;	
(c) the monetary working capital adjustment;	
(d) the gearing adjustment;	
(e) the basis of translating foreign currencies and dealing with gains or losses arising;	
(f) other material adjustments to the historical cost information; and	
(g) the corresponding amounts.	
6. Listed companies should show the current cost earnings per share.	SSAP 16
7. Where the directors' valuation of listed investments (excluding those treated as current assets) differs materially from mid-market valuation, the basis of valuation and reasons for the difference should be disclosed.	SSAP 16
8. Corresponding amounts for the preceding period should be stated. However, unless current cost financial statements are the main financial statements, corresponding amounts need only be included for the first period for which current cost financial statements are prepared if they are readily available.	SSAP 16

TABLE OF PERMITTED TRANSACTIONS CONCERNING DIRECTORS UNDER SS 332 to 338 OF THE COMPANIES ACT 1985

Transactions, agreements, arrangements and guarantees between a company (or its subsidiary) and a director of the company (or a person connected with the director) in relation to loans, quasi-loans and credit transactions are generally prohibited, except as noted below. (Other transactions, etc. are generally permitted, except that special rules apply to directors' service contracts [s 319] and substantial transfers of non-cash assets between companies and directors [s 320]).

Loans, quasi-loans and credit transactions which are permitted are:

<table>
<tr><th>Permitted for:</th><th>Loans</th><th>Quasi-loans</th><th>Credit transactions</th></tr>
<tr><td>1. Any company</td><td colspan="3">A company may make a loan to a director if the aggregate amount does not exceed £2,500. [s 334]

A company may provide a director with funds (up to £10,000 in the case of a public company or the subsidiary of a public company) to meet expenditure for the purposes of the company or to enable him to perform his duties. Approval of the company in general meeting is required, failing which the loan etc. is repayable within six months. [s 337]</td></tr>
<tr><td>2. Public company or member of a group which includes a public company (see note 4)</td><td>Not permitted (except as above)</td><td>Only if reimbursible within 2 months, and the total for the director does not exceed £1,000. [s 332]</td><td>Either (i) where transaction is under normal commercial terms,
Or (ii) where the total for the director does not exceed £5,000. [s 335]</td></tr>
<tr><td>3. Private company not a member of a group which includes a public company (see note 4)</td><td>Not permitted to a director (except as above) May be made to connected person.</td><td>Permitted</td><td>Permitted</td></tr>
<tr><td>4. Moneylending company</td><td colspan="2">Either (i) where loan etc. is under normal commercial terms, with upper limit of £50,000 per director (no upper limit for a recognised bank or for a private company not the subsidiary of a public company);
Or (ii) where loan etc. is on terms available to other employees and is in connection with the purchase or improvement of the director's main residence, with an upper limit of £50,000 per director. [s 338]</td><td>No special rules.</td></tr>
</table>

Notes:

1. Definitions may be found in the Act of the terms 'quasi-loans' and 'credit transactions' [s 331], 'moneylending company' [s 338], 'relevant amount' [s 339], and 'value' of transaction and arrangements [s 340].
2. 'Director' includes 'shadow director' – i.e. one on whose instructions the directors are accustomed to act (excluding professional advice).
3. Other minor exemptions may be found in ss 333 and 336.
4. The term 'public company' in this context includes an overseas private company.

TABLE OF DISCLOSURES OF TRANSACTIONS CONCERNING DIRECTORS (as required by s 232 and Part I of Sch 6 of the Act)

The particulars indicated by the table below should be disclosed by way of notes to the accounts in relation to each transaction, agreement, arrangement or guarantee (or security given) whether permitted or not between a company (or its subsidiary) and a director of the company (or a person connected with the director) in respect of loans, quasi-loans, credit transactions and other transactions. Directors include shadow directors. Corresponding amounts are not required.

Note: There are specific exemptions relating to banking companies and a number of further minor exemptions which are not covered by the table below.

Particulars to be disclosed	Loans	Quasi-loans	Credit transactions	Other material transactions except service contracts*
1. The principal terms of the transaction, etc. including: 2. a statement that the transaction, etc. was made or subsisted during the year; 3. the name of the director (and, where applicable, the connected person);	Yes	Yes	Yes – except where the aggregate outstanding sum for a director did not exceed £5,000 during the financial year.	Yes – except where the aggregate interest in each transaction with a director did not exceed either: (i) the lower of £5,000 and 1% of net asset value or (ii) £1,000 during the financial year.
4. the nature of his interest in the transaction;	N/A	N/A	N/A	Yes – except as above.
5. the amount due (including interest) at the beginning and end of the financial year; 6. the maximum amount due during the financial year; 7. the amount of unpaid interest; 8. the amount of any provision;	Yes	No – but see 9 below.	No	No
9. the value of the transaction, etc;	No (but see 5-8 above)	Yes	Yes – except as above.	Yes – except as above.
And in the case of a guarantee (or security); 10. the amounts guaranteed (secured) at the beginning and end of the financial year; 11. the maximum liability guaranteed (secured); and 12. any amounts paid or incurred since the inception of the guarantee (security).	Yes	Yes	Yes – except as above.	No

If the financial statements do not give this information the auditor must give it in his report (s 237(5)).

*A material transaction is one where the director's interest is material in the opinion of the majority of the other directors.

1985 ACT–ACCOUNTS FORMATS

BALANCE SHEET–Format 1

A. Called up share capital not paid (1)

B. Fixed assets
- I Intangible assets
  1. Development costs
  2. Concessions, patents, licences, trade marks and similar rights and assets (2)
  3. Goodwill (3)
  4. Payments on account
- II Tangible assets
  1. Land and buildings
  2. Plant and machinery
  3. Fixtures, fittings, tools and equipment
  4. Payments on account and assets in course of construction
- III Investments
  1. Shares in group companies
  2. Loans to group companies
  3. Shares in related companies
  4. Loans to related companies
  5. Other investments other than loans
  6. Other loans
  7. Own shares (4)

C. Current assets
- I Stocks
  1. Raw materials and consumables
  2. Work in progress
  3. Finished goods and goods for resale
  4. Payments on account
- II Debtors (5)
  1. Trade debtors
  2. Amounts owed by group companies
  3. Amounts owed by related companies
  4. Other debtors
  5. Called up share capital not paid (1)
  6. Prepayments and accrued income (6)
- III Investments
  1. Shares in group companies
  2. Own shares (4)
  3. Other investments
- IV Cash at bank and in hand

D. Prepayments and accrued income (6)

E. Creditors: amounts falling due within one year
1. Debenture loans (7)
2. Bank loans and overdrafts
3. Payments received on account (8)
4. Trade creditors
5. Bills of exchange payable
6. Amounts owed to group companies
7. Amounts owed to related companies
8. Other creditors including taxation and social security (9)
9. Accruals and deferred income (10)

BALANCE SHEET – Format 1 (continued)

F. Net current assets (liabilities) (11)

G. Total assets less current liabilities

H. Creditors: amounts falling due after more than one year
 1. Debenture loans (7)
 2. Bank loans and overdrafts
 3. Payments received on account (8)
 4. Trade creditors
 5. Bills of exchange payable
 6. Amounts owed to group companies
 7. Amounts owed to related companies
 8. Other creditors including taxation and social security (9)
 9. Accruals and deferred income (10)

I. Provisions for liabilities and charges
 1. Pensions and similar obligations
 2. Taxation, including deferred taxation
 3. Other provisions

J. Accruals and deferred income (10)

K. Capital and reserves
 I Called up share capital (12)
 II Share premium account
 III Revaluation reserve
 IV Other reserves
 1. Capital redemption reserve
 2. Reserve for own shares
 3. Reserves provided for by the articles of association
 4. Other reserves
 V Profit and loss account

References in ( ) are explained on pages 342 and 343.

BALANCE SHEET – Format 2

ASSETS

A. Called up share capital not paid (1)

B. Fixed assets
- I Intangible assets
  1. Development costs
  2. Concessions, patents, licences, trade marks and similar rights and assets (2)
  3. Goodwill (3)
  4. Payments on account
- II Tangible assets
  1. Land and buildings
  2. Plant and machinery
  3. Fixtures, fittings, tools and equipment
  4. Payments on account and assets in course of construction
- III Investments
  1. Shares in group companies
  2. Loans to group companies
  3. Shares in related companies
  4. Loans to related companies
  5. Other investments other than loans
  6. Other loans
  7. Own shares (4)

C. Current assets
- I Stocks
  1. Raw materials and consumables
  2. Work in progress
  3. Finished goods and goods for resale
  4. Payments on account
- II Debtors (5)
  1. Trade debtors
  2. Amounts owed by group companies
  3. Amounts owed by related companies
  4. Other debtors
  5. Called up share capital not paid (1)
  6. Prepayments and accrued income (6)
- III Investments
  1. Shares in group companies
  2. Own shares (4)
  3. Other investments
- IV Cash at bank and in hand

D. Prepayments and accrued income (6)

LIABILITIES

A. Capital and reserves
- I Called up share capital (12)
- II Share premium account
- III Revaluation reserve
- IV Other reserves
  1. Capital redemption reserve
  2. Reserve for own shares
  3. Reserves provided for by the articles of association
  4. Other reserves
- V Profit and loss account

B. Provisions for liabilities and charges
  1. Pensions and similar obligations
  2. Taxation including deferred taxation
  3. Other provisions

C. Creditors (13)
  1. Debenture loans (7)
  2. Bank loans and overdrafts
  3. Payments received on account (8)
  4. Trade creditors
  5. Bills of exchange payable
  6. Amounts owed to group companies
  7. Amounts owed to related companies
  8. Other creditors including taxation and social security (9)
  9. Accruals and deferred income (10)

D. Accruals and deferred income (10)

References in ( ) are explained on pages 342 and 343.

Note – Liabilities may alternatively be shown below assets or on a separate page.

NOTES ON THE BALANCE SHEET FORMATS

(1) *Called up share capital not paid*
(Formats 1 and 2, items A and C.II.5.)

This item may be shown in either of the two positions given in Formats 1 and 2.

(2) *Concessions, patents, licences, trade marks and similar rights and assets*
(Formats 1 and 2, item B.I.2.)

Amounts in respect of assets shall only be included in a company's balance sheet under this item if either:-
(a) the assets were acquired for valuable consideration and are not required to be shown under goodwill; or
(b) the assets in question were created by the company itself.

(3) *Goodwill*
(Formats 1 and 2, item B.I.3.)

Amounts representing goodwill shall only be included to the extent that the goodwill was acquired for valuable consideration.

(4) *Own shares*
(Formats 1 and 2, items B.III.7 and C.III.2)

The nominal value of the shares held shall be shown separately.

(5) *Debtors*
(Formats 1 and 2, items C.II.1 to 6.)

The amount falling due after more than one year shall be shown separately for each item included under debtors.

(6) *Prepayments and accrued income*
(Formats 1 and 2, items C.II.6 and D.)

This item may be shown in either of the two positions given in Formats 1 and 2.

(7) *Debenture loans*
(Format 1, items E.1 and H.1 and Format 2, item C.1)

The amount of any convertible loans shall be shown separately.

(8) *Payments received on account*
(Format 1, items E.3 and H.3 and Format 2, item C.3)

Payments received on account of orders shall be shown for each of these items in so far as they are not shown as deductions from stocks.

(9) *Other creditors including taxation and social security*
(Format 1, items E.8 and H.8 and Format 2, item C.8)

The amount for creditors in respect of taxation and social security shall be shown separately from the amount for other creditors.

NOTES ON THE BALANCE SHEET FORMATS (continued)

(10) *Accruals and deferred income*
(Format 1, items E.9, H.9 and J and Format 2, items C.9 and D.)

The two positions given for this item in Format 1 at E.9 and H.9 are an alternative to the position at J, but if the item is not shown in a position corresponding to that at J it may be shown in either or both of the other two positions (as the case may require).

The two positions given for this item in Format 2 are alternatives.

(11) *Net current assets (liabilities)*
(Format 1, item F.)

In determining the amount to be shown for this item any amounts shown under 'prepayments and accrued income' shall be taken into account wherever shown.

(12) *Called up share capital*
(Format 1, item K.1 and Format 2, item A.I.)

The amount of allotted share capital and the amount of called up share capital which has been paid up shall be shown separately.

(13) *Creditors*
(Format 2, items C.1 to 9.)

Amounts falling due within one year and after one year shall be shown separately for each of these items and their aggregate shall be shown separately for all of these items.

PROFIT AND LOSS ACCOUNT – Format 1 (See note (17) below)

1. Turnover
2. Cost of sales (14)
3. Gross profit or loss
4. Distribution costs (14)
5. Administrative expenses (14)
6. Other operating income
7. Income from shares in group companies
8. Income from shares in related companies
9. Income from other fixed asset investments (15)
10. Other interest receivable and similar income (15)
11. Amounts written off investments
12. Interest payable and similar charges (16)
13. Tax on profit or loss on ordinary activities
14. Profit or loss on ordinary activities after taxation
15. Extraordinary income
16. Extraordinary charges
17. Extraordinary profit or loss
18. Tax on extraordinary profit or loss
19. Other taxes not shown under the above items
20. Profit or loss for the financial year

References in ( ) are explained on page 348.

PROFIT AND LOSS ACCOUNT – Format 2

1. Turnover
2. Change in stocks of finished goods and in work in progress
3. Own work capitalised
4. Other operating income
5. (a) Raw materials and consumables
   (b) Other external charges
6. Staff costs:
   (a) wages and salaries
   (b) social security costs
   (c) other pension costs
7. (a) Depreciation and other amounts written off tangible and intangible fixed assets
   (b) Exceptional amounts written off current assets
8. Other operating charges
9. Income from shares in group companies
10. Income from shares in related companies
11. Income from other fixed asset investments (15)
12. Other interest receivable and similar income (15)
13. Amounts written off investments
14. Interest payable and similar charges (16)
15. Tax on profit or loss on ordinary activities
16. Profit or loss on ordinary activities after taxation
17. Extraordinary income
18. Extraordinary charges
19. Extraordinary profit or loss
20. Tax on extraordinary profit or loss
21. Other taxes not shown under the above items
22. Profit or loss for the financial year

References in ( ) are explained on page 348.

PROFIT AND LOSS ACCOUNT – Format 3 (See note (17) below)

A. Charges
1. Cost of sales (14)
2. Distribution costs (14)
3. Administrative expenses (14)
4. Amounts written off investments
5. Interest payable and similar charges (16)
6. Tax on profit or loss on ordinary activities
7. Profit or loss on ordinary activities after taxation
8. Extraordinary charges
9. Tax on extraordinary profit or loss
10. Other taxes not shown under the above items
11. Profit or loss for the financial year

B. Income
1. Turnover
2. Other operating income
3. Income from shares in group companies
4. Income from shares in related companies
5. Income from other fixed asset investments (15)
6. Other interest receivable and similar income (15)
7. Profit or loss on ordinary activities after taxation
8. Extraordinary income
9. Profit or loss for the financial year

References in ( ) are explained on page 348.

PROFIT AND LOSS ACCOUNT – Format 4

A. Charges

1. Reduction in stocks of finished goods and in work in progress
2. (a) Raw materials and consumables
   (b) Other external charges
3. Staff costs:
   (a) wages and salaries
   (b) social security costs
   (c) other pension costs
4. (a) Depreciation and other amounts written off tangible and intangible fixed assets
   (b) Exceptional amounts written off current assets
5. Other operating charges
6. Amounts written off investments
7. Interest payable and similar charges (16)
8. Tax on profit or loss on ordinary activities
9. Profit or loss on ordinary activities after taxation
10. Extraordinary charges
11. Tax on extraordinary profit or loss
12. Other taxes not shown under the above items
13. Profit or loss for the financial year

B. Income

1. Turnover
2. Increase in stocks of finished goods and in work in progress
3. Own work capitalised
4. Other operating income
5. Income from shares in group companies
6. Income from shares in related companies
7. Income from other fixed asset investments (15)
8. Other interest receivable and similar income (15)
9. Profit or loss on ordinary activities after taxation
10. Extraordinary income
11. Profit or loss for the financial year

References in ( ) are explained on page 348.

NOTES ON PROFIT AND LOSS ACCOUNT FORMAT

(14) *Cost of sales: distribution costs: administrative expenses*
(Format 1, items 2, 4 and 5 and Format 3, items A.1, 2 and 3.)

These items shall be stated after taking into account any necessary provisions for depreciation or diminution in value of assets.

(15) *Income from other fixed asset investments: other interest receivable and similar income*
(Format 1, items 9 and 10: Format 2, items 11 and 12: Format 3, items B.5 and 6: Format 4, items B.7 and 8.)

Income and interest derived from group companies shall be shown separately from income and interest derived from other sources.

(16) *Interest payable and similar charges*
(Format 1, item 12: Format 2, item 14: Format 3, item A.5: Format 4, item A.7.)

The amount payable to group companies shall be shown separately.

(17) *Formats 1 and 3*

The amount of any provisions for depreciation and diminution in value of tangible and intangible fixed assets falling to be shown under items 7(a) and A.4(a) respectively in Formats 2 and 4 shall be disclosed in a note to the accounts in any case where the profit and loss account is prepared by reference to Format 1 or Format 3.

PROPER ACCOUNTING RECORDS

The Auditing Practices Committee of the CCAB has issued a guidance statement on s 12 of the 1976 Act (now contained in s 221 of the 1985 Act) which deals with accounting records. The APC has taken Counsel's opinion on certain points of difficulty arising under this section. The main points dealt with in that statement, (with which Counsel did not disagree), are reproduced below, with references changed to those in the 1985 Act.

QUESTIONS DEALING WITH SECTION 221(2)

1. Q: What does the phrase 'the financial position' of a company mean?

A: In requiring that the accounting records be sufficient to disclose the financial position of the company, the Act recognises that it is not practicable to draw up financial statements giving a 'true and fair' view at any time during the year. The concept of 'true and fair' is extremely wide and embraces information not necessarily contained within the accounting records themselves. Nevertheless, the Act has installed the requirement that the Directors should have available to them an adequate statement 'at any time' of the company's financial position, even though this is drawn up to a less rigorous standard than the 'true and fair' requirement of the company's annual statutory financial statements.

This sub-section appears to require more than mere disclosure of the cash position (as shown in the cash-book) and would seem to indicate that the Directors should be in a position to prepare a statement showing, in addition, the other tangible assets, liabilities and pre-tax results with reasonable accuracy. It follows that in order to do this it will be necessary to be able to form a reasonable estimate of the company's stock position, but this does not necessarily require a physical stocktaking or maintenance of continuous detailed stock records. The method by which the estimate of stock is arrived at will be a matter for judgment, depending on the circumstances.

There appear to be three ways in which an estimate of stock may be reached, depending on the circumstances of the business:

(a) By the use of gross profit margins applied to sales arriving at a cost of stock sold; this may be appropriate if a business has a limited number of product lines and works on the basis of fixed profit percentage.

(b) By maintaining detailed records of cost of sales. In this way the cost of sales may be accurately determined and a residual stock figure arrived at.

(c) By maintaining detailed stock records so as to enable a stock valuation to be performed at any time and used in the compilation of gross margin in the form of a traditional trading account.

The Act clearly recognises that it would be impracticable for the raw data contained in the accounting records to present the true and fair view of the state of affairs and results required for annual financial statement purposes.

2. Q: How is the financial position 'disclosed'?

A: Records must be maintained which provide the basic information from which the financial position can be ascertained. It is suggested that 'disclosure' does not mean that the financial position needs to be displayed after each transaction has been recorded, but that the information from which a statement of the financial position can be prepared is available.

3. Q: Is the phrase 'at any time' to be taken literally?

A: Yes, in so far that the accounting records should be capable of disclosing the necessary information at any point in time. This information does not need to be recorded instantaneously, but should be in a form sufficient to enable a statement showing the financial position at any selected date to be drawn up.

QUESTIONS DEALING WITH SECTION 221(3)

1. Q: What are 'accounting records'?

A: Accounting records comprise the orderly collection and identification of the information in question, rather than a mere accumulation of documents.

The accounting records need not be in book form; they may take the form of, for example, a loose-leaf binder or computer tape; it will even be sufficient if the books of prime entry are in the form of a secure clip of invoices with an add-list attached. The essence of the matter is that the information recorded is organised and labelled so as to be capable of retrieval. A carrier-bag full of invoices will not suffice.

2. Q: Does 'day-to-day' mean hourly, daily, weekly or monthly?

A: Normally, the cash-book taken together with the day books and ledger will provide the information required under Section 221(3)(a). Clearly, transactions cannot be recorded instantaneously. What is necessary is that when the entries are made, each transaction is shown separately and is identified by its date and an explanation of the matter in respect of which it takes place. In the case of retail shops it is likely that a record of the total day's cash taking will suffice.

3. Q: What is meant by 'a record of assets and liabilities'?

A: The sub-section states that the accounting records shall in particular contain 'a record of the assets and liabilities of the company'. Therefore, details must be included of all the company's assets and liabilities, such as debtors, creditors and plant. There is no express requirement that this record should be up-dated on a day to day basis, but the requirement clearly is that a person looking at the accounting records can find recorded therein what are the assets and what are the liabilities of the company at any particular time. For this purpose, the relevant records must be up-dated at frequent intervals and must contain information as to dates of acquisitions and disposals of assets and of the incurring and discharge of liabilities. This sub-section specifically excludes stocks, which are dealt with below.

QUESTIONS DEALING WITH SECTION 221(4)

1. Q: What stock records form part of the accounting records as defined in Section 221?

A: The need to be able to estimate stock in order to provide information from which to prepare a statement showing the company's financial position has been dealt with above. Sub-section (4) requires that statements of stock held at each financial year-end be retained. For this purpose, the term 'statements of stock' is taken to mean a summary supporting the amount included in the financial statements in respect of stock. It is further required that the stocktaking records which support the year-end stock summary - whether these be annual, perpetual or the year-end - shall also be retained. It will be seen that the Act imposes an obligation to retain documentation supporting year-end stock valuations, but allows considerable flexibility in meeting the requirement to disclose the 'at any time' financial position.

2. Q: How detailed should the records of transactions with sellers, goods and buyers be to comply with sub-section (4)(c)?

A: The intention of the Act appears to be to ensure that the substance of transactions is properly recorded. In the case of products where the individual item identity of the product is irrelevant to the seller and purchaser, product type identity will normally be sufficient, whereas in the case of goods where the identity of the individual item is relevant, each particular item will need to be identified. In practical terms, this Section is unlikely to impose a greater obligation than that already imposed by VAT regulations, or the commercial needs of the business. The identity of vendor and purchaser will normally be available from purchase and sales ledgers.'

LEGAL OPINION ON 'TRUE AND FAIR'

THE ACCOUNTING STANDARDS COMMITTEE JOINT OPINION

1. The Accounting Standards Committee ('ASC') from time to time issues Statements of Standard Accounting Practice ('SSAPs'). These are declared in the Explanatory Foreword to be 'methods of accounting approved . . . for application to all financial accounts intended to give a true and fair view of financial position and profit or loss.' They are not intended to be 'a comprehensive code of rigid rules' but departures from them should be disclosed and explained. The Committee also noted in its Explanatory Foreword that 'methods of financial accounting evolve and alter in response to changing business and economic needs. From time to time new accounting standards will be drawn at progressive levels, and established standards will be reviewed with the object of improvement in the light of new needs and developments.'

2. The ASC has recently undertaken a review of the standard setting process and decided that future standards will 'deal only with those matters which are of major and fundamental importance and affect the generality of companies' but that, as in the past, the standards will apply 'to all accounts which are intended to show a true and fair view of financial position and profit or loss'. A SSAP is therefore a declaration by the ASC, on behalf of its constituent professional bodies, that save in exceptional circumstances accounts which do not comply with the standard will not give a true and fair view.

3. But the preparation of accounts which give a true and fair view is not merely a matter of compliance with professional standards. In many important cases it is a requirement of law. Since 1947 all accounts prepared for the purpose of compliance with the Companies Acts have been required to 'give a true and fair view': s 13(1) of the Companies Act 1947, re-enacted as s 149(1) of the Companies Act 1948. In 1978 the concept of a true and fair view was adopted by the EEC Council in its Fourth Directive 'on the annual accounts of certain types of companies'. The Directive combined the requirement of giving a true and fair view with extremely detailed provisions about the form and contents of the accounts but the obligation to give a true and fair view was declared to be overriding. Accounts must not comply with the detailed requirements if this would prevent them from giving a true and fair view. Parliament gave effect to the Directive by passing the Companies Act 1981. This substitutes a new s 149(2) in the 1948 Act, reproducing the old s 149(1) in substantially similar words. The detailed requirements of the Directive appear as a new Eighth Schedule to the 1948 Act. The old s 149(1) (now renumbered 149A(1)) and the old Eighth Schedule (now Sch 8A) are retained for the accounts of banking, insurance and shipping companies. So far as the requirement to give a true and fair view is concerned, a difference between 149(2) and 149A(1) is that the former has come into the law via Brussels whereas the latter has no EEC pedigree.

4. 'True and fair view' is thus a legal concept and the question of whether company accounts comply with s 149(2) (or s 149A(1)) can be authoritatively decided only by a court. This gives rise to a number of questions about the relationship between the legal requirement and the SSAPs issued by the ASC, which also claim to be authoritative statements on what is a true and fair view. What happens if there is a conflict between the professional standards demanded by the ASC and the decisions of the courts on the requirements of the Companies Acts? Furthermore, the ASC issues new SSAPs 'at progressive levels' and reviews established ones. How is this consistent with a statutory requirement of a true and fair view which has been embodied in the law in the same language since 1947? Can the issue of a new SSAP make it unlawful to prepare accounts in a form which would previously have been lawful? How can the ASC have power to legislate in this way?

5. To answer these questions it is necessary first to examine the nature of the 'true and fair view' concept as used in the Companies Act. It is an abstraction or philosophical concept expressed in simple English. The law uses many similar concepts, of which 'reasonable care' is perhaps the most familiar example. It is a common feature of such concepts that there is seldom any difficulty in understanding what they mean but frequent controversy over their application to particular facts. One reason for this phenomenon is that because such concepts represent a very high level of abstraction which has to be applied to an infinite variety of concrete facts, there can never be a sharply defined line between, for example, what is reasonable care and what is not. There will always be a penumbral area in which views may reasonably differ.

6. The courts have never attempted to define 'true and fair' in the sense of offering a paraphrase in other languages and in our opinion have been wise not to do so. When a concept can be expressed in ordinary English words, we do not think that it illuminates their meaning to attempt to frame a definition. We doubt, for example, whether the man on the Clapham omnibus has really contributed very much to the understanding of reasonable care or that accountants have found it helpful to ask themselves how this imaginary passenger would have prepared a set of accounts. It is much more useful to illustrate the concept in action, for example, to explain why certain accounts do or do not give a true and fair view.

7. It is however important to observe that the application of the concept involves judgment in questions of degree. The information contained in accounts must be accurate and comprehensive (to mention two of the most obvious elements which contribute to a true and fair view) to within acceptable limits. What is acceptable and how is this to be achieved? Reasonable businessmen and accountants may differ over the degree of accuracy or comprehensiveness which in particular cases the accounts should attain. Equally, there may sometimes be room for differences over the method to adopt in order to give a true and fair view, cases in which there may be more than one 'true and fair view' of the same financial position. Again, because 'true and fair view' involves questions of degree, we think that cost-effectiveness must play a part in deciding the amount of information which is sufficient to make accounts true and fair.

8. In the end, as we have said, the question of whether accounts give a true and fair view in compliance with the Companies Acts must be decided by a judge. But the courts look for guidance on this question to the ordinary practices of professional accountants. This is not merely because accounts are expressed in a language which judges find difficult to understand. This may sometimes be true but it is a minor reason for the importance which the courts attach to evidence of accountancy practice. The important reason is inherent in the nature of the 'true and fair' concept. Accounts will not be true and fair unless the information they contain is sufficient in quantity and quality to satisfy the reasonable expectations of the readers to whom they are addressed. On this question, accountants can express an informed professional opinion on what, in current circumstances, it is thought that accounts should reasonably contain. But they can do more than that. The readership of accounts will consist of businessmen, investors, bankers and so forth, as well as professional accountants. But the expectations of the readers will have been moulded by the practices of accountants because by and large they will expect to get what they ordinarily get and that in turn will depend upon the normal practices of accountants.

9. For these reasons, the courts will treat compliance with accepted accounting principles as prima facie evidence that the accounts are true and fair. Equally, deviation from accepted principles will be prima facie evidence that they are not. We have not been able to find reported cases on the specific question of whether accounts are true and fair, although the question has been adverted to in the course of judgments on other matters; see for example Willingdale v International Commercial Bank Ltd [1978] A.C.834. There are however some cases on the analogous question arising in income tax cases of whether profit or loss has been calculated in accordance with 'the correct principles of commercial accountancy' and there is a helpful

statement of principle (approved in subsequent cases in the Court of Appeal) by Pennycuick V-C in Odeon Associated Theatres Ltd v Jones (Inspector of Taxes) [1971] 1 W.L.R. 442 at 454:-

> 'In order to ascertain what are the correct principles [the court] has recourse to the evidence of accountants. That evidence is conclusive on the practice of accountants in the sense of the principles on which accountants act in practice. That is a question of pure fact, but the court itself has to make a final decision as to whether that practice corresponds to the correct principles of commercial accountancy. No doubt in the vast proportion of cases the court will agree with the accountants but it will not necessarily do so. Again, there may be a divergency of views between the accountants, or there may be alternative principles, none of which can be said to be incorrect, or of course there may be no accountancy evidence at all . . . At the end of the day the court must determine what is the correct principle of commercial accountancy to be applied.'

10. This is also in our opinion the relationship between generally accepted accounting principles and the legal concept of 'true and fair'. The function of the ASC is to formulate what it considers should be generally accepted accounting principles. Thus the value of a SSAP to a court which has to decide whether accounts are true and fair is two-fold. First, it represents an important statement of professional opinion about the standards which readers may reasonably expect in accounts which are intended to be true and fair. The SSAP is intended to crystallise professional opinion and reduce penumbral areas in which divergent practices exist and can each have a claim to being 'true and fair'. Secondly, because accountants are professionally obliged to comply with a SSAP, it creates in the readers an expectation that the accounts will be in conformity with the prescribed standards. This is in itself a reason why accounts which depart from the standard without adequate justification or explanation may be held not to be true and fair. The importance of expectations was emphasised by the Court of Appeal in what may be regarded as a converse case, Re Press Caps [1949] Ch.434. An ordinary historic cost balance sheet was said to be 'true and fair' notwithstanding that it gave no information about the current value of freehold properties because, it was said, no one familiar with accounting conventions would expect it to include such information.

11. A SSAP therefore has no direct legal effect. It is simply a rule of professional conduct for accountants. But in our opinion it is likely to have an indirect effect on the content which the courts will give to the 'true and fair' concept. The effect of a SSAP may therefore be to make it likely that accounts which would previously have been considered true and fair will no longer satisfy the law. Perhaps the most dramatic example arises out of the recent statement by the ASC in connection with its review of SSAP 16 'Current Cost Accounting'. The Statement puts forward for discussion the proposition that 'where a company is materially affected by changing prices, pure HC accounts do not give a true and fair view'. If this proposition were embodied in a new SSAP and accepted by the courts, the legal requirements of a true and fair view will have undergone a revolutionary change.

12. There is no inconsistency between such a change brought about by changing professional opinion and the rule that words in a statute must be construed in accordance with the meaning which they bore when the statute was passed. The meaning of true and fair remains what it was in 1947. It is the content given to the concept which has changed. This is something which constantly happens to such concepts. For example, the Bill of Rights 1688 prohibited 'cruel and unusual punishments'. There has been no change in the meaning of 'cruel' since 1688. The definition in Dr Johnson's Dictionary of 1755 ('pleased with hurting others, inhuman, hard-hearted, without pity, barbarous') is much the same as in a modern dictionary. But changes in society mean that a judge in 1983 would unquestionably characterise punishments as 'cruel' which his predecessor of 1688 would not have thought to come within this description. The meaning of the concept remains the same; the facts to which it is applied have changed.

13. The possibility of changing accounting standards has been recognised both by the courts and the legislature. In Associated Portland Cement Manufacturers Ltd v Price Commission [1975] I.C.R. 27, esp. at 45-6, the court recognised changes since 1945 in the permissible methods of calculating depreciation. Similarly para 90 of the new Eighth Schedule to the Companies Act 1948 refers to 'principles generally accepted . . . at the time when those accounts are prepared'.

14. We therefore see no conflict between the functions of the ASC in formulating standards which it declares to be essential to true and fair accounts and the function of the courts in deciding whether the accounts satisfy the law. The courts are of course not bound by a SSAP. A court may say that accounts which ignore them are nevertheless true and fair. But the immediate effect of a SSAP is to strengthen the likelihood that a court will hold that compliance with the prescribed standard is necessary for the accounts to give a true and fair view. In the absence of a SSAP, a court is unlikely to reject accounts drawn up in accordance with principles which command some respectable professional support. The issue of a SSAP has the effect, for the two reasons which we have given in para 10, of creating a prima facie presumption that accounts which do not comply are not true and fair. This presumption is then strengthened or weakened by the extent to which the SSAP is actually accepted and applied. Universal acceptance means that it is highly unlikely that a court would accept accounts drawn up according to different principles. On the other hand, if there remains a strong body of professional opinion which consistently opts out of applying the SSAP, giving reasons which the ASC may consider inadequate, the prima facie presumption against such accounts is weakened.

15. We therefore do not think that the ASC should be concerned by the possibility that a court may hold that compliance with one of its SSAPs is not necessary for the purposes of the Companies Acts. This possibility is inherent in the fact that the courts are not bound by professional opinion. The function of the ASC is to express their professional judgment on the standards which in their opinion are required.

16. There are two further points to be considered. The first is the relationship between the 'true and fair' requirement and the detailed provisions of the new Eighth Schedule. The Act is quite explicit on this point: the true and fair view is overriding. Nevertheless it may be said that the detailed requirements offer some guidance as to the principles which Parliament considered would give a true and fair view. In particular, the Schedule plainly regards historic cost accounting as the norm and current cost accounting as an optional alternative. In these circumstances, is a court likely to follow a SSAP which declares that for certain companies, historic cost accounts cannot give a true and fair view? In our opinion, whatever reasons there may be for taking one view or the other, the provisions of the Eighth Schedule are no obstacle to accepting such a SSAP. As we have already pointed out, the provisions of the Schedule are static whereas the concept of a true and fair view is dynamic. If the latter is overriding, it is not impossible that the effect in time will be to render obsolete some of the provisions of the Schedule. But we think that this is what must have been intended when overriding force was given to a concept with a changing content.

17. Lastly, there is the effect of the adoption of 'true and fair view' by the EEC. Because s 149(2) of the 1948 Act now gives effect to a Directive, it must (unlike s 149A(1)) be construed in accordance with any decision of the European Court on the meaning of Article 2.3 of the Directive. In practice we do not think that this is likely to affect the evolution of the concept in England. Just as the concept may have a different content at different times, so it may have a different content in different countries. Although the European Court may seek to achieve some uniformity by laying down minimum standards for the accounts of all EEC countries, it seems to us that they are unlikely to disapprove of higher standards being required by the professional bodies of individual states and in consequence, higher legal criteria for what is a true and fair view being adopted in the national courts of some member states.

18. So for example Article 33 of the Directive gives member states the right to 'permit or require' companies to use current cost accounting instead of historic cost principles. In the UK, as we have said, current cost accounts are permitted by the Eighth Schedule but the only circumstances in which they may be required is if a court should decide, on the basis of prevailing principles, that they are necessary to give a true and fair view. In Germany, on the other hand, the equivalent of the Eighth Schedule does not even permit current cost accounts. In Germany, therefore, the only way they could be permitted would be if the German court applied 'true and fair view' as an overriding requirement. For the reasons given in para 16, we do not regard it as illogical or impossible that even a German court may take this view. But having regard to the Directive, we think it is very unlikely that the European Court would decide as a matter of community law that there are circumstances in which historic cost accounts do not give a true and fair view. Developments of this kind are more likely to be left to national courts to make in the light of local professional opinion.

Leonard Hoffman QC, Mary H Arden.